Goethe and the English-Speaking World

Studies in German Literature, Linguistics, and Culture

Edited by James Hardin
(*South Carolina*)

Goethe and the English-Speaking World

Essays from the Cambridge
Symposium for
His 250th Anniversary

Edited by
Nicholas Boyle
and
John Guthrie

CAMDEN HOUSE

First published 2002
by Camden House

Camden House is an imprint of Boydell & Brewer Inc.
PO Box 41026, Rochester, NY 14604–4126 USA
and of Boydell & Brewer Limited
PO Box 9, Woodbridge, Suffolk IP12 3DF, UK

ISBN: 1–57113–231–7

Library of Congress Cataloging-in-Publication Data

Goethe and the English-speaking world: a Cambridge symposium for his 250th
anniversary / edited by Nicholas Boyle and John Guthrie.
    p. cm. — (Studies in German literature, linguistics and culture)
Sixteen of the 17 papers presented at a symposium held Sept. 22–25, 1999, at
the University of Cambridge
Includes bibliographical references and index.
ISBN 1-57113-231-7 (alk. paper)
    1. Goethe, Johann Wolfgang von, 1749–1832—Appreciation—Great Brit-
ain—Congresses.   2. Goethe, Johann Wolfgang von, 1749–1832—Appreciation—English-speaking countries—Congresses. 3. Goethe, Johann Wolfgang
von, 1749–1832—Knowledge—Great Britain—Congresses.   4. Great
Britain—In literature—Congresses. I. Boyle, Nicholas. II. Guthrie, John,
1953–   III. Studies in German literature, linguistics, and culture (Unnum-
bered).

PT2173.G7 G64 2001
831'.6—dc21

                              2001037456

A catalogue record for this title is available from the British Library.

This publication is printed on acid-free paper.
Printed in the United States of America

Contents

Part II: Goethe and the English-Speaking World: Reception and Resonance(s)

Preface

FROM 22–25 SEPTEMBER 1999, the Department of German at the University of Cambridge held a symposium in Sidney Sussex College on "Goethe and the English-Speaking World" to mark the 250th anniversary of Goethe's birth. This book presents sixteen of the seventeen papers read on that occasion. The organizers of the conference, who are also the editors of its proceedings, are particularly grateful to the Master and Fellows of Sidney Sussex for being our hosts, to David Lowe of the Cambridge University Library who organized an exhibition of the library's rich collection of Goetheana to coincide with the event, to the University of Cambridge, and to the Managers of the Tiarks German Scholarship Fund who made generous grants to support the conference and to help publish the present volume. We could not have staged the conference so successfully, but for the untiring support of our departmental secretaries, Virginia Pearce and Sharon Nevill. We should also like to express our thanks to all the contributors who promptly and meticulously prepared their work for the publisher and put up with our editorial vagaries, to Camden House and Professor James Hardin for their support during the process of production, and to David Campbell (Everyman Library) for permission to reprint in Nicholas Boyle's contribution some pages from the introduction to J. W. von Goethe *Selected Works* (London, Everyman 1999).

N. B.

J. G.

January 2001

Abbreviations

FA: Goethe. Sämtliche Werke, Briefe, Tagebücher und Gespräche. (Frankfurter Ausgabe). Edited by Friedmar Apel et al. 40 vols. Frankfurt am Main: Deutscher Klassiker Verlag, 1987–99.

G: Goethes Gespräche. Edited by Flodoard Biedermann, revised and newly edited by Wolfgang Herwig. 5 vols. Zurich & Stuttgart: Artemis, 1965–87.

GA: Gedenkausgabe der Werke, Briefe und Gespräche. (Artemis Gedenkausgabe). Edited by Ernst Beutler. 24 vols. Zurich: Artemis, 1948–54. 3 supplementary vols. 1960–71.

GG: Flodoard Frhr von Biedermann (Editor). *Goethes Gespräche. Gesamtausgabe.* 5 vols. Leipzig: Biedermann, 1909–11.

GLL: German Life and Letters.

Goethe Jb Wien: Jahrbuch des Wiener Goethe-Vereins.

HA: Goethes Werke. (Hamburger Ausgabe). Edited by Erich Trunz. 14 vols. Munich: Beck, 1948–60.

HAB: Goethes Briefe. (Hamburger Ausgabe). Edited by Karl Robert Mandelkow. 4 vols. Hamburg: Beck, 1962–67.

JEGP: Journal of English and Germanic Philosophy.

LA: Goethe, *Die Schriften zur Naturwissenschaft.* Edited by the Deutsche Akademie der Naturforscher (Leopoldina), 17 vols. of text and 11 vols. of commentary. Weimar, 1947– .

MA: Sämtliche Werke nach Epochen seines Schaffens. (Münchener Ausgabe). Edited by Karl Richter. 20 vols. Munich: Hanser, 1985– .

PEGS: Publications of the English Goethe Society.

WA: Goethes Werke. (Weimarer Ausgabe). 133 vols. Weimar: Böhlau, 1887–1919.

Introduction: Goethe and England; England and Goethe

Nicholas Boyle

THE TOPIC OF THIS SYMPOSIUM is enticing but somehow puzzling. It ought to be deep, but it is actually rather uncomfortable. Goethe's feelings about the three kingdoms (*WA* 4, 47, 17), with the New World looming up behind them across the Atlantic, about everything that for the sake of brevity in my title I have called England, were strangely ambivalent. It would probably be fair to say that the ambivalence has been reciprocated. There is an unease on both sides, a sense of dealing with a power too great to be ignored permanently, at once attractive and alien, and requiring almost too much of an effort of self-redefinition if it is to be made comprehensible. I do not think Goethe's relations with France or Italy, with the Slavonic or the Islamic worlds, complex though they were, were problematic in the same way. His involvement with the culture of classical antiquity was lifelong and intense, but it lacked the challenge of a contemporary, and so permanently changing, political setting.

This volume is concerned equally with Goethe's reception of English-language *Kulturgut* and with the reception of Goethe by the English-speaking world. The first part is devoted to what might loosely be called English influences on Goethe, the second to Goethe's influences on, loosely, us. In both parts, the reader will find occasion to note what I have called the unease in this special relationship. In these opening remarks I shall comment on both sides of the equation and suggest how both sets of ambivalences might be seen to belong together.

First, then, Goethe's reactions to England. On the one hand there is evidence of a distinct power of attraction, leading even to a desire on Goethe's part to identify himself with England and English attitudes. On the other hand — sometimes in the same context, and usually less explicitly — Goethe seems to distance himself from English models, as if, whatever the forces at work in them, they cannot show him the way that he has to go, either personally or as a writer. Let us consider some examples.

One of Goethe's most extraordinary remarks about England, completely private and personal, but of unimpeachable authenticity, is to be found in the travel diary he wrote for Frau von Stein during his journey to Rome in 1786. At the high tide of his existence, plucking at last, he believes, the fruits prepared and tended throughout his early years, putting into effect at last, after at least three previous attempts, the plan his now dead father conceived for him in his childhood, intoxicated with the sensual excitement of the Italian landscape, Palladian architecture, late-summer sunshine, and the personal freedom of his incognito travel, he writes in Venice on 5 October, after a visit to the Arsenal:

> Ich habe schon Vorgedancken und Vorgefühle über das Wiederaufleben der Künste in Italien, in der mittlern Zeit, und wie auch diese Asträa wieder bald die Erde verlies und wie das alles zusammenhängt. Wie mir die Römische Geschichte entgegensteigt! Schade schade meine Geliebte! alles ein wenig spät. O daß ich nicht einen klugen Engländer zum Vater gehabt habe, daß ich das alles allein, ganz allein habe erwerben und erobern müssen, und noch muß. (*WA* 3, 1, 266)

Superficially, Goethe might seem to be expressing here no more than the envious admiration common in German and even French writers in the first two-thirds of the eighteenth century, when Britain, united after its civil war, set about industrialization and global commerce, acquiring first an American and then an Oriental empire, and enjoyed something like the wealth, power, and prestige of the United States in our own day. Would that he had at his disposal the resources that — as he will shortly write from Rome — make only the English and the Russians capable of paying market prices for genuine antiquities, leaving minor German princes like Carl August to scrape around for bargains in unfashionable genres and periods.[1] Would that he could live as he will describe William Hamilton living in Naples, in the lap of beauty, natural, artistic, and human, and with a cellarful of Pompeian treasures. Would that he were a young Englishman on the Grand Tour with a Palladian villa to return to and to furnish with Italian mementoes. In the words in which Pascal expressed the *ressentiment* of hard-worked officialdom towards the inherited wealth and privilege for which it laboured:

> Que la noblesse est un grand avantage qui, dès dix-huit ans, met un homme en passe, connu et respecté, comme un autre pourrait avoir mérité à cinquante ans. C'est trente ans gagnés sans peine.[2]

But the strange explicitness in Goethe's phrasing of unlovely emotional overtones — the seemingly gratuitous involvement of his dead father, towards whom his feelings seem to hover between ingratitude and reproach, the deliberately self-pitying repetitions ("Schade schade," "allein, ganz allein") — betrays that he is not here simply indulging a fantasy, imagining himself into the shoes of the mighty of the earth. He is struggling to make an identity for himself out of the true facts of his situation — his situation as the scion of a bourgeois family, cut off now by his own choice from those roots, writing to the supreme symbolic representative of the courtly world that he has joined, unsupported therefore by any social context, but contemplating now in all its concrete immediacy the cultural achievement of an age in which the individual artist did not have to find his way "alone, completely alone." The passing of that age, the Italian Renaissance, is already for him an image of the passing of the original moment of perfection of the arts in the ancient world, it is a second loss by humanity of its Astraea — or its Pandora as he will in future prefer to call it. From that loss he would be insulated, perhaps even he would not have to experience it at all but would be free and able to realise fully the potential within him, if he had been born into intelligent and cultured surroundings in the nation which seems to hold the future in its hands. Wealthy and confident England provides him with the model of what Germany is not, and so with an image of what separates the Germany in which he has to struggle alone from the fulfilment for which he is looking.

The clearest example of Goethe's dream of an English identity, and of the cultural-historical significance of the dream, is provided by his long-lasting and long-distance "infatuation" with Byron (as Tieck called it to Crabb Robinson).[3] "I have a great curiosity about everything relating to Goethe, and please myself with thinking there is some analogy between our characters and writings," Byron is reported to have said,[4] and I think it better to consider this as a relationship of equality rather than of father and son, as scholarship has usually preferred to see it.[5] Goethe saw himself in Byron — himself as he might have been. Byron had had an intelligent Englishman if not as his father then at least as his great-uncle — intelligent enough to die without issue and unexpectedly bequeath him the title. With the inheritance came wealth and status — wealth that allowed him to travel to Greece and swim the Hellespont at twenty-two, political status which allowed him at twenty-four to speak on matters of pressing concern in the supreme councils of the nation. Trente ans gagnés sans peine. No need for Byron to transfer to another state to acquire influence and experience in the public world — he seemed to have achieved without effort everything that the son of an albeit well-to-do Frankfurt burgher had had to struggle for years to attain, if he attained it at all. Indeed, much of it was not attained but had to remain in the realm of imagination and poetry, like travelling to Greece. Or indeed like the erotic symbol of it all (perhaps) — for the incestuous relationship with his sister, which Byron consummated, had for Goethe to remain only an unspoken poetic inspiration. The erotic charge in Goethe's relationship with Cornelia is alluded to in *Dichtung und Wahrheit* only "between the lines" (*WA* 1, 29, 100, probably written in 1830, when the parallel with Byron could have been conscious), but the scandal surrounding Byron's domestic arrangements was what in 1816 first drew Goethe's attention to him (*WA* 4, 27, 48). Byron, in short, did what Goethe dreamt of doing, and Byron, unlike Goethe, made no secret of it. What Goethe said he admired in Byron's writing is remarkably like a literary self-portrait: the reinterpretative and neo-mythologizing biblical dramas, *Cain*, and *Heaven and Earth* ("A Bishop might have written it");[6] the satirical works, *English Bards and Scotch Reviewers*, *The Vision of Judgement*, and, with reservations, *Don Juan*;[7] the dramas that have a clear relation to *Faust*, namely *Manfred* and *The Deformed Transformed*;[8] and the realistic depiction of the social milieu in *Don Juan* and the dramas.[9] Poetry with a powerfully heterodox theological motivation, realistic instruments, and a strong satirical and comic tone, is certainly a large part of the achievement of the author of *Faust*, even if it does not exhaust his inexhaustible resourcefulness. But Goethe also knows better than Byron how to cover his tracks. His coolness for many years towards *Don Juan*, after initial enthusiasm, has often puzzled critics, but — if I may presume to differ from our great predecessors in the study of Anglo-German literary relations, J. G. Robertson and E. M. Butler[10] — I do not think this had much to do with the lubricious elements in the poem. Goethe — as they point out — had written more explicitly about sexual matters, but he was not being hypocritical in his reaction to *Don Juan*, for he had on the whole refrained from publishing what he had written. In Byron's willingness to publish and, in many senses, be damned, Goethe must have seen a willingness to damage his relations with the public. That intimate relation between writer and public had cost Goethe much pain and many years to establish, and in a German context which in some respects was more tolerant than the English. A writer who savages his public is only a step away from turning on himself. Goethe may have enjoyed the licentiousness of Byron's first canto — why else should he immediately have set about translating it? — but if he soon afterwards called the poem not only "grandios," but "verrückt" (*WA* 4, 32, 205), it must have been because as he read further and came to the second canto with its ruthlessly sadistic account of shipwreck and cannibalism he recognised the self-destructive traits he had already rejected in Kleist or

Runge or Beethoven, or earlier still in the young Schiller and, of course, in the author of *Werther*.

Byron was an image of what an English Goethe might have been, but only up to a point. Goethe knew that a poet could not divorce himself with impunity from his time and his society — that was why to Frau von Stein he had lamented the solitariness wished on him by fate in making him a German poet. Byron lacked that last understanding of his inseparability from the England that had made him. Goethe, near the end of his life, revealed, if Eckermann's report is to be trusted, what the English Goethe would really have looked like — the Goethe who had Byron's inheritance, and Goethe's insight.

> In England geboren [he told Eckermann on 17 March 1830] wäre ich ein reicher Herzog gewesen, oder vielmehr [the point is so mischievous, and sociologically so accurate, that it must be authentic] ein Bischof mit jährlichen 30 000 Pfund Sterling Einkünfte.
>
> Recht hübsch! erwiderte ich; aber wenn Sie zufällig nicht das große Los, sondern eine Niete gezogen hätten? Es gibt so unendlich viele Nieten.
>
> Nicht jeder, mein Allerbester, erwiderte Goethe, ist für das große Los gemacht. Glauben Sie denn, daß ich die Sottise begangen haben würde, auf eine Niete zu fallen? — Ich hätte vor allen Dingen die Partie der 39 Artikel ergriffen; ich hätte sie nach allen Seiten und Richtungen hin verfochten, besonders den Artikel 9, [the article, derived from the Augsburg confession, which deals with the original corruption of man and the lust of the flesh and denounces Pelagianism] der für mich ein Gegenstand einer ganz besondern Aufmerksamkeit und zärtlichen Hingebung gewesen sein würde. Ich hätte in Reimen und Prosa so lange und so viel geheuchelt und gelogen, daß meine 30 000 Pfund jährlich mir nicht hätten entgehen sollen. Und dann, einmal zu dieser Höhe gelangt, würde ich nichts unterlassen haben, mich oben zu erhalten. Besonders würde ich alles getan haben, die Nacht der Unwissenheit womöglich noch finsterer zu machen [. . .] O welch ein Spaß würde es für mich sein, die 39 Artikel auf meine Weise zu traktieren und die einfältige Masse in Erstaunen zu setzen!
>
> Auch ohne Bischof zu sein, sagte ich, könnten Sie sich dieses Vergnügen machen.
>
> Nein, erwiderte Goethe, ich werde mich ruhig verhalten; man muß sehr gut bezahlt sein, um so zu lügen. Ohne Aussicht auf die Bischofsmütze und meine 30 000 Pfund jährlich könnte ich mich nicht dazu verstehen [. . .]

Goethe-Byron in a mitre, and a stole hung with the scalps of deists — it is a wholly plausible picture, and it is plausible because it is based on an extraordinarily accurate cultural-historical diagnosis. The

intellectual energies and personal ambitions that in England were
channelled into building a wealthy empire and maintaining the social
and ideological structure to support it could in Germany find no such
practical expression — constrained by various peculiarities of Germany's
social, economic, and political constitution, they manifested themselves
instead as theological, philosophical, and literary revolution, what we
know now as Enlightenment and Idealism, Classicism and Romanticism. In England the tide of Enlightenment ebbed away around 1740
as the tide of industrialization and imperialism began to flow, and by
the time that France and Germany were in the grip of various revolutionary fevers, English theological and philosophical life was of such
torpidity that Coleridge could seem crazy and eccentric for his interest
in Kant, and well into the nineteenth century a clerical career could be
compromised if in his youth the postulant had been unwise enough to
translate Schleiermacher.[11] The agents of this intellectual oppression
were just such Trollopean prelates as Goethe wickedly characterized —
and to anyone with Cambridge or Oxford connections who doubts the
truth to life of the characterization I would say "and who was Master of
your College between the subscription controversy and 1832?" But it is
not for the light it sheds on England that I quote Eckermann's reconstructed conversation, but for the light it reflects on Goethe. It demonstrates that, whatever he may have dreamt of in 1786, Goethe knew by
the 1820s, and by the time he had to confront the seductive image of
Byron, that an English Goethe was a fantasy — had he indeed been
born with the advantages whose absence he mourned when writing to
Frau von Stein, he would not have reaped the literary and personal fulfilment for which that lonely traveller was looking in Italy. Instead, all
that we know as Goethe would not have been, its place taken by at best
a Paley, a Butler, an Erasmus Darwin — at worst a Warburton, or
George Eliot's Casaubon. Germany, with all its social, economic, and
political constraints, with all its personal frustrations and humiliations,
but also with all its intellectual fertility and freedom, was the condition
for his literary achievement.

In a sense, Goethe had always known that, or at least long before
1786. Consider for a moment some examples not now of the attractive
but of the repulsive effect of England on him. Consider first of all, as
one must, the case of Shakespeare. A percipient observer like Lichtenberg saw at once that there was something amiss with talk of Goethe as
the German Shakespeare, even if he chose to express his insight in fairly
uncharitable terms: "Goethe [. . .] ist zu dem Namen [. . .] des Shakespear gekommen wie die Keller-Esel (Läuse) zum Namen Tausendfuß,
weil sich niemand die Mühe nehmen wollte sie zu zählen."[12] Altogether,

it is surprising how little even the younger Goethe owed to Shakespeare, though that little is of the best, indeed it is quite fundamental: the very idea of *Götz* as a national chronicle, a "history" play in the Shakespearean sense; the episodic structure and mixture of tones in that play and then, supremely, in the *Urfaust;* at a later stage, perhaps motivic structure, tentatively in *Iphigenie*, more systematically in *Tasso*, fully consciously in *Wilhelm Meisters Lehrjahre*. Later still he learned from the coexistence of tragedy and redemption in Shakespeare's later romances when he was planning *Die Natürliche Tochter* and *Faust II* and completing *Faust I*. But from Shakespeare's verse he learnt next to nothing, less even than Lessing — F. Zarncke showed long ago that Goethe's blank verse derives not from Shakespeare but from Italian models[13] — and the rhythms of verse are closer to a poet's heart even than questions of tone and structure. Goethe kept Shakespeare at a distance — the point is a familiar one — just as he kept Spinoza and Linnaeus at a distance,[14] because he did not wish to be overwhelmed by the influence of a spirit with which he had one or two vital ambitions in common. Indeed, the most powerful influence of all these figures was negative, in the sense that they showed him how *not* to proceed towards what may in the end have been a common goal — of Shakespeare and Calderon he remarks that "diese zwei großen Lichter des poetischen Himmels für uns zu Irrlichtern geworden" (*WA* 1, 40, 186), and he repeatedly emphasizes the inappropriateness of the Shakespearean model to German circumstances. But what was it that Goethe did not want to be overwhelmed by? What was it that was peculiar to German circumstances that he knew he could not rise above without losing his own literary identity? As in the case of Byron and the English church, Goethe remains reticent about the self-image with which the English counter-example is incompatible, presenting it only indirectly, through the negation of the counter-example: I am not Byron, nor an English prelate, though in England I might have been. But others could define that peculiarity for him — Wieland, for example, a subtle observer of character, especially of this character, whom he once certainly loved:

> Das Besondere [. . .], was ihn [. . .] fast in allen seinen Werken von Homer und Shakspear unterscheidet, ist, daß der *Ich*, der Ille ego überall durchschimmert, wiewohl ohne alle Jactanz und mit unendlicher Feinheit.[15]

It is subjectivity, the distinctively modern sense of self, that is peculiar to Goethe's writing, supremely embodied in his lyric poetry, but the problematic centre of all his works. To go into the ramifications of this judgement of Wieland's would take us too far from our present theme, but I believe that this infinitely refined yet omnipresent subjectivity is threatened by the remorseless objectivity of Shakespeare's all-penetrating sympathy, and this forces Goethe to keep the English dramatist at a distance. Since the development of a philosophy and a literature of subjectivity was the greatest cultural achievement of Germany in Goethe's lifetime, he was no doubt right to point to an incompatibility between Shakespeare and German circumstances.

The second great English artist from whom Goethe distanced himself even more explicitly than from Shakespeare was Hogarth. Goethe's rejection of Hogarth is, I think, closely related to his failure to respond to the developing English social novel of contemporary manners — Richardson, Smollett, Fanny Burney, and Jane Austen leave him as good as untouched. From the cultural matrix out of which emerged the nineteenth-century novel of urban life, from the commercial and middle-class city, he firmly averted his gaze. On his visit in 1797 to Frankfurt, which thanks to the recent French occupation was culturally almost an outpost of Paris, he became aware of the incompatibility of the literature the modern city was creating with the literature and philosophy of subjectivity being forged in contemporary Weimar and Jena:

> Sehr merkwürdig ist mir aufgefallen [he wrote to Schiller], wie es eigentlich mit dem Publico einer großen Stadt beschaffen ist. Es lebt in einem beständigen Taumel von Erwerben und Verzehren, und das was wir Stimmung nennen, läßt sich weder hervorbringen noch mittheilen, alle Vergnügungen, selbst das Theater, sollen nur zerstreuen und die große Neigung des lesenden Publicums zu Journalen und Romanen entsteht eben daher, weil jene immer und diese meist Zerstreuung in die Zerstreuung bringen. Ich glaube sogar eine Art von Scheu gegen poetische Productionen [. . .] bemerkt zu haben [. . .] Die Poesie verlangt, ja sie gebietet Sammlung, sie isolirt den Menschen wider seinen Willen [. . .]. (*WA* 4, 12, 217)

Isolation, "Sammlung," "Stimmung," and poetry are opposed to the teeming city, "Zerstreuung," the social nexus of production and consumption, and journals and novels. It was precisely the seething, ungraspable, endlessly distracting activity of London life that appealed to Lichtenberg, a frustrated novelist who could not keep his mind on a topic for more than the length of an aphorism. Lichtenberg, however, made his commentaries on Hogarth into an encyclopaedic repository of his own first- and secondhand knowledge of London. Goethe's dismissal of both Hogarth and Lichtenberg may be couched in the language of classicist aesthetics, but it expresses a hostility to the entire concept of literature that underlies the urban novel from Dickens to Döblin — a relentless externality for which character is not simply far more important than subjective "Stimmung" but, in principle at least, replaces it altogether:

> *Lichtenbergs Hogarth* und das Interesse daran war eigentlich ein gemachtes: denn wie hätte der Deutsche, in dessen einfachem reinen Zustande sehr selten solche excentrische Fratzen vorkommen, hieran sich wahrhaft vergnügen können? (*WA* 1, 35, 56)

The English novels of his time on which Goethe can draw are those which stand away from the mainstream, the work of the real eccentric or the outsider, Goldsmith's idyll and, above all, Sterne's ironies, just as in French literature he responds to Diderot rather than to Stendhal or the early Balzac. In Sterne and Goldsmith he finds isolation, "Stimmung," subjectivity; but the urban interaction of producer and consumer, on which France and England were seeking to build their rival empires and which was creating a literature to match, was, like Shakespeare, too vast and alien a phenomenon for the Germany in which alone Goethe could be a poet. To have tried to follow the example set by Hogarth would surely have been to set out after another "Irrlicht," and one cannot say that in the end the case of Lichtenberg suggests anything else.

A third English genius was utterly repellent to Goethe, and more is said about him in Professor Nisbet's essay. Here I should merely like to point out two respects in which Goethe's reaction to Newton fits into the pattern of ambivalence which I have been attempting to discern in Goethe's feelings about England. First, Newton is for Goethe the very type of the hypocritical Establishment prelate, which Goethe claimed he could himself have become had he been born an Englishman. Albrecht Schöne has shown at book length how the form and language of Goethe's writings on colour are those of theological controversy.[16] Newton has the role of defender of the indefensible, maintaining the refrangibility of white light with the same obstinate sophistry used by High Churchmen to assert Trinitarian dogma, while Goethe is the heterodox Unitarian breaking a lance for the original purity and simplicity of the divine. Newton, we may deduce from Goethe's satirical onslaught on the Anglican episcopate, therefore represents in a pure form the English alternative, the counter-possibility to Goethe's German reality — but that means also that he is in Goethe's eyes what Goethe might indeed have become in an English context, and it is striking that the very faults of obstinacy and sophistry which Goethe attributes to Newton are the most prominent features of his own argumentative method in the second, polemical, section of *Zur Farbenlehre*.

Second, though, Goethe carries through the parallel of Newtonianism and Establishment Anglicanism into the social and political sphere. For in the third, historical, section of *Zur Farbenlehre*, he endeavours to show how the foundation of the Royal Society, which becomes the basis for the intellectual hegemony of Newtonian optics, is a stage in the process of consolidation of royal power and the centralization of the kingdom as a necessary preliminary to its political and economic expansion.[17] Newtonianism, therefore, like Trinitarianism, is part of the machinery by which the free and critical operation of the mind is kept subordinate to the practical interests of Britain, whose imperial ambitions lie as much in the intellectual as in the political sphere.

So much for the ambivalences on Goethe's side. In the end, perhaps the most striking feature of Goethe's relations with England is that he never went there. In the course of the eighteenth century, a visit to England became almost as obligatory a part of a European nobleman's education as a visit to Italy. Some of Goethe's closest acquaintances were in Britain for long periods — K. P. Moritz or Fritz von Stein, for example, while Emilie von Berlepsch travelled extensively even in the remoter parts of Scotland — and in his later years Ottilie made Weimar into something of a colony of English expatriates. For both Lichtenberg and Georg Forster, the experience of England had a determining effect on the nature of their intellectual engagement in Germany, and the same could probably be said of Tieck. But these were not examples that Goethe chose to follow, and we must assume — since he did not lack invitations — that he did not wish to follow them. As in the case of Greece, Goethe circumscribed himself: England was a different kind of ideal from Greece, but it too represented other forms of fulfilment than Germany offered, and whether Greek or English they were essentially imaginary, the material of daydreams. Lichtenberg was frustrated, Forster destroyed, by the erroneous belief that English conditions could somehow be a model for Germany, and in that respect their fate was no different from that of Hölderlin who looked out in hopeless yearning to Greece. Patriam fugimus, Lichtenberg thought, was the character of the Germans in two words (1, 422 - E354), but it was not Goethe's character. He stayed on home territory, confining himself almost exclusively to the lands of the Western Empire and its successor, the Holy Roman Empire, of which he was born a subject. Other images beckoned to him, but he recognised their destructive power and resisted them.

I have already suggested that England's reactions to Goethe are marked by the same ambivalence as Goethe's reactions to England, and for much the same historical reasons.[18] Goethe's reception by the English-speaking world like that of Dante — has been intermittent and judgements have been mixed. The full range of his work first became widely known in England in the last years of the conflict with Napoleon, thanks to the efforts of the exiled Mme. de Staël in publicizing the culture of Britain's German allies. In the Victorian period he belonged unquestionably among the great, especially after the death and apotheosis of Prince Albert, and his representation on the base of the Albert Memorial remains the only public monument to him in Britain. For Gwen Raverat's Uncle William, the eldest son of Charles Darwin, "old Go-eethe" was one of the "fine fellows" one had to admire along with Homer, Rembrandt, and Beethoven.[19] The nineteenth-century sages had no hesitation in claiming him as one of their own: to Carlyle, Goethe demonstrated the possibility of retaining moral seriousness in an age of secular modernity; Emerson selected him as his representative "man of letters;" G. H. Lewes made his reputation with his biography and was accompanied on his research trip to Weimar by George Eliot; and Bohn's Standard Library brought out cheap multi-volume editions of Goethe in translation. For Matthew Arnold, "no persons" were "so thoroughly modern, as those who have felt Goethe's influence most deeply," and for them "Goethe's wide and luminous view" was both a consolation and an ideal.[20]

In the last decades of the century, however, economic, then imperial, and finally military rivalry between Britain and Germany clouded the public mind. German culture in general fell into disfavour in England at the very time when Goethe's name and works were being appropriated by the new nation which Bismarck had invented. Under Wilhelm II Goethe was made to serve as the centrepiece of a classical literature which was felt to be as much a prerequisite of nationhood as military heroes, colonies, and a navy. It also happened that Goethe's archives became publicly accessible only in 1885, on the death without issue of his last grandchild, and as a result the systematic study of his life and works was from the beginning made a part of a half-conscious programme of constructing a national mythology. Reactions in England were understandably and increasingly hostile. The British variant of German Idealism, which had dominated university philosophy in the later nineteenth century, was on the defensive after 1900, and as war became more likely, German literary achievements were more stridently and contemptuously dismissed. (Rupert Brooke in a railway carriage: "Opposite me two Germans sweat and snore."[21]) In 1915 Ford Madox Hueffer (eventually to change his name to "Ford," out of hatred for "Prussianism") published a diatribe against the German culture into which his father had been born, under the title *When Blood is their Argument.* "There is no such thing as 'modern German culture,'" he wrote. "The

Goethe legend has done a great deal of harm to the aesthetic standards of the whole world."[22] Goethe's works, in Hueffer's view, will not stand up to critical scrutiny, but their market price is artificially supported by a conspiracy between the German state and its servile jobbers, the German professors. Those who "have invested so many foot-poundals of brain-energy in the author of 'the Sorrows of Werther' . . . dislike seeing what I may call a fall in Goethes" (*When Blood is their Argument*, 280). Hueffer's book was perceptive and well-informed about the political and economic context in which German literature was written and read, but it was also propaganda, and those who win wars do not enjoy the immediate liberation from propaganda which is the fortunate lot of those who lose them. In the decade after 1918, when hundreds of British families of German origin were forcibly repatriated, and those who remained anglicized their names, British intellectual life was ethnically cleansed and the debt of Victorian culture to Germany was erased from memory, or ridiculed. Common sense returned to rule philosophy, Georgian Englishness to rule verse. T. S. Eliot, seeking a new British and post-Victorian identity for himself in the London of the 1920s, adopted Hueffer's estimate of Goethe as a journeyman of letters (283), a prose moralist:[23] Goethe the poet could be disregarded along with the rest of the Romantic generation. (In these circumstances it was a courageous act by our predecessors to refound the English Goethe Society and start the journal *German Life and Letters*, but they did not find the audience outside university circles for which they had hoped.) However, as it became clearer that the age of Empire was drawing to a close and that Britain was culturally no more self-sufficient than she was politically and economically, Germany's experiences became an object of interest again. In the ultra-modern, international, and post-Imperial world of Berlin in the critical years of the Weimar Republic, W. H. Auden and Christopher Isherwood found a release into the twentieth century from the complacency of an English middle class which continued in an essentially Edwardian lifestyle until the demise of domestic service in 1939. Auden's discovery of a world beyond England took him to America and to an environment which had not lost its nineteenth century affiliations with Germany, and at the end of his life he regarded it as achievement enough to become, he hoped, "a minor atlantic Goethe" ("The Cave of Making," 1964).[24] Even Eliot, redefining England and history in the purgatorial fires of the Blitz, changed his view of Goethe completely, and kept a drawing of him on his mantelpiece throughout the war. In the anniversary year of 1949, which also saw Louis Mac-Neice's verse rendering of *Faust*, commissioned by the BBC, Stephen Spender gave a prophetic lecture on "Goethe and the English mind."

He said that the development of the private and self-scrutinizing tone in English poetry had been made possible by the public air of confidence and success in Britain's Imperial epoch, and that "with the catastrophic breakdown of Britain's position in the world," the basis for that private poetry had been withdrawn.[25] Goethe had thereby become extraordinarily topical: "Goethe was evidently close to the problem of Joyce, the problem of the disintegration of a very complex modern consciousness within a world whose values do not provide a structure upon which such complexity can realize itself objectively . . . Goethe's search for a realization of objectivity through subjective experience leads straight into the modern movement in poetry, though very few modern poets realize this" (132, 126). If the British reception of Goethe has made little progress since the anniversary of 1949, it must partly have been because the public and intellectual adaptation to the catastrophe of which Spender spoke has been so slow and the rediscovery of Britain's European and pre-Imperial roots has been so reluctant.

Goethe's achievement is inseparable from the factors which are likely to make him difficult of access for an English audience. In three respects Goethe made himself difficult for the English public to digest, or even to understand: his relation to the Revolution; to religion; and to a reading public. These are also the factors, however, that make for his modernity, indeed his post-modernity.

First, the Revolution. The period of the French Revolution was not a period of revolution for England but a period in which the wealthy English middle class refounded its overseas empire and consolidated it in a series of wars against its French rivals. England knew neither the restrictions and formalities of the *ancien régime,* nor the novelties of political Terror and occupation by the conscript armies of the *levée en masse,* nor therefore the shock of the complete historical disjunction in which, on the continent of Europe, the modern form of the state came into being. That upheaval was the central political event in Goethe's life: it destroyed the Holy Roman Empire, which provided the constitutional framework for the society in which he lived his early years, and though the forms he had been familiar with in his youth were preserved in Restoration Germany, he knew that they were inhabited by a wholly different spirit. To survive the Revolution into the era of European nation-states was to have an experience of collective detachment from an irretrievable past such as England had not known since the Reformation of the sixteenth century and did not have to face again until the final dissolution of the Empire in the twentieth. The self-conscious and semi-serious formality of Goethe's later writing, its ironical juxtapositions of ancient and modern, of the nineteenth and the eighteenth centuries, which nonetheless nearly always refuse the temptation of nostalgia, is the expression of a sensibility which has learnt what it is to be the victim of revolutionary historical change. From the 1840s to the 1940s, from Chartism to the Welfare State, that was not a feeling with which the majority of the English public could, or wished to sympathize. But early and mid-Victorian England also had a small proportion of unflinchingly liberal minds who were aware that their country would not forever remain immune to what had begun on the streets of Paris in 1789, and they saw that Goethe, whatever his public pose, was as modern an intellect as they.

Second, religion. All German literature lay, as far as the nineteenth-century British public was concerned, under the twin suspicions of political Jacobinism and religious impiety. The one was assumed to lead to the other. It is true that the German clergy underwent an Age of Doubt, brought on by biblical criticism and a loss of faith in the scientific evidences for Christianity, in the later eighteenth century, a hundred years before their English counterparts. The result, however, was neither political revolution nor a public outbreak of unbelief, but the rapid growth in philosophy and literature of secular reinterpretations of religion and alternatives to it. The rational and aesthetic rewritings of Christianity by Kant and Schiller and the Idealist generation of philosophers and theologians met a warm reception in America, where they helped to generate a major cultural institution, the Transcendentalist movement, but in England they seemed little better than atheism. In the later part of the century, then, the British mood changed; after the publication of Darwin's *Origin of Species* in 1859, doubts became more widespread and more mentionable, and the German substitutes for belief became the object of serious interest. But it was not long before economic and Imperial rivalry had its intellectual effect, an Anglican school of biblical criticism was founded to counter the German, and isolationism was restored. In one sense it was unfair that Goethe's reputation should have suffered through his being associated with the great philosophical and theological movements of his time and being dismissed as just another irreligious German. Goethe never became a disciple of anyone, not even Kant, and he was never tempted by new restatements of doctrines whose old formulations he had already rejected as absurdities. But his sovereign detachment from the ideologies with which his age teemed made him all but incomprehensible in an England where even unbelief, once it had become respectable, was a specially low form of churchmanship, and certainly was not expected to challenge the social consensus. Goethe had seen through the connection between the

English rejection of theological Enlightenment and the structures of social control which made possible England's industrial and imperial expansion, and there could be no place in his German writings for the
deceptions and self-deceptions of his imaginary life as an English bishop.
The English public could not take him to its heart any more than
Byron, and the nineteenth-century translations of his conversations with
Eckermann, which are still I believe the only ones available today, excised as blasphemous the passage to which I have given attention.[26]

And so, the reading public. "My things can never be popular,"
Goethe confided to Eckermann (11 October 1828), a sentiment which
Germany would have done well to heed in arranging its 250th anniversary celebrations. A third and crucial aspect of the modernity especially
of his later works is their peculiar relation to their audience. In his middle years, and under the impact of both the political and the philosophical revolutions, he at last succeeded in reaching a more or less
stable compromise, a synthesis of the private, courtly writing of the
early Weimar years and the vigorously middle-class works that had preceded it. Reluctantly at first, Goethe committed himself to writing for
the audience he could reach through print, rather than the little public
which surrounded him in Weimar. Increasingly, however, that came to
be an audience of no particular place or time, defined not by any social
or political affiliations, but by a presumptively shared cultural heritage
and cultural concern, the readers of "world literature," "the communion of saints," as he also called them (*WA* 4, 48, 241). They might lie
as far distant from him in time as he was from Hafiz, but they would
find the same delight in discovering him as he had found in that meeting of minds with the Persian poet across the centuries. Goethe in his
maturity, therefore, was not writing for the settled, self-confident, imperialist bourgeoisie of nineteenth-century France and England, and
what he wrote should not be compared with the works of the great realistic novelists whom those societies produced. Nor — more importantly — was Goethe writing for the self-sufficient bureaucratic class,
which in the later nineteenth century created Germany and its national
character in its own image and appropriated Goethe for purposes of
which he could not have approved, or even dreamt. That misappro-
priation in turn had a disastrous effect on Goethe's reputation in England during its long confrontation with would-be imperialist Germany
in the twentieth century. Goethe has suffered — both in Germany and,
by reaction, abroad — from being forced into the role of preceptor of a
nation which he never imagined, the central pillar of a "classical" literature which he declared to be an impossibility,[27] the author of a series
of model or canonical texts — set books for generations of schoolchil-

dren — which were actually unique and highly personal experiments, and many of which had little appeal for his contemporaries. The age of the empires is over, and with it the sense of personal identity which membership in an imperial nation once conferred, or confirmed. That is the solid core of truth within the theorizings of Post Modernism.[28] I hope that the essays in this volume will help to dispel the illusions of the past and to uncover the Goethe who wrote for us, the post-imperial and post-modern English-speaking members of his communion of saints.

Notes

[1] See, for example, *WA* 4, 8, 84–6, 301.

[2] Pascal, *Pensées*, ed. L. Brunschvicg, (Paris: Hachette, 1966), 478, No.322.

[3] J. G. Robertson, "Goethe and Byron," *PEGS* 2 (1925): 50.

[4] T. Medwin, *Journal of the Conversations of Lord Byron* (London, printed for H. Colburn, 1824), 266–67.

[5] See, for example, C. Hentschel, *The Byronic Teuton: Aspects of German Pessimism 1800–1933* (London: Methuen, 1940), 19, and cf. Emil Ludwig, cited Robertson, 121.

[6] *Gespräche* III/2, 457, cf. Tgb 25 August 1828 (*WA* 3, 11, 268); Eckermann 20 June 1827; *Gespräche* III/1, 591, 600; III/2, 450, 456–57 (to Müller 2, 12 October 1823; to Crabb Robinson 13, 16, 17 August 1829).

[7] Tgb 16 August 1829 (*WA* 3, 12, 113); Eckermann 18 May 1824; *Gespräche* III/1, 779, III/2, 437–8, 441, 453 (to Soret and Congreve 28 April 1825; to Crabb Robinson 2, 15 August 1829).

[8] Eckermann 8, 29 November 1824; *Gespräche* III/2, 450, 451–2 (to Crabb Robinson 13 August 1829).

[9] Eckermann 6 (5) July 1827; *Gespräche* III/1, 778, III/2, 583 (to Soret and Congreve 28 April 1825; to Soret 14 March 1830).

[10] Robertson 64, E. M. Butler, *Byron and Goethe. Analysis of a Passion* (London: Bowes and Bowes, 1956), 53–4. Unfortunately, Butler's study draws extensively on Goethe's supposed conversation with Count Stroganoff, which has since been shown to be a forgery: M. von Propper, "Zur Anatomie einer Meisterfälschung: Goethes *Gespräch mit dem russischen Grafen S.*," *Goethe Jahrbuch Wien* 78 (1974): 5–26.

[11] W. H. Bruford, "Some early Cambridge links with German scholarship and literature II" *GLL* 28 (1974–5): 233–45.

[12] Georg Christoph Lichtenberg, *Schriften und Briefe*, ed. W. Promies (Munich: Hanser, 1967–), 1, 357–8 (E70).

[13] F. Zarncke, "Ueber den fünffüßigen Jambus bei Lessing, Schiller und Goethe" *Kleine Schriften I: Goetheschriften*, Leipzig: Eduard Avenarius, 1897, 309–428, esp. 418–23.

[14] Goethe makes the comparison with Shakespeare and Spinoza only after he has remarked of Linnaeus "Ich habe unendlich viel von ihm gelernt, nur nicht Botanik" (*WA* 4, 27, 219). Similarly it might be said he learnt everything from Spinoza except metaphysics, and everything from Shakespeare except how to write plays.

[15] *Goethe. Begegnungen und Gespräche*, ed. E. and R. Grumach (Berlin: De Gruyter, 1965–), 2, 232.

[16] A. Schöne, *Goethes Farbentheologie* (Munich: Beck, 1987), esp. 68–75.

[17] See in particular the sections "Ungewisse Anfänge der Societät," "Naturwissenschaften in England," "Äußere Vortheile der Societät" in the *Geschichte der Farbenlehre, WA* 2, 4, 6–13.

[18] The following thoughts are a somewhat abbreviated version of the argument in my "Introduction" to J. W. von Goethe, *Selected Writings* (London: Everyman, 1999), xxix–xxxix.

[19] G. Raverat, *Period Piece: A Cambridge Childhood* (London: Faber, 1960), 181.

[20] M. Arnold, "Heinrich Heine" in: *Essays in Criticism* (London: Dent, 1964), 113; "Stanzas in memory of the author of 'Obermann'" in: *Poetical Works of Matthew Arnold* (London: Macmillan, 1897), 328.

[21] R. Brooke, "Dawn (From the train between Bologna and Milan, second class)," *The Collected Poems of Rupert Brooke* (London: Sidgwick & Jackson), 1918, 24.

[22] F. M. Hueffer, *When Blood is their Argument: an Analysis of Prussian Culture* (London: Hodder & Stoughton, 1915), 279.

[23] T. S. Eliot, *The Use of Poetry and the Use of Criticism. Studies in the Relation of Criticism to Poetry in England* (second edition, London: Faber, 1964), 99.

[24] W. H. Auden, *Collected Poems*, ed. E. Mendelson (London: Faber, 1976), 522.

[25] S. Spender, *The Making of a Poem* (London: Hamish Hamilton, 1955), 131.

[26] E.g. *Conversations of Goethe with Johann Peter Eckermann*. Translated by John Oxenford. Edited by J. K. Moorhead (New York: Da Capo Press, 1994), "an unabridged republication of the edition published in London in 1930."

[27] See the essay "Litterarischer Sansculottismus," *WA* 1, 40, 196–203.

[28] I have developed this theme further in *Who Are We Now? Christian Humanism and the Global Market from Hegel to Heaney* (Notre Dame: Notre Dame UP and Edinburgh: T. & T. Clark, 1998).

Part I

The English-Speaking World and Goethe:

Meetings and Influences

Wilhelm Meister Reads Shakespeare

Peter Michelsen

"WILHELM MEISTER" is a significant name. If, as Melina says in the *Theatralische Sendung*, names have a great influence on people's imaginations,[1] then we are justified in noting that Goethe gives the hero of his novel the Christian name of a poet he later thought to be part of the *Weltgeist*.[2] Indeed, it is remarkable that ennoblement by this name — "William! Stern der schönsten Höhe"[3] — is bestowed upon a son of the German middle classes, who, from a family of merchants (in the *Theatralische Sendung* he is from a still more humble background), sets out (initially at his father's behest) to follow a most unusual path, beset with errors and remarkable coincidences. The pilgrimage is perhaps not exactly in the direction of a peerage (as Novalis maliciously put it),[4] but it does point towards a lofty goal. His family name is significant too. Goethe may have said in a letter to Schiller that he did not know how Wilhelm had got the name "Meister,"[5] but I am certain he did know. Except that, in 1794 he wanted to forget it, given the change in his conception of the novel, and above all, he did not want the friend who was helping him with the completion of the book to know about it. The intention had probably been that he would begin on his path as a pupil and "prentice" but set his sights on mastery ("Meisterschaft"), even if it remained an open-ended question whether he would reach his goal.

The fact that, even in the *Lehrjahre*, theatre life still takes up considerable space, had already irritated Schiller:

> Das Einzige, was ich gegen dieses Vte Buch zu erinnern habe, ist, daß es mir zuweilen vorkam, als ob Sie demjenigen Theile, der das Schauspielwesen ausschließend angeht, mehr Raum gegeben hätten, als sich mit der freyen und weiten Idee des Ganzen verträgt. Es sieht zuweilen aus, als schrieben Sie *für* den Schauspieler, da Sie doch nur *von* dem Schauspieler schreiben wollen. Die Sorgfalt, welche Sie gewissen kleinen Details in dieser Gattung widmen, und die Aufmerksamkeit auf einzelne kleine Kunstvortheile, die zwar dem Schauspieler und Director aber nicht dem Publikum wichtig sind, bringen den falschen

Schein eines besondern Zweckes in die Darstellung, und wer einen solchen Zweck auch nicht vermuthet, der möchte Ihnen gar Schuld geben, daß eine PrivatVorliebe für diese Gegenstände Ihnen zu mächtig geworden sey.[6]

What Schiller imagined was not far wrong in relation to the early version, which he had probably heard of but did not know. But the novel, as Goethe completed and published it in the nineties, was supposed to show Wilhelm's stubborn endeavours vis-à-vis acting as a long series of errors, which, however, when he recognised and overcame them, led to an entirely different final stage. In this process Wilhelm is secretly steered by a mysterious institution, whose partly disguised representatives — the unknown man Wilhelm met in his home town, the country vicar, the officer who comes to fetch Jarno and embraces Wilhelm, the ghost of Hamlet's father and of course Jarno himself — accompany him at irregular intervals on his path through life or seek him out.

Without particularly dwelling on the influence of the Society of the Tower, I turn to the hero himself, "unser[. . .] Freund," as the narrator regularly apostrophises him (e.g. Book II, 1; *WA* 1, 21, 117; Book II, 2; *WA* 1, 21, 123; Book II, 9; *WA* 1, 21, 185; Book IV, 12; *WA* 1, 22, 68). In the *Lehrjahre*, his earliest aspirations were also directed towards the theatrical: as a child his focus was on puppet shows. Wilhelm tells his beloved about these, but by having her fall asleep at a certain point, the narrator treats this factor with considerable irony and downgrades its significance, and in what follows he will continue to do so. The "wohlgebildete Mann" who joins the small travelling party on the river boat — Wilhelm, Laertes, Philine, Herr und Madame Melina — and, as a ruse, takes the part of the country vicar (Book II, 9: *WA* 1, 21, 188), opposes belief in fate (strangely, by the way, if one considers that he himself belongs to a society devoted to playing the part of fate), and states:

Gesetzt, das Schicksal hätte einen zu einem guten Schauspieler bestimmt (und warum sollt' es uns nicht auch mit guten Schauspielern versorgen?) unglücklicherweise führte der Zufall aber den jungen Mann in ein Puppenspiel, wo er sich früh nicht enthalten könnte, an etwas Abgeschmacktem Theil zu nehmen, etwas Albernes leidlich, wohl gar interessant zu finden, und so die jugendlichen Eindrücke, welche nie verlöschen, denen wir eine gewisse Anhänglichkeit nie entziehen können, von einer falschen Seite zu empfangen. (Book II, 9; *WA* 1, 21, 192)

When Wilhelm asks, in astonishment, how he comes to mention puppet plays, the unknown man states that it is just a random example, "nur ein unwillkürliches [correctly: willkürliches] Beispiel,"[7] but the reader finds the reference unsettling (at least that is the case with me).

The unknown man cannot in fact be right with his assertion, for how else would the author Goethe, with his intensive experiences of puppet plays in his childhood and youth, ever have been able to involve himself in theatre! The narrator spares himself no pains, however, to convince the reader that Wilhelm is nothing more than a dilettante when it comes to acting. Jarno later expresses the opinion that in his case it is "doch so rein entschieden: daß wer sich nur selbst spielen kann, kein Schauspieler ist" (Book VIII, 5; *WA* 1, 23, 214). Now in addition to the actor who can change himself into another person — Goethe admired Iffland for this — there is also the actor whose own personality stands in the foreground and who gives all rôles the stamp of his individuality. But is it clear that Wilhelm has only ever played himself? Several people whom Wilhelm meets on his return visit to the café in town are obviously of a different opinion. They had been pleased to see him on the stage and were sorry to see him leave it. He reports:

> [They] bedauerten [. . .], daß er, wie sie hörten, die Bühne verlassen wolle; sie sprachen so bestimmt und vernünftig von ihm und seinem Spiele, von dem Grade seines Talents, von ihren Hoffnungen, daß Wilhelm nicht ohne Rührung zuletzt ausrief: O wie unendlich werth wäre mir diese Theilnahme vor wenig Monaten gewesen! Wie belehrend und wie erfreuend! Niemals hätte ich mein Gemüth so ganz von der Bühne abgewendet, und niemals wäre ich so weit gekommen, am Publico zu verzweifeln. (Book VII, 8; *WA* 1, 23, 104 f)

According to the text, it was not his insight into his own lack of ability as an actor that caused him to give up a career in the theatre; rather, he doubted whether the audience would be able to raise themselves to the level of inspiration experienced by the actor. But at this point Wilhelm, having gained admittance to the Society of the Tower, is not to be lured back to the boards, which signify the world. The Society to which he belongs from now on is not only antagonistic towards the theatre, but also stands at a noticeable distance from the real conditions that prevailed in Germany in the eighteenth century, as mirrored in the first five books of the novel.

It is surprising, even paradoxical, that a member of this very Society points Wilhelm decisively in the direction of Shakespeare. While in the *Theatralische Sendung* this paradox could not appear (for there is no sign of such a Society), the one source of the recommendation — Jarno — represented even at that point a personality antithetical to the spirit of Shakespeare. Jarno has a low opinion of those figures of the novel — Mignon and the Harper — who seem to have come out of the "schöne[. . .] Raritäten Kasten" that is Shakespeare's world ("Zum Shakespeares Tag," *WA* I, 37, 133); he rebukes Wilhelm for having given his heart to "einen herumziehenden Bänkelsänger und an ein albernes zwitterhaftes Geschöpf" (Book III, 11; *WA* 1, 21, 312). Both of them are therefore provided with terrible incestuous life-stories and excluded from the sphere of the Tower as unsuited for survival; viewed against the Clear and Pure — Mignon against Therese — they must perish. Jarno, in contrast to Wilhelm, would never have taken Mignon under his wing out of pity, but Wilhelm's affection for Mignon is based on a deep sympathetic feeling. "Seine Augen und sein Herz wurden unwiderstehlich von dem geheimnisvollen Zustande dieses Wesens angezogen" (Book II, 4; *WA* 1, 21, 153 f.). Indeed, Wilhelm sees her as his "geliebte Creatur." "Er sehnte sich, dieses verlassene Wesen an Kindesstatt seinem Herzen einzuverleiben, es in seine Arme zu nehmen, und mit der Liebe eines Vaters Freude des Lebens in ihm zu erwecken" (Book II, 8; WA 1, 21, 183). When she let him embrace her closely, with "ihr ganzes Wesen [appearing] in einen Bach von Thränen unaufhaltsam dahin zu schmelzen," he accepts her as "his child," and she answers with "weicher Heiterkeit": "Mein Vater! [. . .] Ich bin dein Kind!" We fully believe the narrator when he assures us that in this experience of fatherhood, accompanied by the Harper's "herzlichste[. . .] Lieder[. . .]," Wilhelm enjoys the "reinste unbeschreiblichste Glück" (Book II, 14, *WA* 1, 21, 229), a happiness that anticipates the later happiness he experiences as an actual father with his son Felix. It must also be emphasised that Wilhelm sticks to the resultant obligation to take care of her. Both Mignon and the Harper are seen by Wilhelm as "Schutzgeister" (Book II, 11; *WA* 1, 21, 205 and Book IV, 12; *WA* 1, 22, 68), and he, together with them, forms a "wunderbare Familie, die Wilhelm [. . .] als seine eigene ansah" (Book III, 9; *WA* 1, 21, 301). It is furthermore significant that Mignon and the Harper alone have access to the room in which Wilhelm locked himself away in order to open himself to Shakespeare's world.

The prejudices that Wilhelm has harboured against Shakespeare, that his characters were monstrous, "seltsame Ungeheuer," "die über alle Wahrscheinlichkeit, allen Wohlstand [i.e. Anstand] hinauszuschreiten scheinen" (Book III, 8; *WA* 1, 21, 290), correspond to notions which, although by no means general in the eighteenth century, could still frequently be encountered. That a work of literature was subject to certain laws seemed obvious, even if there was not complete agreement about the detailed rules themselves. That a poet should have appeared who did not worry at all about such laws, "a genius without rules," whose art owed everything to nature, this initially seemed a provocation of the first order. Yet under the auspices of an increasingly dominant concept of nature, the re-evaluation or triumph of Shakespeare in the eighteenth century followed.[8] With the term "strange" ("seltsame Ungeheuer"), a category vigorously discussed in the Enlightenment is also being addressed: the "miraculous" — something whose validity is either justified or disputed in terms of its verisimilitude. This factor is hinted at when Jarno speaks of the "Zauberlaterne [i.e. laterna magica] dieser unbekannten Welt" (Book III, 8; WA 1, 21, 290). At the same time, by using the attribute "unknown," he alludes to the gamble of venturing into these regions. In a certain respect he is demanding of Wilhelm that he continue along his path into the unknown, but on a higher literary plane.

Thus Wilhelm's admittance to Shakespeare's world is not a break with what has gone before. Indeed, in Shakespeare's plays, which he has read in Wieland's translation of 1762–66 (Book V, 5; WA 1, 22, 168), Wilhelm finds that everything illustrated and depicted there already exists within himself: "Alle Vorgefühle, die ich jemals über Menschheit und ihre Schicksale gehabt, die mich von Jugend auf, mir selbst unbemerkt, begleiteten, finde ich in Shakespears Stücken erfüllt und entwickelt" (Book III, 11; WA 1, 21, 310). That sense of anticipation is linked with its opposite: absolute amazement at the totally new things that are influencing him and impinging upon his mind. As if entranced in a magic circle, Wilhelm feels himself surrounded by a "Geisterfluth," which he was not able to bring "wieder zur Ebbe": "Mit unbekannter Bewegung wurden tausend Empfindungen und Fähigkeiten in ihm rege, von denen er keinen Begriff und keine Ahnung gehabt hatte" (Book III, 9; WA 1, 21, 298–99).

The narrator captures the "Bewegung" that Wilhelm's soul starts to acquire (Book III, 11; WA 1, 21, 309) in various images, beginning with the clock-simile:

> Es scheint, als wenn er [Shakespeare] uns alle Räthsel offenbarte, ohne daß man doch sagen kann: hier oder da ist das Wort der Auflösung. Seine Menschen scheinen natürliche Menschen zu sein, und sie sind es doch nicht. Diese geheimnißvollsten und zusammengesetztesten Geschöpfe der Natur handeln vor uns [. . .], als wenn sie Uhren wären, deren Zifferblatt und Gehäuse man von Krystall gebildet hätte, sie zeigten nach ihrer Bestimmung den Lauf der Stunden an, und man kann zugleich das Räder- und Federwerk erkennen, das sie treibt. (Book III, 11, WA 1, 21, 310)

Alongside this explanation, which seems rather mechanistic, there appear images that indicate the disintegration of all that is permanent and the release of what had seemed to be securely housed within the limits of individuality: Wilhelm was seized by "der Strom jenes großen Genius," which "führte ihn einem unübersehlichen Meere zu, worin er sich gar bald völlig vergaß und verlor" (Book III, 8; *WA* 1, 21, 291). In forgetting and losing the self, something irresistible and unfathomable overwhelms and overpowers the individual, plunging him into the strange and boundless ocean of the world. Does not this image of the "great genius" correspond to the view of the poet that young Wilhelm, after his first great disappointment and serious illness, had enthusiastically sketched during the auto-da-fé of his works? It culminated in these words: "wer hat, wenn du willst, Götter gebildet, uns zu ihnen erhoben, sie zu uns herniedergebracht, als der Dichter?" (Book II, 2; *WA* 1, 21, 131). He lives "den Traum des Lebens als ein Wachender, und das Seltenste, was geschieht, ist ihm zugleich Vergangenheit und Zukunft. Und so ist der Dichter zugleich Lehrer, Wahrsager, Freund der Götter und der Menschen" (Book II, 2; *WA* 1, 21, 129). Whatever the subjectively charged state of inspiration from which these words derive (and which would therefore make them offensive to the strict reason of members of the Society of the Tower), they nevertheless describe their object most appropriately. Such an excess of supreme admiration overcame Wilhelm once again when he made the acquaintance of Shakespeare. "Es sind keine Gedichte! Man glaubt vor den aufgeschlagenen ungeheuren Büchern des Schicksals zu stehen, in denen der Sturmwind des bewegtesten Lebens saus't, und sie mit Gewalt rasch hin und wieder blättert. Ich bin über die Stärke und Zartheit, über die Gewalt und Ruhe [. . .] erstaunt und außer aller Fassung gebracht" (Book III, 11; *WA* 1, 21, 309 f.). Wilhelm immediately connects the profound emotional turmoil, reminiscent of Herder's Shakespeare essay, into which the confrontation with the British poet has plunged him, with practical consequences that he is determined to draw for his own life:

> Diese wenigen Blicke, die ich in Shakespears Welt gethan, reizen mich mehr als irgend etwas andres, in der wirklichen Welt schnellere Fortschritte vorwärts zu thun, mich in die Fluth der Schicksale zu mischen, die über sie verhängt sind, und dereinst, wenn es mir glücken sollte, aus dem großen Meere der wahren Natur wenige Becher zu schöpfen, und sie von der Schaubühne dem lechzenden Publicum meines Vaterlandes auszuspenden. (Book III, 11; *WA* 1, 21, 310 f.)

The consequence of reading Shakespeare is in no sense a self-indulgent cult of inwardness. Rather, it spurs Wilhelm on to production of his own, perhaps to poetic enterprises, but certainly to attempts at practical theatre. Wilhelm lets himself be roused to action with the express intention of influencing the society of his time from the stage.

Let us look further at the effects of Wilhelm's experience of Shakespeare. Jarno welcomes Wilhelm's new frame of mind with the words

"Lassen Sie den Vorsatz nicht fahren, in ein thätiges Leben überzuge-hen, und eilen Sie, die guten Jahre, die Ihnen gegönnt sind, wacker zu nutzen" (Book III, 11; *WA* 1, 21, 311). He immediately connects this with the offer of obtaining Wilhelm a favourable position, although strangely he does not return to this offer in what follows. Wilhelm does not come back to it either, since he feels repelled by Jarno's "hartherzi-ge Kälte" in relation to Mignon and the Harper (Book III, 11; *WA* 1, 21, 313), but he does allow himself to be led by his literary model Shakespeare. He has already acknowledged him as his "godfather" ("Pathen," Book IV, 2; *WA* 1, 22, 14); he has even let himself be in-spired by him in matters of clothing. The model closest to his situation, he felt, was Prince Hal in *Henry IV*. He it was who "sich unter gerin-ger, ja sogar schlechter Gesellschaft eine Zeitlang aufhält, und, unge-achtet seiner edlen Natur, an der Roheit, Unschicklichkeit und Albernheit solcher ganz sinnlichen Bursche sich ergötzt," and was for him "das Ideal, womit er seinen gegenwärtigen Zustand vergleichen konnte" (Book IV, 2; *WA* 1, 22, 14 f.). Was he thereby only promot-ing the "self-deception" to which he "had an almost insuperable lean-ing"? Is this only a case of a dilettantish confusion of art and life?[9] How often did Goethe present himself incognito or dress as someone else! And when Wilhelm puts himself in the role of one of Shakespeare's characters, what is he doing if not playing an "idealized role"? "Alle Menschen guter Art," Goethe says in *Dichtung und Wahrheit*, feel this need, "bei zunehmender Bildung." "Sich etwas Höheres anzubilden, sich einem Höheren gleich zu stellen": "in diesem Gefühl ist der Grund alles Edlen aufzusuchen" (*Dichtung und Wahrheit* III, 11; *WA* 1, 28, 26–27.). And if Wilhelm talks of "Treue" as "Bestreben einer edlen Seele," "einem Größern gleich zu werden," or says of talents that one must "sie um ihrer selbst willen lieben, oder sie ganz aufgeben" (Book IV, 2; *WA* 1, 22, 19–20), then he is not only formulating apho-ristic statements such as could occur in the Lehrbrief, but he is also making an attempt at justifying his present theatrical endeavours, which are oriented around Shakespeare. If it has been maintained that Shake-speare gave new impetus to Wilhelm's "false enthusiasm" and "dilet-tantism," (M. Fick 121), then this of course corresponds to the point of view that the narrator, who constantly adjusts to the perspective of the Society of the Tower, wants to give to the reader. But has this correc-tion of himself from the perspective of the Tower completely pene-trated the text? Is it plausible to see Wilhelm's theatrical career as, from the beginning, a false striving, originating in the obsession with in-wardness? Did he really have, as he thought in retrospect, "nicht die geringste Anlage" for being an actor? Did he seek "da Bildung [. . .], wo keine zu finden war" (Book VII, 9; *WA* 1, 23, 123)? But he did find it! Where else did he find it? Is he only putting into practice "Irrthümer auf Irrthümer, Verirrungen auf Verirrungen" (Book VII, 6; *WA* 1, 23, 45)? Was his life as an actor nothing but a "Grille, etwas Schönes und Gutes in Gesellschaft von Zigeunern hervorzubringen" (Book VII, 3; *WA* 1, 23, 23 f.)?[10] All these malicious commentaries, which the changed conception of the novel as a whole causes the narrator to voice, have to be regarded as mistaken when they are seen in the light of Wilhelm's actual behaviour in the first five books.

The pre-eminence of *Hamlet* in the treatment of Shakespeare is not the fault of Wilhelm. It is not so much the result of his own interests as that of the *Hamlet* fever predominating in Germany in the 1770s and 1780s.[11] The text mainly depicts Wilhelm's practical attempts at achieving an appropriate performance of the play. The interpretation of the play serves primarily this end. "Der Schauspieler," Wilhelm says, "soll von dem Stücke und von den Ursachen seines Lobes und Tadels Rechenschaft geben können: und wie will er das, wenn er nicht in den Sinn seines Autors, wenn er nicht in die Absichten desselben einzudringen versteht?" (Book IV, 3; *WA* 1, 22, 25). Wilhelm's attempts to assimilate himself to the figure of Hamlet outside the theatre as well are part of this desire to penetrate Shakespeare's intentions.

> Auch glaubte ich recht in den Geist der Rolle einzudringen, wenn ich die Last der tiefen Schwermuth gleichsam selbst auf mich nähme, und unter diesem Druck meinem Vorbilde durch das seltsame Labyrinth so mancher Launen und Sonderbarkeiten zu folgen suchte. So memorirte ich, und so übte ich mich, und glaubte nach und nach mit meinem Helden zu einer Person zu werden. (Book IV, 3; *WA* 1, 22, 26)

It is important to recognise that Wilhelm does not exhibit any inner affinity with the figure of Hamlet; the pre-condition of having to do something he is not able to is not there. And his reluctant desire to pursue an acting career is simply not comparable with Hamlet's lack of decisiveness about avenging his father. Wilhelm desires to reach an understanding of the drama, a "Vorstellung des Ganzen" (Book IV, 3; *WA* 1, 22, 26) by attempting to reconstruct Hamlet's character "in früher Zeit vor dem Tode seines Vaters" (Book IV, 3; *WA* 1, 22, 27). This may be — if I may make a critical observation — an interpretative venture that is bound to remain speculative, but for Wilhelm it is a decidedly practical undertaking, directed towards the planned production.

The narrator makes sure that Wilhelm's preoccupation with *Hamlet* leaves its trace in the novel's action. To begin with, the early introduction of a person called "Laertes" — "den wir einstweilen Laertes nennen wollen" (Book II, 4; *WA* 1, 21, 144) — "quotes," as it were,

Shakespeare's play. At an idyllic mountain spot, a true *locus amoenus* on their journey to H., Wilhelm and Laertes practise the duel scene from the play's conclusion "in theatralischer Absicht": "Beide Freunde waren überzeugt, daß man in dieser wichtigen Scene nicht, wie es wohl auf Theatern zu geschehen pflegt, nur ungeschickt hin und wieder stoßen dürfe; sie hofften ein Muster darzustellen, wie man, bei der Aufführung, auch dem Kenner der Fechtkunst ein würdiges Schauspiel zu geben habe" (Book IV, 5; *WA* 1, 22, 37). It is true that, after the surprise attack, as a result of his meeting with the "schöne Amazone," who, with her head surrounded by rays of light, appears to him as a "Heilige" (*WA* 1, 22, 43, 45, 46), Wilhelm's inner sense is steered in a completely different direction, away from Shakespeare, setting his "Jugendträume" alight again. But he nevertheless remains true to his theatrical career after his convalescence. In the *Theatralische Sendung* the conflict in which he found himself was more clearly expressed: "die sehnlichsten Erinnerungen banden ihn wieder an's Theater [. . .]. Nur seit der Erscheinung jener zu bald verschwundenen Heiligen nahm sein Gemüth eine andere Richtung. Sich ihr nahen [. . .] hieß schon aus dem Zustande heraus treten, in dem er sich befand, und ein zwiespältiges Verlangen zog ihn aus einer Welt in die andere" (Book VI, 7; *WA* 1, 57, 222 f.). But his thoughts still revolve around the play *Hamlet*, to which he devotes a long-winded analysis in front of his actor friends and Serlo, and which culminates in this central idea:

> Shakespear habe schildern wollen: eine große That auf eine Seele gelegt, die der That nicht gewachsen ist. [. . .] Hier wird ein Eichbaum in ein köstliches Gefäß gepflanzt, das nur liebliche Blumen in seinem Schoß hätte aufnehmen sollen; die Wurzeln dehnen aus, das Gefäß wird zernichtet. Ein schönes, reines, edles, höchst moralisches Wesen, ohne die sinnliche Stärke, die den Helden macht, geht unter einer Last zu Grunde, die es weder tragen noch abwerfen kann; jede Pflicht ist ihm heilig, diese zu schwer. Das Unmögliche wird von ihm gefordert, nicht das Unmögliche an sich, sondern das, was ihm unmöglich ist. Wie er sich windet, dreht, ängstigt, vor- und zurück tritt; immer erinnert wird: sich immer erinnert und zuletzt fast seinen Zweck aus dem Sinne verliert, ohne doch jemals wieder froh zu werden. (Book IV, 13; *WA* 1, 22, 76)

Friedrich Schlegel's dictum that this view of Hamlet was not so much criticism as higher poetry is surely right. [12] At the same time, it became extraordinarily important in the history of German thought. In Hamlet, as Wilhelm Meister saw him, the Germans — "tatenarm und gedankenvoll" as they still were for Hölderlin[13] — believed they were looking at themselves in the mirror. "Deutschland ist Hamlet!" wrote

Freiligrath in the middle of the nineteenth century: "Du ew'ger Zaude-
rer und Säumer!"[14] But beyond the characterisation of the hero,
Wilhelm interprets the play as a whole as a fate drama.[15] This interpretation of *Hamlet* by Wilhelm is seldom referred to but is so impressive
that I must quote it at length:

> Es gefällt uns so wohl, es schmeichelt so sehr, wenn wir einen Helden
> sehen, der durch sich selbst handelt, der liebt und haßt, wenn es ihm
> sein Herz gebietet, der unternimmt und ausführt, alle Hindernisse ab-
> wendet und zu einem großen Zwecke gelangt. Geschichtschreiber und
> Dichter möchten uns gerne überreden, daß ein so stolzes Loos dem
> Menschen fallen könne. Hier werden wir anders belehrt; der Held hat
> keinen Plan, aber das Stück ist planvoll. Hier wird nicht etwa nach einer
> starr und eigensinnig durchgeführten Idee von Rache ein Bösewicht be-
> straft, nein, es geschieht eine ungeheure That, sie wälzt sich in ihren
> Folgen fort, reißt Unschuldige mit; der Verbrecher scheint dem Ab-
> grunde, der ihm bestimmt ist, ausweichen zu wollen, und stürzt hinein,
> eben da, wo er seinen Weg glücklich auszulaufen gedenkt. Denn das ist
> die Eigenschaft der Greuelthat, daß sie auch Böses über den Unschul-
> digen, wie der guten Handlung, daß sie viele Vortheile auch über den
> Unverdienten ausbreitet, ohne daß der Urheber von beiden oft weder
> bestraft noch belohnt wird. Hier in unserm Stücke wie wunderbar! Das
> Fegefeuer sendet seinen Geist und fordert Rache, aber vergebens. Alle
> Umstände kommen zusammen, und treiben die Rache, vergebens! We-
> der Irdischen noch Unterirdischen kann gelingen, was dem Schicksal
> allein vorbehalten ist. Die Gerichtsstunde kommt. Der Böse fällt mit
> dem Guten. Ein Geschlecht wird weggemäht, und das andere sproßt
> auf. (Book IV, 15; *WA* 1, 22, 90)

Here, in this anticipation of the definition of fate in drama (in the
conversation with Serlo about novel and drama, Book V, 7; *WA* 1, 22,
177 ff.), Wilhelm's ability to interpret is at its height — even if one
must doubt whether he really does justice to the play. Aurelie rightly
gives expression to her admiration: "wenn man Sie Ihren Shakespear
erklären hört, glaubt man, Sie kämen eben aus dem Rathe der Götter,
und hätten zugehört, wie man sich da selbst beredet, Menschen zu bil-
den" (Book IV, 16; *WA* 1, 22, 94). By contrast her criticism, supported by the narrator, that Wilhelm misjudges the people with whom
he lives, I do not find convincing (Book IV, 16; *WA* 1, 22, 94); his
recommendation of Melina and his followers was made more out of
good will than conviction. And with his admission that he always had
"die Augen [seines] Geistes mehr nach innen als nach außen gerichtet"
(Book IV, 16; *WA* 1, 22, 95), he is of course assuming the interpretative perspective of the narrator of 1795–96. It is determined by Schiller's conceptual and schematic explanation of the novel as he expresses

it in a letter to Goethe of 1795–96: Wilhelm was moving "von einem leeren und unbestimmten Ideal in ein bestimmtes tätiges Leben" (Letter of 8 July 1796; NA 28, 254). A close reading of the text does not support his view.

What we have witnessed in the novel up until now is certainly not an introverted life. Characters from the most diverse sections of society have come close to Wilhelm and he has had varying degrees of close contact with them. His energetic efforts towards a production on Serlo's stage, coupled with all kinds of different considerations and concerns — including an appropriate appearance for military characters, and directions for the actors to speak audibly and distinctly — is evidence of fully practical engagement. The production of *Hamlet* is unquestionably the climax of Wilhelm's theatrical career; everything that has gone before points towards it — from puppet play and love of Mariane to his experiences with the troupe of actors (Melina, Philine, and Laertes), but also with Mignon. Did not Wilhelm also show in his acting career something akin to "Entschiedenheit und Folge"?[16] Not so much in outward matters — for in them he is diverted by various forms of chance and necessity — but in his decisive holding on to the theatre and to his talent, or what he thought was his talent. The principle supposedly demonstrating Wilhelm's lack of ability as an actor, later read out by Jarno from the letter of apprenticeship, is this: "Man soll sich [. . .] vor einem Talente hüten, das man in Vollkommenheit auszuüben nicht Hoffnung hat" (Book VIII, 5; WA 1, 23, 215). How could one think of cultivating *any* talent in the light of a principle like this? *Who* can ever hope for "perfection" and *how*? Isn't an unconditional duty being imposed, and of the very kind we are told we should discard? For in the same letter we read: "Der Mensch ist nicht eher glücklich, als bis sein unbedingtes Streben sich selbst seine Begränzung bestimmt" (Book VIII, 5; WA 1, 23, 218). The phrase "unconditional striving" is no doubt intended to apply to Wilhelm's theatrical career, but is it justified? Wasn't this career conditioned by various circumstances? And doesn't Wilhelm consciously and decisively submit to these conditions?

This applies to the production of *Hamlet*, in which both his achievements as an actor and his relationship to Shakespeare reach a climax. The alterations that Wilhelm makes to the text at Serlo's behest are moderate when compared to the norm in German theatres of the eighteenth century. As far as the production itself is concerned, which is preceded by a long, intensive period of rehearsal, it is in essence only the two scenes in which Hamlet's father appears — act 1, scene 4 and act 2, scene 4 — that are closely depicted. Strangely enough, no actor can be found for the role of the ghost, making it necessary to rely on an anonymous letter that promises the ghost will appear. This ghost — an emissary of the Tower, of course — duly appears, and has the greatest possible effect on the audience and a favourable influence on Wilhelm's acting. But most important and marvellous is the veil he leaves behind for Wilhelm with these words sewn into it: "Zum ersten und letztenmal! Flieh! Jüngling, flieh!" (Book V, 13; *WA* 1, 22, 211 f.).

This piece of advice, which we later learn has been devised by the Abbé, does not persuade Wilhelm to leave the theatre. Only after the journey following Aurelie's death does he follow, in any practical way, the advice to flee. What is he fleeing from? We find a short and appropriate answer: from his entire life up to this point and the social circles in which it was situated, but also from the theatre and from the world of Shakespeare. Wilhelm is told he is "zu heilen, wenn sie heilbar wären" (Book VIII, 5; *WA* 1, 23, 215). Because this is intended to be a process of healing, we are obliged to understand the entire course of the novel, even after the significant reference to the sick prince, as a pathological study. But what Schiller calls a "lange Reyhe von Verirrungen" (letter to Goethe of 8 July 1796; NA 28, 254) had left an indelible impression on Wilhelm's life. His career as an actor was a career in the real world. To have an influence in and on the real world through the theatre was his life's ambition. Even if at a later stage he is to decide differently, he cannot reverse this decision. Wilhelm will always have been an actor, whatever he may later become. No one will be able to remove it from him, or release him from it — even the author. And shouldn't one be amazed that Wilhelm, in spite of all the involvements in errors and wrong directions — or perhaps with their help? — becomes that "Persönchen" that Werner looks at with amazement in Book VIII (*WA* 1, 23, 132)? Where his flight takes him — into the Tower's utopia, the land of fantasy — no longer concerns us here. There we find an elitist interest-group, a sort of secret society, whose aims, objectively seen, consist essentially in clinging to cottage industry as an economic structure for society in opposition to the tendencies of the time. In this ideal — not to say unreal — society, it is the spirit of Spinoza that prevails. Shakespeare has no access to it.[17]

Translated by John Guthrie

Notes

[1] *Wilhelm Meisters theatralische Sendung*. Book II, Ch. 7. *WA* 1, 51, 165.

[2] "Shakespeare und kein Ende!" (1813; publ. 1815). *WA* 1, 41, 55.

[3] "Zwischen beiden Welten" (1820). *WA* 1, 3, 45.

[4] Novalis, *Schriften*. vol. 3, ed. Richard Samuel. (Darmstadt, 1968), 646.

[5] Letter of 6 December 1794; *WA* 4, 10, 212. In the annotated editions of Goethe's letters that I have consulted, this passage remains without commentary.

[6] Letter to Goethe of 15 June 1795. Schiller, *Werke*. Nationalausgabe (NA) 27, 197.

[7] *WA* 1, 21, 193. The first edition (Berlin 1795, 307) has "willkührliches" (*WA* 1, 21, 342). Recent editions rightly follow the first edition.

[8] On Shakespeare's reception in Germany cf. my comments in [Review of:] Lawrence Marsden Price. *Die Aufnahme englischer Literatur in Deutschland 1500–1960*. Ins Deutsche uebertragen von Maxwell F. Knight. (Bern and Munich: Francke Verlag, 1961). *Göttingische Gelehrte Anzeigen* 220 (1968): 239–282.

[9] As Monika Fick suggests in: *Das Scheitern des Genius. Mignon und die Symbolik der Liebesgeschichten in Wilhelm Meisters Lehrjahren* (Würzburg, 1987), 122.

[10] That "Zigeuner" is pejorative here is obvious.

[11] See Wilhelm Voßkamp in: Johann Wolfgang Goethe, *FA* 9 1223.

[12] "Über Goethes Meister"; *Kritische Friedrich-Schlegel-Ausgabe*, ed. Ernst Behler, vol. 2 (Munich, Paderborn, Vienna, 1967), 140.

[13] Hölderlin, "An die Deutschen," Sämtliche Werke, ed. Friedrich Beissner, vol. 2 (Stuttgart, 1951), 9.

[14] Ferdinand Freiligrath, *Werke*, ed. Julius Schwering. Part 2 (Berlin, Leipzig, Vienna, Stuttgart, n.d.), 71 ff.

[15] See Hans Jürgen Schings in the commentary to his edition of the novel, MA 5, 761.

[16] "Entschiedenheit und Folge," as the Oheim says in Book VI, is "das Verehrungswürdigste am Menschen" (Book VI; *WA* 1, 22, 334).

[17] As shown by Hans Jürgen Schings in some important essays, which he summarises in his introduction to the novel: "Der Satz des Oheims ["Gedenke zu leben"] gibt die pointierte Essenz einer Propositio aus Spinozas "Ethik" wieder: 'Homo liber de nulla re minus, quam de morte cogitat, & ejus sapientia non mortis, sed vitae meditatio est.'" (641)

Goethe and Newton

H. B. Nisbet

T HAT GOETHE VENTURED to attack Newton at all is remarkable. No individual personage was more venerated by the leading figures of the Enlightenment than Newton, and in scientific circles, his authority was well-nigh absolute. Pope's famous epitaph sums up his standing in eighteenth-century England:

> Nature and Nature's laws lay hid in night:
> God said, Let Newton be! and all was light.

Voltaire, who in 1727 witnessed Newton's funeral at Westminster Abbey, with six dukes and the Lord Chancellor among the pallbearers, endorsed this view, and his *Eléments de la Philosophie de Newton* helped to spread Newton's fame throughout Europe. In Germany too, his works achieved canonic status, especially after Kant, who, in his *Critique of Pure Reason*, set up Newtonian science as the absolute standard against which all empirical knowledge must be measured.

That Goethe's attack on Newton was not confined to his scientific theories but also aimed at his personal character and moral integrity is even more remarkable. In the *Farbenlehre*, for example, Newton's *Opticks* is described as "ein Muster von sophistischer Entstellung der Natur" (*LA* 1, 5, 86); Goethe subsequently declares, with a simile borrowed from the card game of faro in which large sums of money changed hands:

> Man kann [. . .] Newton einem falschen Spieler vergleichen, der bei einem unaufmerksamen Bankier ein Paroli in eine Karte liegt, die er nicht gewonnen hat, und nachher, teils durch Glück teils durch List, ein Ohr nach dem andern in die Karte knickt und ihren Wert immer steigert. (*LA* 1, 5, 157)

For good measure, Newton's optical theories are condemned at various points as "unredlich," "unverschämt," "schändlich," "fratzenhaft," and "närrisch" (*LA* 1, 5, 82, 118, 184–5, 187). Thus, the greatest poet of the eighteenth and early nineteenth centuries, who did not regularly indulge in polemics, repeatedly accuses the world's most re-

spected scientist of fraud and mendacity, and describes a major part of
Newtonian physics as fundamentally mistaken.

This paper will attempt to answer two questions. First, why did
Goethe react so strongly, despite Newton's immense authority, against
Newtonian physics? More particularly, why were his attacks on Newton
no less moral or ethical in character than scientific? The accusations
quoted above plainly suggest that he found something ethically suspect
or unsound about Newton's entire manner of thinking.

The obvious point from which to begin this discussion is Goethe's
famous account, at the end of the *Farbenlehre*, of how he first came to
realise that he disagreed fundamentally with Newton. He tells us how,
during his Italian journey, he had studied the principles of form and
composition in painting (*LA* 1, 6, 415–17). But on the nature and
functions of colour in particular, he had learned nothing of real significance either from the painters he met or from the textbooks he consulted,[1] so he resolved to investigate it himself from first principles as
soon as he returned to Germany. In those days, the authoritative work
on colour theory was Newton's *Opticks*, and Goethe decided to study it
and repeat its central experiments (*LA* 1, 6, 417–21). Before doing so,
however, he glanced casually through a borrowed prism at the wall of
his room, and expected, from his hazy recollections of scientific lectures
at university, to see the whole white surface covered in spectral colours.
He noticed at once that this was not the case, and he describes his astonishment as follows:

> wie verwundert war ich, als die [. . .] weiße Wand nach wie vor weiß
> blieb, daß nur da, wo ein Dunkles dran stieß, sich eine mehr oder we-
> niger entschiedene Farbe zeigte, daß zuletzt die Fensterstäbe am al-
> lerlebhaftesten farbig erschienen, indessen am lichtgrauen Himmel
> draußen keine Spur von Färbung zu sehen war. Es bedurfte keiner
> langen Überlegung, so erkannte ich, daß eine Grenze notwendig sei,
> um Farben hervorzubringen, und ich sprach wie durch einen Instinkt
> sogleich vor mich laut aus, daß die Newtonische Lehre falsch sei.[2]

As Albrecht Schöne has shown in his book on *Goethes Farbentheolo-*
gie, Goethe's account of this aperçu has more than a hint of the religious conversion experience about it.[3] Indeed, Goethe's polemics against
Newton are full of religious language. He obviously viewed himself as a
defender of the true faith in chromatics against the inquisitorial orthodoxy of Newton and his disciples (cf. *LA* 1, 3, 276). He regularly uses
the language of religion throughout his works when dealing with ab-
solutes or ultimate issues, even if these issues are essentially secular in
character as, for example, in his novels, when Werther describes his
feelings for Lotte, or when the narrator in *Die Wahlverwandtschaften*

tells us of Ottilie's saint-like status after her death. Such language serves, among other things, to convey the strength of feeling with which such issues are meant to be viewed, and this applies equally to Goethe's campaign — "crusade" might be a more appropriate word — against Newton. But I am not so much concerned, as Schöne was, with the quasi-religious expression of Goethe's hostility towards Newton, as with the reasons why he felt this hostility strongly enough to use such religious terminology in the first place.

The most immediate reason why Goethe reacted so negatively to Newton's *Opticks* in that flash of inspiration in 1790 lies in the scientific work he had been engaged in over the previous six years. Most of this work had concerned botany and zoology, and more particularly the comparative study of plant and animal anatomy (or "morphology," to use the term Goethe gave to it). Biology, in Goethe's day, consisted largely of natural history, that is, the description and classification of natural forms according to their similarities and differences. Goethe's main objective in morphology was to identify the basic similarities between groups of organisms. He did so for two reasons. First, like Buffon and other natural historians of the time, he sought to classify organisms in "natural" groups or families, with a view to creating a so-called "natural system" of taxonomy (although such a system was not yet conceived in an evolutionary sense).[4] Second, he sought to find support for the metaphysical premise that underlay all his scientific work, namely his conviction that all natural forms, including human beings, are part of a gradual and harmonious series that collectively constitutes the natural world as an organic whole.[5] His discovery of the intermaxillary bone in man, and his theories of the *Urpflanze* (archetypal plant) and the *Urtier* or "osteological type" had served to confirm this conviction. Consequently, when he came to the study of chromatics, he was really looking for a natural history of colour, tracing the metamorphoses of coloured images in a gradual, unified series from pure light at one extreme to darkness at the other. Newton's theory offered something utterly different: darkness played no part whatsoever in it except to denote an absence of light, and colours were simply the visual impressions created by the individual rays into which light could be split by prismatic refraction, each designated by a geometric index within the mathematically based mechanics of light. Newton's colour theory was therefore bound to disappoint Goethe's expectations as a natural historian and believer in the cosmic hierarchy of Leibniz. What it contained was profoundly uncongenial to him for a number of reasons, two of which I shall mention here.

First, he objects to the application of mechanics to nature (except as a means of explaining the simplest kinds of motion). He had been repelled in his youth by the work of the French materialist d'Holbach, who explained the creation and workings of the entire universe as a product of inert matter moving in obedience to the laws of motion (*WA* 1, 28, 70). Goethe particularly disliked the analogy of the machine that thinkers of the Enlightenment had regularly applied to the natural world, for the machine is activated by a force outside itself, and he early concluded that the universe has its own living and creative principle within itself — hence his liking for the pantheism of Spinoza. He preferred to imagine the universe, and the earth itself, as an organism rather than a machine, and he goes so far, in a late essay on meteorology, as to attribute the rise and fall of the barometer to a periodic fluctuation of the earth's attractive force, analogous to the breathing in and breathing out of a living organism (*LA* 1, 11, 244–68). By implication, he dismisses the inverse square law of gravitational attraction, which was the centrepiece of Newton's *Principia*. Newton's mechanical optics was likewise detested by Goethe, because he regarded chromatics not primarily as a branch of physics, but as a science of human visual perception: prisms and angles of refraction may well have an objective existence that physics can investigate, but colour itself exists only if there is an eye to see it. Mechanics, in other words, is of little use to a colour theory whose focus is the study of ocular perception.

Second, although Goethe has no objection to pure mathematics, he disapproves of its application to the study of nature. He believes that the measurements involved in applied physics — for example, in Newton's *Opticks* — supply at best a superficial account of the phenomena in question, and often distort their significance or miss it entirely (as with the reactions of the human eye to colour). As he puts it, "Zahl und Maß in ihrer Nacktheit heben die Form auf und verbannen den Geist der lebendigen Beschauung" (*LA* 1, 9, 367). Goethe's aversion to mathematics had taken shape a few years before the incident with the prism, namely in 1786, when he sought tuition in algebra from a professor of mathematics at the University of Jena. At the end of these lessons, he concluded: "ich werde es zu meinem Wesen nicht brauchen können, da das Handwerk ganz außer meiner Sphäre liegt."[6] He also employs an interesting metaphor to describe his unsuccessful struggle with algebra, saying "daß ich mir selbst einen Weg suche über diese steile Mauren [*sic*] zu kommen. Vielleicht treff ich irgendwo eine Lücke durch die ich mich einschleiche."[7] In the *Farbenlehre* of 1810, he applies this same metaphor, in extended form, to Newton's colour theory. By now, he has convinced himself that the mathematical fortress, which once seemed impregnable, is in reality "ein verlassenes, Einsturz drohendes Altertum" that is ripe for demolition (*LA* 1, 4, 5–6).

Goethe's objections to applied mathematics are closely related to his objections to mechanics: both entail an unacceptable simplification of observed phenomena, because they select very limited aspects. This limitation struck him with particular force in the case of mathematics, for mathematics is a kind of language; as a poet, he was acutely aware of the inadequacy even of natural language, with all its richness, to do justice to the complexity, fullness, and elusiveness of nature. Even poetry — and here, he did know what he was talking about — cannot perform this task adequately; the nearest it can come to doing so is by using concrete images or symbols. By comparison, mathematics seemed to him hopelessly inadequate.

Goethe's objections, then, to Newtonian science may be summarized as follows: all objections were based on pre-existing attitudes, and all are directed against abstraction,[8] the selection of one dimension of nature that corresponds to some particular human interest or need, and necessarily yields an incomplete or simplified picture of reality. If this abstraction is taken as definitive and superior to the intuitive response of the unaided human senses, it involves a serious and possibly dangerous distortion of nature. Above all, this hostility to abstraction gives Goethe's science its distinctive character, and led the scientific establishment of his time — especially the physical scientists — to reject his work as eccentric and misguided.

We may be tempted to conclude from all of this that the distinctive quality of Goethe's science, namely his dislike of abstraction, is due to the fact that he was primarily a poet and artist rather than a scientist. However, his objections to Newton are not fundamentally aesthetic. Indeed, he rarely allows aesthetic criteria to influence his scientific observations directly. A more important factor was that, through developing his morphological approach to nature in the 1780s, he came to realise, unlike most of his contemporaries, that there is no single methodological paradigm for all sciences in all ages, and that not only each particular science, but the scientific method itself, is continually changing and developing throughout history. He consolidated this insight through detailed historical studies, and demonstrates it conclusively in the last part of his work on chromatics, his long and detailed *Geschichte der Farbenlehre*, which is a major contribution to the historiography of science. In this work, he reviews the development of colour theory from antiquity to the present, and shows how different theoretical or ideological presuppositions give it a radically different shape in different ages of history. He also detects in the history of science a cyclic alternation (*LA* 1, 6, 94) of periods of mainly inductive work, periods of intense theoretical activity, and periods in which theory hardens into dogma, until this is in turn undermined by changes in underlying beliefs or attitudes; and he discovers precedents for his own approach to nature, and to colour in particular, in earlier periods of history — especially in ancient Greece. In short, there are different varieties of science, and some are more productive than others.

This historical relativism sounds remarkably modern,[9] but unlike today's historians of science, Goethe gives greater weight to the individual personalities of eminent scientists such as Bacon, Descartes, and Newton, than, for example, to economic and cultural factors (although he by no means ignores the latter).[10] Given this psychological, characterological approach, it follows for Goethe that Newton's *Opticks*, or at least some of the attitudes that underlie the work, must reflect Newton's personal character. He contends that Newton's stubborn and devious character led him to defend mistakes even after he had realised they were mistakes, and that his disciples were credulous enough to accept his pronouncements as Holy Writ.

This brings me back to the second question I raised at the start of this paper, as to why *ethical* considerations predominate in Goethe's condemnation of Newton. He devotes a seven-page section of his history of colour theory, entitled "Newtons Persönlichkeit" (*LA* 1, 6, 295–302), to resolving what he calls "das ethische Hauptätsel," namely how Newton's alleged dishonesty can be reconciled with his otherwise unblemished moral record.[11] Already at the end of the previous, polemical part of the *Farbenlehre*, which contains Goethe's most damning accusations of Newton, he had been uneasily aware that he might have gone too far, saying in apology that his vehemence was partly the result of the violent times in which his remarks were written (*LA* 1, 5, 193–4). (He wrote them soon after the Battle of Jena and the French occupation of Weimar.) His uneasy conscience is even more in evidence in the subsequent section of his history of colour theory on Newton's personality, which begins with praise of Newton as a remarkable man (*LA* 1, 6, 297), interprets the stubbornness with which he defended his alleged errors as merely the downside of his admirable strength of character (*LA* 1, 6, 298–9), reinterprets his alleged dishonesty as for the most part self-deception rather than a deliberate attempt to deceive others (*LA* 1, 6, 299–300), offers the alternative suggestion that he held on to his supposed errors simply because they afforded a greater challenge to his mathematical genius (*LA* 1, 6, 301), adds that his procedures were not very different from those of other contemporary scientists, and concludes (by now describing Newton as "den vor-

trefflichen Mann"): "Auf diese und noch manche andere Weise möch-
ten wir den Manen Newtons, insofern wir sie beleidigt haben könnten,
eine hinlängliche Ehrenerklärung tun" (*LA* 1, 6, 301). Goethe adds for
good measure that the originator of an error is ultimately less reprehen-
sible than those who unthinkingly perpetuate it, and finally places the
entire blame ("alle Schuld") for his own intemperate comments not on
Newton himself, but on his mindless disciples (*LA* 1, 6, 301–2).

These extraordinary tergiversations, which culminate two decades
later in Goethe's suggestion to Eckermann, as his literary executor, that
the polemical part of the *Farbenlehre* might well be omitted altogether
from a posthumous edition of his works (conversation with Eckermann,
15 May 1831), give the game away more by what they imply than by
what they say: it was not a deficiency in Newton's character that led
Goethe to condemn Newton's *Opticks* in the first place, but an alleged
deficiency in the *Opticks* that led him to condemn Newton's character.
That deficiency lay in Newton's implied attitude to nature, an attitude
that Goethe finds ethically unacceptable because he believes both that
it does violence to nature, and that it may have harmful effects on those
who adopt it. Goethe belonged to a generation for whom the concept
of nature was by no means morally neutral, but laden with moral and
even religious values. From the nature-worship of the philosopher
Shaftesbury to the cult of literary sensibility, he had early encountered
that glorification of nature which grew in strength throughout the
eighteenth century. Moreover, his first great literary successes, *Götz von
Berlichingen* and *Werther*, as well as his first excursions into botany in
the early 1780s, were much influenced by the writings of Rousseau, for
whom nature was the supreme ethical norm, violation of which was
synonymous with artifice, decadence, selfishness and deception.[12]

Another significant factor is the way in which Goethe first encountered Newton's theories. There is evidence that he read none of Newton's works, either in Latin or in English, before October 1791, but
gained his first detailed acquaintance with Newton's colour theory from
German sources such as Erxleben's *Anfangsgründe der Naturlehre*[13]
and from a German translation of Priestley's history of optics.[14] The
difference of language is crucial here: whereas the English terms denoting the behaviour of light in optical experiments, such as *refraction,
inflexion, diffraction, dispersion*, etc., sound merely learned and no different from the Latin originals, the German equivalents, such as *Bre-
chung, Beugung, Zerstreuung*, and *Zerlegung* have overtones of drastic
intervention in natural processes, overtones to which Goethe reacted
negatively. He took particular exception to the sixth experiment in
Newton's *Opticks*, which passes light through two prisms and two small

apertures in order to demonstrate that light consists of rays of different refrangibility corresponding to different colours — the so-called experimentum crucis or experiment of the cross — and interprets the metaphor literally as one of torture:

> Es ist dies das sogenannte experimentum crucis, wobei der Forscher die Natur auf die Folter spannte, um sie zu dem Bekenntnis dessen zu nötigen, was er sich schon bei sich festgesetzt hatte. Allein die Natur gleicht einer standhaften und edelmütigen Person, welche selbst unter allen Qualen bei der Wahrheit verharrt. (*LA* 1, 5, 45)

According to Goethe, Newton uses elaborate contrivances to extract one-sided evidence for his predetermined theory, ignoring or suppressing the rest. Goethe's moral objection to Newton's procedure is that it violates the integrity of its object, namely nature — and this integrity is for him a moral value as well as an objective fact. He also believes that Newton's procedure violates the integrity of the subject, of the scientific observer: from the 1790s onward, he notes and deplores the increasing specialisation of the sciences, and the stunting effect which such specialisation is likely to have on the development of the individual. He declares in 1808, for example, "das ist eben das größte Unheil der neuern Physik, daß man die Experimente gleichsam vom Menschen abgesondert hat, und bloß in dem was künstliche Instrumente zeigen die Natur erkennen [...] will" (*LA* 1, 5, 45). By eliminating all but our abstract, rational responses, such science progressively alienates us from nature.

Newton's crime, then, was a crime against nature. The responsibility for it lay not in Newton's personal character — hence Goethe's pangs of conscience about his moral condemnation of him — but in his methods. In his analysis of Newton's personality, Goethe acknowledges that Newton's genius was predominantly mathematical, and he frankly admits "wir maßen uns über dieses sein Hauptverdienst kein Urteil an und gestehen gern zu, daß sein eigentliches Talent außer unserm Gesichtskreis liegt" (*LA* 1, 6, 296–7). He nevertheless goes on in the next paragraph to criticise Newton for applying mathematics to nature. But Goethe could not blame applied mathematics and mechanics at large for the supposed errors of Newton and his followers — although he at times comes close to doing so — without condemning the scientific revolution as a whole, thereby alienating the scientific establishment whom he wished to persuade of the truth behind his own chromatic theory. Hence, he blamed Newton's character instead — and managed to alienate the physicists as completely as if he had condemned modern physics itself.

Goethe's morally loaded view of nature, then, made it impossible for him to assess Newton's physical optics impartially. This view also prevented him from recognising that, beyond the specific issue of colour theory, it might be possible to combine Newton's morally neutral approach to scientific research with a morally responsible attitude towards nature as a whole. In other words, Goethe failed to recognise that Newton's way of looking at nature and his own way of looking at it might be complementary rather than mutually exclusive.[15] In our own times, we have been compelled by changing circumstances to take our moral responsibilities towards nature more seriously than ever before. Therefore, it is no coincidence that Goethe has in recent years been recruited by various (mainly German) writers to the cause of Green and environmental politics.[16] This does not mean, however, that he shared that hostility to technology which we find in some of today's critics of the scientific revolution.[17] In a late essay, he declared himself in favour of controlling the natural elements, even on a large scale, and harnessing them for the benefit of humanity. But he added, significantly, that we should not impose our own order on nature without respecting the order inherent in nature itself.[18] He even captured the consequences of failing to do so in a memorable poem that he wrote in 1797, around the time when he began intensive work on his treatise on colour theory, namely the ballad of "Der Zauberlehrling," who unleashes natural forces that are beyond his capacity to control. What the sorcerer's apprentice — like his present-day progeny — lacks is that comprehensive and morally responsible vision of nature, which Goethe rightly expected to accompany and underlie all scientific activity, and which, despite Goethe's doubts, is not incompatible with the pursuit of exact science.

Notes

[1] Cf. *Beiträge zur Optik*, in LA 1, 3, 12.

[2] LA 1, 6, 120; cf. *Tag- und Jahreshefte*, 1790, *WA* 1, 35, 13–14.

[3] *Goethes Farbentheologie* (Munich, 1987), 15–23 and passim.

[4] LA 1, 10, 326–27, 321; also *Italienische Reise*, 27 September 1786 in *WA* 1, 30, 89–90.

[5] Cf. Goethe to Knebel, 17 November 1784 in *WA* 4, 6, 289–90.

[6] Goethe to Frau von Stein, 25 May 1786 in *WA* 4, 7, 222.

[7] Goethe to Frau von Stein, 23 May 1786 in *WA* 4, 7, 221.

[8] Cf. LA 1, 4, 5; HA, 12, 417, 432 (*Maximen und Reflexionen* nos. 386 and 487); also John Neubauer, "'Die Abstraktion, vor der wir uns fürchten.' Goethes Auffassung der Mathematik und das Goethebild in der Geschichte der Wissenschaft" in *Versuche zu Goethe. Festschrift für Erich Heller*, edited by

Volker Dürr and Géza von Molnár (Heidelberg, 1976), 305–20 and Manfred Wenzel, "'Die Abstraktion, vor der wir uns fürchten.' Goethe und die Physik" in *Freiburger Universitätsblätter*, 35, Heft 133 (1996): 55–79.

[9] On the relationship of Goethe's theory of the history of science to the equivalent theories of Thomas Kuhn and other modern thinkers cf. Karl J. Fink, *Goethe's History of Science* (Cambridge, 1991), 85–90 and Dennis Sepper, *Goethe contra Newton: Polemics and the Project for a New Science of Color* (Cambridge, 1988), 18–19, 186–87.

[10] Cf. LA 1, 6, 87: "Der Konflikt des Individuums mit der unmittelbaren Erfahrung und der mittelbaren Überlieferung ist eigentlich die Geschichte der Wissenschaften." In keeping with this attitude, Goethe's preferred form of historiography is the biographical or autobiographical narrative; cf. H. B. Nisbet, "Goethes und Herders Geschichtsdenken" in *Goethe-Jahrbuch* 110 (1993): 115–33 (131).

[11] Some scholars have admittedly alleged that Newton was not above quoting experimental findings selectively in order to support his contention (later disproved by others) that chromatic aberration in telescopes cannot be corrected by compound lenses; but even if this is the case, such behaviour is uncharacteristic and falls far short of the systematic deception of which Goethe accuses him: see Zev Bechler, "'A Less Agreeable Matter': The Disagreeable Case of Newton and Achromatic Reflection," *British Journal for the History of Science*, 8 (1975): 101–26 (esp. 123); also Michael J. Duck, "Newton and Goethe on Colour: Physical and Physiological Considerations," *Annals of Science*, 45 (1988): 507–19 (esp. 518).

[12] On Rousseau's influence on Goethe's botanical studies cf. LA 1, 10, 327–30; also Goethe to Karl August, 16 June 1782 in *WA* 4, 5, 347–48.

[13] On Goethe's use of Erxleben and other German textbooks cf. LA 1, 3, 15 and LA 1, 6, 418; *HA* 12, 403–4; Sepper, 28; and Jeremy Adler, *"Eine fast magische Anziehungskraft." Goethes "Wahlverwandtschaften" und die Chemie seiner Zeit* (Munich, 1987), 77–78.

[14] On Priestley cf. *HA* 14, 226–27, 335–36 (editor's note); on Goethe's borrowing of Priestley's *History* in Klügel's translation cf. Elise Keudell, *Goethe als Benutzer der Weimarer Bibliothek* (Weimar, 1931; reprinted Leipzig, 1982), 5 (5 July 1791); and on his first borrowings of works by Newton cf. ibid. (5 October 1791 and 26 June 1792).

[15] Cf. Karl Robert Mandelkow, *Goethe in Deutschland. Rezeptionsgeschichte eines Klassikers*, 2 vols. (Munich, 1980–1989), 2, 40.

[16] Cf. Gernot Böhme, "Ist Goethes Farbenlehre Wissenschaft?" in Böhme, *Alternativen der Wissenschaft* (Frankfurt a. M., 1980), 123–53; also various contributions (including those of Gernot Böhme and Klaus Meyer-Abich) to the volume *Goethe und die Verzeitlichung der Natur*, edited by Peter Matussek (Munich, 1998).

[17] On Goethe's generally positive attitude towards industry and technology see *Goethe-Handbuch*, edited by Bernd Witte and others, 4 vols. (Stuttgart, 1996–1999), 4, 104–7 ("Bergbau"), 458–59 ("Handwerk"), 531–35 ("Industrie"), and 689 ("Maschinenwesen").

[18] LA 1, 11, 264 ("Versuch einer Witterungslehre," 1825); cf. my article on that essay in *Goethe-Handbuch*, 3, 778–85.

"Ossian hat in meinem Herzen den Humor verdrängt": Goethe and Ossian Reconsidered

Howard Gaskill

THE TITLE IS MISLEADING. It is not possible to review the significance of Macpherson's blind Gaelic bard for Goethe within a relatively short essay such as this; and a "reconsideration" would imply that the subject had received an appropriate degree of consideration in the first place, which is not the case. Or to be more precise, the only work that concerned itself in any detail with Goethe's reception of Ossian exists in the form of unpublished dissertations and has thus had minimal impact on mainstream criticism.[1] As for the misquotation from Werther's letter of 12 October, suggesting that Ossian has ousted humour rather than Homer from his heart, I'm sure most of us must be grateful to Projekt Gutenberg, and its army of voluntary typists, for making so many of the texts we use available on the Web, but there are inevitably certain errors that will not be picked up by a spellchecker, and this is one of them.[2] At first sight it might seem quite appropriate. Whatever one's view of Ossian may be, no one is going to claim that the work of the doleful bard is conducive to laughter. But then, neither is *Werther*. And on second thought, the notion of anything being able to drive humour out of the protagonist's heart is somewhat incongruous, given that it contained precious little of the kind to begin with. On third thought, however, it is clear that the accidental mangling of Werther's words could have a peculiar relevance to anyone who is misguided enough not to treat Ossian as something of a joke.

Despite welcome signs that an increasing number of critics are taking Macpherson seriously, both as regards his poetic achievement and even his contribution to Gaelic literary culture, old habits die hard. He is indelibly marked with the stigma of the forger, though few of those who call him such are in a position to judge for themselves the degree of his culpability in this respect (assuming that it is even appropriate to talk of guilt in such matters). Too often those who write about Ossian, particularly in Germany, do so as if the issues had all been tied up more than a century ago, and Ossianic research had suddenly stopped in 1895.[3] Admittedly, the more enterprising might venture as far as 1941 and Schöffler's work, for Herbert Schöffler is probably the last critic to have had an adequate conception of the depth and breadth of Ossianic influence in Germany.[4] According to Schöffler, German literature of the 1770s and 1780s is unthinkable without Ossian, as is Hölderlin's *Hyperion*, and Ossian remains at the very heart of German Romanticism (149) — a bold but entirely valid claim, and a truth virtually unacknowledged by postwar critics. Leaving aside the 1780s, Hölderlin's *Hyperion*, and Romanticism (as most do), even for the 1770s the significance of Ossian is constantly underplayed, to the degree that it is tempting to talk of a concerted attempt to write Ossian out of German literary history (though ignorance, rather than suppression, is the more likely explanation). Take, for instance, the refusal to acknowledge the derivation of the phrase "joy of grief," "one of Ossian's remarkable expressions, several times repeated,"[5] for which Michael Denis coined the felicitous translation "Wonne der Wehmut" in 1769 (this, incidentally, in his translation of "Carric-thura"). Why is it that "joy of grief" is continually ascribed — without reference — to Edward Young, particularly in editions of Karl Philipp Moritz's fine psychological novel, *Anton Reiser* (1785–90)? It has taken until 1999 for an editor of the novel (Heide Hollmer, in her edition for the Bibliothek deutscher Klassiker) to get it right. Where is Ossian in the standard works on "Empfindsamkeit"?[6] One would have thought that Herder's first Ossian-essay, in *Von deutscher Art und Kunst* (1773), that major manifesto of *Sturm und Drang* values, is sufficiently important in German literary history to prevent editors from merely taking their annotations from the Suphan edition of a century ago or more. It is becoming increasingly tiresome to find Herder's mention of the "Macpherson'sche Probe der Ursprache" glossed with a reference to scraps of Gaelic quoted in Macpherson's footnotes or the dissertation preceding *Temora*.[7] If one takes the trouble to find and examine the right edition — something that editors seem reluctant to do — it is not difficult to locate the *whole* of the seventh book of the epic given in Scots Gaelic.[8] This is the book from which Goethe translated for Herder, a translation that Herder later adapted and used for his *Volkslieder*. This has been known since at least 1908, and was prominently and accessibly dealt with by Gillies in 1933.[9] Herder, having had his faith in the authenticity shaken by Edmund de Harold from Limerick, tried to bypass Macpherson's English. Yet in the relevant volume of the Klassiker Verlag edition we have to read in detail of Herder's deviations from a text he never trans-

lated: "Man sieht, wie stark Herder die Vorstellungen der Vorlage ab-
ändert."[10] His attribution of the translation of "Erinnerung des Gesan-
ges der Vorzeit" to someone else (i.e. Goethe) is simply not believed:
"Die *Übertragung* ist entgegen der Versicherung Herders [. . .] mit Si-
cherheit von ihm selbst" (1135). The contributions of Heuer and Gillies, not to mention Betteridge, are ignored in the bibliography, and
this is the work of a reputable scholar. Apparently when it is a matter of
Macpherson, normal scholarly standards no longer apply. The editors
of *Der junge Goethe in seiner Zeit* know that Goethe translated the
"Songs of Selma" from the 1765 *Works* edition of Ossian, probably
from a copy he found in his father's library, yet the text they reproduce
is that of 1762.[11]

Given this tendency towards the obfuscation of Ossian, it comes as
no surprise that many Goethe critics — though they cannot deny an
impact on their poet — do their best to minimise it. Some critics, for
example, narrow as far as possible the phase of Goethe's active engagement with Macpherson's text, and blame it on someone else. For
instance, one may read in the Reclam *Erläuterungen und Dokumente* to
Werther that Goethe's first acquaintance with the Ossianic poems came
in Strasbourg and was mediated by Herder, so around the turn of the
year 1770–71.[12] And whilst there is the embarrassment of the letter to
Herder of autumn 1771, in which Goethe's enthusiasm for the "unsur-
passable" Ossian is expressed in unambiguous terms – "denn es geht
doch nichts drüber" – there is also the comfort of a letter written approximately six months later, in which Goethe tells Herder that the
Greeks are now his sole concern, "mein einzig Studium" (*HAB* 1,
131). As Francis Lamport puts it: "Homer and Pindar have (as Goethe
might well have chosen to say) ousted Ossian from my heart."[13] This
sounds plausible enough until one considers that, even had Goethe
wanted to, he could not very well be reading Ossian then: he had no
edition. Herder had it. Goethe had offered him his Ossian in the
autumn of 1771, but underlining that he wanted it back ("ich muß ihn
wieder haben"). It seems that Herder kept it for about a year. Indeed,
the rarity of English Ossians in Germany may have led to Goethe's involvement in the pirated reprint that Merck produced in Darmstadt,
the first volume of which appeared in May 1773, the second at the end
of 1774. Whether Goethe's involvement went much beyond producing
the illustration on the title page and distributing copies amongst his
friends, it is impossible to say. The edition appears to be a reasonably
careful reprint of the *Works of Ossian* of 1765. That is to say, it accu-
rately reproduces Macpherson's own misprints. I think one may be
certain that the Goethe/Merck text is the one used by Lenz for his

complete translation of *Fingal* (though Lenz scholars seem reluctant to admit that he did it at all).[14] Besides the edition, we have the evidence of the Ossianic translations incorporated in *Werther* in 1774, suggesting that Goethe's fascination with Ossian was not as brief as many would have it. Admittedly, one knows what Goethe is alleged to have said to Crabb Robinson about this in old age, but whatever limited truth there may be in the comment that "while Werther is in his senses he talks about Homer, and only after he grows mad, is in love with *Ossian*," the text suggests that Werther is a fan quite early on in the novel.[15] Conventional wisdom would draw a firm line between Werther's reading taste and Goethe's, at least as far as Ossian is concerned – though not Homer, of course. Consequently, the Goethe who now translates the "Songs of Selma" is doing so for a specific literary purpose, and is already inwardly detached from a work that he has now outgrown. On the other hand, one could legitimately argue that the stunning quality of the translation itself must presuppose an intense and prolonged engagement with the text, to which the poet who produces it still responds. This is certainly a fresh translation, not a reworking of the version sent to Friederike Brion from Frankfurt in 1771. With the Ossianic translations in *Werther*, Goethe's active involvement with Macpherson's work effectively ended. But it left its mark, and it was deeper than is generally supposed.

It is quite clearly nonsense to date Goethe's acquaintance with Ossian from the Strasbourg years. Apart from anything else, there is the pre-Strasbourg letter to Friederike Oeser of 13 February 1769 (*HAB*, I, 90), which makes it clear that Goethe has already had access to an annotated version of *Ossian*.[16] If this was the English original — and I suspect it was — he clearly did not have it with him in Strasbourg. Otherwise, he would scarcely have concealed it from Herder, nor would the various translations he made have had to wait until after he left Strasbourg for Frankfurt in August 1771. He and Herder had been looking at — in so far as Herder was capable of looking at anything at the time, given his eye condition — Denis's translation, presumably the review copies sent to Herder by Nicolai. According to a widespread assumption amongst critics, it is through Denis that Goethe became acquainted with Ossian while still in Leipzig, on the appearance of the first two volumes of the translation in 1768. That invaluable Marbach catalogue, *Weltliteratur: die Lust am Übersetzen im Jahrhundert Goethes*, simply states this as fact.[17] I am not aware of any evidence for this assertion, beyond the strongly circumstantial, that Ossianic images and motifs are to be found in several of Goethe's poems from that year, particularly those produced in the autumn. Yet it is ridiculous to assume that Goethe would not at least have known the name of Ossian before then, and had his curiosity aroused.

Wittenberg's translation of *Fingal* had already appeared in 1764, in Leipzig as well as Hamburg. In 1766 the Leipzig-based Christian Felix Weisse had produced his enormous review of the 1765 *Works* edition of Ossian in the *Neue Bibliothek der schönen Wissenschaften*.[18] (This, incidentally, consists largely of paraphrase and direct translation of Hugh Blair's *Dissertation*, which was appended to that edition. That Herder read and repeatedly re-read Weisse's review is evident from the many verbal echoes in his first Ossian essay.) Critics generally accept that the English Ossian, from which Goethe eventually made his translations, was lifted from his father's library. There would seem to be no direct evidence for this, but the fact that he started translating almost as soon as he returned to Frankfurt from Strasbourg in August 1771 presumably tells its own story. One thing is certain: it was the 1765 *Works* edition.[19] We do not know when Goethe's father acquired it or what prompted him to do so. However, since the *Works* did not appear until late autumn 1765, by which time Goethe was already in Leipzig, it seems improbable that he would have had access to that particular copy before returning home in September 1768.

It is interesting that the only two scholars to have examined Goethe's Ossianism in depth, Betteridge and König, are both tempted, independently of one another, to assume — tentatively, it has to be admitted – that Goethe had knowledge of Macpherson before 1768 and the appearance of Denis's translation. Both refer to the passages included in the letter to his sister of 11 May 1766, written in not altogether unimpressive English, particularly to these lines: "Many time I become a melancholical one [. . .] and then a darkness comes down my soul; a darkness as thik as fogs in the October are" (that "are" may well, as Betteridge speculates, be better read as "air.")[20] Could this conceivably have been suggested by Ossian? It is surely Macpherson as much as anyone who gave Goethe the impression that these islands are perpetually shrouded in fog. (Later, in the fifteenth of the Roman Elegies, Goethe claims it is a prominent reason why he would never have followed Caesar here.)[21] The association, at least, between Ossian and fog seems to have become fixed in Goethe's mind. Witness the diary jotting of 18 September 1797: "Gedenke an Ossian. Liebe zum Nebel bei heftig innern Empfindungen." What strikes me in the early English passage, however, is the phrasing: "and then a darkness comes down my soul." A quick check through Ossian produces at least a score of possible models for this, of which I shall quote just three: "Darkness comes on my soul," "Darkness gathered on Utha's soul," "Darkness is blown back on his soul" (114, 163, 274). The closeness to Goethe's English does not prove acquaintance with Macpherson in the original, but it could suggest it, and therefore on Goethe's part a sympathetic reading of Ossian stretching, off and on, for the best part of a decade, rather than the bare year-and-a-bit which some critics would have us believe.

Such protracted contact with the same text in two different languages would be bound to leave its mark. My impression is that this is not a case, such as that of Hölderlin, where the same version of Ossian (Petersen's prose translation of 1782), read repeatedly in adolescence — though of course Hölderlin scholars keep quiet about that — is so totally absorbed into the poet's literary language that conscious allusion may be the exception rather than the rule.[22] I imagine that it was as an English text, rather than a German one, that Ossian left its deepest imprint on Goethe's imagination, and that he would have been at least half-aware of any conversion process. This would apply perhaps to Ossian-inspired neologistic compounds, the best-known being "Nebelkleid."[23] But there are others, for example "Feuerflügel" or "sturmatmend,"[24] "seeumflossen," and "meerumgeben."[25]

It might be an exaggeration to say that Macpherson discovered the moon for modern literature, but his lunar imagery, and his sidereal poetry generally, certainly formed an important part of his appeal and continued to influence major poets through to Leopardi.[26] The young Goethe is no exception (Spinner, 46–50), even managing to inject an Anacreontic note into a voyeuristic Ossianic reminiscence.[27] Naturally, the dispersal of mists by the morning sun may seem to have biblical (if apocryphal) resonances:

> And our name shall be forgotten in time, and no man shall have our works in remembrance, and our life shall pass away as the trace of a cloud, and shall be dispersed as a mist, that is driven away with the beams of the sun, and overcome with the heat thereof. (Wis. 2:4)

Though this reads uncannily as if it could have penned by Macpherson himself, it is the more likely immediate source for the apparent Ossianic echo in "Ode an Herrn Professor Zachariae" (1767):

> Du bist uns kaum entwichen, und schwermüthig ziehen
> Aus dumpfen Höhlen (denn dahin
> Flohn sie bey deiner Ankunft, wie für'm Glühen
> Der Sonne Nebel fliehn)
>
> Verdruß und Langeweile.[28]

The image can easily be paralleled in Ossian, and must have gained increased currency through Macpherson's work. For instance: "like soft mist, that, rising from a lake, pours on the silent vale; the green flowers are filled with dew, but the sun returns in his strength, and the mist is gone" (169).[29] Those caves, too, are not just the abode of "Verdruß und Lange-weile." It is in caves that Ossianic ghosts dwell: "Ghosts fly on clouds and ride on winds [. . .] They rest together in their caves, and talk of mortal men" (66). One may think here of "An den Mond"/"An Luna" (1768):

> Schwester von dem ersten Licht,
> Bild der Zärtlichkeit in Trauer!
> Nebel schwimmt mit Silberschauer
> Um dein reizendes Gesicht.
> Deines leisen Fußes Lauf
> Weckt *aus Tagverschloßnen Hölen*
> *Traurig abgeschiedne Seelen,*
> Mich und nächt'ge Vögel *auf.*[30]

We are familiar with Werther's Ossianic letter of 12 October with its reference to "halb verwehtes Ächzen der Geister aus ihren Höhlen." This is quickly followed by Colma's lament in the translation of the "Songs of Selma," which shall be quoted here in Macpherson's English:

> Oh! from the rock of the hill; from the top of the mountain of winds, speak ye ghosts of the dead! speak, and I will not be afraid. — Whither are ye gone to rest? In what cave of the hill shall I find you? (167)

This seems to be a motif which stuck. It echoes in Faust's opening monologue, with the mention of spirits and mountain caves, "um Ber-geshöhle mit Geistern schweben" (l. 394). One might also think of his later meditations in forest and cave ("Wald und Höhle") and the emer-gence of hovering spirits: "Und steigt vor meinem Blick der reine Mond / Besänftigend herüber, schweben mir / Von Felsenwänden, aus dem feuchten Busch / Der Vorwelt silberne Gestalten auf." The motif fea-tures, albeit ironically, in the second part of *Faust*, too, where the allu-sions to Ossian are of course conscious and highly deliberate.[31] The appearance of spirits of the past in haze and mist is also familiar to us, for example in the dedication preceding *Faust*.

The ghost-world of Ossian is probably one of the least authentic, and therefore most inventive aspects of Macpherson's work, but it clearly appealed, and not just to Goethe. One of the curious things about Ossianic spirits is that they are semi-material and therefore vul-nerable. In the second book of *Fingal*, when Cuchullin is told of the dire warnings issued by Crugal's ghost, his reaction is this: "Hast thou enquired where is his cave? The house of the son of the wind? My sword might find that voice, and force his knowledge from him" (66). Later in the epic we hear of the hero Cormar's confrontation with the spirit of a storm: nothing daunted "When the low-hung vapour passed, he took it by the curling head, and searched its dark womb with his steel. The son of the wind forsook the air. The moon and stars returned" (75). (That image of searching the dark womb with his steel particularly impressed Boswell.) The most famous encounter of a mortal with an elemental spirit, however, occurs in "Carric-thura," when Fingal challenges the spirit of Loda, a Scandinavian deity whom Macpherson supposes to be Odin. (Actually this episode *can* be located amongst Macpherson's authentic sources.) "Do I fear thy gloomy form, dismal spirit of Loda? Weak is thy shield of clouds: feeble is that meteor, thy sword. The blast rolls them together; and thou thyself dost vanish. Fly from my presence son of night! call thy winds and fly!" (161). When the Spirit of Loda resists the invitation to retire to his "calm field above the clouds" and not meddle in human affairs, it comes to a combat in which Fingal's sword passes through the spirit and forces it into ignominious flight. I think there can be no doubt that, along with the "Songs of Selma" and "Berrathon," "Carric-thura" was one of the most important of all the Ossianic poems for Goethe. Interestingly, it contains this image: "warriors fell by the sword, as the thistle by the staff of a boy" (165) — "Knaben gleich, der Diebeln köpft," as we remember from the "Prometheus" poem of 1774. Like Zeus, the Spirit of Loda "üb[t sich] An Eichen [. . .] und Bergeshöhen," but to no avail, and is sent packing. The deity is successfully defied. It is instructive to contrast here what happens in an Ossianic poem written by the young Tieck, a little verse epic of 285 lines, plus footnotes, entitled "Gesang des Barden Congal" — but Tieck scholars do not seem particularly interested in it, given that five or more generations of them cannot even get the title right.[32] Tieck follows the plot of "Carric-thura" very closely, except that, having had the Spirit of Loda retire howling, seemingly with its tail between its legs, he has it strike back. The spirit summons up the mother-and-father of all storms, blasts the now cowering hero with a thunderbolt, and leaves him as an insignificant and frazzled blot on the landscape, whereupon the sun reappears. There, perhaps, one has the essence of the difference between the *Sturm und Drang* Goethe of 1774 and the incipient Romantic Tieck of 1792.

Contrary perhaps to the expectations raised by an essay with this title, I am going to say little or nothing about the role of Ossian in *Werther*. Much that has been written about this is rather good, I think, particularly Trunz's notes to the Hamburger Ausgabe (VI, 575–84). Admittedly, the condescension and ignorance displayed in his opening comment could give offence: "Die überall in Europa lebendig gewordene Suche nach alten Liedern und Epen war auch nach Schottland *ge-drungen*" (my emphasis). This is rather like saying that the study of philosophy had penetrated even as far as Königsberg (Macpherson did study under Blackwell at Aberdeen, after all). But the observations on the Chinese-box structure of the "Songs of Selma" are masterly (581–82). There has also been good work on the role of reading and literary allusion in the novel — I think particularly of Duncan, Wanniek, Pütz, and Wiethölter in the Klassiker Verlag edition of the novel. Nevertheless, some discomfort is naturally caused by the space allotted to Ossian in what is, after all, a very compact novel.[33] It is all very well to take critics to task for imputing to Werther a skewed reading of Homer, as if we moderns knew how Homer ought to be read.[34] If one does so, however, one ought to be wary of falling into the same trap with regard to Ossian — as if we now knew things about the work which Werther did not or could not.[35] After all, what do we know, and how do we know it? But in fact I think Werther's reading of Homer *is* skewed, and his appropriation of Ossian equally so, and that we readers are intended to perceive this. The translation of the "Songs of Selma" may be superb, with only a handful of errors, none of them serious — as Duncan says: after talking about *his* Homer, Werther presents us literally with *his* Ossian (45) — but just look at the letter of 12 October: "Ossian hat in meinem Herzen den Homer verdrängt," so we are told. There follows a passage that increasingly assumes the character of Ossianic pastiche, ending with what is very nearly a quotation from "Berrathon." But then "look" is perhaps the operative word.

> Wenn ich ihn dann finde, den wandelnden grauen Barden, der auf der weiten Heide die Fußstapfen seiner Väter sucht und, ach, ihre Grabsteine findet und dann jammernd nach dem lieben Sterne des Abends *hinblickt*, der sich ins rollende Meer verbirgt, und [. . .] den letzten verlassenen Herrlichen in aller Ermattung dem Grabe zuwanken sehe, wie er immer neue, schmerzlich glühende Freuden in der kraftlosen Gegenwart der Schatten seiner Abgeschiedenen einsaugt und nach der kalten Erde, dem hohen, wehenden Grase *niedersieht* [. . .]. (12 October; my italics)

But Ossian is blind. And so are we, if we do not notice this.

Notes

[1] H. T. Betteridge, "Macpherson's Ossian in Germany, 1760–1775" (Diss., London, 1938), 340–449. Gustav Adolf Koenig, "Ossian und Goethe, unter besonderer Berücksichtigung von Goethes Übersetzungstechnik aus dem Englischen" (Diss., Marburg, 1959).

[2] http://gutenberg.aol.de/goethe/werther/2wert008.htm (at the time of writing).

[3] That is, with Ludwig Christian Stern, "Die ossianischen Heldenlieder." In: *Zeitschrift für vergleichende Litteraturgeschichte 8* (1895): 50–86, 143–174.

[4] Herbert Schöffler, "Ossian. Hergang und Sinn eines großen Betrugs." In *Deutscher Geist im 18. Jahrhundert: Essays zur Geistes- und Religionsgeschichte.* 2nd ed.(Göttingen, 1967), 135–81.

[5] Hugh Blair, "A Critical Dissertation on the Poems of Ossian." In: *The Poems of Ossian and Related Works.* Ed. Howard Gaskill (Edinburgh: Edinburgh UP, 1996), 381. (Future page references in the text will be to this edition.)

[6] See Howard Gaskill, "The 'Joy of Grief': Moritz and Ossian." In: *Colloquia Germanica 28* (1995): 101–25.

[7] For the latest (?) example, see *Johann Gottfried Herder: Schriften zur Ästhetik und Literatur 1767–1781.* Ed. Gunter E. Grimm. (Frankfurt a. M.: Deutscher Klassiker Verlag, 1993), 1139. "Macphersons Proben der gälischen Ursprache, nämlich 32 Verse finden sich in seiner Abhandlung *Dissertation Concerning the Poems of Ossian,* die ebenso wie Hugh Blairs *Critical Dissertation* der Gesamtausgabe, *The Works of Ossian,* translated by James Macpherson, London 1765, vorangestellt wurden." In fact, in the edition in question Macpherson's Dissertation, which does indeed contain some Gaelic (though not what Herder is referring to here), is simply called "A Dissertation"; it precedes the second volume of the *Works* and Hugh Blair's "Critical Dissertation" comes *at the end* of that same volume.

[8] "A Specimen of the Original of Temora." In: *The Works of Ossian, the Son of Fingal, in two Volumes, translated from the Gaelic Language by James Macpherson* (London: Beckett and Dehondt, 1765), vol. 2, 289–309.

[9] Otto Heuer, "Eine unbekannte Ossianübersetzung Goethes." In: *Jahrbuch des freien deutschen Hochstifts* (1908): 261–73. Alexander Gillies. *Herder und Ossian* (Berlin: Junker und Dünnhaupt, 1933), 33–35, 90–92.

[10] *Johann Gottfried Herder: Volkslieder, Übertragungen, Dichtungen.* Ed. Ulrich Gaier (Frankfurt a. M.: Deutscher Klassiker Verlag, 1990), 1133.

[11] *Der junge Goethe in seiner Zeit. Texte und Kontexte. Sämtliche Werke, Briefe, Tagebücher und Schriften bis 1775. In zwei Bänden und einer CD-ROM.* Eds Karl Eibl, Fotis Jannidis and Marianne Willems (Frankfurt a. M.: Insel Verlag, 1998), Eintrag: 24, 881–24, 955.

[12] Kurth Rothmann, *Erläuterungen und Dokumente. Johann Wolfgang Goethe. Die Leiden des jungen Werther* (Stuttgart: Reclam, 1997), 54.

[13] F. J. Lamport, "Goethe, Ossian and *Werther*." In: *From Gaelic to Romantic: Ossianic Translations*. Eds. Fiona Stafford and Howard Gaskill (Amsterdam: Rodopi), 97–106, 103. A similar point is made by Matthew Bell in his introduction to *Goethe: Selected Poems*. Translated by John Whaley (London: J. M. Dent, 1998), xviii.

[14] The translation is discussed in Howard Gaskill, "'Blast, rief Cuchullin . . . !': J. M. R. Lenz and Ossian." In *From Gaelic to Romantic*. 107–118; and in more detail in the forthcoming issue of the *Lenz-Jahrbuch*.

[15] Henry Crabb Robinson visited Goethe on 2 August 1829. The entry in his travel journal is quoted by Lamport, 97 — this is a more authentic version than that reproduced by Trunz, *HA* 6, 536. Werther's remarks on the inappropriate reserve implied by mere liking ("gefallen") in relation to Lotte is equally extended to Ossian, and that already in the letter of 10 July in Book 1: "Gefällt! Neulich fragte mich einer, wie mir Ossian gefiele!" (the last exclamation mark is added in the revised version of 1787).

[16] Surely the implication of: "Wenn Ossian im Geiste seiner Zeit singt, so brauche ich gerne Commentars, sein Costume zu erklären . . . "

[17] *Weltliteratur: die Lust am Übersetzen im Jahrhundert Goethes. Eine Ausstellung des deutschen Literaturarchivs im Schiller-Nationalmuseum Marbach am Neckar.* Marbacher Kataloge 37. Ed. Bernhard Zeller. (Marbach, 1989), 345. (Typically, it goes on to say that, unlike some contemporaries, Goethe soon recovered from his affliction: "Goethe gab Ossian bald den Abschied, hing ihm nicht so lange an wie Herder, Stolberg und andere Altersgenossen.")

[18] *Neue Bibliothek der schönen Wissenschaften und freyen Künste* 2 (1766): 245–61; 3 (1766): 13–38.

[19] *Der junge Goethe*. Eintrag: 45, 068.

[20] *HAB* 1, 29–30. Betteridge, 345; Koenig, 14.

[21] "Cäsarn wär' ich wohl nie zu fernen Britannen gefolget," for the fogs of the North are sad, and as far as the poet is concerned, more hateful "than the assiduous fleas swarming all over the South" (Whaley, 61) — it is just as well Goethe never encountered Highland midges.

[22] Howard Gaskill, "Hölderlin und Ossian." In: *Hölderlin-Jahrbuch* 27 (1990/91): 100–130.

[23] "Willkommen und Abschied" (1771) and "An die Unschuld" (1769). Surely inspired by Ossian's "robe of mist" (125, 146, 187).

[24] Both in "Wandrers Sturmlied" (1774). Cf. Ossian "wings of fire" (75, 106); "breathing gale" (22, 169; cf. Koenig, 39).

[25] Such compounds of noun and past participle, though a feature of Klopstock's poetic language, were certainly still innovative in the German of the 1770s (cf. Koenig, 110), and however Homeric these two may sound, that "seeumflossen" is in fact inspired by Ossian's "sea-surrounded" (73, 169–70, 184, 194) is suggested by its use in Werther's translation of the "Songs of Selma." Whether the same may be claimed of "meerumgeben" in *Torquato Tasso* (II, 1) is moot, though it is interesting that the action takes place in the palace Belriguardo, which Goethe would have known to have been the Italian equivalent of Selma, according to the etymology suggested by Macpherson (452, n. 19): Gaelic *seall* (=look) and *math* (= good).

[26] Van Tieghem credits Ossian with being "son véritable introducteur dans la poésie moderne, où elle devait tenir un si grand rôle" — Paul van Tieghem. "Ossian et l'ossianisme au XVIIIᵉ siècle." In: *Le Préromantisme.* vol. 1. (Paris: Rieder, 1924), 195–287, 280. See Kaspar Heinrich Spinner. *Der Mond in der deutschen Dichtung von der Aufklärung bis zur Spätromantik* (Bonn: Bouvier, 1969), where, for a change, the significance of Ossian is fully acknowledged, see 24.

[27] "An den Mond"/"An Luna" (1768): "Und in wollustvoller Ruh / Säh der weitverschlagne Ritter / Durch das gläserne Gegitter, / Seines Mädgens Nächten zu. / Dämmrung wo die Wollust thront, / Schwimmt um ihre runden Glieder. / Trunken sinkt mein Blick hernieder. / Was verhüllt man wohl dem Mond." Cf. "She bent her head, midst her wandering locks. The moon looked in, at night, and saw the white-tossing of her arms; for she thought of the mighty Crothar, in the season of her dreams" (240).

[28] Contrast Koenig: "Das hier gebrauchte Bild des vor der aufgehenden Sonne dahinschwindenen Nebels ist so typisch für den Ossian, daß man an eine Reminiszenz Goethes denken muß" (15).

[29] Or: "like a mist that fled away, when the blast of the morning came, and brightened the shaggy side of the hill" (88); "He slowly vanished, like a mist that melts on the sunny hill" (113). Naturally, the image may also be found in other works which are heavily imbued with Ossian, such as Miller's *Siegwart* (1776): "dann verschwanden diese Zweifel wieder, wie Nebelwolken vor der Sonne" (Stuttgart: Metzler, 1971, 684); echoed in Moritz's *Andreas Hartknopf* (1786): "verschwanden diese Zweifel wie Nebel vor der Sonne," ed. Hans Joachim Schrimpf. (Stuttgart: Metzler, 1968), 141–42; cf. also Anna Letitia Barbauld's "Seláma: An Imitation of Ossian" (1774): "Try thy strength with the feeble arm, said the rising pride of youth. Thou shalt vanish like a cloud of mist before the sun, when he looks abroad in the power of his brightness, and the storms are rolled away from before his face." (http://miavx1.muohio.edu/ ~leaporm/barbauld/selama.htm).

[30] My emphasis.

[31] Cf. the references to the "Bergvolk," ll. 10427–28. For the ironic use of a stock Ossianic motif — the "narrow house" as the grave — see ll. 11529–30: "Aus dem Palast ins enge Haus/ So dumm läuft es am Ende doch hinaus."

[32] The name has been handed down as *Longal*. For Tieck's Ossianic verse epics (another is called "Iwona") and their relationship to Rambach's novel *Die eiserne Maske*, see Howard Gaskill, "Tieck's Juvenilia: Ossianic Attributions." *Modern Language Review* (forthcoming).

[33] The first version numbers just under 36,000 words, of which the Ossianic passages make up 7%.

[34] Erdmann Wanniek, "*Werther* lesen und Werther als Leser," *Goethe-Yearbook* 1 (1982): 51–92, 60 — taking issue with the reading offered by Bruce Duncan in the same volume, 42–50: "'Emilia Galotti lag auf dem Pult aufgeschlagen.' Werther as (Mis-)reader."

[35] As does Wanniek, 72, where he is equally guilty of a naively normative and unhistorical reaction to Ossian.

Weimar Classicism's Debt to the Scottish Enlightenment

R. H. Stephenson

> "Only the routine and equilibrium which healthy instinct involves keep thought and will at all within the limits of sanity." (George Santayana)

IN THIS PAPER I want to suggest that when Goethe famously defined Classicism as "healthy" (Eckermann, 2 April 1829), he was not so much participating in that emergence in the late eighteenth and early nineteenth-century world of discourse of new norms of "health" and "sickness" to which Clifford Siskin has drawn attention,[1] as indicating his indebtedness to a debate crucially, and seminally, influenced by the Scottish Enlightenment. In other words, in aligning "good sense" with both sensitivity to beauty (see "Ruysdael als Dichter" [1806]; *HA* 12, 142) and the "healthy reason" (the Latin *recta ratio*, translated into German by the Thomasians as *gesunde Vernunft*, which became synonymous in the German eighteenth century with "common sense"), Goethe is throwing an illuminating light on one of the central tenets of Weimar Classicism as it developed in his collaboration with Schiller.

The theory of common sense advocated by the Scots was not always as undifferentiated and naïve as David Hume's rejection of "the reason of the mere vulgar" might suggest;[2] though some of their formulations were undoubtedly open to his charge of mere lazy-minded "prejudice" (146), as is clear from James Beattie's unguarded statement in his *Essay on the Immutability of Truth*:[3]

> . . . I declare, in regard to the few things that I have to say on human nature that I should esteem it a very strong presumption against them, if they were not easy and obvious.

By contrast with the common consent of the *sensus communis*, Lord Kames distinguishes (in his *Loose Hints Upon Education*)[4] between common sense as a faculty and common sense as a set of fundamental, regulative principles, citing as "a principle embraced by all men" the proposition "that nothing can happen without a cause" (156); but noting that "the faculty which regulates belief . . . sometimes leads us into errors" (282). This distinction had been elaborated carefully by Thomas Reid in his *Enquiry into the Human Mind on the Principles of Common Sense* — and, following him, by Beattie (54).[5] While they all seem to be animated by a negative animus against Hume's scepticism[6] — "the demolition of common sense," as Beattie dubbed it (261) — which they saw, following Reid, as essentially Cartesian, even Platonic (Beattie, 234; Reid, 19) — there is, at least in Reid, a more positive epistemological doctrine offered. In opposition to Hume's (Lockean) tenet that "all ideas are derived from impressions, and nothing but copies and representations of them" (*Treatise*, 27), Reid holds that we have, by means of sensation, a direct knowledge of objects. Objects of knowledge are not just "ideas in our minds," as what Reid calls "the ideal system" holds; "impressions" and "ideas" do not intervene between the mind and things.[7] For Reid, common sense is reflected in ordinary language use, precisely because the faculty of sensation plays a crucial role, along with perception, in the acquisition of knowledge.[8] Indeed, for Reid, there is a distinction of kind between perception and sensation, such that neither can be derived from the other (Seth, 87). It is my contention that this epistemological doctrine was what, above all else in Scottish philosophy, appealed to Goethe and Schiller in their formulation of a classical aesthetic.[9]

Goethe's few references to the Scottish philosophers by name — to Adam Smith, Adam Ferguson, and Thomas Reid, for example — almost certainly give a misleading impression of the extent of his familiarity with them. Given their pervasive influence in eighteenth-century Germany, it is nearly inconceivable that he was not at least as well-versed in their cardinal doctrines as were his intellectual contemporaries. It is not just that the roots of Reid's philosophy go back to such major influences as Shaftesbury (often via Hutcheson and Lord Kames).[10] Scottish common-sense philosophy — in effect Thomas Reid, and his followers James Beattie and James Oswald — had an enormous impact on German philosophers preoccupied with the problem of reconciling ordinary perception and the rigour proper to philosophy. Johann Nicolaus Tetens is by no means an unusual figure in being deeply influenced by the Scots; the ramifications of Reid's teachings were assimilated, to varying extents, into the doctrines of all schools of German philosophy.[11] The powerful influence Reid and his followers had in France only consolidated, given the close relationship of French and German thought in the period, the Scots' influence in Germany. Moreover, Scottish common sense infiltrated the German republic of letters as a whole, and quickly won for itself "a wide audience in Germany."[12] As a result of his *Enquiry* of 1764, which was reviewed in Germany between

1764 and 1767, and translated into German in 1768, Reid in particular was highly influential (Kuehn, 15, 52–3, 65); but so, too, were his followers, Beattie and Oswald. The German *Popularphilosophen* turned to the Scots with enthusiasm. Moses Mendelssohn was typical in assimilating Scottish thought to his fundamental Wolffianism, producing an amalgam that, *mutatis mutandis*, was to stamp German philosophy prior to Kant's first Critique. Likewise, Garve devoted an extensive note to Reid's epistemological ideas in his (1772) translation of Ferguson's *Institutes of Moral Philosophy*. Lichtenberg's enthusiasm for Beattie was matched by that of Gerstenberg, who translated Beattie's *Essay*. Hamann and Jacobi were thoroughly familiar with the Scots; Karl Philipp Moritz translated Beattie's *Elements of Moral Science* in the year of its first appearance (1790); and Herder's enthusiastic review of Beattie's (translated) *Essay* in the *Frankfurter gelehrte Anzeigen* of 1772 was, of course, known to Goethe.[13]

Internal evidence of Goethe's intimate knowledge of the characteristic doctrines of the Scottish philosophers is likewise compelling. Similarities and parallels between often-quoted statements by Goethe and those advanced by the Scots seem to be the result of direct, or at least indirect, influence. Consider the fact that the following — notorious! — saying is traceable to the Scottish Enlightenment:

> Es ist besser, es geschehe dir Unrecht, als die Welt sei ohne Gesetz.
> Deßhalb füge sich jeder dem Gesetze.[14]

The doctrine, ultimately derived from Plato, of the supremacy of law, with its amoral-sounding corollary, that injustice is preferable to lawlessness, was systematically elaborated by David Hume.[15] Similarly, the following idea can be found in Lord Kames:

> Wir blicken so gern in die Zukunft, weil wir das Ungefähre, was sich in ihr hin und her bewegt, durch stille Wünsche so gern zu unsern Gunsten heranleiten möchten[16]

Indeed, as I have argued elsewhere,[17] Goethe drew heavily on Scottish philosophers in formulating his *Maximen und Reflexionen*. For example, his defence of analogy is very close to Reid's;[18] and the following saying is a cardinal tenet of Reid's ethics:

> Wo ich aufhören muß, sittlich zu sein, habe ich keine Gewalt mehr. (Hecker, 678)[19]

At other points, the influence is apparently negative, as in Goethe's rejection of Hutcheson's doctrine of a correspondence between mathematical and ethical connectedness (Hecker, 608).

The internal evidence of Goethe's familiarity — and affinity — with the Scottish School seems most compelling with respect to the theory of common sense that runs through his entire work, one which is broadly in agreement with the Scots', particularly with Reid's differentiated account. The "impräscriptible Rechte" of common sense that he recognizes (in a letter to Schiller of 14 February 1798; *WA* 4, 13, 65) are fully consonant with what the Scots claimed for it: it is "natural" (conversation with Riemer, 1 October 1807; *G* 2, 257); it is regulative of thought and action; it is a (preliminary) point of orientation; and it can serve as a test of the truth of such intellectual impositions as some of Newton's theories — as Beattie, too, has it (148) " . . . whatever contradicts common sense . . . is not truth, but falsehood":

> Nirgends war dieses umgekehrte Verfahren trauriger als in der Farbenlehre, wo eine ganz falsche, auf ein falsches Experiment gegründete Lehre durch neue, das Unwahre stets Verbergende und die Verwirrung immer vermehrende, verwickeltere Versuche unzugänglich gemacht und vor dem reinen Menschenverstand düster verhüllt ward. ("Nachträge zur Farbenlehre," *WA* 2, 1, 334)

While it may be useful as a touchstone for error (Hecker, 430), however, common sense, so helpful in practical activity, is inappropriate for higher theorizing (Hecker, 1201). The limitations of common sense (Hecker, 539) express themselves in a smug contentment with immediate, merely apparent causes (Hecker, 597). "Active scepticism" is, therefore, required vis-à-vis common sense, for fear of making serious misjudgements (Hecker, 1203). Hence, while Goethe would never agree with Beattie that "common sense . . . arrives at maturity with almost no care of ours" (42), he is not, in fact, diverging far from the Scottish School in insisting that common sense can be wrong, prove a hindrance, and needs to be "self-rectifying" ("Erfahrung und Wissenschaft"; *HA* 13, 25). Even Beattie had indicated its limitations (" . . . by what criterion shall we know . . . a dictate of common sense from the fallacy of an inveterate opinion?" he asks rather helplessly [162]). And Reid at least was clear that "common sense" and "reason" were co-implicates (Seth, 110). The hierarchy that seems to underlie Goethe's use of the term "common sense"[20] — from "small" common sense (*Dichtung und Wahrheit*, III, Book II; *HA* 9, 471) to the "clearest" (*Italienische Reise*, Neapel, 26. Mai 1787; *HA* 2, 327), to "pure" (*Tages und Jahreshefte*, 1795; *WA* 1, 35, 44) common sense — is entirely compatible with Reid's (if not with Beattie's or Oswald's) view; for Reid, like George Santayana, called for a rational analysis of the principles of common sense as one of the chief desiderata of logic (Kuehn, *Common Sense*, 31, 33).[21]

Such was the pervasiveness of the Scottish doctrines, however, that Goethe could have taken this from almost anywhere in his world of discourse. Besides, "common sense" was not, after all, invented by the Scots (as Beattie freely conceded in his historical discussion of the concept, tracing it in his *Essay* to Aristotle and the Stoics [Kuehn, 33, 274]). [22] "Common sense" already had a distinguished tradition, carried by — amongst others — the Renaissance Humanists, Vico, Buffon, and, not least, Wolff and Thomasius.[23] Common sense as a preliminary test of falsehood was the essence of Wolff's *reductio ad sensum communem*; disagreement amongst adherents as to what common sense really consists of was commonplace in Goethe's intellectual milieu; similarly, Tetens had developed a hierarchy of levels of common sense not dissimilar to Goethe's. Indeed, what else was German *Popularphilosophie* if not a sustained clarification of the nature and principles of common sense? (Kuehn, 81, 131–32, 253).

Important though it is to the tenor and structure of Goethe's thinking, there is, in truth, nothing particularly distinctive about Goethe's undoubtedly Scottish-influenced view of common sense. In fact, it constitutes one of the areas of agreement between him and Schiller — and between him and Kant. "Scholars have not been slow to point out [Schiller's] indebtedness to . . . the Scottish philosophers": his teacher at the Duke of Württemberg's Military Academy had prefaced the *theses philosophicae* his pupils were to dispute during 1776 with the axiom "vera philosophia est philosophia sensus communis quam e.g. Reid pluresque Angli sequuntur"[24] — an influence that was only to be strengthened by Schiller's reading of Garve. It is hardly surprising, then, that Schiller's conception of common sense should, like Goethe's, follow Reid's distinction between, on the one hand, a faculty of the mind and, on the other, the accumulated primary truths that make up the accrued wisdom of mankind (315–16). Nor should it surprise us, given his own debt to the Scots, that Kant himself should consciously attempt to defend and justify common sense, accepting it, qua faculty and qua repository of primary truths, as the field of philosophical enquiry, while rejecting it as a method of philosophy. After all, reliance upon common sense provided the common ground upon which in eighteenth-century Germany the most diverse philosophical minds could meet, the centre of the German attempt to create an "empirical rationalism" (Kuehn, 7, 10).[25] Yet Schiller and Goethe go further than their contemporaries in aligning common sense, not only with a cognitive faculty and traditional sagacity, but with the aesthetic — with that "sinnlich-geistige Überzeugung" (*Italienische Reise*, Bericht, Rom, Dezember 1787; *HA* 2, 456) that results from aesthetic perception.

The authority of the senses championed by the Scottish philosophers had earned them the contempt of Joseph Priestley, who condemned them for considering "the senses as intitled to the same respect, which had usually been appropriated to that superior faculty by which we distinguish truth."[26] But Priestley, like many others, had overlooked the subtlety of Reid's epistemology: the latter, after all, was not arguing for the superiority of either sense or mind, but rather for their coordination in the primary act of apprehension. For Reid, sensation is necessarily accompanied by belief of some kind; such sensation, considered together with such belief, constitutes perception. Thus sensation and thought, though different, are yet united in the act of perception. Sense does not think; thought does not feel. Reid, then, could never have subscribed to J. G. H. Feder's assertion that we know (beauty) through sensation; for Reid, though all knowledge arises in sensation, it is not derived from sensation. Reid's break with Hume (and the whole Western tradition of representationalist epistemology) consists of holding that, by transforming the objective reality known in sensation into mere representation — and "idea" or "image" or "*Vorstellung*" — reality vanishes altogether (Kuehn, *Common Sense*, 14, 23, 25, 30, 77, 140, 241).[27] For this reason, "common sense" is intimately linked in Reid's thinking with sense-experience, since first principles are "suggested" in sensation (though they are not the product of it).

Few in Germany followed Reid in his theory of direct perceptual realism; though the works of British philosophers brought home to Germans the importance of human sensibility, the trend was to accommodate and assimilate sensations to the "superior" faculty of representation that homegrown traditions as diverse as Wolffianism and Pietism upheld (Kuehn, 10). In terms that are uncannily reminiscent of Reid's own, however, Goethe and Schiller formulated an account of aesthetic experience as a coordination of Sense (*Stofftrieb*) and mind (*Formtrieb*) that constitutes the kernel idea of Weimar Classicism. Aesthetic knowledge of objects arises in a coordination of sense and mind, rather than in the initial subordination postulated by Rationalists and Empiricists alike. The epistemological gap of the Cartesian tradition derives for Goethe from the incapacity of discursive reason to connect coherently what the senses – as the organism's media of the mind's interaction with the environment – deliver, from its point of view, as isolated particulars (13, 32); whereas aesthetic experience — *Anschauen* — is the way in which Idea and Experience converge.[28] Similarly — and in terms very reminiscent of Reid — Schiller insists (in a letter to the Duke of Augustenburg, 21 November 1793) that in "presentational thinking" (*darstellend denken*, i.e., aesthetic contemplation) there is no question of sense itself being able to think, though intellect is at work in coordination with sense. By dint of re-establishing the original connection of "common sense" with Aristotle's "koine aesthesis" (Grave, 114), Goethe can speak (Hecker, 344) of common sense as something "innate" that can be developed — in the form of intellectual principle(s):

> Wer nun dieses Besondere lebendig faßt, erhält zugleich das Allge-meine mit; ohne es gewahr zu werden, oder erst spät. (Hecker, 279)

Principles can be deduced from common-sense-as-aesthetic-perception — a capacity of the human mind that Goethe dubs, in the spirit of faculty-psychology, "the highest reason" (to Eckermann, 13 February 1829). Indeed, common sense in the sense of a set of principles can have a settling effect on the inner life (letter to C. F. L. Schulz, 27 June 1826; *WA* 4, 38, 175), just as healthy common sense presupposes a well-tempered inner life (*Dichtung und Wahrheit*, II, Books. 8 and 9). Reid's achievement, in stabilizing the labile relationship between sense and perception in earlier accounts (in Shaftesbury, Hutcheson, and Kames) of that highly influential but murkily vague notion of "inner sense," seems to have offered Goethe and Schiller, severally and jointly, a point of departure for their own clear statement of classical aesthetics.

In aligning common sense — beyond intellectual first principles, beyond even an intellectual faculty — with aesthetic experience, Goethe and Schiller may, at first sight at least, seem to be in total accord with Kant who, in the third *Critique*, all but identified common sense with taste (Kuehn, *Common Sense*, 195, 199). Certainly both Schiller and Goethe seem to have accepted Kant's critical philosophy. Goethe's formulation in the following, though, indicates — as he made clear in conversation with Eckermann (17 February 1829) — that Kant's critique left something to be desired:

> Man hat sich lange mit der Kritik der Vernunft beschäftigt; ich wünschte eine Kritik des Menschenverstandes. Es wäre eine Wohltat für's Men-schengeschlecht wenn man dem Gemeinverstand bis zur Überzeugung nachweisen könnte, wie weit er reichen kann, und das ist gerade soviel, als er zum Erdenleben vollkommen bedarf. (Hecker, 1199)

The fact that "a critique of common sense" is called for at all, even after Kant's *Critique of Pure Reason*, implies that the latter does not, in Goethe's view, exhaust the former; that, as Goethe told Eckermann, the senses have been left out of account:

> Kant hat uns aufmerksam gemacht, daß es eine Kritik der Vernunft gebe, daß dieses höchste Vermögen, was der Mensch besitzt, Ursache habe, über sich selbst zu wachen. Wie großen Vorteil uns diese Stim-me gebracht, möge jeder an sich selbst geprüft haben. Ich aber

möchte in eben dem Sinne die Aufgabe stellen, daß eine Kritik der Sinne nöthig sei, wenn die Kunst überhaupt, besonders die deutsche, irgend wieder sich erholen und in einem erfreulichen Lebenschritt vorwärts gehen solle. (Hecker, 468)

Like Schiller, who felt that one could learn a good deal about human beings in general but all too little about beauty in particular from Kant's aesthetics (letter to Goethe, 19 February 1795), Goethe seems to have accepted Kant as the best available philosophical account of the cognitive aspects of aesthetic experience, while missing a satisfactory treatment of the sensuousness that, for Goethe as for Schiller, is essential to true aesthetic perception. Glad as he is to have Kant's philosophical support for the validity of the aesthetic, Goethe is aware that reason has the upper hand in Kant's account ("taste is formed for us as a regulative principle by a still higher principle of reason": Kuehn, 200), and that the coordination of Mind and Sense, essential to aesthetic experience, is neglected. On the other hand, neither Schiller nor Goethe feel the need to reject Kant's representationalism when applied at the level of theoretical knowledge. Unlike Herder (and Hamann and Jacobi), Goethe and Schiller, following Reid, do not give priority to sensation as the source of knowledge. They, therefore, did not feel that "idealism," at any level of experience, necessarily leads to nihilism in the way Jacobi and Hamann did, even though it represented for Goethe and Schiller a reduction of experience when compared to the fullness of aesthetic perception. Perhaps because Herder seems to have come to Reid late in life (Kuehn, 143); perhaps because he noted Reid's insistence that common-sense principles are *a priori* (Kuehn, 30); perhaps because he was adamant in holding particular experience to be prior to reflexion[29] — for any or all of these reasons, Herder (like Jacobi and Hamann) could not accommodate Kant's critical philosophy in the way Goethe and Schiller managed to do, as a supplement to their own outlook.

In sum, Goethe and Schiller's theory of common sense stands out in its being grounded in a theory of aesthetic experience that is seen, in distinctly Reidian terms, as a coordination of sense and thought, without emphasis being put on either co-implicated element. Some sense of indebtedness to the Scottish School for the strategic poise of this, their shared classical stance, may well explain, in part at least, not only Goethe's advocacy of Scottish philosophy as promising mediation of Idea and Experience in the future (in a schema for *Kunst und Altertum*, "Historische Studien zur Weltliteratur" [1826–32]; *GA* 14, 908), but also his self-ironic description of himself in a late diary entry, dated 11 June 1831 (*GA*, Ergänzungsband 2, 563), as a "Common-Sense Philistine" (*ein Menschenverstands-Philister*).

Notes

[1] Siskin, Clifford, *The Historicity of Romantic Discourse* (New York and London: Oxford UP, 1988), 186.

[2] David Hume, *A Treatise of Human Nature* [1738], ed., A. D. Lindsay (London: Dent, 1911), 7.

[3] James Beattie, *Essay on the Immutability of Truth* (Edinburgh, 1771), 18.

[4] Henry Home [Lord Kames], *Loose Hints Upon Education* (Edinburgh, 1781).

[5] Thomas Reid, *Enquiry into the Human Mind on the Principles of Common Sense* (Edinburgh, 1764), 3, 55, 228. Cf. S. A. Grave, *The Scottish Philosophy of Common Sense* (Oxford: Clarendon Press, 1960), 114.

[6] This despite Hume's use of "the language of a common-sense realism." (Lindsay, ed., xv; cf. xi: "When [Hume] shows that the most fundamental beliefs of mankind cannot be supported by reason, the moral in his eyes is 'so much the worse for reason.'")

[7] Cf. Andrew Seth, *Scottish Philosophy: A Comparison of the Scottish and German Answers to Hume* (Edinburgh & London: Blackwood, 1885), 7, 18–19.

[8] Thomas Reid, *Analysis of Aristotle's Logic* (Edinburgh, 1806), 44–47; cf. Grave, 105.

[9] For a still-useful, broad exposition of the doctrines of the Scottish School, see Henry Sidgwick, *Outlines of the History of Ethics* (London: Macmillan, 1888), 199–225. Alexander Broadie, *The Tradition of Scottish Philosophy: a New Perspective on the Enlightenment* (Edinburgh: Polygon, 1990). See also, *The Scottish Enlightenment: an Anthology*, ed. and introduced by Alexander Broadie (Edinburgh: Canongate, 1997).

[10] See Alfred Bäumler, *Das Irrationalitätsproblem in der Ästhetik des 18. Jahrhunderts bis zur Kritik der Urteilskraft* (Darmstadt: Wissenschaftliche Buchgesellschaft, 1967 [1923]); Ernst Cassirer, *Die Philosophie der Aufklärung* (Tübingen: Mohr, 1932).

[11] See Manfred Kuehn, "The Early Reception of Reid, Oswald, and Beattie in Germany," *Journal of the History of Philosophy* 21 (1983): 479–95.

[12] See Manfred Kuehn, *Scottish Common Sense in Germany, 1768–1800: A Contribution to the History of Critical Philosophy* (Kingston & Montreal: McGill-Queen's UP, 1987), for a detailed account of "the role which Scottish common sense played in the broader development of German thought between 1768 and 1800" (8; see, too especially, 3–12). Kuehn's book effectively refutes Seth's contention (4) that "for the Germans certainly Reid is not of decisive importance." See, too, G. Zart, *Einfluß der englischen Philosophie seit Bacon auf die deutsche Philosophie des 18. Jahrhunderts* (Berlin: Dümmler, 1881), for an account of the influence of Scottish thought in Germany.

[13] See Roy Pascal, "Herder and the Scottish Historical School," *Publications of the English Goethe Society* 14 (1939): 23–42. Cf. Kuehn, 68–72, 140–44.

[14] *Maximen und Reflexionen*, herausgegeben von Max Hecker (Weimar, 1907), (=Schriften der Goethe Gesellschaft 21), 832. For convenience I refer to Hecker's established arrangement and numbering of Goethe's prose sayings; however, volume 13 of the "Frankfurter Ausgabe," ed. Harald Fricke (Frankfurt a. M.: Deutscher Klassiker Verlag, 1993), contains the most reliable edition and commentary yet published.

[15] See George Sabine, *A History of Political Theory* (London: Harrap, 1963), 16, 603–4.

[16] Hecker. Cf. my "'Man nimmt in der Welt jeden, wofür er sich gibt': the presentation of Self in Goethe's Die Wahlverwandtschaften," *German Life and Letters* 48 (1994): 400–6 (404).

[17] R. H. Stephenson, *Goethe's Wisdom Literature* (Bern: Lang, 1983).

[18] Hecker, 532; see Hamilton, Sir William. *Reid's Essays on the Intellectual Powers of Man from his Collected Writings.* (Edinburgh, 1853), 470.

[19] See Sidgwick, 255.

[20] See P. F. Ganz, *Der Einfluß des Englischen auf den deutschen Wortschatz* (Berlin: E. Schmidt, 1957), on "*Gemeinsam*" and "common sense" for the changes in meaning these and related terms underwent in the German eighteenth century.

[21] George Santayana, *Reason in Common Sense* (2nd edition, New York: Dover, 1980).

[22] Cf. Grave, 115: "Reason and common sense go together in nature . . . "

[23] See H. G. Gadamer, *Wahrheit und Methode* (Tübingen: Mohr/Siebeck, 1975), 15–27.

[24] Elizabeth M. Wilkinson and L. A. Willoughby. *Friedrich Schiller: On the Aesthetic Education of Man.* In a series of letters, ed. and translated, with an Introduction, Commentary and Glossary of Terms (Oxford: Clarendon, 1967), xxiii, xxxi–xxxii.

[25] The burden of Kuehn's *Common Sense* is to argue through the implications of Windelband's statement that "Kant begins at the point at which the Scots had stopped.": 7, 10, 191, 202.

[26] Joseph Priestley, *An Examination of Dr Reid's Enquiry into the Human Mind on the Principles of Common Sense, Dr Beattie's Essay on the Nature and Immutability of Truth, and Dr Oswald's Appeal to Common Sense in Behalf of Religions* (London, 1774), 124.

[27] Cf. Seth, 77–79.

[28] See R. H. Stephenson, *Goethe's Conception of Knowledge and Science.* (Edinburgh UP: Edinburgh, 1995), 47–53.

[29] Robert J. Clark, *Herder: His Life and Thought* (Berkeley & Los Angeles: U of California P), 1955, 398.

Faust's Pendular Atheism and the British Tradition of Religious Melancholy

Matthew Bell

Faust's Spiritual Autobiography and the Experience of Pietism in the 1770s

ONE CAN IMAGINE, when in 1797 Goethe returned to *Faust*, that his scientific and other scholarly commitments made the alliance between devil and scholar seem a little less pleasing than it had seemed when he began *Faust* in the anti-university atmosphere of the early 1770s. Evidently Goethe now thought that for a scholar to have any dealings with the devil — and a conventional pact was clearly out of the question — some powerful psychological motivation must be at work. This motivation is what much of the new material with which Goethe filled the "great lacuna" during the final phase of work on *Faust I* was designed to provide. The first piece of infill material, the completion of the scene "Nacht," deals with Faust's reaction to the Erdgeist, and it contains the extraordinary sequence in which Faust decides on suicide, is saved, and then tries to make sense of his salvation. The passage in this sequence that has drawn most comment is Faust's statement of his loss of faith: "Die Botschaft hör' ich wohl, allein mir fehlt der Glaube" (line 765). Nicholas Boyle, for instance, draws attention to the way in which this passage epitomises the moment in German intellectual history at which the process of secularisation became acutely problematic.[1] The lines that follow, however, have drawn comparatively little comment. After confessing to his loss of faith, Faust offers, by way of explanation for his unexpected susceptibility to the Easter Chorus, a kind of spiritual autobiography:

> Zu jenen Sphären wag' ich nicht zu streben,
> Woher die holde Nachricht tönt;
> Und doch, an diesen Klang von Jugend auf gewöhnt,

Ruft er auch jetzt zurück mich in das Leben.
Sonst stürzte sich der Himmelsliebe Kuß
Auf mich herab, in ernster Sabbatstille;
Da klang so ahnungsvoll des Glockentones Fülle,
Und ein Gebet war brünstiger Genuß;
Ein unbegreiflich holdes Sehnen
Trieb mich durch Wald und Wiesen hinzugehn,
Und unter tausend heißen Tränen
Fühlt' ich mir eine Welt entstehn.
Dies Lied verkündete der Jugend muntre Spiele,
Der Frühlingsfeier freies Glück;
Erinnrung hält mich nun mit kindlichem Gefühle
Vom letzten, ernsten Schritt zurück.
O tönet fort ihr süßen Himmelslieder!
Die Träne quillt, die Erde hat mich wieder! (767–784)[2]

So important for the motivation of Faust's behaviour is this flash-back to his childhood faith that Goethe has Faust present another, similar flashback in the next scene, "Vor dem Tor," this time as an explanation for his cynicism about the medication that he and his father had dispensed during the plague:

Nur wenig Schritte noch hinauf zu jenem Stein,
Hier wollen wir von unsrer Wandrung rasten.
Hier saß ich oft gedankenvoll allein
Und quälte mich mit Beten und mit Fasten.
An Hoffnung reich, im Glauben fest,
Mit Tränen, Seufzen, Händeringen
Dacht' ich das Ende jener Pest
Vom Herrn des Himmels zu erzwingen.
Der Menge Beifall tönt mir nun wie Hohn.
O könntest du in meinem Innern lesen,
Wie wenig Vater und Sohn
Solch eines Ruhmes wert gewesen! (1022–33)

The extraordinary thing about these two passages is that here, for the first time in a treatment of the Faust story, Faust is portrayed as a believing Christian.[3] Earlier Fausts had been learned theologians and quick-witted casuists, but not fervent believers, and properly so, for to have portrayed Faust as a believing Christian would have been to fly in the face of the traditional meaning of the Faust story in a scandalous fashion.

Goethe only gives us echoes of Faust's early enthusiasm, but they are enough to establish the outline of Faust's spiritual biography and to affect the way we understand the Faust we have before us. On the face of it, this is a story of a loss of faith. Faust was "im Glauben fest," albeit somewhat desperately so ("mit Tränen, Seufzen, Händeringen"), and now he is an atheist. The story of Faust's loss of faith belongs to a particular species of eighteenth-century spiritual biography, however, the purpose of which is decidedly *not* to illustrate a process of secularisation. To understand Faust's loss of faith, it is necessary to consider its place in Goethe's own work and in the tradition of the Enlightenment. In the early 1770s, Goethe twice treated the theme of the loss of Pietist faith in ways that closely parallel Faust's story. The conceptual framework for these cases of lapsed Pietism may well have come from Goethe's immediate intellectual environment in 1772 and 1773. Whether or not a source can be established definitively, however, is relatively unimportant, for the psychological ideas that Goethe used were part of a broad Enlightenment tradition of the psychological critique of religion, which drew in turn on a seventeenth-century tradition of criticism of melancholy and enthusiasm. This paper aims to show that Faust's psychological condition can be understood in the light of this tradition. The final section of the paper indicates what this might imply for the interpretation of *Faust I*.

The young Faust of the two passages of spiritual autobiography is described as if he were a Pietist.[4] Thus, in a strange incongruity, Faust takes his place alongside that other 1790s Pietist the "schöne Seele" of *Wilhelm Meisters Lehrjahre*. Short of comparing the two, we can see a common reference point for the stories in Goethe's friend Karl Philipp Moritz, whose autobiographical novel *Anton Reiser* was a psychological reckoning with Moritz's own Pietist upbringing. It may be that Moritz provided the immediate impulse for the idea of giving Faust a Pietist past. Moritz died in 1793, and in the following years, it might be argued, Goethe set up a series of literary monuments to his acolyte, which included the Pietist Faust of the 1790s. It is likely, however, that Goethe's interest in Moritz was motivated in part by self-interest, that is to say by Goethe's interest in his own self, in the elements in Moritz's experience that reflected his own experience, the fate that Moritz had suffered and that he, Goethe, had escaped in his own brush with Pietism in the early 1770s.

In the years immediately following his association with Susanna von Klettenberg's circle, Goethe's work showed clear signs of hostility towards the moral and existential straitjacket of Pietism, a hostility that emerged in sharp analyses of the psychological ill-effects of believing too strongly. A conceptual framework into which this experience might have been fitted was provided by deist elements in Goethe's immediate intellectual environment, the circle around Merck and the *Frankfurter*

Gelehrte Anzeigen. In 1772, during Goethe's editorial collaboration, the *Frankfurter Gelehrte Anzeigen* published a review of the infamous *Bekehrungsgeschichte des Grafen Struensee*, a story which, to the reviewer's mind, illustrated the lesson that a morally strict faith was more damaging to the cause of religion than any number of Humes, Voltaires, and La Mettries. The review as a whole is likely to have been a collaborative effort. The resounding final paragraph was almost certainly written by J. G. Schlosser, later to become Goethe's brother-in-law.[5] The reviewer has just delivered a damning verdict on the book and concludes as follows:

> Das ist unser Urtheil über diese Bogen, die wir dessen ungeachtet allen Eltern, Lehrern, Predigern und übertriebenen Devoten angelegentlichst empfehlen, weil sie aus ihnen die große Wahrheit lernen werden: daß allzustrenge, und über die Gränzen gedehnte Religionsmoral den armen Struensee zum Feind der Religion gemacht hat. Tausende sind es aus eben der Ursache heimlich und öffentlich, Tausende, die Christum als ihren Freund geliebt haben würden, wenn man ihn ihnen als einen Freund, und nicht als einen mürrischen Tyrannen vorgemahlt hätte, der immer bereit ist mit dem Donner zuzuschlagen, wo nicht höchste Vollkommenheit ist. — Wir müssen es einmal sagen, weil es uns schon lange auf dem Herzen liegt: Voltaire, Hume, la Mettrie, Helvetius, Rousseau, und ihre ganze Schule, haben der Moralität und der Religion lange nicht so viel geschadet, als der strenge, kranke Pascal und seine Schule. (*WA* 1.37, 255–56)

Struensee is an example of a common Enlightenment type, the "pendular atheist," who swings from enthusiastic belief to atheism and back again. According to this psychological model, then, atheism is a consequence of enthusiasm (or, in the case of Struensee, moral rigorism: to the eighteenth-century rationalist these amounted to the same thing). Enthusiasm breeds atheism, because it encourages wildly optimistic expectations about the providential ordering of the universe and our own moral perfectibility, which, once disappointed as they inevitably must be, send us swinging to their opposite pole, absolute pessimism and/or atheism. It is in this sense that Struensee's story makes Pascal out to be more harmful to religion than Hume.

The first pendular atheist in Goethe's writing is the Prometheus of the 1773 monologue. The monologue and later free-standing poem is usually celebrated for its trenchant and individualized expression of a form of atheism, and this is certainly the first impression that it makes. Prometheus's atheism is Epicurean. He does not believe that the gods do not exist, rather that they should be disregarded, as they are envious and ineffectual.[6] Prometheus's anger, though, is anything but Epicurean. The goal of Epicurus's philosophy was a state of calm (*ataraxia*). The moral gain from disregarding the gods was freedom from the maladaptive passions caused by belief in them. Prometheus has not reached this condition of calm: he is still a slave to the passions created by faith.

Like Faust's monologue, Prometheus's monologue contains a spiritual autobiography:

> Da ich ein Kind war,
> Nicht wußt', wo aus, wo ein,
> Kehrte ich mein verirrtes Aug'
> Zur Sonne, als wenn drüber wär'
> Ein Ohr, zu hören meine Klage,
> Ein Herz wie meins,
> Sich des Bedrängten zu erbarmen.
>
> Wer half mir
> Wider der Titanen Übermut?
> Wer rettete vom Tode mich,
> Von Sklaverei?
> Hast du's nicht alles selbst vollendet,
> Heilig glühend Herz?
> Und glühtest, jung und gut,
> Betrogen, Rettungsdank
> Dem Schlafenden dadroben?
>
> Ich dich ehren? Wofür?
> Hast du die Schmerzen gelindert
> Je des Beladenen?
> Hast du die Tränen gestillet
> Je des Geängsteten?
> Hat nicht mich zum Manne geschmiedet
> Die allmächtige Zeit
> Und das ewige Schicksal,
> Meine Herrn und deine? (21–47)

In the light of this recollection from Prometheus's youth, his atheism, his refusal to honour Zeus, can be seen as the disappointed belief of one who expected too much, one who was — again in Pietist-influenced language — "bedrängt," "beladen," and "geängstet," one who wept but whose "heilig glühend Herz" still gave thanks to the sleeping God in heaven. The implied result of this appeal to a deaf God is disappointment. At some unspecified point Prometheus the Pietist changed into Prometheus the atheist. The spiritual autobiography thus explains Prometheus's un-Epicurean anger. We see in the monologue a riven consciousness, the result of a belief and an expectation that has been disappointed. Indirectly, then, Prometheus with his angry, reactive atheism represents a psychological reason not to suppose that faith makes a difference in the world. Far from undermining Prometheus's atheism, his anger supports it by showing the damage that faith does.

The second case of pendular atheism from the post-Klettenberg years is Werther. Like the young Prometheus, Werther expected too much. He made the mistake of thinking the venerated world would reward its worshipper with transcendent artistic powers, with passionate communion. In his disappointment he turned into a blasphemer, casting himself in the role of Christ sacrificed for the sake of a fallen world. The underlying structure of the novel is of a series of alternating moods of expectation and disappointment, enthusiasm and desperation, euphoria and dysphoria. This is most powerfully expressed in the letter of 18 August. The first half of the letter is a rhapsodic hymn to divine, eternal nature, the second a horrific mirror image of the first, an attack of morbid melancholy, in which Werther imagines a godless and pointless nature, "ein ewig verschlingendes, ewig wiederkäuendes Ungeheuer" (*HA* 6, 53). Between the two halves there is a precise symmetry, for, as Werther writes at the beginning of the letter, "das, was des Menschen Glückseligkeit macht" has become "die Quelle seines Elendes" (52). The hinge that joins the two halves of the letter — and by extension the two aspects of Werther's mood — is something quite intangible, a sudden perceptual shift that turns joy into terror: "Es hat sich vor meiner Seele wie ein Vorhang weggezogen, und der Schauplatz des unendlichen Lebens verwandelt sich vor mir in den Abgrund des ewig offenen Grabs" (52).

Pendular Atheism and the British Tradition of Religious Melancholy

Forerunners of Faust's pendular atheism can be found as far back as Maimonides, but the tradition in which Faust stands can be said definitively to begin with Robert Burton.[7] In his satire on the insufficiency of human knowledge, *The Anatomy of Melancholy* (1621), Burton coined the term "religious melancholy."[8] He distinguished two forms of religious melancholy, the melancholy of "excess" and the melancholy of "defect." The former included superstition, enthusiasm, and all the species of false prophecy; the latter despair, scepticism, and atheism. Both deviations from the sensible middle way were symptoms of the melancholic mind.[9] Burton's satirical analysis could have a polemical function: to stigmatise aberrant forms of belief, "the severall furies of our *Fatidici dii, Pythonissas, Sibyls, Enthusiasts, Pseudoprophets, Heretickes*, and *Schismaticks* in these our latter ages."[10] In the late seventeenth century this polemical function was developed by, among others, the Cambridge Platonist Henry More, and Meric Casaubon, classicist and convert from Catholicism to Anglicanism. More's target was, like Burton's, deviation from common-sense Anglicanism, whether in the direction of fanaticism (especially Puritan fanaticism, but also Catholicism) or atheism. More saw these two deviant tendencies as related, even as consequent upon one another:

> It is too common a disease now adayes to be driven by heedlesse intoxicating imaginations under pretense of higher strains of Religion and supernaturall light, and by bidding adieu to sober reason and a purified mind, to grow first fanaticall, and then Atheisticall and sensuall, even almost to the height of abhorred Gnosticism.[11]

The paradox of the coexistence of belief and disbelief in one person was for More a fact of melancholic psychology. He brought Burton's melancholies of "defect" and "excess" together in a single underlying melancholic syndrome, which explained the apparent paradox of pendular atheism:

> *Atheism and Enthusiasm*, though they seem so extremely opposite to one another, yet in many things they do very nearly agree. For, to say nothing of their joynt conspiracy against the true knowledge of God and Religion, they are commonly entertain'd, though successively, in the same Complexion . . . those that have only a fiery *Enthusiastick* acknowledgement of God . . . will as confidently represent to their *Phansy* that there is no God, as ever it was represented that there is one . . . For the *Atheist's* pretence to Wit and natural Reason . . . makes the *Enthusiast* secure that *Reason* is no guide to God: And the *Enthusiast's* boldly dictating the careless ravings of his own tumultuous *Phansy* for undeniable Principles of Divine knowledge, confirms the *Atheist* that the whole business of Religion and Notion of a God is nothing but a troublesome fit of over-curious *Melancholy*.[12]

Another component of More's synthesis was the tradition of the melancholic thinker, which dated from classical antiquity (the caricature of Heraclitus as the weeping philosopher, for instance).[13] For the seventeenth century, the philosopher qualified as both enthusiast and melancholic, by virtue of his commitment to doubting reality. Descartes was criticised as a melancholic and enthusiast, because his procedure of seeking certainty by means of radical doubt appeared pathological. In his *Treatise on Melancholy*, Meric Casaubon called Descartes a "cracked brain man."[14] Similarly, in the *Treatise on Human Nature*, Hume diagnosed himself in his sceptical mood as suffering from "philosophical melancholy and delirium."[15] By the late eighteenth century, "enthusiast" and "melancholic" had become general-purpose terms of contempt or reproach for anyone who appeared to think too hard. In the original drafts of *Faust*, Faust labels Wagner "der trockne Schwärmer" (line 168).

More moderate were the psychological arguments against enthusiasm in Locke's *Essay on Human Understanding*, the fourth edition of which, published in 1700, contained the celebrated and massively influential associationist critique of enthusiasm. Locke's associationism and, less obviously, Burton's religious melancholy, fed into the mainstream of the British Enlightenment. Whig Anglicans and deists during Queen Ann's reign used the psychological critique of enthusiasm as a weapon against Catholics and Protestant sectarians. John Trenchard's *Natural History of Superstition* of 1709 and Trenchard and Thomas Gordon's periodical *The Independent Whig* were influenced by Burton and Locke. Arguments of this kind can also be found in Shaftesbury's *Letters concerning Enthusiasm* of 1708 and his *Soliloquy* of 1710.[16] From the early eighteenth-century Whig deists, it is a short step to the deists and atheists of the High Enlightenment. Two key works in this spirit were influenced by Trenchard and were thus at one remove from Burton: Hume's *Natural History of Religion* of 1757 and Holbach's 1768 *La contagion sacrée, ou histoire naturelle de la superstition*. The latter advertised itself as a translation from the English of "Jean Trinchard," but was in fact an original work, in which Holbach used Trenchard as, among other things, a smokescreen to preserve his anonymity.

With the pessimism appropriate to a classical moralist, Hume argued that the worst was but a corruption of the best: "corruptio optimi pessima."[17] The most systematic, normative, binding faith, in short the most positive of religions, will yield the worst behaviour, just as, by the same hidden law of compensation, the highest enthusiasm yields to the deepest melancholy. This is the lugubrious conclusion of the *Natural History of Religion:*

> The more exquisite any good is, of which a small specimen is afforded us, the sharper is the evil, allied to it; and few exceptions are found to this uniform law of nature. The most sprightly wit borders on madness; the highest effusions of joy produce the deepest melancholy; the most ravishing pleasures are attended with the most cruel lassitude and disgust; the most flattering hopes make way for the severest disappointments. And, in general, no course of life has such safety (for happiness is not to be dreamed of) as the temperate and moderate, which maintains, as far as possible, a mediocrity, and a kind of insensibility, in every thing. (184)

Faust's Pendular Atheism and Goethe's Classicism

Goethe's first idea of Faust, given form in the great opening monologue, was of a man who oscillated between enthusiasm and pessimism. The monologue was conceived as a succession of alternations between a mood of despair at his physical and spiritual confinement and a mood of elation at the prospect of freedom and discovery. At the end of the first section of the monologue, these alternations appear in a compressed form, as Faust explains how the attractions of magic contrast with the frustrations of scholarship:

> Drum hab ich mich der Magie ergeben,
> Ob mir durch Geistes Kraft und Mund
> Nicht manch Geheimniss werde kund.
> Dass ich nicht mehr mit saurem Schweis
> Rede von dem was ich nicht weis.
> Dass ich erkenne was die Welt
> Im innersten zusammenhält,
> Schau alle Würckungskrafft und Saamen
> Und thu nicht mehr in Worten kramen.
>
> (*Urfaust*, 24–32)

The rhetoric of alternating opposites expresses Faust's emotional dynamic, which is similar to the pendular atheism described by Henry More and the other seventeenth- and eighteenth-century writers considered here. As the monologue develops, its logic becomes similar, too. Enthusiasm, disappointed by reality, is unveiled as an excess of high spirits. The result is a bitter pessimism, which also undermines itself, for if empty bitterness is all that rationality can give, then surely it would be better to be irrational. Thus, the pessimist turns back towards enthusiasm, and the pendulum begins its cycle again.

Goethe had no reason to alter the shape of this emotional dynamic when he came back to *Faust* in 1797. The new "große Lücke" infill material would continue and extrapolate from the pendular model of the original drafts of *Faust*. In the process, Goethe made the significance of the model more explicit in two ways. In the two Pietist-inspired passages of spiritual autobiography, he turned the Pietist metaphors of the original drafts into a literal reality. Faust, from being a frustrated scholar speaking a bizarre hybrid language in which Pietist imagery is one component, becomes an actual ex-Pietist. In a similar fashion, Goethe turns the morbid imagery of the first monologue — the language of dust, worms, mould, confinement, and the Pietist opposition of the wet and the dry — into the literal reality of Faust's abortive suicide.[18] These metaphors, which in the fragmentary original drafts of *Faust* already suggested a morbid mind tending towards self-destruction — as the similar metaphors do very obviously in the finished *Werther*, written during the same period — become symptoms of the "English disease" of suicidal melancholy. The function of the new material was to give Faust's alliance with Mephistopheles a convincing psychological motivation. In order to do this, Goethe found it necessary to draw out the implications of the original 1770s drafts. The opening monologue contained the signs of an illness that would deepen progressively until it became critical.

It is characteristic of Goethe, and of Enlightenment psychology in general, that he should proceed in this way, treating the history of Faust's illness as essentially a problem of cognitive behaviour. At the heart of Faust's problem in the original drafts of *Faust* is the imbalance of expectation and reality. Like Werther, Faust expects too much of the world and of himself. Indeed, one of the dominant themes of Goethe's intellectual development between the mid-1770s and the period of high classicism was the renunciation of these unreasonable expectations. Lofty spiritual goals were renounced in favour of the attainable goals set by natural science, historical scholarship, a poetics of classical moderation, and Epicurean philosophy of healthy, temperate gratification of the senses, and the rationalisation of unwarranted hopes and fears. In the classical 1790s, the Pietist childhood of Moritz seemed to prove the point. To anyone looking for the root cause of Moritz's psychological problems, Pietism was the prime candidate. By 1797, reflecting on the origins of psychological problems had become a favourite mode for Goethe, most recently in the later books of the *Lehrjahre* and in the *Werther* "prequel" *Briefe aus der Schweiz*. In the work on *Faust I*, Goethe used this mode of psychological explanation twice. Given the constraints of the *Faust* drama, as it presented itself to Goethe in 1797, the obvious way to construct this kind of causal story was to have Faust reflect on his youth. The two moments of spiritual autobiography locate the original cause of Faust's sickness in his early Pietism.

Reiner Wild has observed that when Goethe returned to *Faust* in 1797 he came from writing ballads with a distinctly anti-Christian animus, most obviously "Die Braut von Corinth."[19] Other recent work has sought to clarify how Goethe integrated *Faust* into his classicism. The "große Lücke" material is the main vehicle of this integration. It projects an image of Faust's psychology that is thoroughly classical, both typical of Goethe in his classical period and dependent on ideas from classical antiquity, above all the Epicurean psychology of Lucretius.[20] Goethe's classicism married well with the idea of pendular atheism. As it appears in Hume, for instance, the idea of pendular atheism is part of an argument for classical moderation, and this is not far from Goethe's own Lucretian concern with *Gesundheit*. In Hume's version, positive Christianity is socially dangerous and is contrasted with classical reasonableness and restraint. In Goethe's version — in the *Roman Elegies*, the *Venetian Epigrams*, the 1797 ballads, and *Faust* — a strong Christian faith is morbid and psychologically harmful.

The portrayal of Faust as a believer who has been disappointed by his faith is, in the first place, simply a psychological explanation for his morbid state of mind in "Nacht." Faust's habit of lurching from one emotional and cognitive extreme to the other, brought sharply into focus by the abortive suicide and the two fragments of spiritual autobiography, is a continuation of a habit that arose from his childhood enthusiasm. Also, the model of pendular atheism provides the momentum for Faust's final disastrous swing into the wager with Mephistopheles and into his career of amoral striving. Faust's pendular atheism thus assumes a significant place in the moral economy of the drama. It accelerates an existing tendency away from the traditional, theological meaning of the Faust story. If this interpretation is correct, the view of *Faust* as an allegory of secularisation loses some of its attractiveness. There are no grounds for nostalgia about the lost certainties of Christianity. Instead, *Faust I* presents a Lucretian view of religion as the cause of psychological and social ills. The morbid, damaged, amoral Faust is prepared to wager his life with Mephistopheles because he is a psychologically ex-Christian man, not a historically post-Christian man. In this, as in other things, *Faust* seems designed to confound our expectations.

Notes

[1] Nicholas Boyle, *Goethe, "Faust. Part One"* (Cambridge: Cambridge UP, 1987), 37.

[2] Critics have been sceptical about the youthful Faust; see note 5 below. The orthodox view of the function of these lines is that they are a mechanical way of putting Faust in a more life-affirming frame of mind: "Nicht der Inhalt des Osterglaubens, der ja für F. nicht mehr vorhanden ist, sondern die Erinnerung an die mit Ostern verbundenen beseligenden Kindheitserlebnisse ziehen F. ins Leben zurück. In der gleichen Stimmung liegt das Entscheidende" (Theodor Friedrich and Lothar J. Scheithauer, *Kommentar zu Goethes "Faust I"* [Stuttgart: Reclam, 1959], 191). In a sense, of course, this is back to front, for Faust has already been stopped on the brink of suicide before this ration-

alisation. If the lines are to make psychological sense, they must be seen as an explanation of Faust's change of heart, not as its cause.

[3] The point is made by David Luke in the notes to his translation of *Faust. Part One* (Oxford: Oxford UP, 1987), 152.

[4] Stuart Atkins speaks of "pietistic tears and fasting" (*Goethe's "Faust." A Literary Analysis*, Cambridge, MA: Harvard UP, 1958), 35, but other critics are less disposed to take the Pietist language at face value. Erich Trunz takes an existentialist view: "Die Erinnerung an die Jugend ist Erinnerung an die Zeit, da Phantasie die Welt noch als große Aufgabe, nicht als einengende Bedingnis sah. Der Selbstmordgedanke hat das Ich zu seinem tiefsten Wesentlichen gelenkt; die Erinnerung an die Jugend tut es gleichfalls" (*HA* 3, 507). Hans Arens considers that "Gottahnung, Liebesgefühl, Ich-Erlebnis und Naturoffenbarung [verbanden] sich [in] ihm zu Weltlust und Lebensbejahung" (*Kommentar zu Goethes "Faust I"* [Heidelberg: Winter, 1982], 122). Victor Lange in the Münchner Ausgabe sees "[eine] in undeutlich-schwärmerischen Bildern in die Erinnerung zurückgerufene jugendliche Gottesahnung" (MA 6.1, 1001).

[5] See Hermann Bräuning-Oktavio, *Herausgeber und Mitarbeiter der Frankfurter Gelehrte Anzeigen 1772* (Tübingen: Niemeyer, 1966), 556–74.

[6] For the *locus classicus* of this Epicurean argument, see Lactantius's *Treatise on the Anger of God*, chapter 12, in *Works*, trans. W. Fletcher (Edinburgh: T. & T, Clark, 1871), vol. 2, 28.

[7] On Maimonides's psychological critique of false prophets, see Frank E. Manuel, *The Changing of the Gods* (Hanover, NH: U of New England P, 1983), 56.

[8] Burton treats religious melancholy in the fourth section of the *Anatomy*. On the originality of the idea, see *The Anatomy of Melancholy*, 3 vols. (Oxford: Oxford UP, 1994), vol. 3, 330.

[9] See Michael Heyd, *"Be sober and reasonable." The Critique of Enthusiasm in the Seventeenth and Early Eighteenth Centuries*, (Leiden: E. J. Brill, 1995), 66.

[10] *Anatomy*, vol. 3, 331.

[11] Quoted in Heyd, *"Be sober and reasonable,"* 4.

[12] Quoted in Heyd, *"Be sober and reasonable,"* 167.

[13] See for instance Seneca, *Dialogues*, IX.15.2, Juvenal, *Satires*, X.28–35, and Lucian, *Vitarum Auctio*, 13.

[14] Quoted in Heyd, *"Be sober and reasonable,"* 137.

[15] *A Treatise of Human Nature*, ed. L. A. Selby-Bigge, revised by P. H. Nidditch (Oxford: Oxford UP, 1978), 269. See also Donald W. Livingston, *Philosophical Melancholy and Delirium. Hume's Pathology of Philosophy* (Chicago: U of Chicago P, 1998).

[16] See Manuel, *The Changing of the Gods*, 46–57.

[17] *Principal Writings on Religion including "Dialogues Concerning Natural Religion" and "Natural History of Religion,"* ed. J. C. A. Gaskin (Oxford: Oxford UP, 1993), 163 (note), 165.

[18] The address to the moon at lines 386 ff might also be read as a sign of morbidity, as it is characteristic of eighteenth-century representations of suicidal melancholy. See also: dust and worms (l. 403), "Rauch und Moder [. . .] Tiergeripp und Totenbein" (ll. 416–17), confinement (l. 642).

[19] *Goethes klassische Lyrik* (Stuttgart: J. B. Metzler, 1999), 223.

[20] Hans-Jürgen Schings has shown that "die Geschichte der Verzweiflung . . . , die der klassische Goethe in der 'großen Lücke' entfaltet hat" is the exact antithesis of the positive classical model set out in the Winckelmann essay of 1805 ("Fausts Verzweiflung," *Goethe-Jahrbuch* 115 [1998]: 97–123, 123). On Goethe's use of Lucretius's Epicurean psychology, see my forthcoming article "Sorge, Epicurean Psychology, and the Classical *Faust*," *Oxford German Studies* 28 (2000): 83–131.

Goethe and Colonisation:
the *Wanderjahre* and Cooper

Nicholas Saul

THE *WANDERJAHRE* IS perhaps Goethe's most awkward text. It
deals in pioneering fashion with still current problems: technology
and industrialisation, fragmentation of personality, the new utopian orders of mass society and culture, and the role of art in this. Yet with its
decentered authorial perspective, lack of narrative unity or closure,
complex symbolism of contrastive mirrorings, and all the other numerous demands on the reader's initiative, the *Wanderjahre* frustrates conclusive readings.

Above all, there is the matter of America's deeply ambiguous role as
utopian reference point of the novel's logical perspective. America was
of course already that in the *Lehrjahre*, as the major focus of the colo-
nising efforts of the Society of the Tower. Lothario had fought in the
American Wars of Liberation on the American side. But later, in
Europe and from the perspective of the "Turmgesellschaft," he decides:
"*Hier oder nirgend ist Amerika!*" (*HA* 7, 431),[1] so that America becomes more of a metaphor or an ideal than a real place, or at least as
real in Europe as it was across the Atlantic. The utopian conditions that
America alone, as a kind of *tabula rasa*, had seemed to fulfil for a fresh
social, economic, and cultural start seem thereby to be disqualified. All
the more confusing, then, when another member of the Society, Jarno,
decides for entirely pragmatic reasons of mutual security (*HA* 7, 564)
to take his part of the "Turmgesellschaft" back to the States (563–64),
while leaving Wilhelm and Lothario behind in utopian Europe and
sending the Abbé off to the utopian Russia of Catherine the Great. If
this is problematic, the *Wanderjahre* appears to take us little further in
understanding the value of America for Goethe's utopian thought.
Here, as was the spirit of the age, utopian organisations proliferate. The
"Turmgesellschaft" is joined by the patriarchal Enlightenment demesne
of the Oheim, the Pädagogische Provinz, Lenardo's Emigrants League,
and Odoard's inner European colonisers. The Oheim is actually a third-

generation American by birth, yet he follows the Goethean principle whereby the son contradicts the father, prefers the ancient culture of Europe and political accommodation with monarchy to the task of establishing the American nation like another Orpheus or Lycurgus (*HA* 8, 82), and returns to found his own European utopia. His nephew Lenardo, of course, tends in the opposite direction. Lenardo, as his address to the Emigrants League shows (384–92), is committed to the existential, indeed God-given (386) doctrine of continuous emigration and colonisation. Thus the Oheim has donated his old American estate: "ein bisher vernachlässigter Familienbesitz in jenen frischen Gegenden" (142; compare 439). To this place Lenardo will lead the mountain weavers and spinners made destitute by the march of technology and over-population (242). Links are established between the Society of the Tower, which still aims at American colonisation, and Lenardo's group. Lothario's American territory and that of Lenardo are to be linked by a canal for mutual benefit (142, 242). Moreover, links are forged between this alliance and the Pedagogic Province. Wilhelm sends Felix there for a year (167), and there too Lothario recruits suitable artisans (242–44). All this is done in the name of the practical, useful, selfless, universalising activity of the renouncers that the Abbé calls "Weltfrömmigkeit" (243). Thus, when the leading members of the Society of the Tower take ship (436), Lenardo's motto "Gedenke zu wandern!" (318) might seem to infuse the entire work, at least in its practical dimension, with the idea of America — except that of course the text contains counter-indicators undermining this reading.

The first is the unreliably reported and confessedly provisional blueprint (404–8) of Lenardo's new society, the depiction of which we know to have been influenced by Robert Owen's ideas, which in turn Goethe probably encountered through Duke Bernhard's report of his American journey in 1825.[2] I am only reporting the scholarly consensus when I say that this is a very mixed bag of ideas. It contains some likely sounding practical ideas for a pioneering society, such as a relatively informal system of jurisdiction and moderate taxation. On the other hand, there is the lack of a capital (which must hinder the new society's self-understanding and cultural development), also the positively industrialised way they use time, and the apparently anti-Semitic constitution. Secondly, there is Odoard's inner European colonisation project (392–93, 408–13). This is obviously intended to relativise the American project, yet it too is unattractive. Odoard has total control over a distant province, he has a concept and is recruiting disciplined artisans from whom he requires only utmost skill and commitment. The political dimension seems to be covered by the refrain of the communal song: "Heil dir Führer! Heil dir Band!" (413), and with that the regressive, potentially dystopian quality of the project is revealed.

All this still leaves us with America as the perspective of the utopian strivings recorded in the archival novel. What America actually *means*, however, given all the ambivalence and all the transatlantic ditherings, remains unspecified. One way of responding to this challenge to the reader's initiative is to locate the implicit character of the American utopia safely in the dialectic of "Denken und Tun, Tun und Denken" (263) that Montan enunciates, and that characterises in a nutshell the structural principle of the novel, oscillating as it does between reflection and example in both framework and embedded texts of various types. Another way of responding is that of Gerhard Schulz in his most recent essay on the *Wanderjahre*, which is to declare the America theme of subordinate interest.[3] Nevertheless, leaving on one side the well-explored but frustratingly refractive area of Goethe's use of his wide knowledge of American social and economic affairs,[4] there is one further aspect of Goethe's encounter with America, in the years when he was recasting the *Wanderjahre*, that recent scholarship encourages us to explore,[5] that of American letters. I am referring to Fenimore Cooper and the *Wanderjahre*, a question that from Ernst Beutler to Erich Trunz and (most recently) Wynfried Kriegleder has become something of a topos, albeit unresolved. This I wish to explore, and to say something decided about it. American letters and Goethe might be examined under the rubric of "Weltliteratur" that, after all, an epigram from Makarie's Archive admonishes Germans to ignore at their peril (483, No. 151). In his collection of utterances on the notion of "Weltliteratur,"[6] Goethe, it must be noted, omits American literature. This is not, however, in itself a reliable guide. Persian and Chinese literatures are also passed over there, yet the *West-östlicher Divan* and the *Chinesisch-Deutsche Jahres- und Tageszeiten* provide compelling evidence of Goethe's practical intercultural engagement with these literatures. Indeed, it turns out that Goethe, despite his silence at the level of theory, was both formidably well informed about American affairs in general, and deeply interested in the progress of American letters. Here, for example, is something we all know:

> Amerika, du hast es besser
> Als unser Continent, das alte,
> Hast keine verfallene Schlösser
> Und keine Basalte.
> Dich stört nicht im Innern,
> Zu lebendiger Zeit
> Unnützes Erinnern
> Und vergeblicher Streit.

> Benutzt die Gegenwart mit Glück!
> Und wenn nun eure Kinder dichten,
> Bewahre sie ein gut Geschick
> Vor Ritter-, Räuber- und Gespenstergeschichten.
>
>   (*HA* 1, 333)

These lines, written down on 21 June 1827,[7] are usually taken to apply one of Goethe's favourite natural-scientific analogies (the basalt) to the question of America's general social and cultural development. Scholars usually point to a pre-text of this poem in some notes by Goethe on Neptunism from 18 September 1819,[8] with which you are probably also familiar: "Nord Amerikaner glücklich keine Basalte zu haben. / Keine Ahnen und keinen klassischen Boden." Basalt, Goethe scholarship tells us, is a peculiar type of rock that in the scholarship of the day was once taken to be young but was increasingly discovered in older formations, and since then it became identified in Goethe's mind with fruitless controversy.[9] America is blessed with no basalt, and therefore, as a country unencumbered with useless reflection on its nonexistent past, can focus all its vitality on the present.

While that may be so, however, it should be pointed out that the last three lines extend the argument explicitly to cover America's future literary development. In fact, another source of Goethe's makes this plain. He had received a visit from one of his many learned American friends, the Harvard mineralogist J. C. Cogswell, at Weimar in May 1819, around the time of the speculation on basalt. On 11 May 1819 we find, however, the laconic journal entry "Zustand der Litteratur von Cogswell" (*WA* 3, 7, 46), a work that Goethe later praises highly in a letter to Cogswell of 11 August 1819: "[. . .] die schönsten Aufschlüsse [. . .], so daß man ihn nicht genug lesen und wiederlesen kann. Man lernt bedeutende, sich auf eigne naturgemäße Art entwickelnde Zustände kennen" (*WA* 4, 31, 246). The Weimar editors kindly refer us to *Blackwood's Edinburgh Magazine* of March 1819, and there we find an essay by Cogswell (in fact, one of two) "On the State of Learning in the United States of America."[10] The essay is a masterly apologetic presentation and explanation of the state of American letters in general. Cogswell notes proudly that America is strong in "practical cleverness and businessmen" (Cogswell, 641), but also frankly admits that "learning, in its limited and appropriate sense, is not to be found in America" (641), and concedes the "low literary reputation of America" (642): "Franklin is their only philosopher whose discourses have been of much importance to mankind; and if the whole stock of their literature were set on fire tomorrow, no scholar would feel the loss" (646). Cogswell's point, though, is not so much to acknowledge "American barrenness in creative literature" (646), as to defend American creative intellect in principle against the extraordinary imputations widely made by naturalists and cultural anthropologists following Buffon in the latter half of the eighteenth century, and which are amusingly recorded in the opening chapters of James Ceasar's recent book *Reconstructing America*.[11] These held, in Cogswell's words, that "the human mind has suffered a deterioration by being transported across the Atlantic" (647), so that the admitted defects of American letters are due not to circumstantial factors but to the intrinsic "inferiority of the American intellect" (641). The present low state of letters in America, says Cogswell, is due rather to two extrinsic things: first, the "demand for active talent" (647) in practical activity is so great and so well rewarded, that it must for the present divert energies away from learning and writing. Furthermore, while Americans do indeed possess their fair share of native genius, it does not yet receive that stimulation from American life and nature that it needs, so that its development for the present is halted:

> There is nothing to awaken fancy in that land of dull realities; it contains no objects that carry back the mind to contemplation of early antiquity; no mouldering ruins to excite curiosity in the history of past ages; no memorials, commemorative of glorious deeds, to call forth patriotic enthusiasm and reverence; it has no tradition and legends and fables to afford materials for romance and poetry; no peasantry of original and various costume and character for the sketches of the pencil and the subjects of the song; it has gone through no period of infancy; no pastoral state in which poetry grows out of the simplicity of the language, and beautiful and picturesque descriptions of nature are produced by the constant contemplation of her. The whole course of life is a round of practical duties; for every day there is a task for every person; all are pressing forward in the hurry of business; no man stops to admire the heavens over his head, or the charms of creation around him; no time is allowed for the study of nature, and no taste for her beauties is ever acquired. (647)

America will, however, exhibit these (literary) "powers of a higher order" when in due course "a more improved and refined state of society shall bring them into action" (649). In this, she will equal England (649). Goethe's "Amerika du hast es besser," we can now see, echoes not only his own earlier reflection on basalt, but also the early lines of this last extract from Cogswell, which he read around the same time: "[N]o objects that carry back the mind to contemplation of early antiquity; no mouldering ruins to excite curiosity in the history of past ages" — lines, let us note, which contain the promise of an eventual American contribution to "Weltliteratur" following "auf eigne naturgemäße Art." This parallel, then, underscores the emphatically literary function of the otherwise decidedly odd last three lines of Goethe's poem. In June 1827 Goethe evidently recalled his reading of Cogswell from 1819, just as he recalled the speculation on Neptunism from the same year in order to write "Amerika, du hast es besser" for the *Ausgabe letzter Hand*, and he uses it to give the American writers *in spe* a friendly warning to leave out the adventure novels and get on with the "Weltliteratur" as soon as possible. Moreover, it is clear from this extract that Goethe is not only well apprised of the degenerative paradigm widely applied to American nature and culture in the latter half of the eighteenth century, but also that he (on his own natural analogy) prefers the progressivist model of Cogswell.

That said, why should Goethe choose in 1827 to echo Cogswell's vindication of America's potential literary genius from 1819? It may be noted that the day after writing "Amerika, du hast es besser," if the journal is to be believed, Goethe started his final revision of the second, definitive version of the *Wanderjahre* (*WA* 3, 11, 74), beginning as it does in basalt-rich European mountains. But perhaps a better reason is that in those intervening years there appeared the first major phenomenon of American letters, James Fenimore Cooper. Between 30 September 1826 and 29 January 1828,[12] Goethe read no less than six historical novels by Cooper. This represents all of Cooper's novels then in existence save the very first, the unrenowned novel of manners *Precaution* (1821). The most intensive phase of engagement stretches from 30 September to 4 November 1826,[13] when Goethe read, in this order: *The Pioneers, or the Sources of the Susquehanna* (1823), Cooper's third novel and the first Leatherstocking novel; *The Last of the Mohicans* (1826), Cooper's fourth novel and the most famous Leatherstocking novel; *The Spy* (1821), Cooper's second novel and first historical novel, which involves the Major John André case (Benedict Arnold's co-conspirator) and George Washington; and *The Pilot* (1824), a historical novel of the sea involving John Paul Jones. Finally, in June 1827, Goethe reads *The Prairie* (1827), the third Leatherstocking novel, which features Natty Bumppo's death; and in January 1828 *The Red Rover* (1827), another sea novel. These latter novels he seems to have read as soon as they were translated.

Such a pattern of reading suggests at least an unusual measure of enthusiasm and interest on Goethe's part for this first great manifestation of American literature. If we follow the laconic entries in his journal, Goethe is indeed impressed by Cooper's work. He reads and rereads the beginning of *The Pioneers* — a virtuoso presentation of an incident-packed forest sleigh-ride that skilfully introduces all the main characters, themes, and issues of the novel — and copies out the *dramatis personae.* "Auch das Kunstreiche daran näher betrachtet, geordnet und fortgesetzt" (*WA* 3, 10, 251; 1 October 1826), he writes. As he is finishing *The Prairie*, he notes: "bewunderte den reichen Stoff und dessen geistreiche Behandlung. Nicht leicht sind Werke mit so großem Bewußtseyn und solcher Consequenz durchgeführt als die Cooperschen Romane" (*WA* 3, 11, 76). This is little enough to go on and fairly general at that, but it is at least clear that Goethe has recognised not only Cooper's art of form, but also his content and meaning: the richness of material that Cooper treats ("reichen Stoff"), his intellectual stature ("mit so großem Bewußtseyn"), and the power of the arguments that run through his works ("Nicht leicht [. . .] mit solcher Consequenz durchgeführt"). Set against the background of Cogswell's remarks "On The State of Learning in the United States of America," which we know Goethe knew, they make still more interesting reading. If Cogswell had lamented the allegedly unpoetic quality of the American landscape, with its monotonous mountain ranges, featureless prairies, and oceanic forests, then we should recall that one of the triumphs of Cooper's writing achievement is precisely to have supplemented this alleged deficiency with inventions such as the great standing rock, centre of the action in *The Prairie*, the impressively allegorical Glens Falls in *The Last of the Mohicans*, or indeed the symbolically charged forest (or Glimmerglass Lake) in *The Pioneers* (to name but a few).

None of this covers the most striking feature of Cooper's novels, however, if we judge them against another of Cogswell's observations of 1819. Cogswell not only laments the absence of picturesque nature populated with interesting peasants; he also laments the absence of an American past or tradition, historical or legendary. America is paradoxically an adult nation without an infancy — grown up, but lacking the orientation and self-understanding that come from leaving childhood behind. Cooper's novels are of course that very paradoxical thing, historical novels of a nation seemingly without a history, but designed as such to supplement precisely these deficiencies. In a sense, they seek to satisfy in America the conditions Goethe himself set out in *Litterarischer Sansculottismus* for the establishment of a classic national German literature, and are presumably also those of a literature admissible to the canon of "Weltliteratur."

Let us look briefly, then, at some characteristic features of these novels by Cooper. I shall concentrate, because of the confines of this paper, on the landlocked ones, since three of them (*The Last of the Mohicans*, *The Pioneers*, and *The Prairie*) deal with Cooper's major creation, the semi-mythical figure of Natty Bumppo, at various stages of his career, and *The Spy* is of particular interest concerning the question of

American identity. In all of these texts, Cooper supplements missing history in varying degrees with romance, and explores the problem of American identity by setting the romantic action in the transitional zones between two or more orders. In *The Last of the Mohicans*, which features the Leatherstocking as the youthful forty-year-old Hawk-eye in the service of the British in 1757, we are in the primeval forests between the British and French domains, but also between the Mohicans (Chingachgook and the last Mohican Uncas) and the Hurons (Magua). In *The Pioneers*, we are in a literary figuration of the town of Cooper's birth, Templeton, in 1793, where a rough-hewn new town is being established in the area at the sources of the Susquehanna, where forest and settled land merge in a battle of colonisation and the winner is certain. Natty, still bonded with Chingachgook (who is himself now technically the last of the Mohicans), leads a frugal life on the fringe of the struggle between law and nature. This struggle ultimately focuses on his right to hunt on the land its owner and lawgiver, Judge Temple, claims. Traditionally, the land was that of the Indians. While Chingachgook dies as the white man finally usurps his ancient rights at the end of this novel, *The Prairie* takes us to the end of Bumppo's life, now known simply as the Trapper, in 1804. Here he has given up his right and will to hunt, accepted the onward march of civilisation, or colonisation, and moved further west to the prairies to lead a solitary existence among the warring Sioux and Pawnee. He discovers, however, that Ishmael Bush's ruthlessly exploitative settlers are claiming the prairie too, and bidding fair to reach the west coast beyond the Rockies. Even the wilderness will be subjected to the immigrants, he realises; an age has passed, and he, also the last of a particular race, dies. *The Spy* is set in 1780 and the War of Independence, in West-Chester, Neutral Ground between the American and British lines, where the conventional rules of war are suspended. It exploits even more than the others the ambiguity of crossed borders. The Whartons live deep in the Neutral Ground. Mr Wharton is an American whose loyalty, however, is to Britain. Daughter Sarah loves the American Major Dunwoodie and supports the Americans. Son Henry is a British Captain. The house is frequented by both parties — provided that they are uniformed. Nearby dwells Harvey Birch, universally despised as a British spy, but in fact an American double agent. His true loyalty must remain secret till his death, when a note from George Washington reveals the truth. While Birch is the spy of the title and symbol of inextinguishable American identity in adversity and even when it is positively misrecognised, the plot revolves around Captain Wharton, who, though not a spy, ill-advisedly visits his family in disguise, and is taken. Only the united powers of the heroic Americans Birch, Dunwoodie, and Washington can eventually save the Briton from his own folly.

In terms of substantive argument, *The Spy* shows an authentically American identity emerging painfully from the crisscrossing of family and national loyalties, which have genealogies stretching back across the Atlantic. More significantly in this process of finding identity through history, the Leatherstocking novels also invent a history for the nation, but this time in another place — on American soil — and, paradoxically, in the shape of another race — the native American Indians.[14] In each of the three novels sketched here, Cooper sings a sentimental song of the necessary downfall of the Red Indian before the onward march of white colonisation. He is sentimentally unsparing in his criticism of the behaviour of the white colonists, in figures such as Judge Temple of Templeton in *The Pioneers*, whose law, strictly speaking, is based on a crime, the initial taking of the land from those who dwelt there untold thousands of years; or Ishmael Bush, whose colonisation in *The Prairie* consists in shameless predatory despoiling of Indians and whites alike. Cooper is also a sentimental ecologist. *The Pioneers* contains gruesome prophetic images of the white man's slaughter of the passenger pigeon. Billy Kirby, the manic forest feller of *The Pioneers*, is attacked for his ignorance of the consequences of his deeds. It is no coincidence that he is deputed to arrest Natty for the killing of the buck belonging to Judge Temple in the opening scene Goethe so admired, so that poor Natty, who kills only to survive, must defend himself before the white man's law. The Mohicans, Chingachgook and Uncas, or the Pawnee Hard-Heart in *The Prairie*, are veritable paradigms of the noble savage; they live in harmony with nature, they rescue Cora and Alice Munro or Inez and Ellen, and the white race must bear forever the guilt of their destruction. On the other hand, as Stafford argues (Stafford, 243, 256–7, 259), there is no sense that Cooper, in his invented history of the American colonists, ever has more than passing regret for the dispossession and decimation of the Red nations. The "good" Indians are more than counterbalanced by the "bad," Magua and Mahtoree. The Indians, though picturesque and admirable in their own way and formidable in the forest arts, are never shown as being able even to resist white invasion, still less assimilate. As Chingachgook passes from being Chingachgook to Mohegan to Indian John and finally willed self-destruction in Templeton, he is impressively pathetic, yet there is no sense that a cultural integration is possible for him. An amalgam of Indian and white culture seems to be the privilege of the white man Natty, who speaks all the languages, mediates fully between the religions and the cultures, and —

apart from his privileged status — represents as fine an example of cultural hybridity as Homi Bhabha could wish for.[15] Yet it is precisely this
hybrid status that makes Natty an outsider. These novels then, are sen-
timentalist monuments to the passing of the native Americans, but their
deeper purpose is to legitimise the colonists' history and identity as
pioneers, with all their faults and virtues. The novels achieve this, but in
terms of the theories of race of the day, by presenting the Indians as
inferior, and also at the price of destroying the myth of America as a
new country.

There are diverse thematic links between Cooper's and Goethe's
works. We know, for example, that Goethe, in his meditation on culture and nature, *Novelle* (1795–1827), exploited both the puma episode from *The Pioneers* and the (Ossian-influenced) Indian mourning
ritual from *The Last of the Mohicans*.[16] I can add that there is a noteworthy parallel between Goethe's well-known criticism of analytic
medicine (with its rejection of dissecting techniques) in the *Wanderjahre* and Cooper's gruesome corpse-chasing dissector Dr Sitgreaves in
The Spy. But where might traces of Cooper's central problem, the fascinating construction of American identity and history, with its sentimentally tragic legitimisation of white colonisation, be found in
Goethe's late work? Can they be found, for example, in the images of
America in the *Wanderjahre*? Goethe is not blind to the moral problems and racial conflict of American colonisation. The American Oheim
supports his decision to return to Europe by arguing (with obvious
rhetorical emphasis) that accommodation with feudal monarchs is preferable to a situation in which "ich mich mit den Irokesen herumschla-
ge, um sie zu vertreiben, oder sie durch Kontrakte betriege, um sie zu
verdrängen aus ihren Sümpfen, wo man von Moskitos zu Tode gepei-
nigt wird" (*HA* 8, 82). It is noteworthy, however, that this, the site of
Lenardo's colony, and that of Lothario's neighbouring colony, are later
presented as already settled (by tenants, 439). Both are situated "mit-
ten in der vollkommensten bürgerlichen Einrichtung" (439) and next
to a desert ("die noch unangebaute Wüste," 439; "unbebautes und
unbewohntes Land," 242), through which the canal will be built and
next to which the weavers and spinners will be established (242). Under these conditions the Cooperian issues of legitimisation, dispossession and genocide do not for the Emigrants League and the Society of
the Tower seem to arise — or at least not immediately. Goethe does
not entirely evade the buried, yet fundamental issues of colonisation. In
his speech to the Emigrants League (which predates the reading of
Cooper), Lenardo notes: "Haben wir doch den Nordosten gesehen
sich gegen Südwesten bewegen, ein Volk das andere vor sich hertrei-

ben, Herrschaft und Grundbesitz durchaus verändert. Von überbevölkerten Gegenden her wird sich ebendasselbe in dem großen Weltlauf noch mehrmals ereignen. Was wir von Fremden zu erwarten haben, wäre schwer zu sagen" (385). He later enjoins the Emigrants "jeden Gottesdienst" and "alle Regierungsformen in Ehren zu halten" (391). Even so: in Lenardo's later provisional design of the colony (404–8), the focus of regulation is entirely internal and colony-centred — unless we count Lothario's offensive-defensive military manoeuvres, or the ban on alcohol consumption (406). There is no place for a Natty Bumppo, and still less an Indian John, in the New Harmony of Lenardo and Lothario. Thus Lenardo's design for the new colony does not — not yet, at least — have the intercultural generosity that Goethe expresses under the heading "$Tv\chi\eta$, das Züfallige" in the commentary on "Urworte. Orphisch": "[. . .] europäische Nationen, in andere Weltteile versetzt, legen ihren Charakter nicht ab, und nach mehreren hundert Jahren wird in Nordamerika der Engländer, der Franzose, der Deutsche gar wohl zu erkennen sein; zugleich aber auch werden sich bei Durchkreuzungen die Wirkungen der Tyche bemerklich machen, wie der Mestize an einer klärern Hautfarbe zu erkennen ist" (*HA* 1, 404). The painful issues of cultural hybridity, legitimisation, dispossession, and genocide so prominent in these, the first American novels of stature, which Goethe so eagerly read in 1826–27 as he recast the *Wanderjahre*, are in fact marginalised in that book: perhaps because of the colonisers' Goethean need to focus on the present; perhaps to underline just how Eurocentric Lenardo's vision still is, and how much European history he carries with him; perhaps to underscore just how literally Utopian their allegedly American utopia really is. Or has this dimension been positively written out?

This isn't quite the end of the story, however. I mentioned earlier how little evidence there seemed to be for Goethe's practical-intercultural engagement with Cooper (if we admit him to the canon of "Weltliteratur") on the lines of his engagement with Hafiz in the *Divan*. But there is something, produced in one of Goethe's whimsical moments. In *Über Kunst und Alterthum* in the spring of 1827, the high point of his engagement with Cooper, Goethe published a piece of advice for promising German poets under the title "Stoff und Gehalt, zur Bearbeitung vorgeschlagen."[17] Many talented writers today, he laments, waste their gift by treating fashionable, yet unworthy subjects. He offers three subjects from books recently published that merit profounder treatment than they received in their current form, and one of them is the Protestant pastor Ludwig Gall's *Auswanderung nach den Vereinigten Staaten* of 1822, a self-pitying 800-page "lament" about a failed emigration project.[18] The precondition of this re-writing exercise, says Goethe, is "das vorzüglichste Talent" (296) coupled with the ability to acquire extensive and deep knowledge of the material:

> Der Bearbeitende müßte den Stolz haben, mit Cooper zu wetteifern, und deßhalb die klarste Einsicht in jene überseeische Gegenstände zu gewinnen suchen. Von der frühesten Colonisation an, von der Zeit des Kampfes an, den die Europäer erst mit den Urbewohnern, dann unter sich selbst führten, von dem Vollbesitz an des großen Reichs, das die Engländer sich gewonnen, bis zum Abfall der nachher vereinigten Staaten, bis zu dem Freiheitskriege, dessen Resultat und Folgen: diese Zustände sämmtlich müßten ihm überhaupt gegenwärtig und im Besonderen klar sein. In welche Epoche jedoch er seine Behandlung setzen wolle, wäre mancher Überlegung werth. (296)

Goethe leaves the choice of epoch (mirroring as it does those selected by Cooper for his novels) up to the writer, but he does suggest plot and mode for the new work. The main figure, the emigrant pastor, is to be a cross between Moses, leading his people into the desert, and Dr. Primrose (the Vicar of Wakefield), with his disproportionate combination of culture and naivety. Thus the plot will move through comic disaster to a tolerable solution back in Europe, and this will necessarily involve the depiction of a vast panoply of (usually dissatisfied) characters from both sides of the Atlantic. All Goethe does is promise to pass judgement according to his best ability on the results, but it seems clear to me that this is a concept for a great unwritten intercultural German-American comic novel. If I may borrow Suzanne Zantop's felicitous neologism, it would have been a kind of prose Occidentalist[19] equivalent to the Orientalist *Divan*, and might have provided a useful counterweight to the history of nineteenth-century German literary misapprehensions of North America from Sealsfield to May, reconstructed by Jeffrey Sammons.[20] We can only wish that Goethe himself had had time to write it.

Notes

[1] On utopias in *Wilhelm Meisters Lehrjahre* and *Wilhelm Meisters Wanderjahre* see especially Wilhelm Voßkamp, "Utopie und Utopiekritik in Goethes Romanen in *Wilhelm Meisters Lehrjahre* und *Wilhelm Meisters Wanderjahre*," in *Utopieforschung. Interdisziplinäre Studien zur neuzeitlichen Utopie.* ed. W. V. 3 vols. (Stuttgart: Metzler, 1982), vol. 3, 228–49.

[2] This included a description of Owen's American colony New Harmony, which sought after New Lanark to realise the vision of Owen's *New View of*

Society; see too: *Reise des Herzogs Bernhard zu Sachsen-Weimar durch Nord-Amerika*, ed. H. Luden, 2 vols. (Weimar, 1828); on Goethe and America see Ernst Beutler, "Von der Ilm zum Susquehanna. Goethe und Amerika in ihren Wechselbeziehungen.," in E. B., *Essays um Goethe*. Fifth edition. (Bremen: Schünemann, 1957), 580–629; Wynfried Kriegleder: "Wilhelm Meisters Amerika. Das Bild der Vereinigten Staaten in den *Wanderjahren*.," *Jahrbuch des Wiener Goethe-Vereins* 95 (1991): 15–32; Waltraud Maierhofer, "Perspektivenwechsel: Zu *Wilhelm Meisters Wanderjahre* und dem amerikanischen Reisetagebuch Bernhards von Sachsen-Weimar-Eisenach," *Zeitschrift für Germanistik*, N.S. 3 (1995): 508–22; for an up-to-date overview: Erhard Bahr, *The Novel as Archive. The Genesis, Reception, and Criticism of Goethe's "Wilhelm Meisters Wanderjahre"* (Columbia, SC: Camden House, 1998).

[3] "Zwar ist der Plan der Auswanderung nach Amerika ein Handlungsfaden im Hintergrund des Buches, und es ist gerade für das Deutschland des frühen 19. Jahrhunderts ein geschichtlich sinnreicher epischer Vorwurf, aber er bleibt letztlich unausgeführt [. . .] Das eigentlich poetische Leben des Buches liegt in einer Reihe von Erzählungen, die dann ihrerseits in den Zusammenhang des Buches überlaufen." Gerhard Schulz, *Exotik der Gefühle* (Munich: Beck, 1998), 133.

[4] Leaving aside mineralogical works, he studied amongst numerous other similar works: D. B. Warden, *Statistical, Political and Historical Account of the United States of North America* (Edinburgh, 1819) (*WA* 3, 7, 46–7); and David Ramsay: *Geschichte der Amerikanischen Revolution aus den Acten des Congresses* (Berlin, 1795) (*WA* 3, 10, 261–62); William H. Keating: *Narrative of an Expedition to the Source of St. Peter's River, Lake Winnipeek [. . .]* 2 vols. (Philadelphia, 1824) (*WA* 2, 10, 165); Henry Bradshaw Fearon: *Scizzen von America, entworfen auf einer Reise durch die Vereinigten Staaten in den Jahren 1817 und 1818* (Jena, 1819) (*WA* 3, 8, 198).

[5] See Kriegleder, "Wilhelm Meisters Amerika," 29, Note 70; also: James Boyd, *Goethe's Knowledge of English Literature* (Oxford, 1932), 266–68; Erich Trunz, commentary on *Wilhelm Meisters Wanderjahre*, *HA* 8, 675 (Nachtrag).

[6] On "Weltliteratur": Fritz Strich, *Goethe und die Weltliteratur* (Bern: Francke, 1946); most recently: Henrik Birus: "Am Schnittpunkt von Komparatistik und Germanistik. Die Idee der Weltliteratur heute," in H.B. ed., *Germanistik und Komparatistik. DFG-Symposion 1993* (Stuttgart, Weimar: Metzler, 1995), 439–57.

[7] *WA* 4, 42, 378 (draft letter to Zelter).

[8] *WA* 2, 13, 314.

[9] Trunz, HA, 1, 653; compare *WA* 2, 9, 183–95; 10, 273.

[10] *Blackwood's Edinburgh Magazine*, no. 24 (March 1819): 641–49; compare: "On the Means of Education, and the State of Learning, in the United States of America," *Blackwood's Edinburgh Magazine*, no. 23 (February 1819): 546–53.

[11] James W. Ceasar, *Reconstructing America. The Symbol of America in Modern Thought* (New Haven, London: Yale UP, 1998).

[12] See Boyd, 266–9.

[13] September-October 1826 was clearly a period of renewed intense study of America. Around this time we find Goethe reading not only the four Cooper novels, but also Warden, *Statistical, Political and Historical Account* (vol. 3, 10, 249, passim), Ramsay: *Geschichte der Amerikanischen Revolution* (*WA* 3, 10, 261–62); he also re-read and pondered the publication plans of Duke Bernhard's American travel journal (*WA* 3, 10, 253–54, 6 October 1826; 259, 19 October 1826, passim).

[14] See Fiona J. Stafford, *The Last of the Race. The Growth of a Myth from Milton to Darwin* (Oxford: OUP, 1994), esp. 232–60.

[15] Homi Bhabha derives his concept of hybridity in part from Goethe's concept of "Weltliteratur." See H. B., *The Location of Culture* (London, New York: Routledge, 1994), 11–12.

[16] See Jane K. Brown, "The Tyranny of the Ideal: The Dialectics of Art in Goethe's *Novelle.*" *Studies in Romanticism* 19 (1980): 217–31, esp. 227–28, note 21, 229–30. Also commentary in Goethe, *Werther. Die Wahlverwandtschaften*, ed., Waltraud Wiethölter and Christoph Brecht (*FA* I/8: 1054–55, 1080–81).

[17] *WA* 1, 41.2, 293–97, dated Weimar, 28 February 1827 (*WA* 1, 42.1, 264).

[18] *Meine Auswanderung nach den Vereinigten-Staaten in Nord-Amerika im Fruehjahr 1819 und meine Rueckkehr nach der Heimath im Winter 1820* (Trier: Gall, 1822).

[19] On the phenomenon of German Occidentalism see Susanne Zantop, *Colonial Fantasies. Conquest, Family and Nation in Precolonial Germany, 1770–1870* (Durham, London: Duke UP, 1997).

[20] Jeffrey Sammons, *Ideology, Mimesis, Fantasy: Charles Sealsfield, Friedrich Gerstäcker, Karl May, and Other German Novelists of America* (Chapel Hill, London: U of North Carolina P, 1998).

Johann Christian Hüttner (1766–1847): a Link Between Weimar and London

Catherine W. Proescholdt

IN THIS ESSAY I will speak first about Johann Christian Hüttner, the man, and his early career as a journalist in London. Second, I will deal with his *Englische Miscellen* and its predecessors, and with the political and economic circumstances that led to its closure. Finally, I will focus on Hüttner's contacts with the court in Weimar, and with Goethe in particular, in order to evaluate the significance of Hüttner's work for Weimar and for Goethe.

Early Career

There are entries for Hüttner in both the German and the English National Biographies. In the *Allgemeine Deutsche Biographie*, vol. 13, 1881, he is described as a "Reisebeschreiber und Tagesschriftsteller;" in the *Dictionary of National Biography* as "miscellaneous writer." Both entries mention his career as a translator for the British Foreign Office.

Hüttner was born in Guben, about 120 km southeast of Berlin in 1766, the son of a cantor. He studied classics at Leipzig University, where he graduated in 1788. He then worked as a private tutor in Leipzig, moving in 1791 to London to take up a position as private tutor in the household of the British diplomat Lord (George) Staunton. His ten-year-old pupil shared Hüttner's interest in languages and literature. In his capacity as tutor Hüttner travelled widely in Britain, and the social position of the Stauntons enabled him to establish contacts with eminent scientists and public figures. He travelled with the Staunton household to Switzerland, France, and Italy. The most important journey, however, occurred when he was invited to accompany Lord Maccartney — together with Lord Staunton and his son — on his diplomatic mission to China in 1792–93. During this journey Hüttner, together with his pupil George Staunton, learnt Mandarin and was given the chance to talk to the emperor in his own language. Hüttner's description of this journey received much critical praise in the contemporary press, in particular for its clarity of style and detailed observation.[1]

In 1796, he left his position as a tutor in order to devote himself entirely to writing. He began to contribute regularly to several German papers and journals, the *Bayreuther*, *Braunschweiger*, and *Hamburger Neue Zeitung*. He became the chief foreign correspondent for the journal *London und Paris*.[2] He wrote for the magazine *Allgemeine Geographische Ephemeriden*, and occasionally for the *Journal des Luxus und der Moden*,[3] which were published in Weimar. In addition to all this, Karl August Böttiger,[4] a school friend of Hüttner's, had introduced him to Wieland, and contributions from Hüttner began to appear in Wieland's *Neuer Teutscher Merkur*, and in the *Allgemeine Zeitung*,[5] which Cotta had founded in 1798.

The "*Englische Miscellen*" and Its Predecessors

It is clear then, that apart from his work as a translator and occasional language teacher, Hüttner's main occupation after 1796 was in journalism. He wrote contributions on English topics for German readers, and accordingly it comes as no surprise that in 1800 he became the editor of the newly founded *Englische Miscellen*.[6] This type of magazine was not entirely new. Eschenburg was the first to publish a similar journal between 1777 and 1781 in Leipzig under the title *Britisches Museum für die Deutschen*. In 1793 Ludwig Schubart started a similar venture, his *Englische Blätter* (of which only two volumes appeared), and Archenholz published the magazine *Annalen der Britischen Geschichte* from 1788 until 1796. In January 1798 Cotta began to publish a big, political daily paper under the title *Neueste Weltkunde*, which in September of the same year was renamed *Allgemeine Zeitung*. It contained articles written by foreign correspondents, amongst them Hüttner. In June 1800 Hüttner suggested to Cotta that he start a paper devoted exclusively to news from England:

> Sie sehen, wie in viel deutschen Flugschriften und Zeitungen unsre hiesigen Magazine, Reviews usw. mit Vorteil geplündert werden; alle stehlen daraus und manche sättigen sich völlig damit. . . . Könnte man nicht von hier aus an Sie posttäglich außerordentlich verschieden und sehr interessante Materialien schicken, welche . . . unter irgend einem beliebigen Titel, z. B. eines Englischen Magazins, Museums, Repertoriums etc. erscheinen könnten?[7]

In October 1800 Cotta published the first number of such a magazine under the title *Englische Miscellen*. For years German magazines had copied from English magazines, but now Cotta, with Hüttner as editor, was able to publish English news much earlier than his competitors. He intended to direct this magazine at a wide range of educated people and to offer them both "entertainment and instruction." This explains his wide range of topics. In his preface to the first volume Hüttner wrote:

> Der Gelehrte darf nämlich erwarten, von allen erschienenen oder unter Arbeit befindlichen Werken in diesen Miscellen die frühesten Nachrichten zu erhalten und mit dem Wesentlichen ihres Inhalts bekannt zu werden. . . . Und welchen Stoff zur Unterhaltung und Belehrung wird überhaupt jeder gebildete Leser in diesen Miscellen finden, da nichts davon ausgeschlossen bleibt, was zur Darstellung der sittlichen, intellektuellen und physischen Kultur dieser interessanten Inselbewohner gehört. Nur die Politik werden wir nicht darinnen aufnehmen, da über diese die Allgemeine Zeitung hinlänglich Auskunft gibt.

As we can deduce from this preface, the journal was indeed a miscellany, the contents of which at times seem randomly put together. Hüttner reported everything that he considered in the least interesting or worth knowing: inventions, announcements and excerpts of newly published books, biographical sketches, summaries of the latest stageplays, cultural news from around the world, moral anecdotes, and stories more suited for the general reader. For the ladies and courtiers he included excerpts from novels along with reports about the latest fashion, luxury items, and newly invented gadgets. Most articles were short and entertaining in order to avoid boredom. Each volume had an engraving as a frontispiece. From volume 25 onwards an index was added, enabling the reader to use the *Miscellen* as an encyclopaedia of sorts. The magazine was intended to provide regular readers with a wealth of information, and to familiarise them with British characteristics, even those which might be considered trivia.

The last volume of the *Englische Miscellen* was published in 1807, although it seems certain — when compared with the frequently short periods of publication of similar contemporary magazines — that they must have been successful. This is supported by reviews of the *Miscellen* in other publications. The main reasons for its ultimate closure were political. In November 1806 Napoleon succeeded, with the help of his coalition partners (Confederation of the Rhine), in enforcing the Continental System, a general embargo on British goods in order to undermine Britain's economic domination. As well as serious negative economic consequences, the ban made all other contacts, private and cultural, much more difficult and, at times, impossible. Establishing contacts via Holland or Denmark was slow and expensive. In 1807, when the *Englische Miscellen* ceased publication, Cotta did not inform his subscribers about these problems; instead, he told them he did not

want to make them pay twice, for he would now publish similar material in his newly founded *Morgenblatt*. Indeed, Hüttner started writing
for the *Morgenblatt* and the *Allgemeine Zeitung*, but this was not a full-
time job as the editing of the *Englische Miscellen* had been. In order to
improve his income, therefore, he looked for work elsewhere, and in
1809 started work as a translator at the British Foreign Office.

Hüttner's Contacts with the Weimar Court, and with Goethe

It could be argued that the Grand Duke of Weimar, Carl August, was a
complete anglophile. Not only did he greatly admire the British industrial advance, but also, because of his love of botany, he kept in regular
contact with Kew Gardens. As soon as political circumstances allowed,
he travelled to London and Birmingham. On his way back he wrote to
Goethe, from Aachen on 6 August 1814, about his time in England.[8]
He praised the abundance of works of art, complained about the
weather, and showed himself to be greatly impressed by technical inno-
vations that he had been shown on his visit to Watt in Birmingham. He
did not, though, mention his meeting with Hüttner, whom he had engaged as an agent there and then. He had agreed to pay Hüttner £50
p.a. in return for weekly reports in German about British historical, political, scientific, and literary events and publications, and for his help in
procuring books. This agreement between Carl August and Hüttner
was diligently kept by the latter from 1814 until 1829, a little beyond
Carl August's death (16 June 1828). Apart from the manuscripts of
Hüttner's weekly reports, a large body of correspondence between him
and various members of the Weimar Court is kept in the Thüringische
Hauptstaatsarchiv. Unfortunately, this material was not available to me.
I will therefore concentrate on Hüttner's letters to Goethe, the manuscripts of which are kept in the Goethe-Schiller-Archiv.

Goethe mentions Hüttner's name for the first time in an entry in his
diary dated 9 March 1797.[9] Goethe had met Hüttner at the house of
Justizrat Hufeland in Jena. Like Goethe, Hüttner had studied at Leipzig University, and it is quite likely that he visited Leipzig after his return from China, so that he and Goethe would have had common
interests. At that time, Hüttner may have also established first contacts
with Cotta.[10] Goethe's and Hüttner's first encounter did not immediately result in further personal contacts between them. However, we
know that Goethe regularly read Hüttner's articles, which appeared in
the *Morgenblatt* and the *Englische Miscellen*. He borrowed the first issues during the winter of 1802 and mentioned them in his letters to

Frau von Stein. Entries in his diary show that from 1814 onwards, Goethe regularly perused Hüttner's weekly reports sent from London, and read the English journals and magazines that Hüttner sent regularly, soon after their publication. The personal correspondence between the two men only started in 1817 and is not extensive. I will deal with each letter separately, giving a resumé of its contents.

The first known letter written by Hüttner to Goethe is dated 19 September 1817. In it, Hüttner answers earlier queries about sending mineralogical samples; and about books ordered, some of which are out of print, and some are yet to be published, including several volumes of the *Philosophical Transactions*, a work on *Chinese Drama*, and volume 12 of the *Adriatic Researches*. He also reports to Goethe that Mawe, the mineralogist, has gone to Cornwall again. On 10 October 1817, Hüttner assures an impatient Goethe that Mawe will be back in a week's time and most likely will bring with him the desired collection of samples. The *Sanskrit-English Dictionary*, which Goethe desperately wants, is still unavailable. In answer to Goethe's earlier request for some drawings of the Elgin collection, Hüttner now reports that Bewick is recommending Landseer's drawings of Proserpina, of Ceres, and of the three Fates; he encloses a notice by Bewick that reads: "I think them very reasonable; and you may depend upon their being as correctly copied as they can be done in London." On 24 November 1817 Goethe writes in this matter to Vogel:

> Man ist auf Herrn Bewicks Zeugniß gar wohl zufrieden, daß der jüngere Landseer die gewünschten Zeichnungen übernehme. Herrn Bewicks Billet liegt wieder bey und Herr Hüttner verbindet mich abermals durch diese für mich höchst interessante Besorgung. (*WA* 4, 28, 304–5)

The first two letters written by Hüttner to Goethe in the following year, 1818, are dated 7 and 14 August 1818. Hüttner begins his letter of 7 August with these words: "Seiner Excellenz dem Geheimen Rath von Göthe dient folgendes zu aller unterthänigsten Nachricht." He goes on to tell him that Landseer[11] feels flattered by Goethe's commission, and he will start work in two weeks' time. He assures Goethe that Mawe[12] himself will soon be writing to Goethe, since he intends to supply an article for the journal of the *Mineralogische Gesellschaft*. At this time, Goethe was exchanging mineralogical samples with Mawe. In his letter of 14 August 1818, Hüttner again writes about the planned drawings of the Elgin marbles, and explains that Haydon, whom he had earlier recommended for this commission, is unable to start work on the project before next spring.[13] He had, however, already completed a drawing of the Fates and was prepared to draw Ceres and Proserpina. Hüttner informs Goethe about possible sizes of those drawings and their price: 25 guineas. Haydon recommends through Hüttner the purchase of Bewick's drawing of Theseus for 15 guineas.[14] In the margin of the letter is a handwritten notice by Carl August: "Es geschehe! C. A." In his answer to this letter, Goethe writes on 21 September 1818 that Hüttner's suggestions have been accepted, that is a life-size drawing of the Fates at 10 guineas, and a life-size drawing of Theseus at 15 guineas; the prices have been dropped surreptitiously.

The last letter of 1818 is very short, dated 8 December, and deals with an enclosed article — not identified in the text of the letter — that had been published in an English magazine, and — so Hüttner writes — had given much pleasure to English friends of Goethe's. He ends the letter with the remark: "Der anonyme Verfasser ist ganz unbekannt." During my research on the reception of Goethe in British periodicals, I identified the article as one written by John Gibson Lockhart published in *Blackwood's Magazine* (4, 1818) in which Goethe was strongly defended in answer to an attack on him published in the *Edinburgh Review* the previous year.[15] Lockhart had visited Germany, and Goethe, in 1817.

The first personal contact between Goethe and Hüttner in 1819 was as late as November, when Goethe wrote to Hüttner telling him that Kanzleirath Vogel,[16] who had been Hüttner's main contact at the Weimar Court from the start, had died. Goethe uses the occasion to thank Hüttner profusely for all he had done for him so far. Several letters of spring 1820 have survived: Goethe wrote on 6 March 1820 in order express his gratitude to Miss Dawe (sister of the painter George Dawe) for a portrait of General Hill,[17] and to let her know how much Goethe had enjoyed her brother's visit to Weimar.[18] He puts an order in for several prints, and encloses two letters to be handed on to Dr. Noehden and Mr. Bohte.[19] At the end of the letter Goethe comments on Retzsch's[20] Faust drawings:

> Die kleinen Kupfer zu Faust, welche derselbe in England bekannt machen will, sind wirklich geistreich und geben einen guten Begriff vom Charakter des Gedichtes. (*WA* 4, 32, 181)

Two letters written by Hüttner in April 1820 have been preserved: in the first, dated 18 April 1820, he informed Goethe that the copperplate engraver's wife had died, and he had been unable to do any work, but he was now about to start again. Another important piece of news, for which Goethe had been waiting, was that the ships of the East India Company were expected to arrive any moment now, and therefore Goethe might soon receive the desired copy of the *Sanskrit Dictionary*. In his second letter, Hüttner acknowledges the receipt of Goethe's letter of 5 March, and confirms the handing over of the enclosed letters. He also informs Goethe that he has opened a subscription for two portraits, one of the Duke of Meiningen and the other of Goethe.

During the summer of 1820 the correspondence between Goethe and Hüttner was frequent because Vogel's successor, Haage, was accompanying the Grand Duke on a journey to the Bohemian spas. Before setting off, Carl August visited Goethe in his garden on 24 July 1820 and, as we know from Goethe's diaries, they discussed the latest news received from Hüttner. The Weimar archives contain a folder with the inscription: "Acta die Korrespondenz mit Herrn Hüttner in London in Abwesenheit Serenissimi, ingleiche nachher 1820." On 4 July 1820, Hüttner wrote to Goethe directly and sent copies of Retzsch's *Outlines* on behalf of Boosey, the London bookseller. He also confirmed the completion of the plates from two portraits, the Duke of Meiningen and Goethe, so that printing had now begun. Miss Dawe — so Hüttner writes — has sent the first copies to her brother, who is in St. Petersburg, in order to ask his opinion about possible changes.[21] Goethe received this packet on 29 July and acknowledged receiving it the next day. Earlier, however, on 9 July, Goethe had sent a list of requests to Hüttner in which he asked for copies of oriental literature, made inquiries about Dawe's portraits (about which Hüttner had written to Goethe already), and required the transfer of letters to Noehden and Henry Crabb Robinson.[22] On 30 July, Goethe thanks Hüttner for the *Faust* illustrations and asks to see more of them, in particular the accompanying text. He would also like to know who the author is. Only on 4 August does Hüttner acknowledge the receipt of Goethe's letter sent from Jena on 9 July, and he promises to carry out the requests. In this letter he makes a reference to the "Prozeß der Königin der die ganze Aufmerksamkeit des Publikums verschlingt." The *Sanskrit* books, so he writes, have been posted, the letters delivered, and Miss Dawe wants to confirm that she has nearly completed the portraits and asks what captions they should bear, since her brother had not decided. Goethe answered on 18 August 1820:

> Was die Unterschrift unter mein Bild betrifft, so sollte glauben, daß der Name, ganz einfach, dem gegenwärtigen Zweck entspräche. Denn da hier eigentlich nur der bekannte Schriftsteller erscheint, so ist von seinen übrigen äußeren Verhältnissen nicht die Rede. Empfehlen Sie mich Miss Dawe; wollte sie mir einen Probedruck schicken, so wird es mir sehr angenehm seyn . . . Ich gedenke aller Freunde in London gar oft in den jetzigen unruhigen Zeiten. Dabei fällt mir ein: haben Sie doch die Gefälligkeit, manchmal eine bedeutende Carricatur zu schik-

ken; die gegenwärtigen Zustände geben, wie ich aus den Zeitungen sehe, hiezu manche Gelegenheit.[23]

Goethe is referring to the events following the death of George III and those at the coronation of George IV. The latter had separated from his wife, Caroline of Brunswick, in 1796. She had returned to England in 1820 to establish her position as queen. There were rumours that she was not to be allowed to be present at the coronation in Westminster Abbey. However, George IV was very unpopular and the people and the press were on Caroline's side. The court proceedings that Hüttner had mentioned to Goethe were an attempt by George IV to have his marriage dissolved and annulled by the Government. Caroline had to appear as a witness. Eventually the attempt to have the marriage annulled was abandoned. Caroline, however, died in the following year, in August 1821.

On 22 August 1820, Hüttner writes in great haste — his handwriting is even more illegible than usual — and wants to know which signature should go under Goethe's portrait. He reports that the bookseller Boosey is glad that Goethe liked the *Outlines to Faust*; a letter is enclosed which throws some light on the anonymous author of the text.

In his letter of 22 September 1820, Goethe once again takes the opportunity to thank Hüttner personally for all his help because, from now on, Finanzrat Haage will take charge of the correspondence. Goethe makes a list of further requests regarding the purchase of magazines and reviews, and the portraits of the Duke of Meiningen and of Goethe by Dawe. He raises the question of a present for Dawe's sister and suggests the originals of Retzsch's etchings to *Faust*.

After receiving the trial print of his portrait, Goethe asks that Miss Dawe should be thanked and comments:

> Man hält es für das beste, was von mir existirt, nur wollen Freunde behaupten, daß ich nicht immer so gutmüthig aussähe." (*WA* 4, 33, 317)

In December 1820 Hüttner asks Goethe to make some changes to his poem "Howards Ehrengedächtnis"[24] because:

> In dem bewussten Gedicht hat keiner von uns hier Spürkraft genung, die Beziehung auf Howard ausfindig zu machen. Wollen Ew. Excellenz geruhen, ein paar Winke darüber zu ertheilen, so dass die Verse auch einem grösseren Publicum verständlich werden, so wird man die Übersetzung derselben (welche in meinen Händen und von einem geschickten Linguisten Bowring verfertiget ist) mit Vergnügen lesen.

In his letter to Goethe of 5 June 1821 Hüttner returns to the subject. He thanks Goethe for his letter of 4 April and shows himself pleased with the "kindly added verses," since it is now obvious that the poem is referring to the meteorologist Luke Howard and not to the late philologist of the same name. Hüttner goes on to inform Goethe that Soane is working on a translation of *Faust* and that the prints of his portrait by Dawe are selling well. On 7 June 1821 Goethe orders six copies of his portrait; and asks whether a translation of his Memorial Poem to Howard exists and if so, whether he might have a copy. He concludes by thanking Hüttner and asks him to stop sending political pamphlets.

The following letter by Hüttner is dated 10 July 1821 and deals with a number of practical items. On 24 July he sends an answer to Goethe's letter of 7 June 1821. It is the letter of 22 February 1822, however, which contains interesting enclosures for Goethe: these include an autobiographical sketch by Luke Howard and a copy of his two-volume work *The Climate of London* (1818–20), the receipt of which Goethe notes in his diary on 6 March 1822: "Gegen Abend kam Sendung von Hüttner aus England." Goethe writes by return of post:

> Nur mit den wenigsten Worten vermelde eiligst, daß mir lange nichts so viel Freude gemacht als die erhaltene Selbstbiographie des Herrn Howards, die ich seit gestern Abends durchlese und durchdenke. . . . Auch hier ergibt sich die Erfahrung aufs neue, daß zarte sittliche Gemüther für Naturerscheinungen die offensten sind. (*WA* 4, 35, 278-9)

He asks Hüttner to thank Howard, to whom he will personally write in May once the new number of *Zur Naturwissenschaft überhaupt* has been published. Hüttner's letter to Goethe of 19 July 1822 contains a short notice about Vertue's out-of-print *Catalogue and Description of King Charles the First's Capital Collection*,[25] which he will try to acquire at an auction.

Hüttner's last letter to Goethe, to be found among the manuscripts in the Goethe-Schiller-Archives in Weimar, is dated 30 August 1822. It is short and the script is faint and difficult to decipher. Hüttner informs Goethe that a book for which he has been searching on behalf of Goethe for a long time has finally been found. Goethe last wrote to Hüttner in August 1825, about the society fhe founded with Noehden to promote "Continental-Literatur" (*WA* 4, 40, 29). In a letter to Knebel of 17 May 1823, enclosing a letter for Noehden, Goethe writes:

> An Herrn Hüttner wollt ich nicht schreiben, denn ob er gleich ein vortrefflicher Commissionair ist, so wird man ihm durch Empfehlung von Fremden, wie ich aus Erfahrung weiß, nur lästig. (*WA* 4, 37, 42-3)

Perhaps Hüttner had reacted negatively to this sort of request in addition to all the other demands made on him, and Goethe is careful not to impose unnecessary additional duties. This might explain why there are no further direct communications between the two men.

The connection with the Weimar court, however, remained intact until a few months after the Grand Duke's death. During the whole period 1814–1829, Goethe only approached Hüttner directly if it concerned personal issues or something of particular urgency, and during the absence of Vogel, or later of Haage, who were in charge of the correspondence.

Hüttner's letters to Goethe are matter-of-fact, precise, and do not show any exaggerated respect. Goethe's personal letters to Hüttner are usually short, and to the point, and always written in a modest and friendly manner. Usually Goethe ends with expressions of great gratitude, such as: "Der ich mich mit den aufrichtigsten Wünschen für Ihr fortdauerndes Wohl mich zu bleibendem Antheil empfehle," or "Nur meinen vielfachen Dank lebhaft wiederholend," or "Erhalten Sie auch im nächsten Jahre mir ein geneigtes Andenken und gönnen mir eine fernere freundliche Fürsorge." Goethe seems well aware how much he owes to Hüttner's help: regular information from all manner of areas and topics in which Britain played a leading role — the arts, history, ethnography, literature, politics, and sciences — in particular, botany for the Grand Duke and mineralogy and meteorology for Goethe. He also supplied books, often soon after their publication, and he served as a link with other people by delivering letters or fulfilling various commissions. Between 1814 and 1829 Hüttner sent thousands of books to Weimar, and as a result the library contains the best collection of English books from this period. It is all the more surprising considering that the Grand Duchy only had about 100,000 inhabitants.[26] This link with Britain involved considerable sums of money in those years, and Vogel, in charge of finances, frequently expressed his concern at the amounts spent.

Carl August and Goethe were not the only ones, however, who profited from Hüttner's service to the Weimar court. Other people were interested in a variety of subjects. Amongst these was Friedrich Alexander Bran,[27] to whom Goethe, on the orders of the Grand Duke, sent Hüttner's list of books for the first time in December 1819, so as to support Bran's work in the newly founded journal *Ethnographisches Archiv*. Bran frequently published translations of, or excerpts from, English books, travelogues, and works on topics of more general interest which Carl August, who did not speak English, liked to read. An enthusiasm for everything British was widespread in Weimar. Carl August was a member of the English Botanical Society and imported expensive and rare plants from Kew Gardens for his own botanical garden. He sent young men to England for their education, introduced the Lancaster educational system in Weimar (he personally corresponded with Hüttner about it), experimented with the new gas street lights in Weimar, and had some of the roads covered with the newly developed macadam. Another indirect result of these regular and frequent contacts with Britain was the formation of the so-called English colony.

Through his association with Hüttner, Goethe had intense, frequent, and regular contact with London, even though he never visited it in person. Hüttner procured for him a rich harvest of books, magazines, reviews, and artefacts that helped to shape Goethe's thinking. As a consequence, Goethe became an admirer of English pragmatism, and this influenced his own methods of research. It is arguable that his vision of a world literature, and his idea of world citizenship, were developed and illuminated by the flow of cultural exchange so continuously nurtured by Johann Christian Hüttner. The result was the establishment of an informative link between Weimar and London during a period of considerable upheaval in Europe.

Notes

[1] *Nachricht von der brittischen Gesandtschaftsreise durch China und einen Teil der Tartarei* (Berlin, 1797).

[2] This journal is very similar to the *Miscellen*; it was published in Weimar from 1798 until 1815; Hüttner wrote all articles for the London section for vols. 1–20.

[3] Both were edited by Friedrich J. Bertuch (1747–1822).

[4] Karl August Böttiger (1760–1835), archaeologist, classical philologist, journalist and editor, inter alia, of the *Merkur* from 1779–1809.

[5] This is supported by a letter from Hüttner to Cotta, dated 31 October 1809 (kept in the Cotta Archives, Stuttgart).

[6] *Englische Miscellen* (Tübingen, 1800–1807). The British Library has copies of vols. 5–25; the comment in the catalogue reads: "This may be regarded as a continuation of the "Annalen der brittischen Geschichte."

[7] Quoted from Pia Müller, *Joh. Chr. Hüttners Englische Miscellen* (Würzburg, 1939). The letter, dated 3 June 1800 is kept in the Cotta Archives, Stuttgart.

[8] *Briefwechsel des Herzogs-Großherzogs Carl August mit Goethe* (Bern, 1971), vol. 2, 111–12.

[9] *WA* 3, 2. It is most likely that Hüttner was looking for a publisher for his report on his journey to China, and also for his translation of Sir William Jones's version of the Hindu Law.

[10] John Hennig's article: "Goethe's Relations with Hüttner," *Modern Language Review* 46 (1951), also believes that this was the case. Hennig only knew Goethe's letters to Hüttner, not those from Hüttner to Goethe.

[11] This most likely refers to Charles Landseer (1799–1879), famous for his genre and historical paintings, or to his brother Edwin Henry (1802–1873) equally well known for his animal paintings.

[12] John Mawe (1764–1829), English mineralogist.

[13] Benjamin Robert Haydon (1786–1846) English painter.

[14] Thomas Bewick (1753–1828), English graphic artist, famous for his wood-engraving techniques and his illustration of birds.

[15] For further detail see: C. W. Proescholdt, *Goethe and his British Critics* (Frankfurt a. M.: Peter Lang, 1992).

[16] Christian Georg Karl Vogel (1760–1819), Kanzleirath in Weimar, in charge of Hüttner's activities.

[17] Viscount Rowland Hill, English officer (1772–1842).

[18] George Dawe (1781–1829), English painter and engraver; on his visit to Weimar in May 1819 he painted a portrait of Goethe.

[19] Georg Heinrich Noehden (1770–1826) philologist and art historian, in 1818 tutor to the Weimar princesses Maria and Augusta, from 1822 librarian at the British Museum in London; J. H. Bohte, German bookseller in London.

[20] Friedrich August Moritz Retzsch's (1779–1857) *Outlines to Faust* had been published in Germany in 1816 with Goethe's approval.

[21] It is sometimes claimed that Miss Dawe produced those prints but she was only the mediator; the printer was Thomas Wright.

[22] Henry Crabb Robinson (1775–1867), English lawyer, studied in Jena from 1800–1805, worked hard on the dissemination of German literature, in particular Goethe's, in Britain.

[23] *WA* 4, 33, 119.

[24] Luke Howard (1772–1864) British chemist and meteorologist; in 1816 Goethe had read one of Howard's articles on cloud formation in *Gilbert's Annalen* — see his letter to Döbereiner of 25 May 1816, *WA* 4, 27, 20 — and in January 1817 he asks Louise Seidler to send him the article.

[25] *A Catalogue and Description of King Charles the First's Capital Collection of Pictures, Limnings, Statues, Bronzes, Medals, and other Curiosities; Now first published from an Original Manuscript in the Ashmolean Musaeum at Oxford.* The whole transcribed and prepared for the Press, and a great part of it printed, by the late ingenious Mr. Vertue (London, 1757).

[26] According to Bruford, the combined duchies of Weimar and Eisensach had 106,398 inhabitants in 1785, and Weimar about 7,000 in 1796. Walter H. Bruford, *Culture and Society in Classical Weimar* (Cambridge: Cambridge UP, 1962), 59, 69.

[27] Friedrich Alexander Bran (1767–1831) ethnographer and historical re-searcher, editor of the *Ethnographisches Archiv*, *Minerva* and *Miscellen für die neueste ausländische Literatur*.

Destination Goethe: Travelling Englishmen in Weimar

Karl S. Guthke

A Cultural Institution: The Travelling Englishman in Goethe's Weimar

AS GOETHE LAY DYING (if I may mention this at a birthday party), his speech failed him; to communicate his last words and possibly his legacy, he raised his right hand and "wrote" words in the air — indecipherable, alas, except for one letter: W. Speculation about the meaning of this W has been a minor cottage industry ever since.

The word so rudely truncated by the Grim Reaper — was it Wolfgang? Or Weimar? Or was Professor Friedenthal clairvoyant when he guessed that it was *Weltliteratur*, in the Goethean sense not of "Great Books" but of "geistiger Handelsverkehr" (*WA* 1, 42, 187)[1]: that worldwide interconnectedness of national cultures, brought about by boundary-crossing intermediaries. Perhaps the W was the ultimate shorthand for all three. Wasn't Wolfgang the catalyst for the inauguration of that age of World-Literature, and wasn't Weimar its prime venue? Of course it was — and not least by virtue of its own version of a specific cultural institution of the time, known on the continent as "the travelling Englishman." In what follows, I'd like to assess this unique phenomenon: the travelling Englishman in Goethe's Weimar — an institution that is hard to miss, though that is exactly what the most recent cultural history of Weimar manages to do.[2]

In principle, the institution was not new in Goethe's day. As early as 1734 an anonymous book had appeared, entitled *Der reisende Engländer*. A guidebook and travelogue rolled into one, it attributed the English penchant for travel to melancholia and the attempt to overcome it, rather than to a propensity (as we might think) for do-it-yourself empire-building or a yen for salacious off-the-beaten-track specials (as

Mephistopheles thought when he looked for Britons in the Classical Walpurgis Night, "sie reisen sonst so viel").[3] Goethe himself slipped into what was by his time a familiar type of common casting, when he, the author-to-be of *Der Groß-Cophta*, visited the Cagliostro family in Palermo in the guise of "Mr. Wilton" from London (*WA* 1, 31, 133, 300) — W again: the plot thickens. "Ein reisender Engländer" was also the identity chosen by Melina in *Wilhelm Meisters Lehrjahre* when the acting troupe decided to enliven their pleasure-boat trip by adopting improvised roles (*WA* 1, 21, 189). The term is used frequently by Goethe himself as a designation for a known quantity, all but collapsing Englishness and travelling into one, as is still the case in a remark made to Eckermann a year before his death.[4] To this day, Goethe's editors and commentators know the type, thinking that the tag "reisender Engländer," attached to this or that person in Goethe's life, says it all.

Yet it doesn't. The itinerary changes. Up to the end of the eighteenth century, the typical English tour of the Continent would include the usual assortment of waterfalls, cathedrals, castles, and mountain peaks (once they were no longer thought to be dotted with dragon's nests). Jeremy Black's book *The British Abroad: The Grand Tour in the Eighteenth Century* (1992) even adds a chapter on "Love, Sex, Gambling and Drinking," for good measure. But neither Weimar nor Goethe make it into the index of this reference work. By the early nineteenth century, after the lifting of the continental blockade, this has changed. Weimar is definitely on the map now, perhaps replacing the odd waterfall. Considering that even the 1734 *Reisende Engländer* had included "conversation[s] with persons of various classes" in its bill of fare displayed on its very title page, we may be sure that what accounted for the change was not the Grand Duchess's needlework, but the hoped-for chance to meet the author of *Werther* and *Faust*, rumoured to be so attractively immoral. After all, Madame de Staël's book, published in London in 1813, with all 1,500 copies sold in three days, presented Goethe as a genius of conversation, and French conversation at that, not even hinting that his French was as Teutonic as a nineteen-year-old whippersnapper named William Makepeace Thackeray proudly reported it was.[5] It was Madame de Staël's image of Goethe, the wise and scintillating causeur, that lured Americans like Bancroft and Cogswell to Weimar, even from Göttingen.[6] (That image was long-lived. It may have even motivated a recent American president to have a letter sent to 170 Beacon Street in Boston, Massachusetts, inviting "Dear Goethe" to the White House for a kaffeeklatsch with the inner circle — so, perhaps it was all right after all to start out with a reminder of Goethe's death.) Be that as it may, a steady stream of visitors poured into Goethe's house at Frauenplan (which one visitor, George Calvert, insensitively translated as "women's place" [G 3/1, 759]). They ranged not exactly from Madame de Staël's enemy Napoleon, but certainly from Madame de Staël's English publisher to the local butcher's wife eager to meet the author of "Die Glocke,"[7] from the disgraced Vice President of the United States, Aaron Burr (who didn't say a word about his conversation with Goethe in his diary, but did record a lot of gossip about other Weimarians, whose names he misspelled without fail), all the way to the sixteen-year-old Weimar high-school student who, having paid half a guilder to see a tiger and a bear in a circus, jumped at the opportunity to see the "great man" with that "fiery eye" for free, if only from under the shrubs in a consenting neighbour's garden.[8] But by far the most plentiful category in this wide range of visitors was the travelling Englishman. Goethe's diaries abound with routinely uninformative entries such as "Obrist Burr aus Nordamerika," "der Engländer Swift," and "Herr Ticknor aus Boston" (though some documented visitors, like George Butler, from Cambridge, didn't even rate this much indifference; conversely, comparatively few visitors jotted down their impressions of Goethe's conversation, thus preventing me from sparing you this talk). Also, Goethe, Eckermann, Riemer, Soret and others frequently mention travelling Englishmen or the like as guests at tea-time or lunch-time, in Goethe's or in Ottilie's, his daughter-in-law's, quarters (e.g. G 3/2: 148); one day in 1823 Kanzler von Müller recorded no less than "countless newly arriving Englishmen, some of them just passing through," at a soirée at the court (G 3/1: 606), and in 1830 the Goethe household, ever orderly, had to compile a "list of travelling Englishmen."[9] Goethe inquired about them, even asked to be introduced to them, if only "by and by."[10] Unlike the other company registered in such diary entries on social events, these (probably short-term) English visitors are usually nameless, much like the visiting fireman of American social mythology; often they appear in the plural, in those days of incipient group travel,[11] and perhaps they are not really human. At any rate, Ottilie suggested as much when she wrote to Goethe's spare Eckermann, Soret, on 16 August 1826: "Weimar ist so still und menschenleer, das [sic] wirklich nur Engländer hier sind." Soret for his part agreed with Ottilie that the English in Weimar would not significantly "zur Menschenkenntnis beitragen," but they did dance well.[12]

Human or not, "von Engländern wimmelt's in Weimar," Duke Carl August remarked to Knebel as early as 1797; by 1830, Goethe summarised, in a letter to Carlyle, "seit vielen Jahren werden wir von den Einwohnern der drey Königreiche [and of the U. S., we may add] besucht, welche gern eine Zeit lang bey uns verweilen und guter Gesellschaft genießen mögen" (*WA* 4, 47, 17) — and gave a boost to the otherwise parochial marriage market, as Thackeray observed.[13] Of fourteen of them, Goethe commissioned the court painter Johann Joseph Schmeller to do portraits.[14] For while he enjoyed complaining about the bother of often plainly curious English visitors, Goethe suggested that they were, after all, his favourite strangers. As one of them, R. P. Gillies, noted, Goethe "seldom refused to see" them (*G* 3/1: 253), as long as they didn't bring their dogs. Indeed, far from being averse to such visitors, Goethe seems to have had a sort of mail-order business to get a steady supply of them, writing to Professor Charles Giesecke in Dublin for yet another shipment of "suchlike worthy persons" (*WA* 4, 40, 28), or receiving word from Soret that two young Englishmen were being dispatched from Geneva "als Ersatz für Barry und Michelson" (Soret, 205; cf. *WA* 4, 41, 6–7). This is surprising, since not all conversations with English visitors were worth writing home about. Think of the hapless Brit who felt that Erlkönig was unduly concerned about the death of his child, considering that he had at least eighteen children ("Er hält in den Armen das achtzehnte Kind" [*G* 3/2, 700]); note, too, that the only recorded conversation with Mellish, that long-time Weimar resident of great culture and taste, consists of just one, if heady, word, Goethe's exclamation: "Champagne."[15]

It is also worth remembering that several important English and American travellers to Germany, or indeed to Weimar, chose *not* to approach the threshold that, famously, said "Salve," and was commonly considered worth a detour: Wordsworth, William Taylor, Longfellow, R. W. Emerson, J. F. Cooper, and Washington Irving, among others. Nor was Goethe necessarily the reason why a traveller from England or America followed the semi-beaten track to Weimar. To be sure, Lord Gower, the translator of *Faust*, claimed that he journeyed to the Continent "with the sole object" of visiting Goethe,[16] and Göttingen Professor Sartorius, with nice self-effacement, stated the same on behalf of his students Ticknor and Everett (pretending to know more than they did).[17] There were other reasons for going to Weimar, however. Around 1800 it was Jean Joseph Mounier's academy in the Belvedere Castle, designed primarily for young Englishmen of good family and gifted with what Trevor Jones's research identified as a sense of "very Britannic horseplay."[18] Pillars of Weimar society like Böttiger and Melos offered them room and board plus punch in the evenings, with daily German lessons by Eckermann thrown in for twelve thaler a month.[19] Even after the closing of Mounier's institute in 1801, though, the stream of British youngsters (as well as more mature visitors) continued to pour into Weimar, the "colony" "perpetuating" itself and resulting in "eine geistreiche interessante Unterhaltung," as Goethe said (*WA* 4, 39, 167). This was not because, as a German critic thought, Weimar was "die wahre Hauptstadt" of Germany; no: "Word had gone around in Oxford and Cambridge that life in Weimar was both pleasant and cheap," as Professor Willoughby observed.[20] Maybe not cheap. True, it was a Scot, James Macdonald, who showed his appreciation by augmenting the rent with a locket containing a snip of his own hair;[21] but Thackeray complained about the high price of his sauerkraut-cum-culture package deal.[22] Not cheap, perhaps, but pleasant certainly, and this was largely due to Ottilie, who loved everything English, especially men. The rounds of teas and lunches and *thés dansant* in her attic apartment in Goethe's house were never-ending, with the indefatigable hostess overshadowing the man who allegedly overshadowed everyone else, even at his own dinner table. On 31 August 1827, for example, "several times during the meal Englishmen were announced who had taken lodging in the Hotel Erbprinz and wished to call on Frau von Goethe" (*G* 3/2, 193). There were several dozens of them in Ottilie's orbit over the years; some well-behaved, some not (like the obstreperous "scion of quality" who, according to George Downes, threatened the police with a rare musical instrument). Some scholars have counted them, with preliminary investigations indicating that Thackeray was "one of the very few Englishmen in Weimar who did not make love to Ottilie."[23]

Ottilie's eros-driven "Treiben," as Goethe called it with discreet irritation (*G* 3/1, 622), did, however, have its literary side in the form of the journal *Chaos*, soon to be followed in 1831 by the equally short-lived *Creation*, when interest in Byron mysteriously gave way to concern with religion.[24] *Chaos* was a multicultural enterprise, founded on an afternoon in 1829 when conversation ran the gamut from "es regnet" via "it rains" [sic] to "il pleut."[25] The only qualification required of contributors was that they had spent a minimum of three days in Weimar.[26] The pages of *Chaos*, therefore, were graced with numerous pieces of prose and poetry in English, penned by the Weimar colony of horseplaying teenagers and twenty-somethings, from Thackeray on down. This could be eminently forgettable, of course, if it weren't for the numerous reminders, throughout *Chaos*, that English had become the language of Weimar. "Deutsch ist aus der Mode" in Weimar, complained Gries, the translator, hoping that it might soon "als fremde Sprache Mode werden" (1, 48). Take, too, the dismay of an as yet unresearched maiden aunt, on hearing that her niece, who up to now had been so good, embroidering Byron's portrait on a footstool and all, now wants to move to Weimar to learn English. Is she aware, cautions her aunt, that the English are conspiring to ruin Weimar, sending "all evildoers of their country" there, where "nobody is safe any more now"? Charles Knox, the son of the Bishop of Derry, seems hell-bent on tearing down all churches in town; Walter Scott's Robin the Red now resides in the culture capital under the name of Campbell, "fortunately, I hear, without his bloodthirsty wife"; and then there's Captain Parry with his polar bears and that sex-starved fellow Robinson from his "desert island with those wild animals." "Oh my daughter, I am warning you against Weimar! Your aunt, who has always wanted what is best for you" (1, 142–43).

Goethe was tolerant about *Chaos* and the social whirl around Ottilie, but when it came to his own accessibility, he was a stickler for protocol, befitting the "Dichterfürst" he was so enjoyably believed to be. There is something mock-heroically Kafkaesque about the attempt of a would-be celebrity tourist, described in a letter to Goethe in 1822: "I was once on my way to Goethe's dwelling — What imports it to recollect that I could never reach it — And the hope is extinguished for ever."[27] Whatever funny thing happened on the way to Frauenplan in this case, "there are forms which one must go through to see the great Patriarch," wrote Granville, a visitor whose attempt was successful. "He likes not being taken by surprise" (*G* 3/2, 246). A letter of introduction — "from great personages or intimate friends," Charles Murray, the publisher, was told by his Weimar landlord (*G* 3/2, 707; cf. 3/1, 759) — was normally a *sine qua non* even for a chat in the vegetable garden. In a pinch, a good word from Müller, Soret, Peucer, Bertuch, Froriep, or even Ottilie might do; but in addition to this local infrastructure of busybodies, there was a worldwide network of former visitors introducing prospective ones in writing. Even so, it could take "much negotiation," as Francis Cunningham found in 1827.[28] Fortunate the traveller who could add a meaningful present to his letter of introduction, such as a message from Scott or Byron,[29] a new book by Byron,[30] or a stellar item for the Geheimrat's autograph collection, like an envelope addressed (to someone other than Goethe) by American President Monroe (no letter inside),[31] or specimens of minerals[32] or "Cannings kleine Büste" (*WA* 3, 11, 135). In the case of R. P. Gillies, even a written allusion to *Faust* did the trick (*G* 3/1, 254). Charles Murray had none of the above handy, so he sent his passport to Goethe with a letter, saying that if Goethe were not willing to see him and his companion, would he please tell them so in writing, rather than through the valet, so that Goethe's note might be preserved in perpetuity as a family heirloom (*G* 5, 260). They were admitted, heirloomless. But the rule remained in effect, for unannounced visitors had to be discouraged so as not to be interrupted by "fremde Gedanken," as it was difficult enough to cope with one's own (*G* 3/1, 735–36). In 1826 Douglas Kinnaird was formally and quite seriously instructed to advise potential English visitors to use "Anmeldungscharten," apparently provided by the Goethe Admissions Office and eerily reminiscent of the ritual for admission to "kaiserliche Fußwaschungen" under Franz Joseph (*WA* 4, 41, 7). It was worth the effort, however. The more informative ones among the preregistered visitors were rewarded with quotable quotes and a souvenir: a bronze medal or two, an autographed poem, or, American-President-style, a portrait engraving (*G* 3/2, 457, 250, 709, 157). H. C. Robinson got three continental kisses, which was the local maximum (*G* 3/2, 441; cf. 438).

World Literature as "Intellectual Trade Relations"

Time to ask: what was in it for Goethe? Looking back on the summer of that Brit-ridden year 1827, he wrote to Sulpiz Boisserée on 12 October of the "unzählige Engländer und Engländerinnen, die bey meiner Schwiegertochter gute Aufnahme fanden, und die ich denn auch mehr oder weniger sah und sprach. Weiß man solche Besuche zu nutzen, so geben sie denn doch zuletzt einen Begriff von der Nation, . . . und so kommt man gar nicht aus der Gewohnheit, über sie nachzudenken" (*WA* 4, 43, 107–8). One thing to think about in this connection was *Weltliteratur*, the pet project first mentioned that year. The English visitors proved useful in the promotion of this "geistiger Handelsverkehr," mediation, or "Communication," which was to create the mutual familiarity, tolerance, and appreciation that Goethe thought was "the great benefit that world literature has to offer."[33]

The English visitors' contribution to such a worldwide literary life took many forms. The act of — entirely unmetaphorical — conversation was the basic ingredient, in this age when social culture was developing even among the normally solitary German intellectuals cooped up in their small and cantankerous worlds.[34] Hence Goethe's eagerness to meet the English travellers — now and then.

> Seht, lieben Kinder, was wäre ich denn, wenn ich nicht immer mit klugen Leuten umgegangen wäre und von ihnen gelernt hätte? Nicht aus Büchern, sondern durch lebendigen Ideenaustausch, durch heitre Geselligkeit müßt ihr lernen![35]

Many of his English and American visitors were well-informed and highly educated, in touch with the literary scene at home; they brought literary gossip, local minerals, and English books, which they sometimes read to Goethe, often following up with correspondence, more books, and journals. Thus, Goethe learned a lot from his visitors about English literature and culture, and life in the colonies, not to mention American and Irish mineralogy.[36] Conversely, the visitors, back home again or earlier, would bubble over, in letters and conversation, with reports of their encounters with the "majestic" man whom Fritz Strich was to call the "Oberhaupt" of the intellectual capital of Europe (68). More likely than not, Goethe would have read and interpreted his writings to the intermediaries, correcting misunderstandings as he went along — *Werther* to Lord Bristol (*G* 3/2, 593–95), *Hermann und Dorothea* to James Macdonald (*WA* 3, 2, 65). He even explicated his "connection" with Byron to Robinson, (*G* 3/2, 451), thus giving a helpful hand in shaping his own image abroad. The visitors, moreover, as well as translating some of Goethe's works into English, would eventually publish books and essays on Goethe and his works. These were then sometimes brought to his attention so that he could inform himself first hand about the progress of *Weltliteratur*, comment on it, and thus promote it (and himself) even more.

This exchange is "ein weites Feld," irresistible to the accident-prone. I'll limit the damage to a very few examples. By all accounts, Goethe was eager for "information" rather than opinion (*G* 3/2: 249, 670; 3/1, 255). Calvert, an American blue blood from the South, de-scribed him at their first meeting as an "expectant naturalist, eagerly awaiting the transatlantic phenomenon" (*G* 3/1, 760). Most welcome, always, was news about Byron and his literary and other activities, with the Irishman Charles Sterling as the most important, though by no means only intermediary (*WA* 1, 42/1, 101–3). Scott ran a close sec-ond, with R. P. Gillies introducing himself as a friend of Scott, Lady Jane Davy, and no doubt Lockhart, Scott's son-in-law, reporting the latest.[37] Captain David Skinner brought news from Carlyle (*WA* 4, 44, 137; 45, 302); H. C. Robinson was in touch with, and could give in-formation about, Lamb and Coleridge, Southey, Wordsworth, Scott, and Carlyle, telling Goethe, for example, that Byron's *The Deformed Transformed* owed much to *Faust*, whereupon Goethe praised it to the high heavens (*G* 3/2, 452). He also read Byron, Coleridge, and Milton to Goethe (*G* 3/2, 455–58). Charles Murray even helped him with Anglo-Saxon literature (*G* 3/2, 708). More tangible was information through books that Goethe received from his English visitors: a volume of Byron from Ticknor (*G* 2, 1168); O'Halloran's *Antiquities* from Anthony O'Hara (*WA* 3, 4, 130, 133); Charles Dupin's *Voyages dans la Grande Bretagne* from Des Voeux (*WA* 3, 11, 46, 332); and a vol-ume on mineralogy and geology, published in Boston, from Cog-swell,[38] who also sent his essay "On the State of Literature in the

United States." On his visit he had presented D. B. Warden's *Statistical . . . Account of the United States of North America*, which Goethe assured him he had "auf's fleißigste studirt."[39] Journals, those all-important agents of *Weltliteratur*, were sent by Randall Edward Plunkett,[40] etc. etc. Such was the inflow of information that Goethe claimed to be quite at home in England, while American visitors time and again commented on Goethe's thorough familiarity with conditions in their own country, down to the layout of the University of Virginia.[41] Goethe did seem to think, though, that life in the state of Indiana was such that women were driven to the spinning wheel (*G* 3/1, 69), which is not generally believed to be true.

Let's examine the flow in the other direction. The best known visitors passed their impressions of Goethe and his work on to those who mattered in the literary life of their country. H. C. Robinson apparently gushed about his conversations with Goethe at the slightest provocation, or even without it, and "with disconcerting regularity,"[42] to Carlyle and Madame de Stael most notably, but also to Wordsworth, Lamb, Hazlitt, and, perhaps most effectively, Sarah Austin. Her *Characteristics of Goethe* (1833) was authoritative for a long time — until G. H. Lewes' biography (1855), in fact, which in turn contained a famous letter from Thackeray about his encounters with Goethe in Weimar. Lockhart reported to Scott (*G* 3/1, 271), as did James Henry Lawrence. Charles Murray reported to Carlyle,[43] M. G. Lewis to Byron, etc. Lewis, famously, also translated parts of *Faust* to Byron when he was turning *Manfred* over in his mind, and Goethe was pleased with what came of it — so much like his own *Faust*. Other visitors subsequently published translations of Goethe's works: Mellish tackled *Hermann und Dorothea*, Des Voeux *Tasso*, benefiting from feedback from Goethe (*G* 3/2, 193–94); George Seymour translated *Dichtung und Wahrheit*; Calvert translated some poetry and the correspondence with Schiller; and Samuel Naylor was encouraged by Goethe to undertake an English rendering of the medieval *Reineke Fuchs* (*G* 5, 144). Calvert, who visited in 1825, was to be the author of the first American biography of Goethe (in 1872, by which time North America was no longer "stumbling over the correct pronunciation of his name"[44]). William Fraser, who visited in 1827, no doubt for longer than the "few minutes" requested, was editor and — with R. P. Gillies, another Goethe visitor — cofounder of the *Foreign Review*, where Carlyle's essay on *Faust II* appeared.[45] Robinson wrote on Goethe in journals, as did Gillies, preparing the way for Carlyle, it has been said.[46] Everett and Bancroft published widely noted articles on Goethe in the *North American Review* in 1817 and 1824. The former is considered to be "the first significant paper on Goethe in an American journal."[47] Of the latter, Goethe received two copies within hours of each other: *Weltliteratur* in high gear (*G* 3/1, 762). This was Bancroft's review of *Dichtung und Wahrheit* — an essay that heaped fulsome praise on Goethe. In a letter to Varnhagen, Goethe, without irony, took this as an indication of transatlantic "Verstand und Einsicht" (*WA* 4, 39, 167), delighted that his works were making an impact not just on the world, but the New World. As Robinson observed, also without irony, Goethe "ardently enjoyed the prospect of his own extended reputation,"[48] or of his very own *Weltliteratur*. Then, too, American professors who had talked to Goethe, George Ticknor and Calvert definitely, but no doubt also Everett, Cogswell, and Bancroft, lectured on or at least mentioned Goethe in their lectures, though, regrettably, "with the even then critical eyes of Boston and Harvard," according to Professor Jacob Beam of Princeton University.[49] *Weltliteratur* academic style. Finally, my academic dean will take pleasure in my mentioning that Joseph Cogswell introduced Goethe to American undergraduates by arranging for the gift, in 1819, of 39 volumes of his publications to Harvard College, bookplated to this day as "The Gift of . . . John W. von Goethe, of Germany." It was meant, Goethe said, as a token of recognition for the "promotion of solid and elegant education"; Cogswell, anticipating the spirit of *Weltliteratur*, thanked Goethe in 1819 on behalf of "the whole literary community of my country."[50]

This was the time when the tide of Goethe's reputation in the English-speaking world was beginning to turn, for the better; the contributions of his English-speaking visitors to this reversal of fortune, while hard to quantify, are also hard to ignore.

The World and the *Dichterfürst*

The panorama of *Weltliteratur*, with Goethe as its central massif and English visitors as the principal mountaineers, is as vast as it is diffuse, eluding any attempt to gain an overview. Still, rushing in where surveyors fear to tread, one might ask some specific questions, which in turn may allow us to perceive some structure and meaning in this cultural institution, the Goethe stop on the Grand Tour. What do the principal actors in this interaction represent to one another? What did Goethe see in the English visitors that beat a track to his house, and what did they see in him? And what is the significance of that encounter of cultural images? The short and incomplete answer is this: for Goethe, cooped up in the narrow world of acute provinciality German style, the English, much more than the French or Poles or any other nationals, provided an opportunity to get in touch, firsthand, with what he called the world, that is, not so much with the sophisticated cosmopolitan ambience of the European metropolises but, more importantly, with "die große weite Welt" out there beyond the confines of Germany or even beyond Europe. This was a world which, by definition and often in practice, was *not* beyond the confines of the experience of the English, those enterprising citizens of a far-flung empire over which the sun was not about to set. Goethe, the "Weimaraner," was ever eager to be a "Weltbewohner," and talking to travellers from the English-speaking world was the next best thing. Thus, they were unabashedly pumped for information about the outlying regions beyond Weimar. England, after all, unlike virtually all other countries, was "nach allen Weltgegenden thätig" (*WA* 1, 41, 56).

But what was in it for the visitors? Surely most of them were in no position to appreciate Goethe's works, for they were what academic correctness calls linguistically challenged; lucky the visitor who could pronounce his name. What they came to see, and sometimes literally just to see, to gawk at, like another waterfall on the itinerary, was not Goethe but Goethe's nimbus. Nimbus is defined in Funk and Wagnall's *Standard College Dictionary* (1957) as "a luminous emanation . . . believed to envelop a deity or holy person; glory" or, secularised, an "atmosphere or aura, as of fame, glamour, etc., about a person." In short, this is what in the seven German-speaking countries is called a *Dichterfürst*, a term applied to Goethe to this day, but an outlandish notion to the English, a bit like something out of Gilbert and Sullivan. In any case, one sees the irony of the constellation: the "world," not just well-travelled Londoners but also Australians and Americans, as well as English residents of places like Jamaica or Egypt or Brazil, made its way into Goethe's house to pay homage to a world-class power of a different kind, believed to rule over the world of inwardness and culture, from this (as Professor Bruford established[51]) three-shop town. The age of global empire was also the age of Goethe, with its belief that the "universe" was "within" — and the two met in Weimar. Thomas Mann got it right (the Gilbert and Sullivan side of it, that is) when in *Lotte in Weimar* he had August von Goethe ask his self-absorbed, self-important father on behalf, not of himself but of the "entire world" out there: "Hat dir das Frühstück geschmeckt?"[52]

Let's have a closer look at this encounter, this unique constellation in the cultural history of the two countries. First, the English and the world; then the *Dichterfürst* and *Krähwinkel*; and finally the *significance* of their encounter in the eyes of the cultural historian.

The English World and the German Province

The world belonged to the English, it seemed to Goethe, and as one of his Irish visitors, William Swifte, put it: "travelling Englishmen," unlike continentals, would "take their country along, wherever they go" (*G* 3/2, 156). Thus, as the world (which Goethe also read about voraciously, in travelogues, ever since he devoured Anson's *Voyage Round the World* as a boy)[53] came to Weimar, it would — in those coveted conversations — reveal its unfamiliar glories to the possessor of a "glory" just as unfamiliar to the visitors. Much as Alexander von Humboldt (whom Ottilie in *Wahlverwandtschaften* is dying to listen to) could tell Goethe more about the real world in an hour than he could read in books in a week, or more in a day than he could have discovered on his own in years,[54] and just as Johann Georg Forster, when Goethe sought his company in Kassel in 1779, was "viel ausgefragt . . ., wies in der Südsee aussieht" (*WA* 4, 4, 61–62), so, too, the English visitors were systematically pressed into service to enlarge Goethe's knowledge of the "große weite Welt" out there, especially the world beyond Europe.

Who but the English could have told the author of the *Novelle* those stories about the "lion-hunting" English that he then proudly repeated to Edmund Spencer (*G* 3/2, 925). Even as a teenager Goethe was able — or so he claimed in *Dichtung und Wahrheit*, written at the high tide of English pilgrimages to Weimar — to use his teacher Harry Lupton to soak up a lot of information about his country and its people (*WA* 1, 27, 26). William Hamilton's company was appreciated in Naples, primarily because he had roamed through "alle Reiche der Schöpfung" (*WA* 1, 31, 68). To return to Weimar, however, Charles Gore, a temporary Weimar resident, was to be ranked high among Weimar's "bedeutende Vortheile" because he had "vieles gesehen, erlebt" on his extensive travels in southern Europe (*WA* 1, 46, 337). Two Australians, "zwey Herren Macarthur aus Sydney," were eagerly admitted on 15 December 1829, without regret: they "erzählten viel Interessantes von ihren dortigen Zuständen, Landesart der benachbarten Wilden" (*WA* 3, 12, 166) — which compares favourably with Dr. Johnson's alleged remark about the exploration of Australia: too much bother for just one new animal. The conversation was hardly less informative when, in August 1827, a "Madame Vogel, Schottländerin, welche die Reise nach Brasilien gemacht hatte," was invited for the evening (*WA* 3, 11, 98), or when, the following year, Dr. Michael Clare, whom Weimar Prince Bernhard had met at the Niagara Falls, turned up in nearby Dornburg and proved "unterrichtet und mittheilend. Das Gespräch bezog sich meist auf Jamaica, wo er mehrere Jahre residirt hatte" (*WA* 3, 11, 262). Similarly, Goethe wrote to his son that Cogswell, "ein freyer Nordamerikaner [and soon to be director of Harvard College Library] hat mich auf der Durchreise besucht, schöne Bücher und Aufsätze mitgebracht, auch viel Erfreuliches von dort her erzählt" (*WA* 4, 31, 154). This is followed by a letter to Cogswell himself, requesting that he report more, from time to time, "aus jener Weltgegend," which is surely not a euphemism for Harvard College Library (246). Granville, who presented his *Essay on Egyptian Mummies* to Goethe in 1828 (*WA* 3, 11, 158), reported on Goethe's "great eagerness after general information," not so much about mummies as about St. Petersburg, where Granville had spent some time a little earlier (*G* 3/2, 249). James Henry Lawrence, the Chevalier Lawrence, returned to Weimar in 1829 after a nine years' absence and "erzählte uns von seinen vielfachen Reisen" (*WA* 3, 12, 145). So did Captain Reding "der viel Welt mit klaren Augen gesehen hat" in 1831 (*WA* 3, 13, 119), as well as Anthony O'Hara, an Irish adventurer who had travelled extensively in Eastern Europe and had been the tsar's last ambassador to the Sovereign Order of the Knights of Malta; he resided in Weimar for a time in 1811, repeatedly treating Goethe to "die Geschichten seiner vielfältigen Irrfahrten" and to the best mocha in town (*WA* 1, 36, 70–71; cf. *WA* 3, 4, 126). On 21 May 1825 the diary records: "Herr Stratford Canning [the diplomat and former ambassador to Constantinople] von Petersburg kommend" (*WA* 3, 10, 58), and again, on 4 July 1831: "Ein gesprächiger Engländer, der . . . die Mitternachtssonne zu Torneå gesehen hatte" (*WA* 3, 13, 104). On 28 October 1818 it was "Der Engländer Hare Naylor, . . . der Europa durchreist und Asien berührt" (*WA* 3, 6, 258). Another English visitor, Ottilie's would-be beau Charles Sterling, arrived in Weimar in 1823 on horseback straight from the Mediterranean, and talked, if not about real experiences, then about his pipe dreams (plausible, being British) of living among exotic "savages."[55] (This Sterling eventually did, in fact.) Englishmen, these examples suggest, were world-travellers almost by definition in Goethe's eyes, and Goethe benefited from their expeditions by hearing "wie es auf irgend einem Puncte der bewohnten Welt aussieht" (*WA* 4, 47, 31). He also loved to have his geographical expertise confirmed: "Mit Sir Clare habe ich die Antillen in möglichster Geschwindigkeit recapitulirt und, indem ich zu einiger Zufriedenheit fand, daß ich dort ziemlich zu Hause bin, machte ich mir durch seine Mittheilung noch einiges Besondere zu eigen" (*WA* 4, 44, 276).

One could go on. But let's not. Let me simply add that the world, as seen through English eyes, was not necessarily accepted as heaven on earth by Goethe (right or wrong, my visitor's country). Goethe did muster up the courage to tell off Lord Bristol, the bishop of Derry, in 1797 on the general subject of the morality of world domination, bringing up colonial exploitation and wars of conquest (*G* 2, 904; *G* 3/2, 593–95; Eckermann, 17 March 1830); on another occasion he held forth on the commercially profitable evils of slavery (Eckermann, 1 September 1829); and *Werther* was not as harmful as British commercial practices, we hear in a curious exercise in comparative literature (*G* 2, 904). The point is, however, that even in the case of Lord Bristol, whom he calls "grob," "starr," and "beschränkt," such "nationale Einseitigkeit" is typically made up for by "große Weltkenntniß" (*WA* 1, 36, 256–57).

In this respect, then, even the lord of the eccentric Hervey family conformed to Goethe's image of the English, which he had begun to form early on, and which he was apparently determined to have confirmed by any and all English visitors. This image was the obverse of his image of the Germans, and both images had more than a nodding acquaintance with well-established national clichés, tiresome even then.[56] In short, the British had "knowledge of the world" and the ever-ready self-confident common sense that comes with it, symbolised by the umbrella; Germans had a speculative and introspective bent of mind, highlighted by reading glasses. The British, as citizens of a worldwide empire, though "ohne eigentliche Reflexion" (Eckermann, 24 February 1825), were "von Jugend auf von einer bedeutenden Welt umgeben," even if they stayed put, simply by absorbing the imperial atmosphere: they grew up with daily news from the far corners of the world; many had family connections with the colonies; and virtually all could see exotic wares, artefacts, and people around them, day in, day out.[57] In a word, they had experience in "Weltgeschäften" (*WA* 1, 28, 212). Germans, by contrast, might have moral and aesthetic *Bildung*, like Wieland, but even Wieland lacked Shaftesbury's "Weltumsicht" (*WA* 1, 36, 323); Germans "sehen nichts von der Welt."[58] "Während die Deutschen sich mit der Auflösung philosophischer Probleme quälen, . . . gewinnen die Engländer die Welt" (Eckermann, 1 September 1829). No wonder his English visitors, who, it will be remembered, brought their country with them, struck Goethe as acting "als gehöre die Welt überall ihnen" (Eckermann, 12 March 1828), even if they were not colonial administrators themselves but Ottilie's heartthrobs hoofing it in her quarters upstairs. No philistines, they were "komplette Menschen"; to be sure, there were some fools among them, but they, too, were complete, "komplette Narren" — a state of grace Germans evidently aspired to in vain. Indeed, to the extent that "the old heathen" believed in a second coming, he is on record as thinking that the new saviour would be British, and theory-resistant (Eckermann, 12 March 1828).

There is a touch of personal ambition in all this. Goethe was fond of fantasising along the lines of "Wäre ich aber als Engländer geboren . . ."[59] or "Was möchte daraus geworden sein, wenn ich . . . vor dreißig Jahren nach Amerika gegangen wäre und von Kant usw. nichts gehört hätte" (G 2, 1028). Vicariously, of course, he had gone to America and had been born English — through his conversations with his English visitors (and "der Amerikaner ist im Grunde Engländer," according to an eminent German Goethe specialist).[60]

Being only vicarious, Goethe's experience of the "world" and its "bedeutendes Leben" (Eckermann, 15 May 1826) rubbed in the corresponding feeling of provinciality in Weimar-Krähwinkel. "It is scarcely possible to mention one without thinking of the other," reported a visitor, George Downes (G 3/2, 65). When Hebbel said he could not have survived in Weimar for more than a week, he was affecting cosmopolitanism Wesselburen-style; there is no denying, however, that even the young among the English visitors possessed a real sense of urbanity as well as a cosmopolitan perspective (which is surprising only if they truly came to Weimar in search of "letzten gesellschaftlichen Schliff," as a much-used source has it).[61] In their eyes, Weimar, "the German Athens" by the "muddy stream," with "scarcely a straight street," where "knitting and needlework know no interruption,"[62] was the "village-like capital" of a miniature state, with a "miniature palace," a "miniature theatre," and miniature everything else, as Charles Lever noted in 1829[63] — miniatures compensated for by huge titles. George Butler (see n. 87) committed Böttiger's three-part title to memory, and all doors opened, while Lockhart got nowhere when he inquired about Goethe as simply "Goethe" or even "Goethe, der große Dichter": "Geheimer Rat" was the key to name recognition (G 3/1, 271). One hears Lord Chesterfield chuckling in his grave. Professional charity requires one to be brief on this point, and in any case who could hope to equal Vanity Fair's vignette of the Duchy of Kalbsbraten-Pumpernickel, with its court teeming with assorted homely but stuck-up "Transparencies" — the court that Goethe himself had described as well-meaning, but not quite rising above mediocrity yet (WA 1, 53, 383). Monk Lewis, heir to loads of Jamaican sugar, arriving in 1792 and eager to "speak very fluently in my throat," reported that "some things" were "not quite so elegant . . . as in England: for instance, the knives and forks are never changed, even at the duke's table; and the ladies hawk and spit about the room in a manner most disgusting."[64] Weimar Professor Melos thought that the young Englishmen who boarded in his house made unheard-of demands: "jeden Tag neues Tischzeug und neue Servietten," and this was only "z.B."[65] Aaron Burr, passing through in 1810, found that nobody at the hotel "Elephant" understood what he considered to be French, and that his room there was triangular. He also managed to mistake the Grand Duchess for a chambermaid.[66] Ticknor in 1816, every bit the Harvard-trained American, was "displeased" by the parochial "servility" shown to his baronial host as well as to the baron's "dinner."[67] Thackeray, of course, Weimar class of 1831, takes the prize. He, too, found the court "absurdly ceremonious," presided over by "as silly a piece of Royalty as a man may meet," with the local "delights" running the narrow range from schnaps and "huge quantities of cabbage" to stoves and rheumatism, not to mention that "great bore," Madame de Goethe, though she did have three volumes of Byron sitting on her coffee table. Here is Thackeray, the anthropologist from the world's greatest metropolis, studying "the manners of the natives": required court dress suggests "something like a cross between a footman and a Methodist parson"; the moment an Englishman arrives, "the round of mothers offer the round of daughters who are . . . by this time rather stale" as so many Englishmen arrive; and lots of tea and card games and French with an oddly un-English pronunciation, but mercifully, or maybe not, at half past nine "all the world at Weimar goes to bed."[68] If one were anything but clever, one could go on like this forever. In matters cultural, as Goethe said to Eckermann, German life was indeed "isoliert, armselig" (3 May 1827).

"Inward Culture": The *Dichterfürst*

Weimar did have something to offer, though, something to offset this mutually enhancing interplay of the English world and the German province. That was Goethe himself. He was the *Dichterfürst* — which is what put him on the tourist itinerary as a "sight worth a detour," authentically German. To this day, the series of recordings of Goethe's conversations with famous visitors that the tourist is invited to listen to in front of Goethe's house is advertised, irresistibly, as "Wallfahrt zum Dichterfürsten." No wonder *Der Spiegel* could report as late as 1999 (24, 69) that the Allensbach Institute found that Goethe comes second on the list of things that make Germans proud to be German, preceded by postwar reconstruction and followed, amusingly, by "Professors." "In other countries they have other things," as Innstetten observed in *Effi Briest* (ch. 19).

There isn't even a satisfactory English translation of the term *Dichterfürst.* "Prince of poets" wouldn't do, as a *Dichterfürst* commands respect not just among poets and their readers, but in the world at large, in the real world. The language of German advertising makes that clear to this day (when one is invited to invest not only in a *Goethe-Lexikon* offering information on "Der Dichterfürst von A bis Z," but also in a culinary handbook with 260 illustrations in colour, entitled *Zu Gast bei Goethe: Der Dichterfürst als Genießer*, "mit 40 Rezepten," by Joachim Nagel, Heyne Verlag 1998). Let me try again: the scope and nature of *Dichterfürst* is more than simply literary. The metaphor (*Fürst*) is reified; as such, it gains real power, real status and authority in matters other than literary, and the person so identified becomes a power to be reckoned with, comparable to the real article. This was noted by Gerhart Hauptmann — who in turn was proclaimed King of the Weimar Republic by none other than Thomas Mann. Hauptmann naturally had Goethe in mind when he defined the *Dichterfürst*, and indeed the *Dichterfürst* was a powerful cultural (not just literary) institution in Goethe's own lifetime, with Goethe as the primary specimen of the species.[69] As George Downes noted, in an unanthologized passage of his *Letters from Continental Countries* (1832), "Goethe still reigns the intellectual sovereign of Germany" (2, 438) — unthinkable, at the time, in a country commanding real global power.

One of the visitors, John Russell, a young Scottish lawyer taken in tow by Viscount Lascelles on his grand tour in 1821, captured this status in a vignette that has escaped anthologization in Goethe's *Gespräche*: a concert in Weimar, given at the court in honour of somebody's birthday (not Goethe's). The music starts, Goethe arrives late, everybody rises, the music stops. "All forgot court and princes to gather round Gothe [sic], and the Grand Duke himself advanced to lead" Goethe to his seat, with all the deference of a professional usher.[70] The *Dichterfürst* is "honoured by sovereigns," Russell adds, rather unnecessarily (*G* 3/1, 243). Remember also the ceremony worthy of a prince required to secure admission to Goethe's "presence." This feudal expression is actually used in English accounts of an "audience" with Goethe.[71] The word "majestic," too, is used in the descriptions of Goethe's personal appearance[72] — much as if they all had consulted the same guidebook to cram for the occasion. Grillparzer put it in a nutshell: Goethe received him "wie ein Audienz gebender Monarch" (*G* 3/2, 79). Imagine Sheridan doing that at the time. On 27 January 1830, Goethe was at last able, with mock modesty, to impress Eckermann with proper documentation of his rank — showing him a letter addressed "Seiner Durchlaucht dem Fürsten von Goethe," pleased with the postal delivery service. ("Fürst der Poeten" would be more correct, Soret thought.)[73] The letter, like the visitors struck by Goethe's sovereign majesty in and out of the concert hall, came from Britain where the title *Dichterfürst* (awarded by Germans, out of "allzu große Liebe," Goethe believed) was not a household word.

Of course, in England there was Shakespeare; but the trouble with Shakespeare (as with Harry) was that he was dead. Besides, as Goethe enlightened Eckermann on 2 January 1824, Shakespeare was not perceived to be such a "miracle" because he was surrounded by at least the semi-great, a bit like Montblanc: to be perceived as "gigantic," Montblanc/Shakespeare would have had to be in the lowlands of the Lüneburger Heide (a fate that Goethe would not have wished on his worst enemy); and in any case, "in today's England, in 1824," there was no Shakespeare, no *Dichterfürst* (cf. *G* 3/2, 449). In Weimar, things were different. Here, in the metaphorical language of the English (who might actually have gone lion-hunting in real life), "lion-worship" was rampant, as *Chaos* reported (1, 54). The English visitors wrote home that they had actually "stared at" the "lion" in his own habitat, the lion wearing a dressing gown and a "clean shirt, a refinement not usual among German philosophers";[74] one could even touch the lion: "I have been vain enough to think proudlier of myself ever since the hand that penned *Faust* . . . friendlily retained my own in its mighty grasp," wrote Samuel Naylor, understandably lapsing into Germanism, as did others affected by the "presence."[75]

There is a touch of secularised religion about this princely presence of Goethe as experienced by the English visitors. Naylor saw a "halo,"[76] others "worship" the "oracle" (*G* 2, 845–46), "idolatry" is the order of the day, not to mention pilgrimage; the house is a "temple" (*Chaos*, 1: 54); even the garden cottage is "sacred" (*G* 3/2, 457), etc. — somewhat unsettling, all this, for the clerical establishment. (The Rev. Herder, Goethe's dependably uncharitable neighbour, wrote to Knebel on 11 September 1784 that Goethe's house was a Bethlehem, adding his pious hope that the visitors would "allmählich die Krippe leer finden u. die Wallfahrt unterlaßen.")

Secularised religion, but no less disturbing are the *purely* secular circumlocutions used by English visitors to convey the German idea of *Dichterfürst*. They are all fulsome, so I'll be brief. "The sublime man — [not only] honored by all the hundred millions in Christendom," but also "wiser than the wisest of the seven sages of Greece" or even "the wise [professors] of Goettingen" (*G* 3/1, 760–61); "the world's greatest luminary";[77] "the first man on earth . . . caressed by all the ladies of Germany" (*G* 3/1: 243), or just plain "immortal" (Russell, *Tour*, 39); "the greatest poet of his age," "the very greatest of mankind" (*G* 1, 818; 3/2, 440), "the first literary character of the age" (*G* 3/2, 247).

Even Thackeray stooped to "the Patriarch of letters" in his letter to
Lewes, appended to Lewes' biography of Goethe. Talking to Goethe
was like talking to Shakespeare, Plato, Raphael, and Socrates all at once,
Robinson confided, as though speaking from experience, after getting
over his initial tongue-tied condition (*G* 1, 945). Meeting such a phenomenon was, as Granville put it, "one of the highest gratifications
which a traveller can enjoy, . . . seeing and conversing with a genius
whose fame, for the last fifty years, had filled all civilized Europe."[78]

"Seeing": There were indeed those in the stream of English visitors
who merely wished to *see* Goethe, like yet another waterfall. One day in
1828, Goethe's diary records, among other guests, "ein stummer
Schottländer" (*WA* 3,11, 205). But another encounter, this time in
1831, takes the prize in this category of the, shall we say, uncharismatic
Brit: Ottilie had asked Goethe

> einen jungen Engländer anzunehmen; es sei ein geistreicher, liebens-
> würdiger, sehr unterhaltender, lebhafter junger Mann. Da mußte ich,
> so ungern ich es tat, mich fügen. So willst du doch, dachte ich, einmal
> von dieser geistreichen, liebenswürdigen, lebhaften Unterhaltung
> profitieren und kein Wort sprechen. Der junge Mann wird mir gemel-
> det; ich trete zu ihm heraus, nötige ihn mit höflicher Pantomime zum
> Niedersetzen; er setzt sich, ich mich ihm gegenüber, er schweigt, ich
> schweige, wir schweigen beide; nach einer guten Viertelstunde, viel-
> leicht auch nicht ganz so lange, steh' ich auf, er steht auf, ich emp-
> fehle mich wiederum pantomimisch, er tut dasselbe, und ich begleite
> ihn bis an die Tür. Nun schlug mir doch das Gewissen vor meiner
> guten Ottilie, und ich denke: ohne irgend ein Wort darfst du ihn wohl
> nicht entlassen. Ich zeige also auf Byrons Büste und sage: Dies ist die
> Büste des Lord Byron. — "Ja," sagte er, "er ist tot!" — so schieden
> wir. (*G* 3/2, 806)

Even Gillies, later an articulate writer on Goethe, preparing the way for
Carlyle,[79] admitted that he had merely "set my heart on seeing Goethe"
and was struck by near-terminal speechlessness when he sensed that he
was expected to say something (*G* 3/1, 257). H. C. Robinson, too,
just "gaze[d] on him in silence" on his first visit, dumbfounded by the
upscale freak show (*G* 1, 820).

What did they see?

To some extent, it depends on the eye of the beholder. Still, basic
features recur, and they do not include that humble, perfectly ordinary
construct of the poet popularised at the time in the preface to the second edition of the *Lyrical Ballads*. Rather, it seems as if the "unacknowledged legislator of mankind" had stepped out of the pages of
Shelley's essay in defence of poetry and had become acknowledged —

not so much as a poet (only a few of the English visitors were particularly interested in literature), but as a worldly power. "Majestic" is the word used time and again to describe Goethe's bearing and his "imposing" or "grand" figure (*G* 3/1, 243; 2, 1181). The Irishman Charles Lever, whose account of his visit in 1828 has not found its way into the collected *Gespräche*, summed it up in his description of Goethe as "a man of grand presence and imposing mien, with much dignity of address."[80] This is particularly true of Goethe's well-practised dramatic entree into the reception room. "The door was opened before me by the servant," Calvert remembered, "and there, in the centre of the room, tall, large, erect, majestic, Goethe stood," approaching "silently," Gillies continues, "at a slow majestic pace . . . much like an apparition from another world," "with a demeanour as if completely absorbed in his advanced thoughts, yet . . . considering whether the strangers . . . were, or were not, worthy of being honoured even with a single word" (*G* 3/1, 760; 254–55). He kept his "hands behind his back," noted Thackeray, adding "just as in Rauch's statuette" (*G* 3/2, 670), referring to Christian Daniel Rauch's much-reproduced little statue of Goethe wearing a house-coat and a laurel wreath.

This is a reference to life imitating art, and it is only one of many suggestions that there was something unreal and stagey about the encounter, some role-playing or self-fashioning. Robinson, quite without irony, thought of Jupiter (*G* 3/2, 441), as did Grillparzer, Heine, Victor Cousin and Mickiewicz, and others. Granville thought that Goethe was "exposed to be stared at as a lion" (*G* 3/2, 246). It might have been more accurate to say that Goethe trotted himself out, to be stared at, as a lion or a leviathan (*G* 3/2, 67). He admitted himself that Robinson was an exception in that "ich ihm, . . . wie man wohl gegen Fremde zu thun pflegt, keinen blauen phraseologischen Dunst vor die Augen bringen durfte" (*WA* 4, 46, 54). More than one of Goethe's English guests were reminded, by his bearing and motion about the room, of specific theatrical scenes they had seen on the London stage — be it John Kemble playing the Duke in *Measure for Measure* (the Duke!), or Mrs. Siddons "with all the pomp and corroborative scenery and decorations" (*G* 1, 819–21; 3/1, 254): the *Dichterfürst* as a public icon, known from "pictures, busts, and prints" (*G* 3/2, 708).

It is true that some visitors found their host quite "affable" (*G* 3/1, 140), "gracious" (*G* 3/1, 116), or "unaffected" (*G* 3/2, 247), putting them at their ease (*G* 3/2, 708); but the point is that that needs saying, given the contrary expectation of solemn majesty or hauteur. And when, more often than not, Goethe did live up to that expectation,[81] the princely role is perceived (by the worldly eye from overseas) to be not quite appropriate for a mere poet — and therefore rather funny.

Even Robinson, easily the most sycophantic of the lot, was aware that Goethe's "deportment to strangers had often been the subject of . . . satire" (*G* 1, 820). Robinson himself comes close to reporting comedy, the Gilbert and Sullivan side of the institution of *Dichterfürst*, when he notes with a straight face that "Goethe said nothing which *un de nous autres* could not have said too [including "gossip" and "scandal"-mongering], and yet everything was of infinite importance, *for Goethe said it*" — clearly, the princely medium becomes the message (*G* 1, 945, 946), though not a significant message.

Robinson's report is, of course, not meant to be funny. Other visitors, however, can't resist the temptation to cut the "giant" (*G* 2, 1181) figure down to size. The nimbus is not inviolable when Goethe's ruffled shirt strikes one visitor, Bancroft, as "not altogether clean" (*G* 3/1, 141), when the famous fiery eye is perceived to be "watery," and hair becomes remarkable for its absence; when some of the oracle's front teeth are reported gone, his mouth "somewhat collapsed," and when Jupiter is observed to be hard of hearing and to walk "with the genuine shuffle of a German 'Gelehrte,'"[82] to say nothing of his French (*G* 3/2, 235, 598, 671). Majesty is a little paltry, "pedantic" (*G* 2, 845), or even farcical. The habitat contributes to this effect, not just the town, with the farmyard smells hanging about its streets, as Professor Bruford determined (59): Goethe's house, the most sumptuous in town, would be undistinguished even in Bury St. Edmunds, one hears from Robinson, the son of a tanner (*G* 1, 948, cf. 820; see also Gillies *G* 3/1, 256); it is too flimsily built for vigorous dancing, Calvert noted, and remained seated (*G* 3/1, 763); the furniture is reported to be Spartan, "most plain," no "luxurious or costly appliances," the floors uncarpeted (*G* 3/1, 254, 256), nothing but "tausendfacher Tand," said Ticknor.[83] Still, this is the house that (Froriep, speaking for the inner circle, confided to Samuel Naylor) stands for Weimar, just as Louis XIV stood for the state.[84]

The intellectual environment is no better. It is curious how the word "jealousy" turns up when English visitors to Goethe's Weimar describe its cultural atmosphere. The writers residing in the "German Athens" make snide remarks about each other, with Herder classically ridiculing Goethe as Jupiter minus the "flashes of lightning"[85] and the "erudite professors of Jena" writing and doing "mortifying things against him," while others augured "that the best of his fame is past."[86] George Butler, whose diary notations on his Weimar visits around 1800 have only recently come to light, makes the most of this jealousy and "envy" among great writers in and around the "Musen-Sitz" behaving as though they were in Krähwinkel. (Remember Herder's remark about the Bethlehem next door.) "Sad Pity, that Genius should debase itself by the alloy of so mean a Passion as Envy!" While Butler stands in awe of the towering cultural achievements, he is appalled by the small-mindedness that comes with them.[87] (This is not to say, though, that Butler for his part was someone with whom one would enjoy being stranded in a small airport.)

Small-mindedness — the *Dichterfürst* himself is no exception. Gillies noted a certain carping spirit in his conversation: he "could by no means be led into hearty praise" of the works even of Scott or Byron, feeling "disgusted, or at least disappointed, with all the literary productions which he had read" (*G* 3/1, 255). John Russell, like Cogswell (*G* 1, 905), went into his audience with Goethe, having heard of "the jealousy with which he guards his literary reputation." True, in the passage excerpted in the canonical *Gespräche*, Russell tries to exonerate Goethe for this failing as well as for the lack of "genius" in his conversation (*G* 3/1, 243–44). But a suppressed passage from his *Tour in Germany* notes the grim comedy of celebrity status: "Like an eastern potentate, or a jealous deity, he looks abroad from his retirement on the intellectual world," expecting to be worshipped as an oracle by princes and others, pronouncing "doom" or sending forth "revelation."[88] No wonder Goethe thought that the German version of Russell's book was unsuitable for excerpting in a sort of festschrift in his honour (*WA* 4, 40, 227; 3, 10, 331).

Russell also gets some comical mileage from the well-known story about the mastiff and the theatre director. He describes Goethe as the supreme ruler over the austere temple to the Muses, the Weimar Court Theatre, where it would have been "treason" to applaud before Goethe had given his "signal of approbation." "Yet," Russell goes on, "a dog . . . could drive him away from the theatre and the world" because Goethe "esteemed it a profanation" that "a mastiff played the part of a tragic hero" in a French melodrama, where the dog had to ring a bell by snapping at the sausage tied to the bell rope (*Tour* 49). So a dog makes Jupiter resign his directorship of the Weimar theatre and prompts him to withdraw to Jena in a huff: Cogswell thought it was this contretemps that motivated "the very favorable reception" Goethe accorded him and Ticknor, both dogless (*G* 2, 1182).

The comedy of the inappropriate celebrity status of the *Dichterfürst* continues with Gillies, in his account of his "audience," as he called it, with Goethe in 1821. He can't even say "the great man" without arousing a suspicion of mockery or irony (*G* 3/1, 253). On the other hand, when he says that the "majestic," slow-moving figure was "much like an apparition from another world," "ghostlike" (254), he really means it. "He had veritably the air and aspect of a revenant. His was not an appearance, but an apparition. Evidently and unmistakably he had belonged to another world which had long since passed away," "perversely antique" with his powdered hair and grossly mismanaged neckcloth (254, 257). Gillies all but suggests that if Goethe should open his mouth, a moth might come fluttering out. In any case, "after the manner of ghosts in general, he waited to be spoken to," "spirit" that he was, "evoked from his other world" (257). Goethe does speak, eventually, moth-free; but Gillies skilfully sharpens the irony of what the oracular celebrity has to say in this long-awaited moment of revelation. What Goethe has to say concerns largely the riding boots of a former Weimar visitor, Sir Brooke Boothby. Sir Brooke had made a fuss about not wanting to appear at court wearing the required silk stockings. "*Ganz richtig,*" intones the oracle, "he complained of our cold winters, disliked silk stockings" — which is why he wore his riding boots. "This important fact disposed of," Gillies continues, the conversation turned to *Werther, sans* boots; but the irony remains unabated. Sir Brooke had received a copy of *Werther* from the author's own hands, but never got around to reading it, we hear. Goethe, according to Gillies, was mystified by such negligence: Sir Brooke, Goethe said, "never would take the trouble of studying our language so as to comprehend our best authors" (258–59). (If there is a plural of modesty, this must be it.)

Finally, before *Dichterfürst* bashing becomes even more tiresome, let's listen to Thackeray. Professor Prawer had a good ear for the ironic undertones in the young visitor's descriptions of the "great lion," who was more likely an "old rogue," with his "little mean money-getting propensities" — again, a report that didn't make it into the sacrosanct *Gespräche.* One does hope, though, that Thackeray's obiter dictum, conveyed by his biographer, Gordon Ray, is authentic: "If Goethe is a god, I'm sure I'd rather go to the other place."[89]

Cultural History: Global vs. Humanist Education

There is a touch of comedy, then, in this encounter of "the world" and the "Dichterfürst" — but the comedy points to an underlying significance, as any spoilsport would hasten to add. Goethe's encounter with his British visitors occurred at a crucial moment in cultural history. Ulrich Im Hof in a different context called that moment "die große Öffnung in die weite Welt," meaning the expansion of geographic knowledge to overseas continents: an event that brought about a revolution of self-perception in the West. "The proper study of mankind is man" now pointedly includes an awareness of those non-European populations that came into full view in the age of Goethe — the period that John Parry identified as the second age of discovery (distinguishing its anthropological interest from the exploitative motivation of the earlier explorers). As Wieland put it in 1785, knowledge of human nature ("Menschenkenntnis") is now becoming "Völkerkunde," ethnology; Georg Forster agreed: the focus on human nature is now the focus on the "other" in distant parts of the world, or, at the very least, it must include it. This is the defining experience of the time, as Felipe Fernández Armesto has recently reminded us in his *Millenium* (1998). (What was the proudest moment in the life of Louis XVI? That day in La Rochelle when he dispatched La Pérouse to the South Seas.) The British, as rulers of a vast empire, were more aware of this shift than the Continentals (though ethnology did take root in Germany as well at the time, with Blumenbach and, alas, Meiners). Here is Edmund Burke, writing to William Robertson on 9 June 1777:

> We possess at this time very great advantages towards the knowledge of human Nature. We need no longer go to History to trace it in all its stages and periods. History from its comparative youth, is but a poor instructour. [. . .] But now the Great Map of Mankind is unrolld at once; and there is no state or Gradation of barbarism, and no mode of refinement which we have not at the same instant under our View. The very different Civility of Europe and of China; barbarism of Persia and Abyssinia [. . .]. The Savage State of North America, and of New Zealand.[90]

What is signalled here is a fundamental change in concepts of what it means to be educated or concepts of the proper study of mankind: global awareness of the "other," including the savage, vs. traditional, humanist ideas of human nature derived from history, particularly from classical antiquity. Proper knowledge of human nature now involves worldwide breadth of awareness rather than depth of introspection or depth of historical knowledge. In a sense, this is the clash of what anthropologists call "wide" culture, on the one hand, and "deep" culture on the other — a pair of terms recently appropriated for cultural history by Hans Ulrich Wehler.[91]

It is this contrast or historical sea-change that played itself out in Goethe's encounters with the British. (When Burke, glorifying the new global perspective, said "we," he meant the British, of course.) Let me repeat: this was not necessarily a contrast between the globetrotters and the stay-at-homes. It was a matter of awareness: of being open to whatever information was available, firsthand or secondhand; and this is where the British had the edge — simply because of what Goethe called the "bedeutende Welt" in which many educated Britons grew up.

In this sense, then, as Goethe saw it, the British, with their global education or experience, brought the world to Weimar. It is to Goethe's credit that — in a land of "ungewöhnlicher Unbekanntschaft mit der Welt" (Lichtenberg)[92] — he opened himself eagerly to this world. Indeed, though not a theorist, he even conceptualised the conflicting ideas of education or culture: Germany (where life was "isoliert" and "armselig" for intellectuals) had humanist "innere Cultur" or at least aspired to it, he said in his notes for a continuation of his autobiography (*WA* 1, 53, 383). This was *Bildung* in the sense of self-cultivation (as Bruford translated the term, qualifying it as a "German idea"). The opposite of such "innere Cultur" Goethe (in these notes) called "weltbürgerlich," and this is what, by and large, the British represented to him, with their "knowledge of the world" and of mankind.

Moreover, this kind of *weltbürgerlich* culture (not urbane, or not always urbane but familiar with New South Wales or Brazil), Goethe felt, was not just an alternative to conventional humanist education but a culture whose time had come. In his *Novelle* there is the memorable sentence, addressed to the Duchess, "Wen Ihr beehrt, Eure Gesellschaft unterhalten zu dürfen, der muß die Welt gesehen haben" — the world, namely other "Welttheile," other continents — a veiled statement about his own ideal choice of company or culture (*WA* 1, 18, 334–35).

Nevertheless, it still seems to be widely agreed that when the chips were down, the culture that Goethe found most congenial in his own personal terms was not global; it was humanist "innere Cultur": that worldless *Bildung* focused on the self, on Europe and its history — "deep" rather than "wide," the preference of the bespectacled Germans he so disliked. Just as Iphigenie cannot really learn anything new from Thoas as long as he remains a "barbarian," so everything exotic that could not be assimilated (like Persian culture) remained alien, indeed repulsive to Goethe: Indian or Egyptian art, for example (as Crabb Robinson reported with proper British dismay [*G* 1, 946, 948]). Remember the conclusion of *Campagne in Frankreich*:

> Wir wenden uns, wie auch die Welt entzücke,
> Der Enge zu, die uns allein beglücke. (*WA* 1, 33, 271)

Why? Because Goethe believed that as a humanist he already had the world within himself, or so he told Eckermann on 26 February 1824 (see also *WA* 1, 35, 6).

This, then, is the Goethe the British visitors saw when they described their encounters as something straight out of comic opera: the public icon of private "deep" culture — humanist self-cultivation (self-absorbed inwardness) perversely trotted out to be lionised. (Inwardness, in Goethe's case, did not exclude activity; but the "tätig" Goethe, active in a limited sphere, to be sure, rather than "nach allen Weltgegenden," the visitors did not catch sight of.) As a result, in their perception, majesty changed surreptitiously into pomposity, German self-cultivation into self-importance: a mere poet who hadn't been anywhere, really, whose journeys, even if ostensibly to Italy, had been (I'm overstating the case from the perspective of the visitors) essentially trips into the interior of the self. To them, who knew the world, this was outlandish, even amusing.

This image of Goethe, minus the comedy of it (the man of self-cultivation and humanistic education rather than of global culture, in my terminology) is compatible with that of generations of scholars; it was recently analysed most competently by Gerhard Schulz in his book on Goethe and *Exotik der Gefühle* — where it is pointed out that there is an element of Goethe's own wisdom in "Es wandelt niemand ungestraft unter Palmen."[93] Jochen Schütze, in his engaging *Goethe-Reisen* (Wien: Passagen, 1998), agrees, as does Jörg Aufenanger (who reports that while Goethe travelled a total of 37,765 km, which is once around the globe, he nevertheless had no curiosity about "die Fremde").[94] Indeed, when in 1792 Goethe is required to set out for France — Paris even — what does he look forward to? To returning and closing the garden gate behind him (letter to Jacobi, 18 August 1792). That's the man who, when he wishes a young woman *bon voyage*, tells her: don't look right or left, look into yourself (*WA* 1, 4, 36).

Such introspective self-cultivation may have been a specifically German aberration at the time, and Goethe may have shared it; but it is more correct to say that Goethe was sitting on the fence, as I have been suggesting all along. He welcomed the English visitors, pumping them for information about the continents that were brought into their view by the second age of discovery; he readily acknowledged how much he had learned about the world from his English contacts. He also devoured Hüttner's reports on books about the far corners of the world; he studied journals such as *Le Temps* and *Le Globe*; and travelogues were serious reading for him — all of which suggests a balance of the two concepts of culture distinguished here.

Conversely, there is a comparable balance on the part of his visitors: they left their island not just to see the Sphinx or fabled maharajas but also to see Goethe — respecting, with some effort, the icon of that peculiar German inwardness that was the very antithesis of what they had been brought up to value. Remember Burke, with the map of the world unrolled before him.

In retrospect, what we appreciate about this encounter, then, is the *balance* of those two concepts of education or culture, which were in competition at the time. But as we look at this epoch-making constellation from our own vantage-point, which is post-colonial and post-Holocaust, we are aware of something else as well: both concepts of what it means to be educated reveal shortcomings when they occur in their "pure state," that is, when they lack that Goethean balance or complementarity. "Inward culture," championed by Weimar Classicism, when left to its own devices, neglected the active, outer-directed, public or civic virtues that make the world bearable: in the face of barbarism (Burke's word) in social or political life, "innere Cultur" may tend to stand by passively — think of Zeitblom vis-à-vis the Nazis in Thomas Mann's *Doktor Faustus*. Zeitblom is the representative of humanist culture, demonstrating the same lack of civic virtue in the face of evil that American press officer Saul K. Padover found when he interviewed educated Germans in 1945 about their attitude during the previous years. (Rediscovered by Enzensberger, Padover's book, *Lügendetektor*, was a big hit in Germany in 1999.)[95] On the other hand, we know by now that "Weltkenntnis," so admired by Goethe, was all too often world domination, and, as such, repressive and exploitative as Goethe knew very well: he confronted Lord Bristol with that charge in no uncertain terms.

These, then, are the shortcomings, incomparably different ones of course, that may be associated with pure states of one or the other of the two concepts of what it means to be educated or cultured; associated, that is to say, with the lack of that balance that Goethe and his visitors, in some modest way, at least aspired to.

Looking back, for the last time, in this year of free-for-all Goethe-bashing,[96] we may see something commendable in Goethe's outlook. He valued his encounters with the British (and Americans), his preferred "others," because they gave him the chance to question his own *Bildung* or values and identity. How? By thinking about theirs. Goethe summed up the net benefit of his encounters with his visitors from the English-speaking world in this way: "Man kommt gar nicht aus der Gewohnheit, über sie nachzudenken" (*WA* 4, 43, 108).

And that, as a German equivalent of *1066 and All That* — that classic antidote to self-importance — might say (if only there were one!) "was a *good* thing."

Notes

[1] Guthke, *Die Entdeckung des Ich* (Tübingen: Francke, 1993), 268. "Weimar": Frederick Norman, "Henry Crabb Robinson and Goethe: Part II," *PEGS*, New Series, 8 (1931): 35.

[2] Norbert Oellers and Robert Steegers, *Treffpunkt Weimar: Literatur und Leben zur Zeit Goethes* (Stuttgart: Reclam, 1999). George Butler is mentioned in passing.

[3] Cf. R. R. Wuthenow, "Reisende Engländer, Deutsche und Franzosen," in *Rom-Paris-London*, ed. Conrad Wiedemann (Stuttgart: Metzler, 1988), 100; *Faust*, l.7118.

[4] 3 March 1831. See L. A. Willoughby, "Goethe Looks at the English," *MLR*, 50 (1955): 480.

[5] *De l'Allemagne*, pt. 2, ch. 7: "un homme d'un esprit prodigieux en conversation." Thackeray: *Goethes Gespräche*, ed. Wolfgang Herwig (Zürich: Artemis, 1965–87), 3/2: 671. References to *Gespräche* (G) are to this edition. Vol. 3 is in two parts, referred to as "3/1" and "3/2."

[6] Ernst Beutler, *Essays um Goethe*, 4th ed. (Wiesbaden: Dieterich, 1948), 1: 481, 509.

[7] Willibald Franke, *Die Wallfahrt nach Weimar* (Leipzig: Dieterich, 1925), 2–3.

[8] Johannes Falk, *Goethe aus näherem persönlichem Umgange* (Berlin: Morawe u. Scheffelt, 1911), 199.

[9] Frédéric Soret, *Zehn Jahre bei Goethe* (Leipzig: Brockhaus, 1929), 436.

[10] Eckermann, 24 November 1824; 10 January 1825.

[11] *WA* 3, 11: 257; *G* 3/2: 431.

[12] Soret, 189, 190, 137.

[13] S. S. Prawer, *Breeches and Metaphysics: Thackeray's German Discourse* (Oxford: Legenda, 1997), 26. Cf. *WA* 4, 43: 173. Carl August's remark: Alexander Gillies, *A Hebridean in Goethe's Weimar* (Oxford: Blackwell, 1969), 24.

[14] R. G. Alford, "Englishmen at Weimar," *PEGS*, 5 (1889): 191–92.

[15] D. F. S. Scott, *Some English Correspondents of Goethe* (London: Methuen, 1949), 15.

[16] Scott, 60.

[17] Frank Ryder, "George Ticknor and Goethe: Boston and Göttingen," *PMLA* 67 (1952): 961.

[18] Trevor D. Jones, "English Contributors to Ottilie von Goethe's *Chaos*," *PEGS*, New Series, 9 (1931–33): 69.

[19] A. Gillies, 8; Soret, 208–209.

[20] L. A. Willoughby, 482; Eduard Engel, *Goethe* (Berlin: Concordia, 1910), 554.

[21] A. Gillies, 11.

[22] See S. S. Prawer, "Thackeray's Goethe: A 'Secret History'," *PEGS*, New Series, 62 (1933), 26.

[23] Jones, 81. On the musical instrument, a serpent, see George Downes, *Letters from Continental Countries* (Dublin: Currie, 1832), 2: 433.

[24] *Chaos* (1829–32, reprint, Bern: Lang, 1968) 2: 34.

[25] Soret, 325–26.

[26] *Chaos*, Postscript by Reinhard Fink, 45.

[27] Scott, 46.

[28] Jacob N. Beam, "A Visit to Goethe," *Princeton University Library Chronicle*, 8 (1947): 116.

[29] *WA* 3, 12: 144–45; *WA* 1, 42, 102.

[30] Theodore Lyman brought *Manfred*; see Leonard L. MacKall, "Mittheilungen aus dem Goethe-Schiller-Archiv," *Goethe-Jahrbuch* 25 (1904): 6.

[31] MacKall, 5.

[32] *G* 3/2: 66 (Downes); *WA* 3, 10: 60 (George Knox); John Hennig, *Goethe and the English-Speaking World* (Bern: Lang, 1988), 125.

[33] Eckermann, 15 July 1827; *WA* 1, 41, *WA* 2, 299, 348; *WA* 1, 42, 187; *WA* 4, 44, 257. See the collection of Goethe's remarks on *Weltliteratur* in Fritz Strich, *Goethe und die Weltliteratur* (Bern: Francke, 1946), 397–400; also Reiner Wild, "Überlegungen zu Goethes Konzept einer Weltliteratur," in *Bausteine zu einem transatlantischen Literaturverständnis*, ed. Hans W. Panthel and Peter Rau (Frankfurt: Lang, 1994), 3–11.

[34] *Strich*, 64, 77; Walther Killy, *Von Berlin bis Wandsbeck* (Munich: Beck, 1996), passim.

[35] *G* 3/1: 48; see also Strich, 55–58 on the value Goethe put on conversation. "Goethe's knowledge of . . . most subjects was personal rather than bookknowledge" (Hennig, 126).

[36] "In time Goethe became known in America as an authority on European and American mineralogy, long before he was acknowledged for his literary genius" (Walter Wadepuhl, *Goethe's Interest in the New World* [1934, reprint, New York: Haskell House, 1973], 43).

[37] Scott, 36; *WA* 3, 9, 266; *G* 3/1, 271.

[38] Leonard L. MacKall, *Goethe-Jahrbuch* 25 (1904): 8.

[39] *WA* 4, 31, 246, 394–95.

[40] John Hennig, *Goethes Europakunde* (Amsterdam: Rodopi, 1987), 68.

[41] England: Eckermann, 10 January 1825; America: *G* 2, 1180–81; 3/1, 140; Univ. of Virginia: *G* 3/2, 598.

[42] F. Norman, *PEGS*, New Series 8 (1931): 105; Hertha Marquardt, *Henry Crabb Robinson und seine deutschen Freunde*, vol. 1 (Göttingen: Vandenhoeck u. Ruprecht, 1964), 17; W. D. Robson-Scott, "Goethe through English Eyes," *Contemporary Review*, No. 1005 (Sept., 1949): 151. Norman's article provides the most plentiful documentation of Robinson's "conversational activities."

[43] Scott, 33; Herbert Maxwell, *Sir Charles Murray* (Edinburgh and London: Blackwood, 1898), 78.

[44] Orie W. Long, *Literary Pioneers* (Cambridge, Mass.: Harvard UP, 1935), 196.

[45] Scott, 69–70, 73–74.

[46] On Gillies, see Scott, 43, and Scott, "English Visitors to Weimar," *GLL*, New Series, 2 (1949): 337.

[47] Long, 68.

[48] *G* 3/2, 438. Cf. 3/2, 448: "interested in the progress of his fame in England."

[49] Beam, 118; see also 116–18; Frank Ryder, "George Ticknor and Goethe: Europe and Harvard," *MLQ* 14 (1953): 421; Harry W. Pfund, "George Henry Calvert, Admirer of Goethe," in *Studies in Honor of John Albrecht Walz* (Lancaster, PA.: Lancaster Press, 1941), 138.

[50] *Goethe-Jahrbuch* 25 (1904): 17, 14.

[51] W. H. Bruford, *Culture and Society in Classical Weimar* (Cambridge UP, 1962), 58.

[52] *Lotte in Weimar,* Frankfurter Ausgabe, 1982, 326.

[53] Arthur R. Schultz, "Goethe and the Literature of Travel," *JEGP* 48 (1949): 445–68; Uwe Hentschel, "Goethe und die Reiseliteratur am Ende des achtzehnten Jahrhunderts," *Jb.d.FDH* 1993: 93–127. An important purveyor of such books was J. Chr. Hüttner; see Walter Wadepuhl, "Hüttner, a New Source for Anglo-German Relations," *GR* (1939): 23–27; Hennig, *Goethe and the English-Speaking World*, 37–51.

[54] *WA* 4, 12: 54; Eckermann, 3 May 1827.

[55] Hennig, *Goethe and the English-Speaking World*, 13–16.

[56] See David Blackbourn, *The Long Nineteenth Century* (London: Fontana, 1997), 270–71; see also Richard Dobel, *Lexikon der Goethe-Zitate*, Zürich: Artemis, 1968; H. B. Nisbet in *Goethe-Handbuch* (Stuttgart: Metzler, 1996–1999), 4/1, 257–58.

[57] *WA* 1, 28, 212; see also *WA* 1, 46, 337, 338; Eckermann, 15 May 1826.

[58] Soret, 630.

[59] Eckermann, 2 January 1824; Soret, 405.

[60] Beutler, 511. See also Goethe's similar remarks on Stefan Schütze (Eckermann, 15 May 1826) and Jean Paul (Xenion "Richter in London").

[61] Hugo Landgraf, *Goethe und seine ausländischen Besucher* (Munich: Deutsche Akademie, 1932), 48. On Hebbel, see Guthke in *Hebbel-Jahrbuch 2001*.

[62] John Russell, *A Tour in Germany [. . .] in the Years 1820, 1821, 1822,* (Boston: Wells and Lilly, 1825), 35, 55. "The German Athens" also in Downes, 2, 438.

[63] W. J. Fitzpatrick, *The Life of Charles Lever* (London: Chapman and Hall, 1879), 1, 77; cf. Downes, *G* 3/2, 65.

[64] *The Life and Correspondence of M. G. Lewis* (London: Colburn, 1839), 1, 71, 80.

[65] Soret, 208.

[66] Erwin G. Gudde, "Aaron Burr in Weimar," *South Atlantic Quarterly* (1941): 384, 388.

[67] Ryder, *MLQ,* 415.

[68] I take these quotations from Prawer's *Breeches and Metaphysics,* 16–18, 26, 31.

[69] Eberhard Lämmert, "Der Dichterfürst," in *Dichtung, Sprache, Gesellschaft: Akten des IV. Internationalen Germanisten-Kongresses 1970 in Princeton,* ed. Victor Lange and Hans-Gert Roloff (Frankfurt: Athenäum, 1971), 439–55, also on the Hauptmann-Mann constellation mentioned in what follows.

[70] Russell, *A Tour,* 48–49.

[71] Willoughby, *Samuel Naylor and "Renard the Fox"* (London, New York: Milford 1914), 11; "audience": *G* 3/1, 254; 3/2, 670.

[72] "Majestic": Beam, 116, 118; *G* 1, 819; 3/1, 254, 271, 760; 3/2, 671.

[73] Soret, 359, cf. 358.

[74] *G* 3/2, 246 (cf. 3/1: 253); 3/2, 538. See also note 89 below on Thackeray's "lion."

[75] Willoughby, *Naylor,* 11; cf. Bancroft: *G* 3/1, 242; Robinson: *G* 3/2, 449.

[76] Willoughby, *Naylor,* 11.

[77] Swifte, *Wilhelm's Wanderings* (London: Remington, 1878), 34–35; cf. *G* 3/2, 155.

[78] A. B. Granville, *St. Petersburgh: A Journal [. . .]* (London: Colburn, 1828), 2, 671.

[79] Scott, "English Visitors to Weimar," 337.

[80] John Hennig, "Irish Descriptions of Goethe," *PEGS,* N.S., 25 (1956): 123.

[81] The charitable interpreted this as defence against rampant adulation (*G* 2, 845); or as embarrassment (see Beam, 121; *G* 2, 1167; 3/1, 141; 3/2, 62, 598).

[82] Beam, 116 (Cunningham); *G* 2, 1167 ("front teeth," "watery"); 3/2, 597 ("somewhat collapsed"); *G* 3/2, 439 ("hard [of] hearing").

[83] See Ryder, *MLQ,* 422.

[84] Willoughby, *Naylor*, 11.

[85] Robinson, *G* 1, 819, cf. *G* 3/2, 452 and Norman, *PEGS*, N.S., 8 (1931): 20.

[86] Russell, *A Tour*, 49–50, 52.

[87] See Guthke, "Mißgunst am 'Musensitz': Ein reisender Engländer bei Goethe und Schiller," *GLL*, N.S., 51 (1998): 15–27; also in Guthke, *Der Blick in die Fremde* (Tübingen: Francke, 2000), 281–91.

[88] *A Tour*, 52, but see the contrary statement on p. 41. For a similar, if more forgiving, statement on the "oracle," see General George Jackson's account (*G* 2, 845–46).

[89] I am following Prawer, "Thackeray's Goethe," 28–30. The final quip is in the second volume of Ray's biography, *Thackeray* (New York: McGraw-Hill, 1958), viii.

[90] *The Correspondence of Edmund Burke*, vol. 5, ed. George H. Guttridge (Cambridge UP, 1961), 351. This is the motto of P. J. Marshall and Glyndwr Williams, *The Great Map of Mankind: British Perceptions of the World in the Age of Enlightenment* (London: Dent, 1982).

[91] Wehler, *Die Herausforderung der Kulturgeschichte* (Munich: Beck 1998), 147–48. For documentation of statements made in this paragraph, see my essay "Goethes Weimar und Hebbels 'Welt,'" in *Hebbel-Jahrbuch 2001* as well as the first section of my book *Der Blick in die Fremde* (see note 87 above).

[92] Lichtenberg, *Schriften und Briefe*, ed. Wolfgang Promies (Munich: Hanser, 1967–1992), 3, 269.

[93] Schulz, *Exotik der Gefühle* (Munich: Beck, 1998), 70.

[94] *Hier war Goethe nicht: Biographische Einzelheiten zu Goethes Abwesenheit* (Berlin: Kowalke, 1999), 7, 14, 40.

[95] Berlin: Eichborn, 1999.

[96] W. Daniel Wilson, *Das Goethe-Tabu* (Munich: DTV, 1999).

Part II

Goethe and the
English-Speaking World:

Reception and Resonance(s)

The "Confessions" of Goethe and Coleridge: Goethe's "Bekenntnisse einer Schönen Seele" and Coleridge's *Confessions of an Inquiring Spirit*

E. S. Shaffer

IN VICTORIAN ENGLAND, Goethe became the object of a cult of hero-worship initiated by Thomas Carlyle, but he was equally attacked by others for loose morals and irreligious thinking. His was a strange, ambiguous, yet looming presence in the work of the major Victorian writers. Coleridge, the major advocate for German literature and thought in the early nineteenth century, after whom J. S. Mill spoke of "the Germano-Coleridgean tendency," is well known for his absorption and reinterpretation of the major thinkers, especially Kant and Schelling, but also the critics A. W. and Friedrich Schlegel, and a host of literary figures. The extent of his immersion in German thought and indebtedness to these writers has been a continuing source of controversy, though one man to whom he has been least often linked is Goethe. As we shall see, however, Coleridge was one of the first in this instance, as in so many others, to grasp and develop a major aspect of Goethe's practice as writer and thinker. It was in the last productive phase of his own career, in the early 1820s, that Coleridge took up *Wilhelm Meister* again, recalled to it by Carlyle's presentation copy of his translation, and found new resources in it, particularly in book 6, the "Confessions" ("Bekenntnisse"), for his own culminating work. As he had led the way for the Romantics, he now became one of the begetters of the Victorian age through his own *Confessions of an Inquiring Spirit* and *Aids to Reflection*.

The most familiar pairing of Goethe and Coleridge is a negative one, involving the unhappy story of how Coleridge failed to translate *Faust*. From a late (1833) record of his *Table Talk*, Coleridge appeared to castigate *Faust* for language that was "vulgar, licentious, and blasphemous," and refused to set pen to paper. This is misleading, however, for two reasons. In 1814, Coleridge approached the publisher John Murray with the proposal that he translate *Faust*, having heard indirectly that Murray was seeking a translator for the work. The correspondence makes clear that Coleridge agreed to do it, and was offered £100 for it, but when he tried to increase the sum and make complicated terms, Murray backed out. Thus, his negative remarks in 1833 were, at least in part, "sour grapes"; he was concealing his own disappointment at the rejection of his offer. His assessment of the poem, in a letter to Murray, shows his customary critical perspicacity, both in recognizing the genius of the work and in assessing the public's likely reaction to its several scenes. He compared Goethe to Shakespeare, describing him as one of "the living Stars, that are now culminant on the German Parnassus."[1]

Despite Byron's championship of Coleridge, which led Murray to publish Coleridge's *Poems*, the publisher remained wary. Disappointed by the reception of the *Poems*, especially *Christabel*, which received slashing attacks from the pen of Hazlitt, he was eventually completely alienated. Coleridge's project of translating *Faust* foundered as a result of the more general difficulties that undermined his enterprises. Even so, he did not abandon his interest in *Faust*; later, in 1820, he approached another publisher with the proposal that he write an introductory essay that would depict Goethe as "man, philosopher, & poet," and *Faust* itself as "a German Poem, with it's high merit on this very account. . . ."[2] This introductory essay would have been for Boosey's edition of *Faust*, accompanied by Retzsch's drawings. As Shelley said in 1822, on reading an inferior and truncated translation published with the popular Retzsch drawings, which was destined to reach a wide circulation, "The translations are miserable. Ask Coleridge if their stupid misintelligence of the deep wisdom and harmony of the author does not spur him to action."[3] Shelley tried his own hand at both the Prologue and the Walpurgisnacht scene, but held that Coleridge, the translator of Schiller's *Wallenstein* into English, which Carlyle himself pronounced "the only sufferable translation from the German with which our literature has yet been enriched," was the only one who could hope to compass *Faust*.[4]

The view that Coleridge rejected Goethe is also misleading for a second reason: the accuracy of the late, reportedly negative remarks by Coleridge about *Faust*, as on a variety of topics, has been called into question by the re-editing of his *Table Talk*, which has revealed the manipulation of the text by the family editor Henry Nelson Coleridge, to give Coleridge's utterances a more conservative cast.[5] This bowdlerizing affected the presentation of Coleridge's religious, political, and literary views.

There is a less familiar and much more agreeable tale to tell of the relationship between Goethe and Coleridge than that of the *Faust manqué*. With his translator's and poet's discerning eye, Coleridge read Carlyle's translation of *Lehrjahre*, which Carlyle presented to him in June 1824. At the time, Coleridge was in the throes of work on several manuscripts whose exact form and relationships he had not yet settled. An essay he had begun earlier under the title "Letters on the Old and New Testament . . ." and laid aside, probably as early as 1820, he took up again in the month he received *Wilhelm Meister's Years of Apprenticeship*, and under its stimulus he wrote his own version of the *Confessions* in the next six months. That he was already familiar with Goethe's *Wilhelm Meister* is certain. He was in Germany in 1798–99, enrolled at the University of Göttingen; he was a reader of *Die Horen*. He discussed Goethe with Tieck in Rome in 1805. Indeed, he had translated "Mignons Lied." In 1813 Henry Crabb Robinson visited Coleridge — this was one of his darkest periods — and found him discussing music and reciting Mignon's song "Kennst du das Land," in his own fine translation, with tears in his eyes: [6]

> Know'st thou the land where the pale citrons grow,
> The golden fruits in darkest foliage glow?
> Soft blows the wind that breathes from that blue sky!
> Still stands the myrtle and the laurel high!
> Know'st thou it well, that land, belovéd friend?
> Thither with thee, O, thither would I wend![7]

This does not establish the extent of Coleridge's familiarity with *Wilhelm Meister*, for the tale of Mignon was the part of the novel that was best known in England, and it was often singled out by the reviewers; but its fame in England came later, with the reception of Carlyle's translation. During the teens he repeatedly sought a copy of Goethe's *Works*, usually a sign with him that he wished to reread in the most recent edition a work he had known earlier. A notebook entry in October 1821 indicates among his many projects a translation of *Wilhelm Meister*.[8]

The novel had already had a major impact on his criticism as well as his poetry. Crabb Robinson in November 1810, at one of their meetings at Lamb's, discussed Goethe's views on *Hamlet* with him as expressed through Wilhelm Meister, in response to which Coleridge offered the ideas delivered the next year in his lecture on *Hamlet*. This became the most resonant and most renowned of his Shakespeare interpretations. Hamlet was not a "beautiful vase" liable to break amidst the unwonted political circumstances in which he was suddenly placed, but one "whose internal images (ideas) are so vivid, that all actual objects are faint &

dead to him . . ." As the original notes taken at the lecture have it, Hamlet was "a person in whose view the (external) world and all its incidents (and objects) were comparatively dim, and of no interest in themselves, and which began to interest only when they were reflected in the mirror of his mind."[9] It appears that whenever Coleridge came upon Goethe's work, it had the effect of bringing forth his own creativity and originality in reponse. This was no less true in his later years.

The understanding of Coleridge's writings in the 1820s has been obfuscated by the fact that the *Confessions of an Inquiring Spirit*, written between 1820 and 1824 and intended to be published with *Aids to Reflection* (1825), was withheld and published only well after Coleridge's death. To withhold it may have been the better part of wisdom on Coleridge's own part.[10] *Aids to Reflection* was well received on its first appearance in 1825, more favourably than any other work in his lifetime, and it held its ground as his major and most influential book throughout the nineteenth century (to be replaced by *Biographia Literaria* only in the twentieth century). Its good reception was such that the parade of visitors to "the Sage of Highgate" began in response to public acclaim. The publication with it of the *Confessions* could well have jeopardized this result. When the latter was published in 1840 it received the kind of obloquy in the press that Coleridge had evidently feared, and which threatened to change the public perception of *Aids to Reflection*. When the *Confessions* received support from Thomas Arnold and from J. C. Hare, the result was an attack entitled "On Tendencies towards the Subversion of Faith," which identified Coleridge as the founder of the English school of biblical interpretation that, if followed, would lead to "complete Infidelity."[11] Only in 1854 in the Bohn edition did the two Coleridge texts briefly appear together. In the *Collected Coleridge*, unfortunately, they have been kept apart, with *Aids to Reflection* published as a separate volume containing no discussion of the *Confessions*, and *Confessions* relegated to volumes too modestly entitled *Shorter Works and Fragments*.[12] One gain from this procedure is that the manuscript of *Confessions* is now published, offering a fascinating display of the progressive alterations in the draft text of one of Coleridge's most controversial writings.

This continued suppression of the link between *Confessions* and *Aids to Reflection* resulted, among other things, in curtailing the awareness and influence of the reference to Goethe. No critical work that I have found on the reception of Goethe in England in the 1820s or later has referred to Coleridge's vital text. In fact, however, Coleridge's text circulated in manuscript among major Victorian thinkers on Biblical criticism — not only Hare, but also F. D. Maurice, Connop Thirlwall (the translator of Schleiermacher, whose excellent introduction to Schleiermacher's *On Luke* Coleridge had read), John Sterling (who had been allowed to transcribe it), and Thomas Arnold, all of whom made public acknowledgement of their debts to it.

The *Confessions* offers one of the most attractive and persuasive statements of the position (which most moderns would now accept) that the Bible is not infallible, not an example of "plenary inspiration" by the Holy Spirit, but a human text, to be treated accordingly. It was to be treated as a historical text, to which the canons of evidence applied; and, even more momentously, it was to be read as a work of literature, to be compared with other works of literature. That the Bible was not inspired in every word and detail was scarcely a new argument by 1822; Spinoza in the *Tractatus* had queried "infallibility" in the late seventeenth century, and a series of eighteenth-century writers and biblical critics had taken up his ideas (sometimes without naming their dangerous source), including the English Deists, the French philosophes, the German Enlightenment thinkers, notably Lessing and Reimarus, and scholarly biblical critics like Eichhorn. Coleridge had known their arguments since the 1790s.[13] The acknowledgement that the Bible was a series of historical texts led to an intense critical scrutiny of the texts, which convinced Lessing of the necessity of relinquishing any argument for Christianity based on "historical evidences." That it was a work of literature was an argument first employed in sceptical and sardonic comparisons of the Bible to other works of notoriously unreliable Oriental fantasy, and to convert it into an affirmative view required a long and arduous process of mythologizing and literary valuation.

Confessions is presented as a series of "Letters to a learned and religious Friend." As is often the case with Coleridge, this is probably an imaginary "Friend" and he is replying to an imaginary letter; "Friend," nevertheless, had a considerable significance for him as a hermeneutic conception, conveying the circumstances of intimacy and full understanding which alone enabled true communication to take place. Moreover, the original context of the essay was his formal and informal teaching of a group of young men in 1820 who were seeking a vocation. The theme of the problematic vocation that is so searchingly probed by Goethe in the *Bildungsroman* was already one of his concerns. He opens with a reference to Goethe's *Bekenntnisse einer schönen Seele* in Carlyle's imperfect translation of the title as "Confessions of a Fair Saint," developing it immediately into an account of his own experience, that of one who is "neither fair nor saint." In another letter, he tried out the translation "Experiences of a fine and sensitive Spirit," which "your friend Carlyle, somewhat strangely renders by, the Confessions of a Fair Saint."[14] In the *Confessions* he uses the best rendering he can devise, "The Confessions of a Beautiful Soul," but maintains "fair" and "saint" as pointing a stark contrast to his own state:

Dear and honored Friend

I employed the compelled and most unwelcome Leisure of severe Indisposition in reading "the Confessions of a Fair Saint" in Mr Carlile's [sic] recent translation of the Wilhelm Meister, ~~I should myself have ventured the literal rendering~~ which might, I think, have been better rendered literally, viz. "The Confessions of a beautiful Soul)." ~~It will doubtless appear to English Readers as a most interesting Chapter~~ This, however, acting in conjunction with the concluding sentences of your letter, threw my thoughts inward on my own religious experience, and gave the immediate occasion to the following Confessions of one who is neither fair nor saintly but who groaning under the deep sense of infirmity and manifold imperfection feels the want, the necessity, of religious support; [of one] who cannot afford to lose any the smallest buttress; ~~or staff, and would be willing to believe the Reed, which others profess to have found a staff, is a Reed only for him & owes its apparent flexure to its being seen thro' the refractive medium of "the unstable waters"[Gen 49.4(var)] of his own mind~~; but who not only loves Truth even for itself, and when it reveals itself aloof from all interest, ~~moral no less than personal, the functions of a Number or the properties of a transcendent Curve~~, but who loves it with an indescribable awe, that far too often withdraws the genial Sap of his activity from the columnal Trunk, the shelt'ring Leaves, the bright and fragrant Flower; and the foodful or med'cinable Fruitage, to the deep root, ramifying in darkness and labyrinthine Way — winning —

> ~~Dead to the World~~
> In darkness there to house unknown
> Far underground
> ~~by sound~~
> That listens for the up ~~turn'd~~ torn
> Mandrake's parting Groan!

Coleridge goes on:

I should,[perhaps,] be a happier, ~~probably a better, certainly~~ at all events a more useful man, if ~~it²~~ my mind were otherwise constituted. But so it is: and even with regard to Christianity itself, like certain Plants, I creep towards the Light, even tho' it draws me away from the more nourishing Warmth. ~~and~~ Yea, I should do so, even tho' the Light ~~should~~ had ma ~~ke~~ de its way thro' a rent or cranny in the wall of the Temple. Glad and grateful am I that not in the Temple itself but only in one or two of the side chapels, ~~which~~ not essential to the Edifice, and probably not coëval, have I found the light absent, and the Cranny in the wall has but admitted the free light of the Temple itself.[15]

Thus Coleridge, upon the spur of, and under cover of criticism of, Carlyle's mistranslation, appropriated Goethe's title and set out in a white heat of composition on his own "Confessions." He had found a way — in the fictional form of the confessional letters — to present his own inward experience, and his own long-nurtured thoughts, and to give an accounting of "the state of my faith." (1118)

In this guise, moreover, he could present the thoughts that he knew were considered dangerous. The *Confessions* would in turn introduce the *Aids to Reflection*, which would be finely tuned to the "state of his faith" after the work of biblical criticism — the state of the modern mind. Thus Coleridge cast himself into a fictional form of Goethe's own character in order to express his own "vulgar, licentious, and blasphemous" thoughts. These very thoughts, turned through the prism of aesthetic reflection, might lead to the only possible form of modern spirituality.

It has often been remarked that Goethe, in drawing on his personal acquaintance with Susanna Katharina von Klettenberg, the strongly religious pietist friend of his mother, for the *Bekenntnisse*, was locating the centre of spiritual experience in a place of its own apart from the active world. This may be seen in gender terms; more importantly, however, it is expressing the crisis of religious belief in his time. For him, as for Coleridge, the life of the spirit in a religious sense belonged to the past, to another world. Coleridge in *Aids to Reflection* constructed the work around a series of aphorisms drawn from the seventeenth-century Archbishop Robert Leighton: the rich spiritual experience of a past age.

No one writing in Goethe's and Coleridge's time (they died within two years of each other) could match Leighton's direct access to the realities of a spiritual life. Coleridge's own text is a commentary growing out of carefully selected aphorisms from Leighton. In the original edition Leighton's passages were clearly marked as his; in the American edition of 1828, which was powerfully influential on the New England transcendental movement, Leighton's passages were not clearly marked, and the whole text was received as an expression of Coleridge's mind. But while this added to Coleridge's reputation, it obscured the fact that he was trying to make a past spiritual experience available to an age whose definitions of rationality were putting such immediacy beyond possibility.

Equally, Goethe places the "schöne Seele" in the past, a generation ago, in a secluded place, in his mother's world. The world of one's parents' generation is a world even more dramatically and as it were intimately dead than the historical past of the seventeenth century that Coleridge conjures up. Yet the "puritan diary," the record of inward experience, was itself a phenomenon of the seventeenth century, as has been abundantly shown; and it had already abundantly flowed into the English and the German novel through Richardson. For Coleridge, who was deeply read in the poetry and divinity of that century (including the "Metaphysical poets," Donne and Herbert, on whom he wrote with insight and approbation), it represented the last age before what T. S. Eliot, borrowing as so often from Coleridge, called the "dissociation of sensibility." Coleridge was diagnosing a condition of his own age; both the fragmented form, and the attempt to build a new whole out of the shards, were an expression of that condition.

Moreover, both Goethe and Coleridge are writers presenting an aesthetic form of a lost experience. Only in an aesthetic form was this experience still retrievable. The pressure behind this is powerfully displayed in the originality of the forms employed. Paradoxically, the embedding of past forms — the puritan diary of the *Stiftsdame*, the aphorism of Leighton — highlights the innovation in form of the *Bildungsroman* in the one case and the critical reflections in the other. Coleridge's handling of the aphorism, the embedding of past aphoristic insights within his own, bears comparison to the contemporary German development of the aphorism from Lichtenberg through Novalis (and pointing on to Nietzsche).

Coleridge, while assuming the role of the "schöne Seele," nevertheless transforms her into an "Inquiring Spirit." This is not simply a recognition of the author's gender (for a "schöne Seele" could in pietist terms be masculine). Whereas in *Aids to Reflection* Coleridge presented seventeenth-century religious experience through Leighton, the intended prefatory essay, the *Confessions of an Inquiring Spirit,* gives us the protagonist of the modern critical search, the spirit of Kritik itself. The very question, what will the "Confessions" of an "Inquiring Spirit," that is the spirit of their own age, be like, the problematic of the modern form, perhaps returns for both Goethe and Coleridge to Rousseau. For Coleridge, however, both the critical intellect of Lessing and the philosophical critiques of Kant were more significant than Rousseau. These parallels and resonances between the imaginative and the critical-philosophical work of the period are familiar, especially in German. Schelling's *System des transcendentalen Idealismus (System of Transcendental Idealism)* has been likened to Goethe's *Lehrjahre*[16] — and we know how closely Goethe's poetic plans were linked to Schelling (and, as Jeremy Adler has shown, for a longer period than usually thought).[17] Coleridge (immersed in Schelling 1808–12) found in the System the aesthetic solution to the problem of the conjunction of the self with the external world. More locally, Coleridge is also presenting his characteristically richer and more profound commentary on the topic of his former acolyte Hazlitt's more popular *Spirit of the Age*, published in the same year.

The role of the *Confessions of the Inquiring Spirit* bears closer comparison with the role of the *Bekenntnisse einer Schönen Seele* in the economy of the larger works of which they are a part. The "Confessions" in both cases do not stand on their own, but serve a function in a larger whole. Some readers have puzzled over this; even Schiller thought the "Confessions" might be perceived as an "interruption" in *Wilhelm Meister*. George Henry Lewes, Goethe's first biographer, flatly dismissed the Confessions as having nothing to do with the rest of the work and held that book 6 simply interrupts the story in "a most inartistic manner." Many readers shared this view.[18] Coleridge, on the contrary, saw its true function; as Wilhelm himself said, it was an "interruption that marks the beginning of a new epoch." The new epoch is the phase of Wilhelm's experience presented in the final two books of the novel. Similarly, Coleridge introduced a new epoch in thought unfolded in *Aids to Reflection*. In both cases the operative factor is the subjectivity of the faith of the "schöne Seele." As Nicholas Boyle has pointed out in his subtle analysis of the way the "Confessions of a Beautiful Soul" play into the last two books (7 and 8) of *Wilhelm Meister*, and help to transform the significance of his earlier encounters, almost the first words Wilhelm utters in book 7 are directly linked to the canoness's account of the last stage in her religious pilgrimage, and they show he is right to say the memory "had an effect on my whole life." He draws the imperative from her memoirs: "Retire into yourself." The new phase, then, is one of subjectivity; it is not free-floating subjectivity, but one in which we have learnt "the deepest lesson the Confessions have to teach: that we alone are responsible for interpreting the story of our life; and yet always implicit in any interpretation will be the faith that somewhere, ultimately, it is solidly grounded outside our sensibilities."[19] It is this double notion that Coleridge draws upon for his "Confessions": that there can be no rational proof of religious faith, yet that an imaginative construction of such a view could animate and underpin a life. Coleridge's own experience of need and despair lays the foundation for the imaginative construction of the "Inquiring Spirit," and Goethe's fictional character gives him the courage to draw on it openly.

Throughout his analysis, Boyle draws on Kant to explain Wilhelm's exploration of the role he plays in the interpretation of his own experience. "Like the Beautiful Soul at the last — and of course, like Kant — Wilhelm finds in moral and aesthetic experience the confirmation that this faith has 'a real object'" (367–391). But what can be meant by "real object"? Coleridge was one of the main exponents of Kant's view that aesthetic and moral objects had to be created as works of art or of will in the world; they did not otherwise exist. Thus to have full effect, they must emerge again from self-interpretation and subjectivity into works of art in the world, into objects visible and experienciable by others. It is in this sense that Coleridge employs the Bible as the work of art beyond all others that enables the objectification of this experience. Only Shakespeare is admitted into this class. Coleridge's *Confessions*, like his private notebooks and some of his personal letters, tells of his own sense of weakness, his inability to construct through his will the moral realm of autonomous reason. Because of this weakness — which he keenly felt as his own, but which is also a general human frailty — he took Kant's cautious admission of "aids to reflection" and developed it in *Aids to Reflection* beyond the strict limits of reason to strengthen the soul that was neither beautiful nor saint. To the extent that Kant admitted the need for "aids," Coleridge's *Confessions* and *Aids to Reflection* is both a critique of Kant's moral philosophy and a subtle extension of possibilities within it. Finally, the fiction of the "beautiful soul" plays its role in the philosophical sphere of the "inquiring spirit."

The use of the form of the aphorism repays attention. It has had considerable notice in German studies, yet Coleridge has not been seen in this context. Goethe's employment of maxims and aphorisms in the *Bildungsroman* has been seen to reflect his mature desire "to convey general insights without usurping the primary status of specific experiences,"[20] the *Sendung* (*Wilhelm Meister's Theatrical Mission*) providing the experience, the *Lehrjahre* and even more the *Wanderjahre* working up the general insights. This does scant justice, however, to the complex history of the aphorism as a vehicle of thought from classical antiquity, and its development since Lichtenberg into a vehicle for experiential thought. A reference to "aphoristic, generalising devices (notably the *Turmgesellschaft*)" shows how far the word "aphorism" is stretched by critics[21] — an unjustifiable stretching, if "aphorism" is merely equated with "maxim." Rather, we may conjecture that Goethe's active use of aphorism came vividly before Coleridge again as he examined Carlyle's translation.

Coleridge gradually changed his conception of the form, at first suspicious of it as likely to be superficial, merely witty — "aphorisming," as he termed it[22] — and then adapting it to a full-scale work. Familiar with a wide variety of contemporary aphorisms — including the *Athenaeumsfragmente* (which he annotated), Novalis' *Blütenstaub*, and probably Fuseli's aphorisms on art, from which (in their English version) Blake drew the form — as well as Schelling's justifications of the fragment as "epitome," it lay ready for his working of it. It provided one of his most successful solutions to the question of how to cast philosophical thought into literary form, how to present the imaginative moment or "seed" of thought together with its discursive train, which had proved so vexing in *Biographia Literaria*.

The image of progressive or organic growth — metamorphosis — is central to the notion of the imaginative spirit for both Goethe and Coleridge. *Aids to Reflection* is subdivided into twelve "chapters," arranged in three main sections: "Prudential Aphorisms," "Moral and Religious Aphorisms," and "Spiritual Aphorisms." The arrangement represents Coleridge's usual, surreptitiously Kantian, mode of organization, according to an ascending hierarchy of the faculties of the mind.[23] This in turn represents the gradual progress of the reader toward spiritual enlightenment. In explaining the order of the aphorisms, Coleridge wrote that he had been "determined by the following convictions":

> 1. Every state, and consequently that which we have described as the state of religious morality, which is not progressive, is dead or retrograde. 2. As a pledge of this progression, or, at least, as the form in which the propulsive tendency shows itself, there are certain hopes, aspirations, yearnings, that with more or less of consciousness rise and stir in the heart of true morality as naturally as the sap in the full-formed stem of a rose flows towards the bud, within which the flower is maturing.[24]

The stages of spiritual progress, then, as represented in organic metaphor, should grow easily, even inevitably out of each other. But they are marked off by formidable obstacles. At the point of transition from "prudential" to "moral" looms the obstacle of the impossibility, within a system of cause-and-effect, of free will, without which there can be no moral life; and at the still more crucial transition from the moral religion of reason made possible by Kant to true "spiritual religion" looms the necessity of criticizing Kant's religious ethics. *Aids to Reflection* grapples with the Kantian arguments, as I have shown elsewhere; Coleridge chose Kant's most extreme statement of the destructive effect on traditional religion of the application of reason to it, *Religion within the Limits of Reason Alone* (*Religion innerhalb der Grenzen der bloßen Vernunft*). He was keenly aware, through his own intellectual anguish, that religion must meet the sharpest attacks of the Enlightenment, or go under.[25] But his mature work — *Confessions* taken together with *Aids to Reflection* — presents the activity of argument in a matrix of an aesthetic form bent on the unfolding of individual growth.

In order to grasp the full set of aesthetic frames within which Coleridge enacts his arguments, then, it is essential to restore the connection between the *Confessions* and the *Aids to Reflection*, and to restore the stimulus and the occasion of Coleridge's most fully realized critical work, the one that was for the nineteenth century his masterwork, in Goethe's *Bildungsroman*, in the inward life of the "schöne Seele."

In conclusion, both Goethe and Coleridge invent a new form of "Confession" — Goethe within a *Bildungsroman*, in which the spiritual "confessions" of another mark a new phase in the protagonist's subjective understanding of his own experience; and Coleridge in a work validating literary criticism as an authentic mode of biblical interpretation and self-exploration. In both cases, style is of central importance; and style embraces sententious qualities that permit the projection of personal experience into statements approaching philosophy, that is, aesthetic statements which in Kantian terms are asymptotic to knowledge claims. This explores the Romantic theme of the relation between philosophy and poetry, and lays the groundwork for the many Victorian prose forms, including the novel, that attempt to tread this fine line between subjective and objective modes of cognition.

Notes

[1] *Collected Letters of Samuel Taylor Coleridge,* ed. E. L. Griggs, 6 vols. (Oxford and New York, 1956–71), III, To John Murray, 12 September 1814. This fine letter on *Faust* is quoted by Richard Holmes in the second volume of his biography, *Coleridge: Darker Reflections* (London: Harper Collins, 1998), 367. Rosemary Ashton omitted it in "Coleridge and *Faust*," and allotted only one sentence to Coleridge's offer to translate *Faust*, in *The German Idea* (Cambridge UP, 1980), 56–66 (56), which perpetuated the negative view of the relations of the two writers. She has given a fuller account of his offer, as well as of his own Faust drama, in her *Life of Samuel Taylor Coleridge: A Critical Biography* (Blackwell, 1996), 290–3.

[2] *Collected Letters* V, 43–44, Letter of 10 May 1820.

[3] *The Letters of Percy Bysshe Shelley*, ed. Frederick L. Jones, 2 vols. (Oxford: Clarendon Press, 1964), Letter of 12 January 1922.

[4] Carlyle, "Life of Schiller," *The Works of Thomas Carlyle* XXV, Centenary edition, 30 vols., ed. H. D. Trail (London, 1896–9), 151n.

[5] See the introduction by the Editor Carl Woodring to the *Table Talk*, vol. XIV in the *Collected Works of Samuel Taylor Coleridge*, ed. Kathleen Coburn (Princeton, N. J.: Princeton UP; London: Routledge, 1969).

[6] *Henry Crabb Robinson On Books and their Writers*, ed. Edith J. Morley (London, 1922), 119–128.

[7] Coleridge, *Poetical Works*, ed. Ernest Hartley Coleridge (Oxford: Oxford UP, 1912), 311. The Editor dated the translation to Coleridge's time in

Germany; Ashton points out that there is no evidence in Coleridge's German notebooks, but that is not conclusive. In any case, between 1799 and 1813, when Crabb Robinson heard him reciting it, he did indeed translate it.

[8] *Shorter Works and Fragments (SWF)*, eds. H. J. Jackson and J. R. deJ. Jackson (*The Collected Works of Samuel Taylor Coleridge*, Vol. XI), (Princeton, NJ: Princeton UP; London: Routledge, 1995), 2 vols., II, 955 and 955 n6.

[9] *Lectures 1808–1819 On Literature*, ed. R. A. Foakes, 2 vols. (*The Collected Works of Samuel Taylor Coleridge*, LXXV) (Princeton, NJ: Princeton UP; London: Routledge, 1987), I, 386.

[10] The editor of *Aids to Reflection* (*AR*) believes that Coleridge withheld the *Confessions;* the editors of the *Confessions* believe the failure to publish it was owing to the financial crisis and dissolution of the partnership of his publishers Taylor and Hessey in 1825.

[11] *The English Review* x (1848): 399–344 (416). The anonymous essay is attributed to William Palmer, and reviewed a group of works of the English and the German schools of biblical criticism. (*SWF(CC)*, 1115n1).

[12] See E. S. Shaffer, review of *SWF(CC), Review of English Studies* NS 49 (1998), 96–97.

[13] E. S. Shaffer, "*Kubla Khan" and The Fall of Jerusalem. The Mythological School in Biblical Criticism and Secular Literature 1770–1880* (Cambridge: Cambridge UP, 1975), 17–61.

[14] *SWF(CC)* II, 1171. The addressee is probably Edward Irving.

[15] *SWF(CC)* II, 1117–1118.

[16] Michael Minden, *The German "Bildungsroman": Incest and Inheritance* (Cambridge: Cambridge UP, 1997), 9.

[17] Jeremy Adler, "The Aesthetics of Magnetism: Science, Philosophy and Poetry in the Dialogue between Goethe and Schelling," *The Third Culture: Literature and Science*, ed. E. S. Shaffer (Berlin and New York: Walter De Gruyter, 1998), 66–102. For the original German version of this paper, see *Goethe-Jahrbuch* 112 (1995): 149–165.

[18] A generation after Coleridge, George Eliot famously demurred from Lewes's view, as her thoughtful affirmation of the novel in her essay "The Morality of Wilhelm Meister," published just before the biography in July 1855, holds that the novel must be understood on the basis of its construction as a whole rather than judged on particular incidents: Goethe's "large tolerance" "waits patiently for the moral processes of nature as we all do for her material processes." (*Essays of George Eliot*, edited by Thomas Pinney (New York: Columbia UP; London: Routledge and Kegan Paul), 143–47 (146–47).

[19] Nicholas Boyle, *Goethe: The Poet and the Age. II. Revolution and Renunciation (1770–1803)* (Oxford: Clarendon Press, 2000), 367. See Boyle's whole exposition "*Wilhelm Meister*, Concluded," 367–391.

[20] Clemens Heselhaus, "Die Wilhelm-Meister-Kritik der Romantiker und die romantische Romantheorie," in *Nachahmung und Illusion*, ed. H. R. Jauß, (Munich 1964), 113–27 (114).

[21] Minden, 18.

[22] Several instances of this deprecating usage are given in Coleridge's Marginalia (*CM(CC)* III, 141n13), including one by Milton.

[23] This ascending hierarchy is, of course, not exclusively Kantian, but was widespread in the eighteenth century; it lent itself both to empiricist epistemology and to the progressive history of culture.

[24] *AR*. Ed., Henry Nelson Coleridge. 5th ed. (1843), 70; *AR(CC)*, 103. The earlier editions have not been superseded by the *Collected Coleridge* in that neither *AR(CC)* nor *SWF(CC)* contains J. H. Green's valuable introduction to the *Confessions*, which set out Coleridge's concurrence with the main lines of Lessing's criticism of "historical evidences" of Christianity, nor Sara Coleridge's "Note" on the *Confessions*, which first appeared in the 1849 edition, defending Coleridge against the more intemperate attacks on his advanced position. The only modern edition of *Confessions* containing these essays is that by H. St. J. Hart (Stanford UP, 1957). Moreover, some may also prefer to read the text in the form in which it became known, from which Coleridge's emphatic MS underlinings and capitalizations were removed, and I have accordingly maintained the 1843 text while indicating useful information supplied by the *Collected Coleridge*.

[25] E. S. Shaffer, "Metaphysics of Culture: Coleridge and Kant's 'Aids to Reflection,'" *Journal of the History of Ideas* (April-June, 1968): 199–218.

The Winkworth Sisters as Readers
of Goethe in Mrs. Gaskell's Manchester

Peter Skrine

Elizabeth Gaskell's foreign languages were French and, to a lesser degree, Italian. Despite her fondness for Germany, she owned up to a "no-knowledge" of German, and even her reading knowledge of it was, by her own account, scant.[1] Yet three of her five novels contain specific references to Goethe, as does *Cranford*. Some of these references are epigraphs, and others are authorial allusions, while the one in *Cranford* is made by one of its many memorable characters. What does this tell us? The epigraph — a fascinating feature of much nineteenth-century fiction, and one too often overlooked — provides rare glimpses, we might say, into the author's commonplace book; it indicates a range of literary awareness and, perhaps, hints at associations between what the author has read and the work taking shape. The textual allusion, on the other hand, implies a frame of reference shared by author and reader, whereas references and quotations placed in a character's mouth suggest that they can also be plausibly associated with persons other than the reader and author. Mr. Holbrook, the "old bachelor" visited by the narrator in Chapter 4 of *Cranford*, may have "pronounced the name of Goethe strictly in accordance with the English sound of the letters," but what is significant is that he is ready and able to mention him, and indeed to quote him, albeit in English, alongside Shakespeare, Herbert, and Byron. What is even more significant is that Elizabeth Gaskell feels able to include such a reference in a book that is built on her recollections of people and places in and around Knutsford, the Cheshire town in which she had spent much of her youth.[2] *Cranford* first appeared in *Household Words* between December 1851 and May 1853, the year in which it was published in book form.[3] Two years later, George Henry Lewes's pioneering *Life of Goethe*, dedicated to Carlyle, sold over 1,000 copies within three months of its publication,[4] yet only six years before, in July 1846, Baron Bunsen, the influential Prussian ambassador in London, had written a letter to a German author proposing to give literary lectures in London, warning him that "ein englisches Publikum noch viel zu wenig vorgebildet für Goethe und dergleichen sei."[5]

Mrs. Gaskell's German may have been deficient, but there was ample compensation for this deficiency in her immediate circle. In 1843, when Carlyle was encouraging Lady Harriet Baring to learn German in order to read Goethe in the original, the fifteen-year-old Catherine Winkworth (born on 13 September 1827) noted in her diary for 30 July: "I am going to learn German next Thursday."[6] A month before, in Carlyle's *Miscellanies* (1839), she had already read *The Tale*, his translation of *Das Märchen*, first published in 1832 in *Fraser's Magazine*, No. 33. She was clearly eager to make rapid progress and alive to Carlyle's stimulus. A diary entry for 2 July 1843 reads: "I have also read Carlyle's 'The Death of Goethe' and 'The Works of Goethe,' which are inspiriting, as it ever is to read of goodness and greatness. [. . .] Carlyle's writings have a spiritual tendency which makes them valuable to me. They tend to draw off one's attention from merely outward and material things, and to show the reality of the inner world, and the spirituality of all the circumstances going on either in common life, or great men's lives or history — I mean spirit here as opposed to matter" (68–69). Looking back over her first year of German at the end of September 1844, Catherine acknowledges that her teacher is good: he was none other than Mr. Gaskell, with whose family Mr. Winkworth and his gifted children had begun to form a warm relationship in 1842. One is reminded of the parallel cases of Marian Evans and Margaret Fuller. The future George Eliot started Italian lessons with Mr. Brezzi of Coventry in 1839, added German in February 1840, and after her fourth lesson wrote that she liked the language extremely. By October 1840 she was expressing the view that "there seems a greater affinity between German and my mind than Italian. [. . .] I am reading Schiller's *Maria Stuart* and Goethe's *Tasso*."[7] Earlier still, in Groton, Massachusetts, just a few months before Goethe's death, Margaret Fuller and her friend James Freeman Clark, encouraged by Carlyle's earlier essays on German Romantic writers, had plunged into the study of German at the deep end by reading Goethe, an intellectual and linguistic challenge that was to lead seven years later — and a mere three years after the publication of the German original — to the publication of Margaret's pioneering translation of *Eckermann's Conversations with Goethe in the Last Years of his Life* in George Ripley's *Specimens of Foreign Standard Literature* series (Boston: Hilliard & Co.), a remarkable achievement, which was later paid the compliment of being plagiarised by John Oxenford in his version. This was to become the standard version for English-speaking admirers of Goethe for the next hundred years and more.[8]

Catherine's elder sister Susanna (1820–84) had already begun to learn German with Mr. Gaskell in 1841. By 1843 she was ready to visit Germany for the first time, where she spent the summer months in Mannheim with her widowed aunt, Eliza Winkworth. Mrs. Winkworth had gone to Mannheim to superintend the education of her three nieces, Susanna's first cousins; she needed a companion who was able to speak German, of which she herself was ignorant.[9] During Susanna's stay she took singing lessons from a Madam Meyer, who in her youth had known Beethoven. "She was a very highly cultivated woman to whom I owe much," Susanna wrote later. With her, Susanna sang chiefly the songs of Schubert, of which she brought home a large repertory.[10] Young Catherine was enthusiastic: "I admire him exceedingly," she exclaims in January 1844; "perhaps I like his 'Gretchen am Spinnrade' the best of all his songs" (72). At that time, the Winkworth family had a "Chamber Concert" on Wednesday evenings at their home at the corner of the Polygon, in the southeast Manchester suburb of Ardwick, "Papa being sometimes sole audience, but often friends came. Susanna [. . .] sang" (66). No doubt she sang Schubert. In the days of the drawing room, when musical and artistic accomplishments were the hallmark of a good upbringing, vocal music could be as ready a channel of literary transmission as books, particularly where lyric poetry was concerned. It is not surprising, therefore, that Elizabeth Gaskell, the sisters' friend and mentor, used the lines "My rest is gone/My heart is sore,/Peace find I never,/And nevermore" as the epigraph for chapter 21 of her first major novel, *Mary Barton*, which caused such a sensation when it was published in October 1848. Most of the novel had almost certainly been written between the last months of 1845 and the first months of 1847.[11] The presence of Gretchen is even more palpable in *Ruth*, Gaskell's story of a seduced girl and betrayed mother, published in October 1853. Schubert's Goethe setting may well have been sung in the drawing room of Plymouth Grove, the Gaskells' Manchester home, while *Mary Barton* and *Ruth* were being written.

William Gaskell (1805–84) was Catherine Winkworth's first German teacher, and he taught her sisters, too. But what qualified him for the task? In all probability he had acquired his knowledge of German — a literary rather than a bread-and-butter one — from his older friend and colleague John Kenrick (1788–1877). Like William Gaskell, Kenrick had studied at Glasgow and had then taken up a post as tutor in classics, history, and literature at Manchester New College, an illustrious Unitarian academy and training college founded in Manchester in 1786 but located at York between 1803 and 1840. In July 1817 Kenrick had been granted a year's leave of absence to study at Göttingen. He moved on to Berlin for the summer semester of 1818, where he heard Schleiermacher lecture on philosophy. Thus he was able to transmit something of the great new German academic tradition to pupils and colleagues such as William Gaskell, who began to train for the Unitarian ministry there in 1825 and who in turn passed it on to his eager pupils, such as Catherine and her sisters, if only at second hand. Then in February 1844, Catherine acquired a second German teacher, whom she soon came to regard with equal respect. This was Tobias Theodores, a Berlin Jew, who was to become Manchester University's first German teacher after its foundation in 1851. He was "a man of very acute intellect and a most wonderful linguist" in Susanna Winkworth's estimation, and one who accelerated the mental and linguistic development of her sister (73, 78). Before the year was out, Catherine was reading Goethe's *Aus meinem Leben*: it was to prompt her first recorded response to a work by Goethe. "It is very amusing and interesting; raises my ideas of Goethe's powers, but does not please me, from the total want of Christian feeling and principles. It is really astonishing to see how many books are destitute of these, and makes one very unhappy" (80). The point she makes is crucial, and characteristic of the reception of Goethe in mid-nineteenth-century England.

By now Susanna, with her Mannheim experience behind her, was teaching German to her younger siblings, Alice and Stephen, while Catherine and her sister Selina set off in their turn for Germany, again, like Susanna, to keep their aunt Eliza company, though this time in Dresden. It was an experience Catherine would always look back on as an important epoch in her mental development. "As long as I am here," she wrote to her sister on 6 May 1846, "I know pretty well what I have to do, viz., to get as much knowledge as ever I can about Germany and its inhabitants. [. . .] I am afraid when I get back to England I shall find no one who can give me much information about German books — unless it be Mr. Theodores" (109). By mid-August 1845 she can confide to her diary that feeling of satisfaction which many readers will know from experience: "I find that I can speak German pretty easily" (97). Her state of mind, when she returned to England, was later recalled by Susanna, who writes: "The various influences under which she came at Dresden had thrown her out of the old traditional grooves of thought and feeling in which her childhood had moved, and her whole intellectual being was now in a state of ferment." And at the centre of it was Goethe: "Goethe was her chief instructor and guide," Susanna tells us, "her early beliefs had been rudely shattered, and she

was much inclined to replace them by the worship of Art and Culture."
In a word, "her philosophy was a chaos" (120). Catherine, for her part,
took a more reflective and long-term view of what her sister called the
"*Sturm und Drang Periode*" of her life. Writing up her journal at the
end of 1846 she comments: "These two years have certainly been
among the most eventful of my life, since they include my first long
visit abroad. [. . .] It would take too long to describe the new world
opened to me by my improved knowledge of German, and residence in
Dresden, the books I read through, the lessons I took, and the intercourse with our friends" (121). As Theodores had taught her, and as
he was to point out in 1851 in "On the Study of the German Language," his inaugural lecture as Professor of German at the Victoria
University (published 1852), "among all the tongues of the modern
world there is none that possesses stronger claims on the attention of
Englishmen than the German." He had gone on to tell his audience, "I
am bold enough to maintain that England stands in a closer and more
generally perceptible intellectual connexion with Germany than any
other foreign land."[12] He was heartened by the growing "multitude of
those who, from all parts of England, and from all classes of English society, repair to German seats of learning for the acquirement of that
intellectual culture which has already exerted so appreciable an influence on the state of the English mind." But his vision saw further as he
went on: "More momentous by far is the influence obtained for German thought and feeling on the culture of this nation, by the rapidly
increasing diffusion of the literary productions of Germany, over the
length and breadth of this land, through the instrumentality of the
most potent spirits of the British intellectual community." It was an
obvious allusion to Carlyle, but also to others closer to hand in Manchester, such as the Gaskells' wide circle of Manchester German friends
and acquaintances.[13]

Goethe was central to the growing appeal of German thought and
feeling as well as of German literary productions in mid-nineteenth-
century Britain. This is made clear when, reviewing *Jane Eyre* in *Fraser's
Magazine* No. 36 in December 1847, George Henry Lewes observed
that Goethe was now a normal element in critical discourse ("A canon
that excludes *Faust*, must *ipso facto* be suspicious") and that "*Hamlet,
Don Quixote, Faust*, marvellous creations as they are, with roots diving
deep into the profoundest regions, and with branches rising into the
highest altitudes of thought, do, nevertheless, powerfully interest even
the foolishest readers."[14] "Foolish" is not a term one would think of
applying to the Gaskell circle in Manchester, but Lewes's remark puts
into broader context the intellectual and emotional self-confidence with

which that circle was beginning to treat Goethe's intellectual and literary legacy. Their ongoing debate about the exact nature and importance of that legacy is evident when in May 1848 Emily, another of the Winkworth sisters, writes to tell Catherine about a discussion she has just had with her friend Emma Shaen "who has the impudence to hate and despise Goethe" because he had the "wickedness of making self-development the object of life" (145). In discussions such as these, the Goethean philosophy of life was percolating through the well-ordered existence of these young female representatives of the first truly Victorian generation, and sometimes disturbing its inherited assumptions. His presence in their private world surfaces, too, when in November of the same year, Elizabeth Gaskell, writing to Catherine, affectionately calls her "Kate-Bettina" — adding in parenthesis "for somehow you two are inextricably blended" — a clear indication that *Goethes Briefwechsel mit einem Kind* (1835) by Bettina von Arnim was familiar to them both.[15] When, in a letter of 7 May 1849, Matthew Arnold described Goethe as "writing about nothing he had not experienced," he put his finger on a quality which Elizabeth Gaskell, too, possessed, as those in her Manchester ambience knew from experience. The combination of introspection and objectivity associated with the great German author was as central to her fiction as it was to the translations of German hymns that Catherine Winkworth was working on at the time, and which she began to publish to mounting acclaim in 1855. They were as much the product of her deepening realisation that mental and spiritual growth is a lifelong quest, as of her growing command of the German language in its many registers and historical phases, and of her deepening insight into Germany's religious heritage.[16]

In the spring of 1851, Catherine and her circle of siblings and friends were reading *Eckermann's Conversations with Goethe* in John Oxenford's Fuller-based translation, which had been published the year before.[17] Anna Jameson, who was soon to become a friend of Elizabeth Gaskell and stood up for *Ruth* when its publication met with widespread critical and moral contempt, had written in 1838 that "a translation of Eckermann would hardly please in England; it deals in 'notions rather than facts,' and in 'speculation and ideas, more than in anecdotes and personalities.'" She went on to say that "it is necessary to take a strong interest in German literature and society, and in the fine arts generally, to care about a great deal of it."[18] Catherine, however, with her strong interest in Germany and its culture, found it "exceedingly interesting." Though she had only read part of the way through the first volume, we find her writing to her friend Emma Shaen to say "Somehow, whenever I read anything of Goethe's, it takes hold of me as almost nothing else ever does. All that he says is so deep and significant that it keeps growing in one's mind, and the whole gives one an impression of life so rich and varied, and a range of perception so infinitely beyond anything you ever conceive of, that you feel dwarfed into nothing before it, and as if no power of self-assertion were left you." Despite her admiration, however, she is not bereft of critical reservations. The future champion of women's secondary and higher education in Bristol and Cheltenham cannot refrain from pointing out that "some things he says are very unsatisfactory, — for instance, almost everything he says about women, — if not downright bad." Yet, born during the reign of George IV, she is close enough to the Regency to be able to add, "Still it is very easy to see what power he must personally have exercised over any woman when he chose, or even without choosing. Other things again sound cold-hearted, yet how could he be cold-hearted and have so many friends?" At this point the modern reader's appreciation of her range of potential awareness grows still further: "It is curious," she writes, "to observe how he seems to regard his Theory of Colours as amongst the greatest achievements of his life, and yet how rarely one hears of it." Her healthy curiosity then prompts a telling question: "I wonder if it ever has made any progress among scientific men; do you know?"

The most telling document to survive of this Manchester circle's *Auseinandersetzung* with Goethe revolves around a work whose centrality may come as a surprise in this context. During the three weeks between 22 October and 12 November 1853, a remarkable three-way exchange of letters took place between Catherine, Susanna, and their sister Emily, in which they discuss their impressions of *Die Wahlverwandtschaften*. Their letters give an unusually vivid picture of the responses of three intelligent young women at the height of the early Victorian period to a major text by Goethe. Like George Eliot at about the same time, they could claim that "Mr. Goethe is one of my companions" (October 1853). Emily, who had married, left Manchester, and now lived in London, starts the conversation off in a letter from her home in Bedford Row by telling Catherine "I am reading the '*Wahlverwandtschaften*.' What an exquisite story it is!" Catherine's reply, dated Alderley, 30 October, is of the kind to generate discussion. "Which side do you take about the '*Wahlverwandtschaften*'?" she writes. "Do you think it highly moral or immoral?" The question is a leading one still, but was all the more so when posed by a young woman in Victorian England; but before jumping to conclusions, we should read on, for Catherine now throws the name of James Anthony Froude into the discussion. Froude was well known as the author of

The Nemesis of Faith, a "loss of faith" novel in the epistolary form made fashionable by Goethe's *Werther*, which, like *Mary Barton*, was a controversial product of 1848, the "Year of Revolution." In a letter to Catherine dated 21 August 1849, the author of *Mary Barton* had used unmistakably Faustian terms to describe its author: "If any one under the sun has a magical, magnetic, glamour-like influence, that man has. He's 'aut Mephistophiles aut nihil,' that's what he is." Now, four years later, in October 1853, while Catherine was writing to Emily, Froude was working on the final stages of *Elective Affinities*, his translation of Goethe's 1809 masterpiece, which was to appear — anonymously — one year later, in *Novels and Tales by Göethe* [*sic*] in the Bohn's Standard Library series.[19] "You know Mr. Froude thinks the Germans were very stupid not to find out that it is the highest morality possible about marriage, and that English people would see it better," she tells Emily. It is a view with which she, as a young Englishwoman, cannot agree, as her estimate of Ottilie shows: "I can't say that I am much cleverer than the Germans, for it seems to me that Ottilie is the person Goethe cares most for, and I think she did behave very badly, though she is better than Edward." It is not so surprising that this future friend and confidante of Charlotte Brontë goes on to say, "But I do admire Charlotte exceedingly, for she could not help liking the 'Hauptmann' better than that weak Edward, and she gave him up as soon as she found it out. Her character I think very fine and very interesting." The fact that she and her sisters are reading the novel in the original German — Froude's translation had not yet appeared — becomes clear when she turns to matters of narrative style: "What exquisite writing there is in the book, is there not?" she writes; "that part where Ottilie and the child are in the water is perfectly written I think." Her admiration, however, is not unreserved: "But I never could understand what was the use of the young architect or Lucilla (isn't that her name?) to the plot of the story. I suppose a man who cared so much about the rules of art, had a very good reason for putting them in, but it seems to me like what Papa calls 'a second effect' in a pattern" (414–15), an *aperçu* which reminds us that Mr. Winkworth was involved in the Macclesfield silk business.

Emily had presumably already received Catherine's letter when, on 3 November 1853, she revealed to Susanna that Goethe's novel was much on her mind. This may have been for personal reasons. Writing about a recent dinner party in London, she says: "Went to dine at the Wm. Ashursts'; Mazzini there, and there was a quantity of general making-fun conversation, so of course it was nice, only, unluckily, when tea came, and he was beginning to talk in a corner quietly with me about the '*Wahlverwandtschaften*' and marriage, and in praise of 'grace before meat,' I turned poorly, and had to leave the room" (416). Could such Ottilie-like behaviour have been caused in part by the burgeoning friendship between Emily, who had married William Shaen two years before, and Giuseppe Mazzini (1805–72), whose political career, like the fate of Italy itself, the Winkworths and Gaskells were following with passionate interest? At all events, this conversation between Emily and her Italian hero about Goethe's novel is evidence that *Die Wahlverwandtschaften* was already the subject of lively interest in some English and Italian circles. Emily's reply to Catherine's letter is dated 12 November. Her reading of the novel is remarkable for its sensitivity and open-mindedness. "I don't think the '*Wahlverwandtschaften*' sets me moralizing any way," she writes, "except exciting my horror at the German Divorce Law, which could open the door to such a tragedy. But now I come to think of it, it does seem to me that the two things it shows very plainly are very good; first, that the real true love — the pairing in heaven — is the supreme thing that triumphs in its own strength over all earthly arrangements; such a love as Edward's and Ottilie's, for instance, which all outward things opposed and set aside, but which rose over all like the sea over wrecks, and penetrated through everything like a perfume out of sight; and also the danger, and perhaps final immorality of ever marrying without this love; — for even Charlotte and Edward, sensibly as they are married, found as soon as the true love came along, that they had committed a sin. And, secondly, that when marriage has once been made, it is so sacred that even this love may not, in this life, infringe upon it. For as soon as Ottilie comes to herself, — when through the dying of the child her conscience awoke, — she sees this plainly; and she acted on it, though her love killed her in the acting. Charlotte and the Captain show the same thing in a secondary degree. One feels that Charlotte could never have loved Edward as she fancied she did before, after the 'Hauptmann' has come, yet she saw that the marriage must be held up, and not broken. The 'Hauptmann' and Edward seem to show the manly and less pure view of the matter on its two sides, — the 'Hauptmann' the estimable, and Edward the rascally." This is surely critical interpretation of a high order, observant, responsive, and worthy to be set alongside Lewes's longer yet no more perceptive analysis of the novel in chapter 4, Book 7, of *The Life and Works of Goethe*. It also marks the climax of the Winkworth sisters' recorded *Auseinandersetzung* with Goethe. Catherine was soon to become preoccupied with her life's work, the translation of German hymns into English, while Susanna was already involved in translating the *Theologia Germanica* and Bunsen's topical *Die Zeichen der Zeit. Briefe über die Gewissensfreiheit und das Recht der christlichen*

Gemeinde.[20] When they finally left Manchester to settle in Clifton in 1862, higher education for women was to become the central concern of the one, public health and housing the preoccupation of the other.

The triangular correspondence between the three Winkworth sisters about the implications of Goethe's novel took place while Mrs. Gaskell was working on her own great novel, *North and South.* It is therefore, not so strange that Goethe's presence can be felt in the letter that Catherine wrote to Emma Shaen on 25 March 1851, in which we find an unexpected but significant comparison between Lily (the name by which Elizabeth Gaskell was affectionately known by those close to her) and the two classics of Weimar. "One thing that I read yesterday reminded me of Lily," she writes. "He [Eckermann] says that when Schiller wrote his plays, he used to tell Goethe the plan of them beforehand, and discuss all the separate scenes with him, but that when he himself [Goethe] wrote, he could never speak of his productions till they were finished, but carried them about with him always in silence." As she continues, we find ourselves transported to Plymouth Grove, Manchester, the home of the Gaskells. "I can't help fearing that we shall spoil 'Ruth' in itself, as well as for ourselves," she writes, "by talking it all over with Lily as it goes on, and being summoned to give judgment and advice upon it. The latter I always give with a fervent desire that it may not be taken" (285). Thus the great writers of Weimar become prototypes and exemplars of the artistic process, and reading them helps Catherine and her circle to understand the artistic and psychological make-up of the great creative artist in their midst. There is a good deal of evidence to indicate that Elizabeth Gaskell did indeed consult friends such as Catherine Winkworth when writing her books, and that she was highly responsive to motifs and ideas that fitted in with her vision. A case in point occurs in an important passage in *North and South*, the novel which she began in the late spring of 1853, and which was serialised by Dickens in *Household Words* during the winter of 1854–55. This is the explicit authorial reference to *Hermann und Dorothea*, the "German idyll" which comes vividly into Margaret Hale's mind alongside Longfellow's much more recent *Evangeline* as she revisits Helstone, her childhood Hampshire home, just before the dénouement of the story. Later, in her correspondence with her American friend, Charles Eliot Norton, resonances of these earlier conversations about Goethe involving the Winkworth sisters and, perhaps, their mutual friend, Charlotte Brontë, surface again when, discussing the problems of her daughter, she writes: "Meta conscientiously in her artistic conscience — disapproves of washes — is she to draw to give pleasure to others, or to improve herself? You see the complexity of the question, as to selfishness, Goethean theories of self development. I believe it to be *right* in all things to aim at the highest standard; but I can't quite work it out with my conscience."[21]

In *North and South* there is another passage where, though he is not directly alluded to, we can sense Goethe's presence — the Goethe who commanded the respect and admiration of so many of Britain's cultural élite during the age of Prince Albert. In chapter 40, Mr. Thornton, the mill-owning male protagonist of Elizabeth Gaskell's genial blend of *Bildungsroman* and the epic of social collision and the inevitability of progress, champions the vision he and his like have for Britain at the height of its industrial and imperial expansion. The words she finds for him are an eloquent testimony to the Mancunian reception of Goethe, but this time it is the Goethe of *Faust Part II*. Mr. Bell, an elderly Oxford classicist, suggests that Manchester men care only for money and outward appearances. Mr. Thornton's response reveals a very different interpretation. "Remember," he tells Mr. Bell, "we are of a different race from the Greeks, to whom beauty was everything. [. . .] I don't mean to despise them, any more than I would ape them. But I belong to Teutonic blood; it is little mingled in this part of England to what it is in others; we retain much of their language; we retain more of their spirit; we do not look upon life as a time for enjoyment, but as a time for action and exertion. Our glory and our beauty arise out of our inward strength, which makes us victorious over greater difficulties still."[22] There can be no doubt that this vision of Victorian England owes a good deal to Goethe and the new *Weltanschauung* that Faust seemed to personify, that is the Faust of the last act of Part II as understood by its mid-nineteenth-century admirers and interpreters.[23] Faust's last speech resonates powerfully through the opening sentences of chapter 50 where, near the end of the novel, the Goethean notion of 'Streben' and the futuristic images of Faust's 'great works' become audible and visible in Elizabeth Gaskell's depiction of nineteenth-century Manchester approaching its apogee as the powerhouse of the industrial revolution: "Meanwhile, at Milton [Manchester] the chimneys smoked, the ceaseless roar and mighty beat, and dizzying whirl of machinery, struggled and strove perpetually." With visionary realism Manchester's greatest nineteenth-century writer recognizes that the striving and struggling epitomised by Mr. Thornton is more needful than the nostalgia of Margaret Hale's *Biedermeier* "German idyll" for the citizens of a city increasingly conscious of its industrial and commercial destiny in Britain's dawning Age of Empire. But Margaret, as she leaves her pastoral idyll behind, will ensure that wealth and vigour are tempered by feminine kindness and the courage of a social conscience.

Notes

[1] See her letter to her daughter, Marianne, written from Heidelberg in early August 1860, in which she owns up to her "no-knowledge of German" and her letter to her publisher, George Smith, dated [?5] May 1858, in which she writes that German is a language "which unfortunately I cannot read." Elizabeth Gaskell, *Letters*, ed., J. A. V. Chapple and Arthur Pollard (Manchester: Manchester UP, 1966, nos. 475 (p. 625) and 286 (p. 389).

[2] For a detailed discussion of Elizabeth Gaskell's use of German sources and allusions in her creative writing see my article "Mrs. Gaskell and Germany" in *The Gaskell Society Journal*, 7 (1995): 37–49.

[3] The publication history as well as the *Entstehungsgeschichte* of *Cranford* is covered in J. G. Sharps, *Mrs. Gaskell's Observation and Invention* (Fontwell: Linden Press, 1970), 125–35.

[4] Rosemary Ashton, *George Eliot: A Life* (London: Hamish Hamilton, 1996), 151.

[5] Wilma Höcker, *Der Gesandte Bunsen als Vermittler zwischen Deutschland und England*, Göttinger Bausteine zur Geschichtswissenschaft, 1 (Göttingen: Musterschmidt, 1951), 129.

[6] Quotations from the Winkworth sisters are taken from the first volume of Susanna Winkworth's *Letters and Memorials of Catherine Winkworth* (Clifton: R. Austin and Son, 1886), 2 vols. 70.

[7] See Gerlinde Röder-Bolton, *George Eliot and Goethe. An Elective Affinity* (Amsterdam/Atlanta: Rodopi, 1998). Susanna Winkworth also started to learn German in 1840.

[8] Charles Capper, *Margaret Fuller: An American Romantic Life. The Private Years* (New York and Oxford, 1992), 253. Oxenford's *Conversations of Goethe with Eckermann and Soret* (London: Smith, Elder, 1850) was, for example, re-issued in an edition by Roy Pascal in 1971.

[9] *Letters and Memorials*, 68.

[10] *Letters and Memorials*, 72.

[11] Sharps, 52.

[12] Tobias Theodores, "On the Study of the German Language," in *Introductory Lectures on the Opening of Owens College, Manchester* (London, Cambridge, Manchester, 1852), 139–40.

[13] Some of these were members of the Manchester Foreign Library, which was established in 1830 to cater for the needs of Manchester's growing French and Italian population and especially for its German cultured middle class, estimated to be around 10,000 by 1864.

[14] Lewes's review of *Jane Eyre* and his essay "Schools of Poetry" (1853) are reprinted in *Versatile Victorian: Selected Writings of George Henry Lewes,* ed., Rosemary Ashton, 81–87, 132–36 (here, 84, 135).

[15] *The Letters of Mrs. Gaskell,* 61.

[16] Her *Lyra Germanica,* First Series, was published in 1855; the Second Series followed in 1858. They were later followed by *The Christian Singers of Germany* (London, 1869), a study of German hymn texts in the context of their times and the lives of their authors.

[17] See Catherine Winkworth's letter to Emma Shaen dated 25 March 1851, *Letters and Memorials,* I, 285.

[18] Anna Jameson, *Winter Studies and Summer Rambles in Canada* (3 vols., 1838, reissued 1852), I, 230.

[19] London: Henry George Bohn, 1854.

[20] Susanna's translations were published in 1854 and 1856 respectively.

[21] Letter of 27 August 1860, *Letters of Mrs. Gaskell and Charles Eliot Norton, 1855–1865,* ed., Jane Whitehill (London, 1932, reprinted by George Olms: Hildesheim and New York, 1973), 65.

[22] *North and South* (Harmondsworth: Penguin, 1995), 326.

[23] There had been many translations of *Faust Part I* into English, but the most successful and respected mid-nineteenth-century translation of the complete work was by Elizabeth Gaskell's Liverpool acquaintance and fellow-Unitarian, Anna Swanwick.

Goethe and American Literature:
The Case of Edith Wharton

Jane K. Brown

IN THE FOUR DECADES before the First World War, the familiarity of the American reading public with German literature reached an all-time high. Auerbach, Freytag, Reuter, Spielhagen, and the popular women authors of the period were widely read in North America, and not simply by German emigrants; Schiller and Goethe had their place among the great writers of world literature. Edith Wharton (1862–1937), one of the most famous American writers of her time, had especially thorough knowledge of German literature. This scion of New York society was eventually named a *Chevalier* of the French Legion of Honour, received an honorary doctorate from Yale, and the Pulitzer Prize. Her novels and stories, which appealed to a broad public, refer constantly to Goethe, her favourite author. I shall use her here to illustrate and, in a certain sense, assess the reception of Goethe in the United States at this time.

I begin with the cultural situation that made possible both Wharton's familiarity with German literature and her public's receptivity for her allusions to German texts. After a brief presentation of her knowledge of German literature, I will discuss her well-known best-seller, *The House of Mirth* (1905), for which she used Goethe's *Wahlverwandtschaften* as a source. Investigation of conspicuous parallels and striking differences between the two novels suggests that her reading of the novel was rather superficial, and that she used it primarily as a source of figures and events, and secondarily as a kind of legitimation of her own novel. Finally, I shall draw a comparison with the reception of *Die Wahlverwandtschaften* by Walter Benjamin and Ford Madox Ford (in his novel *The Good Soldier*, 1927), in order to clarify the differences in Wharton, who seems to have read *Die Wahlverwandtschaften* exclusively as a novel of manners.

Knowledge of German culture among educated Americans not of German origin increased substantially in the second half of the nineteenth century. The earliest encounters with German culture in the seventeenth and eighteenth centuries had been restricted primarily to theology and alchemy, although the *Faust* chapbook (in English translation) was fairly popular in puritan New England.[1] Actual reception of contemporary German literature began somewhat tentatively at the end of the eighteenth century with Gessner, Wieland's *Oberon* (translated by the future president of the United States, John Quincy Adams), *Werther*, and the best-known Weimar dramatist of the period, August von Kotzebue, whose plays dominated the New York stage from 1799 to 1804, and continued to be played afterward with considerable success. Not until the appearance of Mme. de Staël's *De l'Allemagne* (1813, first American translation 1814) were Goethe's other works, as well as those of Schiller and the German Romantics, brought to the attention of American readers. Through the annual lectures of the poet Henry Wadsworth Longfellow, Professor of Modern Languages at Harvard University, Goethe was elevated to the same position that he occupied in Germany in the later nineteenth century.

The familiarity of educated Americans in Edith Wharton's milieu with German culture can be assessed most effectively in the popularity of the German language theatre in New York in the early twentieth century: from the mid-1850s until the First World War there was always at least one professional German theatre operating in New York. The repertoire consisted mainly of comedies and operettas, but some German classics were staged as well.[2] It is a sign of true breeding in Wharton's novels to be familiar with Goethe's *Faust* (not just in Gounod's setting) and to have seen the most recent serious play on the German stage in New York.[3] We can distinguish three respects in which the German-language theatre was acknowledged by English-speakers.

Wagner performances first brought the English- and German-language publics together. George Templeton Strong, taken aback by the quaintness of the experience, reported as follows on the first performance of an entire Wagner opera (*Tannhäuser*) in the New York Stadttheater in 1859: "A great crowd, Teutonic and generally frowzy . . . Lager beer and cakes handed round between acts. Audience grimly attentive to the music, which is grim likewise."[4] Nevertheless, Mr. Strong considered the chorus, a New York *Gesangverein*, the best he had ever heard in opera. The premier of *Lohengrin* in 1871 again brought English-speaking visitors to the (now) Neues Stadttheater. The Metropolitan Opera House, which opened in 1883, was fundamentally a German house from 1884 to 1891 under the German conductors Leopold Damrosch and then Anton Seidl. German-speakers regularly visited the numerous Wagner performances, where the wealthy box-holders were shushed by the frowzy interlopers from the German ghetto (Horowitz 79–80).

The second aspect of this history is the high standing of Heinrich Conried, who directed the German-language Irving Place Theater from 1893 to 1907. (The span corresponds approximately to the years of Edith Wharton's residence in New York as an adult.) Born in Silesia in 1855 as Heinrich Cohn, Conried acted for the Vienna Burgtheater at age nineteen, and three years later became acting director (and saviour) of the Bremen Stadttheater. When he was told he was too young to be named Oberleiter, he left for America, and soon became one of the most influential agents and producers for German-language theatre in the U. S. — an activity that he subsidised, by the way, with deck-chair concessions on ocean-liners. The Irving Place Theater, famous for its outstanding ensemble-work, was a repertory theatre on the pattern of the great German stages, a model that, except for the Metropolitan Opera in New York, didn't take root in the United States. Because, like every other American theatre, it had to survive without subventions, Conried could not afford to maintain the ambitious program that his high ideals of the stage as academy of morals demanded. Nevertheless, every Tuesday, known as "Klassikerabend," his company played Goethe, Schiller, Lessing (whose names were mounted above the proscenium arch), or some other European classic. The Irving Place Theatre thus functioned as an educational model (in the sense of *Bildung*) rather in the same sense as Goethe's and Schiller's stage.

The American public recognised the exemplary role of this theatre. Shortly before his death Conried was asked to develop a plan for an American (English-language) National Theatre and was named general director of the project.[5] In 1903 he was offered the general direction of the Metropolitan Opera, and served in the position until 1908 with considerable success (indeed éclat in the case of the first staging of *Parsifal* outside of Bayreuth), while he continued to run the Irving Place Theatre. When the famous English actress Mrs. Patrick Campbell wanted to stage Sudermann's *Es lebe das Leben* in New York — in a translation she had commissioned from Edith Wharton — Heinrich Conried trained her in her role (Moses 94). The English-language reviews by Norman Hapgood of the productions at Irving Place testify to the status of the German classics for the American public. Both the number and tone of the reviews make clear that Hapgood assumes his audience will be able to follow the performances without difficulty and understand almost everything; he comments specifically that the superb declamation in Hauptmann's *Furhmann Henschel* makes even the difficult Silesian dialect readily understandable.[6] He gives German titles (and French titles) without translation, while Russian and Norwegian titles are given only in English. He dispenses with plot summaries of the famous German plays, and even his asides assume that his audience knows the German classics.[7] He closes his chapter on foreign tragedy with the assertion that tragedy flourishes best in New York at Irving Place.[8] Conried's theatre was not only acknowledged as exemplary, but was seemingly accessible to New York audiences.

Conried's work at American universities constitutes a third aspect in this discussion. He spoke at several of the most important universities in the country — Harvard, Yale, Columbia, Cornell, and the University of Pennsylvania. Professors sent their students to his theatre with the discounted tickets he offered. He helped establish German clubs at several colleges (Moses 115). His production of *Iphigenie auf Tauris* at Harvard for the sixty-eighth anniversary of Goethe's death was greeted, we are told, with "genuine delight" by "throngs" of students, the entire faculty and the intellectual elite of Boston and Cambridge,[9] with the proceeds going to the Germanic Museum at Harvard. The following year Conried repeated his generous gesture with *Minna von Barnhelm*, and he celebrated the opening of the museum with three one-acters, among them Goethe's *Geschwister* (Moses 133–34). He staged similar benefits at Columbia, the University of Pennsylvania, and Yale. These universities were at the time the leading institutions of higher education in the country, the places where the intellectual and social elite (to a large extent the same) sent their sons (daughters were still the exception) to be educated. It is perhaps less surprising that the *Faust* course at the University of Michigan was — according to oral tradition — the single largest course on campus just before the First World War, for it served a region heavily populated by German emigrants. In the Ivy-League schools of the Northeast, however, it was primarily old families of the colonial period, the American equivalent of aristocracy, to whom Conried brought the best and newest in German theatrical life. The performances were received with lively interest, as the well-informed reviews in the Yale student newspaper of Conried's performances and talks demonstrate (Moses 125, 137). Moreover, Harvard and Pennsylvania offered Conried honorary MAs. On a related note, Schiller's *Jungfrau von Orleans* was performed in English in 1909 before 15,000 spectators in the Harvard football stadium with a cast of 1,500.[10] Though Conried was not connected with this production, it does show the widespread interest in the German classics during the period.

Now let us turn to Edith Wharton to illuminate the individual side of this phenomenon. As the daughter of an old wealthy New York family,

she belonged to a social class that consumed more culture than it produced. Men of this class owned fine libraries, and collected — sometimes
in earnest — books or various *objets d'art*,[11] men and women attended
the theatre and especially the opera, if only to be seen. The young men
studied at the colleges and universities mentioned above. Nevertheless,
Wharton emphasises in her autobiography that anything more than dilettantish interest in culture violated the code of manners for men as well
as for women. Thus, as a woman and talented writer Wharton is not so
much typical — when is genius ever typical? — as representative. The
tendencies of the period appear concentrated in her and are revealed in
concentrated form in her works, which mercilessly expose this society.

The same could be said of her knowledge of German. She learned
German at age eight while on a cure in the Black Forest. Her family resided at the time in Paris: the devaluation of the American currency at
the end of the Civil War had driven them, like so many of their friends
and relatives, whose wealth was vested primarily in real estate, to rent
their various homes to the *nouveaux riches* and take refuge in Europe in
1866.[12] When the family returned to New York in 1872, ten-year-old
Edith had already mastered French, German, and Italian.[13] Her knowledge of German literature was extended considerably by lessons taken
with the German governess of the neighbouring family when she was
fifteen. The latter, Anna Bahlmann, became her secretary in 1904 and
remained with her till her death (Lewis, 150). All her life Wharton read
German books, "from the minnesingers to Heine" (as she said [*A Backward Glance*, 48], but actually to Nietzsche).[14] Her best-known work,
Ethan Frome, is obviously based on Gottfried Keller's *Romeo und Julia
auf dem Dorfe* (Lawson 51–70); another novel, *The Custom of the Country*, plays cleverly and repeatedly on Fouqué's *Undine* (Lawson 109–19).
The importance of the German language for her is illuminated by a diary
that she kept during the beginning of her one extramarital affair: the passages on the beloved are mostly in German, as if, according to her biographer, she wanted to "enshrine" such moments (Lewis 203).

Goethe remained her favourite poet and *Faust* her favourite work
until her death. Quotes from Goethe appear everywhere in her work —
in the autobiography (even on the title page), in the novels, in the letters. Often they involve witticisms, such as "a London dinner reminds
me of Klärchen's song; they could be so "*freudvoll*" or so "*leidvoll*" —
but seldom "*gedankenvoll*," (*A Backward Glance*, 218); or another
time in a letter: "*Zwei Seelen wohnen, ach, in meine* [*sic*] *Brust* and the
Compleat Housekeeper has had the upper hand for the last two weeks"
(quoted by Lewis 111). Many of the allusions are intended seriously:
the Mothers from *Faust II* are a leitmotiv in *Hudson River Bracketed*

(1929) and the hero is advised to read Goethe's masterpiece. At the high point of her love affair, Wharton sent her lover a poem on which he jotted a note that the metre derived from Goethe's *Römische Elegien* (Lewis 260). It seems likely that Goethe had been discussed during their nights together. In any case, the repeated allusions make clear both that Wharton knew her Goethe chapter and verse, and that she used him in a manner typical of the time. Like so many Germans of her generation, she had a Goethe quote for every occasion. Wharton says in her autobiography that she had no interest in drama (*A Backward Glance*, 160). Goethe appears in her poetics of the novel, *The Writing of Fiction* (1924), as one of the "true pioneers, who are never destined to see their own work fulfilled, but build intellectual houses for the next generation to live in."[15] Her Goethe was above all the great sage, the philosophical poet celebrated in 1910 by the then famous philosopher and Harvard professor George Santayana.[16]

The only exception seems to have been her appreciation for *Die Wahlverwandtschaften*, the single German work that she mentions twice in *The Writing of Fiction*. The references to *Die Wahlverwandtschaften* in and of themselves demonstrate exceptional knowledge of Goethe, for the novel was marginal to the Goethe canon of the period and was only just being recovered by the modernists in the twenties. Her use of *Die Wahlverwandtschaften* for *The House of Mirth* in 1905 is even more remarkable. Since the novel is probably unfamiliar to the nonspecialist, I will describe it briefly. The lovely orphan Lily Bart seeks a husband of the proper class with no assistance from the wealthy aunt who is her guardian. Her hunting expeditions take place on visits to the country places and yachts of various motherly friends. Despite great beauty and exceptional social skills, Lily is too intelligent and too impatient to comply fully with the usages of her dull surroundings and hence deliberately spoils or lets slip several advantageous matches. The one man she can truly love (and who loves her) lacks sufficient wealth to come into consideration. Without doing anything actually immoral, she slips into ambiguous relations with the husbands of two of her older friends; in the second case the husband wishes to divorce his wife and marry Lily, but Lily does not agree. Without quite deserving it, she loses her reputation, her inheritance from her aunt, and her social position. Only her boring and penniless cousin Gerty stands by her, but with little real aid to offer. Lily could still recover her position by blackmailing her worst enemy through letters that have accidentally come into her possession, but she is too noble to do so. In any case, the letters also compromise the man she loves. She destroys the letters without his ever knowing she had them. She finally dies of an overdose of a sleeping draught and is mourned by the cousin and the beloved.

What, one might wonder, has this novel to do with *Wahlverwandt-schaften*? The unambiguous references to Goethe's novel are first the theme of divorce and second a scene in which *tableaux vivants* are the central motif — Lily Bart is of course the great star. Once the allusion is recognised, others spring to mind: Lily is, like Goethe's Ottilie, an orphan who must find her place in the world, her *Bahn*. Both novels begin with the orphan's visit at the country house of an older couple; in both cases the husband falls in love with his wife's protégé. Wharton uses the gesture twice, and the second time the situation carries the figures, as in Goethe, to the brink of divorce, which has already been mentioned in both novels by minor characters. Furthermore, both Ottilie and Lily are loved by men who are socially (or financially) below them — Ottilie actually has two, the architect and the assistant from the pension. Toward the ends of both novels the heroines try to serve their fellows; Ottilie acts more definitively in this regard, but the motif is more striking in the case of Lily, since nothing in the novel prepares us for it. Both novels end, finally, with the voluntary death of the heroine, who is visited after her death by a lover who never really articulated his love. The novels are thus remarkably similar with respect to themes, motifs, episodes and, also partly, organisation.

In spite of these parallels, the experience of reading Wharton's book is completely different from Goethe's. Lily Bart has much more in common with the insufferable Luciane of *Die Wahlverwandtschaften* than with Ottilie, while boring cousin Gerty seems to play Ottilie's role. Only gradually does Lily take on the qualities of Goethe's heroine. Just as her name moves from the first sound of Luciane to the final syllables of Ottilie, so, too, does Lily develop in the course of the novel from Luciane's egotism and social flair to Ottilie's moral purity. Even more significant is the different conduct of the narrative. The episodes of Wharton's novel turn on the one protagonist and follow a single falling line of development. In Goethe's novel, however, the real action takes place behind the scenes, while the narrative seems to wander aimlessly or even to stagnate. As a result, the narrative perspective is totally different. Wharton alternates between the point of view of the heroine and of her beloved; the narrator often reports skipped episodes in retrospect but seldom comments on the action. The narrator of *Die Wahlverwandtschaften* is, by contrast, anything but neutral, and the narrative perspective is often ironic and notoriously unstable — there are insertions in different voices, like Ottilie's diary and the novella, whose point of view is not clearly defined, and the narrator's own position seems to wander. *The House of Mirth* represents and critiques a particular segment of a particular society at a particular time. Goethe, on the contrary, represents the universal in the particular and simultaneously investigates the parameters of such a representation — and, finally, calls its very possibility into question.

We are dealing here with two distinct traditions of the novel. Wharton writes in the realistic tradition of the nineteenth century as it developed especially in France and England. With her focus on the life of the great city and her sense for the evil inherent in society, she is closest perhaps to Balzac. Goethe writes partly in this tradition, where he is most like Jane Austen in tone and in his choice of a setting on an isolated estate.[17] Both novels are novels of manners and of the critical sort, but the social criticism is more visible in Wharton than in Goethe. Goethe addresses so many other issues — the analysis of Romanticism, epistemological issues, the relationship of the scientific and moral spheres, etc. — that the social issues are overshadowed. Goethe has thus integrated the achievements of the less structured philosophical novel of the eighteenth century — Laurence Sterne's *Tristram Shandy* or his own *Wilhelm Meisters Lehrjahre* — into the linear structure of the novel of manners. In this union, the form of the novel of manners is scarcely recognisable: Wharton's *House of Mirth* renders this veiled aspect of the *Die Wahlverwandtschaften* visible again.

Wharton's reception of *Die Wahlverwandtschaften* differs from the important reactions to the novel in the 1920s by Walter Benjamin and Ford Madox Ford. In his essay "Goethes Wahlverwandtschaften" (1924), Benjamin identifies impenetrable depths in the novel as he seeks the truth (Wahrheitsgehalt) behind the realities (Sachgehalt).[18] The characters in the novel fall victim to mythic Nature (132), this "verborgene[n] Macht im Dasein der Landedelleute" (133), "dem Unergründlichen" (133). Benjamin finds the ineffable everywhere, whether "in der rätselhaften Stille" of the water (133), or in formulations like these: "Dabei ist das Spiel am Tage und der Ernst geheim" (137), "als ein mythisches Schattenspiel in Kostümen des Goetheschen Zeitalters erscheint sein Inhalt" (140–41), "Alle mythische Bedeutung sucht Geheimnis" (146), "Der Mensch erstarrt im Chaos der Symbole" (154), and "Macht der Zweideutigkeit" (183). In the course of the essay, Benjamin redefines the word "olympisch": it refers no longer to the superior clarity and repose of the great poet; instead, it identifies

> die dunkle, in sich selbst versunkene, mythische Natur, die in sprachloser Starre dem Goetheschen Künstlertum innewohnt. Als Olympier hat er den Grundbau des Werkes gelegt und mit kargen Worten das

Gewölbe geschlossen. In dessen Dämmerung trifft der Blick auf das, was am verborgensten in Goethe ruht. (147)

Benjamin's programme of assimilating the novel to the opacity of modernity comes into the open here: Goethe shall henceforth justify the austere, rigid style of modernity.

Ford Madox Ford's novel *The Good Soldier* attempts something similar. It deals with the dissolution of the marriage between an Edward and a Leonora (an allusion to *Tasso*) instead of a Charlotte. The novel takes place on Edward's estate where the narrator — a wealthy American, who also plays the role of Goethe's captain — writes down this "saddest story of all";[19] the narrated action takes place primarily in a German spa shortly before the First World War. It describes Edward's more or less innocent, sentimental love affairs and the attempts of his apparently cold wife to win him back by her patience and general capability. Edward's affairs reach their climax in his consuming love for a girl who stands in the same relationship to him as Goethe's Ottilie does to Edward and Charlotte. Both try to resist their love; as a result the girl descends into incurable insanity and Edward commits suicide. Leonora marries her neighbour; the narrator spends the rest of his life caring for the mad girl, whom he would happily have married, on Edward's former estate, now the narrator's own. Goethe's pleasantly ironic gesture toward an eventual reunion of the dead lovers and Wharton's openly sentimental ending are both revealed in Ford to be either banal (through Leonora's second marriage) or completely incommensurable.

The most interesting aspect of *The Good Soldier*, however, is the narrative stance. Ford narrates through a naive American, who initially understands nothing of the circumstances he reports, not even that his own wife has been Edward's mistress during the entire nine-year friendship between the two couples. His plaintive "I don't know" echoes through the obscure windings of his reflections. Only in the course of his narrative does he realise what has actually transpired, and even then he can make no sense of the events. His judgements of his fellow actors change from one chapter to the next; the general opacity of the social condition thus becomes a theme, and the process of bringing-to-knowledge becomes the central focus. In this respect, Ford's reading of *Wahlverwandtschaften* is much closer to Benjamin's than to Wharton's. Concealment, epistemological difficulties, ambiguity, and the incommensurability of the human condition are central to both in their understanding of Goethe's novel.

Before rejecting Wharton's *House of Mirth* as a banal simplification of Goethe, however, it is necessary to acknowledge that her turn away from the representation of opacity is not random. At the beginning of

The Writing of Fiction, Wharton characterises *Die Wahlverwandtschaf-ten* as "uncannily modern" (10). Seven years after *The House of Mirth*, in *The Reef* (1912), the heroine comes to realise, "The truth had come to light by the force of its irresistible pressure; and the perception gave her a startled sense of hidden powers, of a chaos of attractions and re-pulsions far beneath the ordered surfaces of intercourse."[20] Wharton was aware of the phenomenon and was at least able to describe it: the fact that she dealt with Goethe's material so differently in *The House of Mirth* probably had more to do with her loyalty to the realistic novel. Her sparse comments on *Die Wahlverwandtschaften* in *The Writing of Fiction* are illuminating in this respect. Wharton distinguishes there between novels of character and novels of situation, and says with re-gard to the second:

> One of the earliest, as it is the most famous, is Goethe's "Elective Af-finities," where a great and terrible drama involves characters of which the creator has not managed quite to sever the marionette wires. Who indeed remembers those vague initialled creatures, whom the author himself forgot to pull out of their limbo in his eagerness to mature and polish their ingenious misfortunes? (90)

Shortly after she continues:

> Balzac alone, perhaps, managed to make of his novels of situation — such as "César Birotteau" or "Le Curé de Tours" — such relentless and penetrating character studies that their protagonists and the diffi-culties which beset them leap together to the memory whenever the tales are named. But this fusion of categories is the prerogative of the few, of those who know how to write all kinds of novels, and who choose, each time, the way best suited to the subject in hand.

With this, Wharton reveals her most deeply held principles: despite the two-part typology, she actually considers the novel of character to be superior; the novel of situation is only truly great when it is also a novel of character. The novelists she cites repeatedly are probably for this reason first Balzac and Thackeray; then Tolstoy, Eliot, and Austen; then Flaubert. Despite her lifelong admiration for Goethe, and despite her lifelong engagement with German literature, there was in fact not one German novel in her canon.

It is well known that classical German literature disappeared from the American intellectual horizon after the First World War, practically without a trace. The collapse is normally explained, doubtless correctly, as the result of the war itself. One might nevertheless wonder why it happened so rapidly and so thoroughly, especially since German music did not suffer a comparable decline. The paradoxical situation pre-sented above with regard to Edith Wharton allows us to offer at least a hypothesis, which might eventually be confirmed: knowledge of German literature declined so precipitously after the First World War because its reception in the United States, despite all appearances to the contrary, focused more on its content than on its stance. Wharton derived her ideas of form and purpose entirely from the French and English novel. Goethe interested her — and her fellow Americans — exclusively as thinker.

It is of course bold to generalise so much from this single example. One could immediately argue that this example is a woman who never attended a school of any sort, much less a university. That is, however, not untypical, even for very wealthy men of her time and class. The important issue here is her demonstrated familiarity with German literature on the one hand, and, on the other, her demonstrated poetic achievement. The confirmation of my hypothesis would depend on an investigation of both American literature, and of academic and nonacademic discussion of German literature, in the second half of the nineteenth century — more than can be addressed here. Americanists have taken essentially no interest in the reception of Goethe in America. I hope I have shown that this lack of interest is inexcusable for the nineteenth century. Unfortunately, it may not be completely unjustified for the twentieth.

Notes

[1] Henry A. Pochmann, *German Culture in America: Philosophical and Literary Influences 1600–1900* (Madison: U of Wisconsin P, 1957), 26–28.

[2] A detailed chronology of the German-language stage in New York may be found in Edwin Hermann Zeydel, "The German Theater in New York City, with Special Consideration of the Years 1878–1914," in *Deutsch-Amerikanische Geschichtsblätter. Jahrbuch der Deutsch-Amerikanischen Historischen Gesellschaft von Illinois* 15 (1915): 255–309.

[3] The hero is advised to read *Faust* in *Hudson River Bracketed*; *The Age of Innocence* begins at a performance of Gounod's *Faust*; in *The Custom of the Country* the heroine demonstrates her lack of social qualifications through her ignorance of New York's German-language theatre.

[4] Quoted in Joseph Horowitz, *Wagner Nights: An American History* (Berkeley: U of California P, 1994), 42.

[5] Montrose J. Moses, *The Life of Heinrich Conried* (New York: Thomas Y. Crowell, 1916), 270–281.

[6] Norman Hapgood, *The Stage in America: 1897–1900* (New York, London: Macmillan, 1901), 229.

[7] For example: "What makes this, in all probability, the greatest tragedy since Goethe and Schiller" (Hapgood 220).

[8] And after that, remarkably enough, in the Yiddish theatres on the Bowery (Hapgood 247).

[9] Kuno Francke, Professor of German at Harvard University. Quoted Moses 126.

[10] Albert Bernhardt Faust, *The German Element in the United States*, vol. 2 (Boston: Houghton Mifflin, 1909), 334.

[11] The motif occurs in almost all of Wharton's novels.

[12] Edith Wharton, *A Backward Glance* (New York, London: D. Appleton-Century, 1936 [first edition 1933]), 44.

[13] R. W. B. Lewis, *Edith Wharton: A Biography* (New York: Harper & Row, 1975), 19.

[14] Richard H. Lawson, *Edith Wharton and German Literature*. Studien zur Germanistik, Anglistik und Komparatistik, Vol. 29 (Bonn: Bouvier, 1974), 30–40.

[15] Edith Wharton, *The Writing of Fiction*, (New York: Simon and Schuster, 1997), 83.

[16] George Santayana, "Goethe's Faust," in *Three Philosophical Poets: Lucretius, Dante, and Goethe*. (Cambridge: Harvard UP, 1945), 139–99.

[17] I have analysed this relationship at greater length in "*Die Wahlverwandtschaften* and the English Novel of Manners," *Comparative Literature* 28 (1976): 97–108; in German as "*Die Wahlverwandtschaften* und der englische Sittenroman," in Jane K. Brown: *Ironie und Objektivität: Aufsätze zu Goethe* (Würzburg: Königshausen & Neumann, 1999), 135–47.

[18] Walter Benjamin, "Goethes "Wahlverwandtschaften," in *Gesammelte Schriften (Werkausgabe)*, ed. Rolf Tiedemann und Hermann Schweppenhäuser, vol. 1 (Frankfurt a. M.: Suhrkamp, 1980), 123–201(here 123).

[19] Ford Madox Ford, *The Good Soldier* (New York: Vintage, 1983), 3.

[20] Edith Wharton, *The Reef* (New York: Collier, 1986), 339. This is considered the novel in which Wharton most closely approaches the style of Henry James — James, of course, because critics tend not to be aware of *Die Wahlverwandtschaften*.

The Authority of Culture:
Some Reflections on the Reception
of a Classic

James Simpson

IN HIS ESSAY "Goethe as the Sage" (1955), Eliot famously declared Goethe to be one of a triad of great Europeans, Dante and Shakespeare being the others, the three essential poets who have by their work "helped [. . .] to explain European man to himself."[1] The configuration of these three classic poets has become commonplace, but in respect of their reception by foreign linguistic cultures they constitute very different cases. Whereas German literature, for example, absorbed Shakespeare into itself almost as one of its own, transforming him according to the particular needs of the time, and made all but a German classic out of him, the same cannot be said of Goethe's reception in England, or, rather, his reception in English literature. In this essay, I want to summarise my thoughts on the central problem of the response to Goethe in English literature. For many influential figures of the nineteenth century, Goethe formed an important, indeed, essential part of their literary culture: the German poet was simply a massive presence in the literature of England at this time. By contrast, in the twentieth century he is, if not an invisible presence in English literature, certainly no longer a dominant one, and no more celebrated than numerous other foreign classic authors. In order to analyse this curious historical circumstance, it will be necessary to sketch the stages of Goethe's reception, and at the same time suggest reasons for its particular shape and features. Simplification, perhaps tendentious simplification, seems unavoidable.

Matthew Arnold, one of Eliot's predecessors as a poet, who also had considerable influence as a critic, likewise proclaimed the centrality of Goethe in modern culture. According to Arnold's own testimony, Goethe was one of the major influences on Arnold's own work. Considering that he saw himself as one of Goethe's advocates in England, however, he had surprisingly little to say about the man in his published criticism. His most famous utterances are contained in the *Essays in Criticism* (1865). In the essay "Heinrich Heine," Arnold announces Heine as Goethe's successor in what he describes as the main current of Goethe's activity and significance for the present time. Arnold names Goethe as "a soldier in the war of liberation of humanity."[2] Goethe as liberator, then — but liberator from what? Arnold explains:

> Modern times find themselves with an immense system of institutions, established facts, accredited dogmas, customs, rules, which have come to them from times not modern. [. . .] yet they have a sense that this system is not of their own creation, that it by no means corresponds exactly with the wants of their actual life, that, for them, it is customary, not rational. The awakening of this sense is the awakening of the modern spirit [. . .] the sense of want of correspondence between the forms of modern Europe and its spirit, between the new wine of the eighteenth and nineteenth centuries, and the old bottles of the eleventh and twelfth centuries, everyone now perceives [. . .]. To remove this want of correspondence is beginning to be the settled endeavour of most persons of good sense. Dissolvents of the old European system of dominant ideas and facts we all must be [. . .] what we have to study is that we may not be acrid dissolvents of it.[3]

For Arnold, the great break in modern history is marked by the French Revolution, and while it was easy for him to depict Heine as the vehicle of the democratic modern spirit, one senses in reading Arnold's essay a certain discomfort or embarrassment that Goethe cannot be claimed as a democrat as well. Instead, Goethe is characterized as "that grand dissolvent in an age when there were fewer of them than at present," yet Arnold seems to be aware that the Goethe who was a minister in one of the thirty-odd German courts makes an odd candidate for a "dissolvent" of the old European order.

Nevertheless, the image of Goethe that Arnold offers here does not come from ignorance or some simple misunderstanding. The image of Goethe as "dissolvent" was not new. Indeed, Arnold's comments address, in part, a significant element in the reception of Goethe from the earliest time. Just as Shakespeare's reception in Germany was a political as much as an aesthetic phenomenon — because the example of Shakespearean genius was used to license the liberation of a generation of bourgeois writers from the dominance of a courtly culture where French neo-classical tastes set the tone — so Goethe's reception in England has an unexpected political dimension.[4] Goethe had become known in England first and foremost as the author of *Werther*, and it is not an exaggeration to say that at first the novel was better known than the author. Early discussion of the work followed the pattern established in France, which in turn echoed the controversy in Germany. On the surface, at least, there was no political dimension to this controversy. The reviews that greeted the novel in England tended to focus on one issue only, the supposed immorality of its attitude in apparent defence of suicide. The contemporary reviewer who complained of the "pernicious tendency" of the work and agreed "with those who consider Mr Goethe [. . .] as the apologist of suicide" was typical.[5] Goethe was from the first identified as a "dissolvent," then, and what he dissolved was "morality." This is important in two respects. First, it set the tone for the general reception of Goethe, who remained in English eyes a dangerous and immoral writer: this was an accusation that could be heard in various forms well into the nineteenth century. To an important degree, it was the focus of the entire critical reception of Goethe. Second, and more interestingly, the question of immorality is a screen for much more urgent anxieties concerning the source and location of moral authority in society. One can illustrate the quasi-political nature of aesthetic responses to *Werther* in England simply by asking who was enthusiastic about the novel and who was not.

The short answer is this: the same groups that either enthusiastically greeted the discovery of German theatre in the 1790s, that "loud trampling of the German Pegasus on the English stage," or deplored it.[6] In the 1790s, openness to German literature generally was tantamount to an admission of republican or Jacobin sympathies. The famous satirical spoofs attacking Goethe and the fashion for German theatre, which were published by the pro-government weekly *The Anti-Jacobin*, may not have shown much understanding of the German literary scene, but the magazine had a good nose for its political enemies closer to home. William Taylor, who was one of the earliest translators of Goethe and an enthusiastic if not especially perceptive critic, with his nonconformist provincial background — like Henry Crabb Robinson, a Norwich man — had republican sympathies, as did many of the first-generation Romantic poets. One thinks of Robert Southey, by his own admission going up to Oxford as a young student, his head full of Rousseau and Werther,[7] or the young Wordsworth and Coleridge and their response to Schiller's *Die Räuber*. By the time Wordsworth and Coleridge travelled to Germany in 1798, the early radicalism of the two poets had already begun to wane, and by different routes both of them found their way back, as did Southey, to religious and political orthodoxy, or at least something very close to it. In the course of time, both Southey and Wordsworth became Laureates and were thought of as representatives, even spokesmen, of a conservative establishment.

Naturally enough, the curious misunderstanding that equated Goethe and German literature with Jacobinism, and that was characteristic of the exaggerated insularity and nationalism fostered by the circumstance of war with Napoleonic France, gave way gradually to a more discriminating view. Important, naturally, was the alliance with Prussia in the defeat of the common enemy, but hardly less so was Mme. de Staël's *De l'Allemagne*, which even then was widely seen as having contributed significantly to this process. A reviewer of the book noted in 1813 that equating German literature with revolutionary politics was an error of the past,[8] but as late as 1820 Hazlitt was affirming, half flippantly as he acknowledges, the link between the German poets, Goethe and Schiller included, and "the only real school of Radical Reform." His comments on *Werther* are particularly telling, for they reveal that he read the novel not in terms of romantic agony or pathological sensibility, or the rights and wrongs of suicide, but rather as a work of social protest against an oppressive class system in Germany:

> Is it wonderful that the poets and philosophers of Germany, the discontented men of talent, who thought and mourned for themselves and their fellows, the Goethes, the Lessings, the Schillers, the Kotzebues, felt a sudden and irresistible impulse by a convulsive effort to tear aside this factitious drapery of society, and to throw off that load of bloated prejudice, of maddening pride and superannuated folly, that pressed down every energy of their nature and stifled the breath of liberty, of truth and genius in their bosoms?[9]

Not that Werther was any longer the issue. Mme. de Staël had brought *Faust* to the notice of the English reading public, and before long, in 1820, the first of a string of translations of Part I appeared. This had the effect of rekindling the controversy over Goethe's moral character and the irreligious tendency of his work. As in Germany, the "Prolog im Himmel" excited particular indignation, and it was not only the first translator who omitted this scene out of considerations of propriety. The kind of anxiety that Goethe aroused is typified by the reactions of the first-generation Romantic poets. Coleridge was the expert Germanist among them, but even his attitude to Goethe was at best deeply ambivalent.[10] In conversation with Crabb Robinson, we find him urging the supposed immorality of Goethe as proof that he was not a good poet,[11] but in the same year to the same man "he acknowledged the genius of Goethe in a manner he never did before." However, Coleridge added, and it was a telling reservation, that Goethe "lacked religion."[12] Likewise, his comments on *Faust* vary so much between enthusiasm and hostility that it is difficult to ascertain what his real opinion was. What is certain, however, is that the failure of the projected translation to become a reality was a significant loss to English literature.

Ambivalent is hardly the word one would apply to Wordsworth's attitude. His comments on Goethe arc as virulent and unpleasant as any that one encounters in the nineteenth century, and they are not mitigated by his admitted ignorance of Goethe's writings. One notices that the issue is again the question of morality:

> [. . .] there is a profligacy, an inhuman sensuality, in his works which is utterly revolting. I am not intimately acquainted with them generally. But I take up my ground on the first canto of Wilhelm Meister; and, as the attorney-general of human nature, I there indict him for wantonly outraging the sympathies of humanity.[13]

These are late comments, dating from a time when Wordsworth was firmly back within the fold of the established church. Extreme as this response to *Wilhem Meister* was, it was not at all exceptional. Carlyle's translation of the *Lehrjahre* (and Wordsworth knew the work only in translation) had received a savaging at the hands of Thomas De Quincey in 1824 in a review that is a model of sneering arrogance and incomprehension.[14] The novel, surprisingly, did not succeed in shaking off its reputation as an immoral work until considerably later in the century.

The contrast with Goethe's reception by the second generation of Romantic poets is startling. Both Byron and Shelley were outcasts from English society, in rebellion against the political and moral order of their homeland. Their political outlook, especially Shelley's, was more congenial to Brecht (who admired his "brother" Shelley's *Masque of Anarchy* greatly[15]) than it would have been to Goethe. Yet their enthusiasm for *Faust* was, at this point in time, as politically significant as the enthusiasm for *Werther* and *Die Räuber* had been for the generation of 1790. This generation, which included Wordsworth and Southey, was now the enemy. Shelley's translation of the scenes that caused offence to English readers (and that were omitted from the first translations) was in its way a political statement.[16] The journal in which they were published reinforces the impression, for they appeared in Leigh Hunt's *The Liberal*. (The magazine, which was planned as a countervoice to the conservative *Quarterly Review*, survived for only two years.) Hunt was a journalist and would-be poet, who had been imprisoned for opinions that were considered seditious by the authorities, and it was in *The Liberal* that Byron published his hilarious *The Vision of Judgement*, a satire on Southey — now, as Poet Laureate, the visible representative of the literary and political establishment — which made ironic play of not repeating the offence of the "Prolog im Himmel" where the deity actually speaks.[17] Byron understood that *Faust* would be repugnant to the tastes of the general reading public in England. From his exile he remarked: "What would the Methodists at home say to Goethe's *Faust*?

His devil not only talks familiarly *of* Heaven, but very familiarly *in* Heaven! What would they think of the colloquies of Mephistopheles and his pupil, or the more daring language of the prologue, which no one will ever venture to translate?"[18] He was wrong, of course. In the light of Byron's almost nonexistent German, it is easy to smile ironically at his extravagant dedications to Goethe, but one should not forget that this chapter represents the first, and perhaps only occasion, when Goethe as poet exercised a significant influence on the greatest poets, as poets. As far as I know, Keats died without ever reading a word of Goethe, but one thing is certain. If he had lived, his closeness to Hunt, Shelley, and this circle would have made the name of Goethe as familiar to him as that of Dante. It seems certain to me that the history of Goethe's reception in England would have been different but for the early deaths of these second-generation Romantic poets.

W. B. Yeats, who declared himself among the last Romantics, chose as an epigraph to a 1914 collection of verse an enigmatic quotation from an old play: "In dreams begins responsibility." I take this to be a late formulation of the Romantic intuition that the educated imagination is the foundation of the moral self. The logic of this is that masters of imagination, the poets, are in Shelley's famous words "the unacknowledged legislators of mankind." It is useful to bear this in mind when considering the case of Carlyle. One is tempted to think of him as a somewhat dour Victorian, but he was in fact born in the same year as Keats. His series of essays on Goethe is generally credited with having transformed English opinion of Goethe, and having opened the way to Goethe's pre-eminence in the literature of mid-Victorian England. But it is doubtful whether these essays would have made the lasting impression they did, had Carlyle not achieved prominence independently with *Sartor Resartus* and *On Heroes, Hero-Worship and the Heroic in History*. It was this success that justified the republication of the fugitive magazine pieces on Goethe in his *Critical and Miscellaneous Essays*. The tenor of Carlyle's "agitprop" on Goethe's behalf was determined by the need to counter his reputation as irreligious and dangerously immoral. Hence his insistence that the opposite is true. A key feature of his representation of Goethe is the emphasis laid on the German poet's status among his own people: Goethe is depicted as a kind of intellectual authority transformed by personal suffering into a kind of spiritual authority as well.

> A man who, in early life, rising almost at a single bound into the highest reputation over all Europe; by gradual advances, fixing himself more and more firmly in the reverence of his countrymen, ascends silently through many vicissitudes to the supreme intellectual place

among them; and [. . .] still reigns, full of years and honours, with a soft undisputed sway; still labouring in his vocation, still forwarding, as with kingly benignity, whatever can profit the culture of his nation.[19]

Not so much a *Dichterfürst* as a *Dichterkönig* in this portrayal. Crucial, too, is the fact that Carlyle's advocacy of Goethe in *Sartor Resartus* and *On Heroes* occurred in a context where Carlyle was setting out his own solution to the crisis of faith. Christianity is untenable, he affirms, but religious belief is still both necessary and possible: Carlyle is one of its prophets. In essence, the new credo is that of the response to Gretchen in Faust's speech "Wer darf ihn nennen?/Und wer bekennen." It may not be possible, as Faust implies, to attach a name to God or confess faith in him in the traditional ways, but for Carlyle the divine order is visible in nature — the living garment of God — and the divine plan revealed in human history. There is no need for Holy Writ, and the great poets, now acknowledged as the legislators of mankind, stand in for the saints and prophets of old:

> But is there no religion? [. . .] Fool I tell thee there is. Hast thou well considered all that lies in this immeasurable froth-ocean we name LITERATURE? Fragments of a genuine Church-Homiletic lie scattered there, which Time will assort: nay fractions even of a Liturgy could I point out. And knowest thou no Prophet [. . .] to whom the Godlike has revealed itself [. . .]? Knowest thou none such? I know him and name him — Goethe.[20]

So Goethe's role in Carlyle's own spiritual development is that of redeemer, and Carlyle makes Goethe into the embodiment of intellectual greatness and wisdom: in so doing he creates the dominant icon of the mid- to late nineteenth century — Goethe as teacher and sage.

The 1840s marked Carlyle's greatest impact, and the influence of his writing was attested by George Eliot in 1855, the year of Lewes's pioneering biography.[21] It is no coincidence that the mid-nineteenth century is also the high-water mark of Goethe's reputation in England. Carlyle had made it virtually impossible for any serious writer or intellectual to be unaware of Goethe, and we have the testimony of many central figures of the age — figures like John Stuart Mill, George Henry Lewes, George Eliot, Matthew Arnold, and Walter Pater — that it was Carlyle who made Goethe's name known. He did more than make it known; he set the pattern for the reception of Goethe, and for many he had succeeded in making Goethe into a figure of spiritual and intellectual authority, so that response to Goethe was a litmus test of where writers stood in relation to the crisis of faith and the problem of religion. The above roll call tells its own story. The German poet was no figure of authority for those who retained their links with orthodoxy; but for liberal freethinkers and agnostics, the figure of Goethe was a reassuring example of the possibility of a successful transcendence of Christianity.

In common with most other liberal intellectuals, Matthew Arnold eventually became disillusioned with Carlyle and dismissive of him, especially of his writings on Goethe,[22] but in ways he may not have cared to acknowledge he was Carlyle's inheritor. True, Arnold's tone as a critic is more measured and urbane than Carlyle's hectoring, but if one ignores this difference there is much in common: Arnold's Goethe was also primarily the sage rather than the poet and was valued by him chiefly for his intellectual pre-eminence, even though he believed it had been harmful to Goethe as a poet.[23] In another respect, too, Arnold was indebted. Like Carlyle, he was concerned to find a new ground for social and moral authority now that the props of religious faith were giving way. Arnold's ground was culture, in his definition "the best that has been thought and known," into which the Bible, but only as literature, and Goethe are subsumed. "The strongest part of our religion today is its unconscious poetry," he writes, and predicts that as time goes on poetry will assume ever greater importance.[24] From Arnold, who emphasises Goethe's "Hellenism" — what Goethe liberates us from is the narrowness of Philistinism — it is only a short step to the image of Goethe cherished by Walter Pater and the Aesthetic Movement. Pater seems to have been the last of the major nineteenth-century figures for whom Goethe played a significant part in their intellectual development.[25] It is the serene Goethe, the apostle of Hellenic paganism, who is referred to in Yeats, and Oscar Wilde, who had every need of serenity in Reading Gaol where he studied German, also asked for a copy of *Faust* to be sent to him.[26]

The twentieth century, Eliot remarked in 1920, is still the nineteenth.[27] With respect to Goethe's reputation in England, this is less than half true. It is difficult to find a convincing explanation of why Goethe suddenly relinquished the position of esteem that he'd enjoyed in the nineteenth century, but that he did so seems undeniable. Perhaps once again the international climate of growing Anglo-German rivalry played a part here: certainly, the repatriation of Shakespeare from the hegemony of German criticism occurred under this aegis.[28] But even with writers whose literary culture was broadly European and who were far removed from any taint of jingoism, this loss of esteem was the case. D. H. Lawrence and James Joyce make interesting test cases of the new attitude. Both had a command of German, and as exiles fleeing a suffocating cultural situation and sexual scandal respectively, and seeking to exchange a narrow provincialism for the greater freedom of continental Europe, they could almost pass for revenants of Byron and Shelley:

even Stephen Daedalus's declared intention "to forge in the smithy of my soul the uncreated conscience of my race" reads like a variant of the Romantic claims for the imagination. But what does one find? Joyce is obviously familiar with Goethe's work, but refers to him as "a boring civil-servant,"[29] while Lawrence praises De Quincey for his attack on Goethe, and in a letter to Aldous Huxley we find him complaining, hard though it may be to believe, about the immorality of *Wilhelm Meister*. If the novel was too sensual for Wordsworth, for Lawrence it was not sensual enough. He objected to "the perversity of intellectualised sex" and, clearly ignorant of Goethe's great erotic poetry, complained that Goethe lacked "phallic consciousness."[30]

In the nineteenth century, the image of Goethe that had become established was that of Goethe as intellectual authority, a modern who had moved beyond Christianity while retaining a serious religious sensibility: Goethe the literary artist, the novelist, say, was of importance chiefly in relation to this icon, and Goethe the lyric poet hardly figured at all. It is no exaggeration to say that after *Faust I* and *Wilhelm Meister*, the most influential Goethe text of the nineteenth century was the Eckermann conversations.[31] What had clearly not occurred was that absorption of a classic's writing into the linguistic culture of the receiving nation, such as was the case with Shakespeare in Germany, and this must have something to do with the failure of Goethe's *translated* work to achieve classic status in its own right. Not that there was a shortage of translations of *Faust*, say. On the contrary, there was a plethora of versions, but there was no undisputedly great version by a Coleridge or a Shelley to naturalise the text in the corpus of English literature.

Nevertheless, a more subtle and perhaps more important factor may have been at work. The abrupt diminution in Goethe's prominence at the start of the twentieth century has to do, it seems, with the passing of that acute crisis of faith, which was both a characteristic of the individual development of many leading literary figures, as well as a characteristic of the intellectual and cultural climate generally.[32] Perhaps, then, it is not by chance that where faith remains an issue for a writer, there one can still find a reaction to Goethe. Paradoxically, in the twentieth century, the reaction to Goethe in English literature has principally been confined to poets, like Eliot, Auden, MacNeice, and Ted Hughes, for all of whom in varying degrees Goethe has been accessible in the original German. The Goethe to whom Auden responded, rather late in life, was the prose writer and sage rather than the poet, and the title of Eliot's essay, "Goethe as the Sage," which was my starting point, also seems to indicate some continuity with the nineteenth century.

The title might suggest that Eliot was merely repeating one of the tired clichés of the previous century, but this would be unfair. One of the interesting features of the essay is Eliot's struggle to reach a just and generous appraisal of a writer, towards whom he confesses a feeling of antipathy. Whatever one thinks of the essay, the appraisal is generous; but the antipathy, if the private comments of letters are set against the public statement, was stronger than he confesses.[33] Naturally, in a public tribute, Eliot does not dwell on antipathy, but he does indicate its roots, and these are relevant: "For anyone like myself, who combines a Catholic cast of mind, a Calvinistic heritage, and a Puritanical temperament, Goethe does indeed present some obstacles to be surmounted."[34] There is more than a faint allusion here to the religious controversies of the previous century, and Eliot could be severe on the agnostics Arnold and Pater, who embraced the secularising "modern spirit" too readily, rather than resisting it like his admired Cardinal Newman. For the poet of *The Waste Land*, any attempt to locate spiritual authority in the cultural products of a fallen humanity must be inherently flawed. Indeed, at the bottom of Eliot's quarrel with Goethe lies a fundamental difference of religious vision. His comparison of Goethe with Wordsworth shows this most clearly: both men, according to Eliot, had experienced something in nature which, he tells us, he had not experienced, and this we must surmise was God or the Divine.

It was Thomas Carlyle who remarked that "no hammer in the Horologe of Time peals through the universe when there is a change from Era to Era." The implications of such a change from era to era are the subject of Ted Hughes's centenary tribute to Eliot. Hughes interprets Eliot's Christian vision as a response to a crisis that was historical as much as personal. Hughes himself did not share that vision, but he did share Eliot's sense of what was at stake. The change in question is that long process of secularisation, which most would date from the Enlightenment, but in Hughes's description that process was somehow completed with extraordinary rapidity and finality at the beginning of the twentieth century, as if the First World War were a physical symbol of the shock waves emanating from Darwin and Nietzsche. The triumph of secular materialism resulted in, or is synonymous with, a quite radical desacralisation in which "the whole metaphysical universe centred on God had vanished from its place."[35] Hughes has to be mentioned here as a rare example of a great poet whose literary culture is very broad, not exclusively European, and includes Goethe. One can infer this from the scattered references to Goethe in Hughes's critical writings. These do not add up to a *Bild* of Goethe, nor do they suggest that Goethe was a creative influence in the way that Dante was to Eliot.

But what Hughes writes about Goethe and religious experience in the centenary essay allows us an insight into the possible significance of Goethe for a post-Christian poet like Hughes, whom it would be fair to call a nature poet and a religious poet.

For Hughes, the dreadful reality of what he thinks of as a radically desacralised world is inescapable. But then Hughes moderates his proposition by arguing that this world had not been destroyed but re-located, "interiorised," and he identifies Goethe as one who understood the authority of the poetic self, the god within.[36] Though Hughes does not articulate this, Goethe's relevance to a nature poet such as Hughes lies in part in the central role that science played in Goethe's work as poet. This was something that was also recognised by Eliot, who felt drawn to Goethe's science precisely in proportion to the rejection that it had met with among modern scientists. To Hughes, science is no more the enemy of poetry than it was to Goethe. Not that Hughes practised scientific research in the way Goethe attempted, but his poetry draws repeatedly on the sciences as a source of metaphor. Perhaps the most important model for Hughes's effort to respiritualise the desacralised universe of modern physics and biology was, surprisingly, the occult Neo-Platonism of the sixteenth and seventeenth century, and it appears from Hughes's references to Goethe that he interprets Goethe's activity as a scientist at least partly in this context.[37]

I began this attempt at an overview with a reference to what I called the unexpected political dimension of Goethe's reception in English literature. One can see now, I hope, that the word "political" is inadequate, because the issue that has been predominant in Goethe's reception transcends the narrow scope it suggests. Goethe has interested English writers chiefly in relation to the overriding issue of secularisation and its consequences. The nineteenth-century attempt, in a variety of forms, to relocate spiritual authority in human culture will at the end of the twentieth century seem to many untenable, to others as, in some form or other, still an inescapable necessity. This overview suggests, however, that the abrupt displacement of Goethe from his position close to the centre of English literary consciousness, which took place at the beginning of the twentieth century, was a direct consequence of the fact that the religious crisis experienced so acutely by many nineteenth-century writers in England simply ceased to be an issue of overriding importance. For those poets for whom that crisis and its consequences were still a live issue, however – Yeats, Eliot, the later Auden, and Ted Hughes – the relevance of Goethe, and his controversial status, has remained undiminished.

This overview cannot offer any perspective on the future of Goethe's position in English literature. At the outset of this essay, Dante was mentioned, and it is worth recalling that the Italian classic was largely unknown in England until the beginning of the nineteenth century when he was "discovered" by the Romantics. Since then, he has been a pervasive presence in English poetry. This signals to us that Goethe's relative obscurity in the context of English poetry is not necessarily a permanent one. Certainly, an English rediscovery of Goethe is long overdue.

Notes

[1] T. S. Eliot, *On Poetry and Poets* (London: Faber, 1957), 213.

[2] *The Complete Prose Works of Matthew Arnold*, ed. R. H. Super (Michigan: Ann Arbor, 1962), 3, 108.

[3] *Complete Prose Works*, 3, 109–10.

[4] For some interesting remarks on this and the political dimension of the rise of bardolatry in eighteenth-century England, see Jonathan Bate, *The Genius of Shakespeare* (London: Picador, 1997), 165–84.

[5] *The Critical Review*, 47 (1779): 477.

[6] The phrase is Hazlitt's, who testified to the huge impression made on him in his youth by Schiller's *Die Räuber*. See "On the Spirit of Ancient and Modern Literature — On the German Drama, contrasted with that of the Age of Elizabeth," in *Collected Works*, ed. A. R. Waller and Arnold Glover, vol. 5 (London: J. M. Dent, 1902), 359–62.

[7] See Richard Holmes, *Coleridge: Early Visions* (Harmondsworth: Penguin, 1989), 62.

[8] *Edinburgh Review*, 22 (1813): 201. The reviewer was James Mackintosh.

[9] "On the Spirit of Ancient and Modern Literature — On the German Drama, contrasted with that of the Age of Elizabeth," in *Collected Works*, vol. 5, 362.

[10] For a detailed treatment of Coleridge's relationship to Goethe and German literature, see Rosemary Ashton, *The German Idea: Four English Writers and the Reception of German Thought 1800–1860* (Cambridge: UP, 1980), 27–66.

[11] See *Diaries, Reminiscences, and Correspondence of Henry Crabb Robinson*, ed. T. Sadler, vol. 1 (London: Macmillan, 1869), 388.

[12] See *Henry Crabb Robinson on Books and their Writers*, ed. E. J. Morley, vol. 1 (London: Dent, 1938), 107.

[13] See *Wordsworth's Literary Criticism*, ed. Nowell C. Smith (London: Henry Frowde, 1905), 260.

[14] See Thomas De Quincey, "Goethe as reflected in his novel of Wilhelm Meister," in *Collected Works*, ed. David Masson, vol. 12 (Edinburgh: A. & C. Black, 1897), 222–58.

[15] Brecht's poem "Der anachronistische Zug oder Freiheit und Demokratie" is clearly inspired by and modelled on Shelley's work. See Bertolt Brecht, *Gesammelte Werke*, ed. Elisabeth Hauptmann and Rosemarie Hill, 10 (Frankfurt a. M.: Suhrkamp, 1967), 943–9.

[16] Shelley's relationship to Goethe and his translation of scenes from *Faust* are ably discussed in Timothy Webb, *The Violet in the Crucible: Shelley and Translation* (Oxford: Clarendon Press, 1976), 141–203.

[17] Both Byron's preface to the poem and stanza 33 in particular seem to make indirect allusion to the "Prolog im Himmel."

[18] See Thomas Medwin's *Conversations of Lord Byron*, ed. Ernest J. Lovell, Jr. (Princeton, NJ: Princeton UP, 1966), 130. On the subject of the early translations of *Faust*, see William F. Hauhart, *The Reception of Goethe's Faust in England in the First Half of the Nineteenth Century* (New York: Columbia U P, 1909).

[19] "Goethe" (1828), in *Critical and Miscellaneous Essays*, 2nd ed., 1 (London: Chapman and Hall, 1842), 251.

[20] *Sartor Resartus* and *On Heroes, Hero-Worship and the Heroic in History* (London: Dent, 1964), 190.

[21] "For there is hardly a superior or active mind of this generation that has not been modified by Carlyle's writings; there has hardly been an English book written for the last ten or twelve years that would not have been different if Carlyle had not lived." See "Thomas Carlyle," in *Essays of George Eliot*, ed. Thomas Pinney (London: Routledge and Kegan Paul, 1963), 213–14. Lewes's *Life of Goethe*, as its generous dedication to Carlyle indicates, was one such book. For the background to Lewes's biography, see Ashton, *The German Idea*, 131–46.

[22] See *The Letters of Matthew Arnold 1848–88*, ed. G. W. E. Russell, vol. 2 (London: Macmillan, 1895), 144. For a full treatment of Goethe's influence on Arnold, see James Simpson, *Matthew Arnold and Goethe* (Cambridge: Modern Humanities Research Association, 1979).

[23] See, for example, *The Letters of Matthew Arnold*, ed. C. Y. Lang, vol. 2 (also vols. 3, 4) (Charlottesville and London: UP of Virginia, 1996–), 43, 339.

[24] See "The Study of Poetry," *Complete Prose Works*, vol. 9, 161.

[25] Pater's relation to Goethe is explored in some detail by David J. DeLaura, *Hebrew and Hellene in Victorian England: Newman, Arnold and Pater* (Austin and London: U of Texas P, 1969), 207–222.

[26] See *The Letters of Oscar Wilde*, ed. Rupert Hart-Davis (London: Hart-Davis, 1962), 416–17.

[27] See the essay "Dryden," in *Selected Essays*, 3rd ed. (London: Faber, 1951), 305.

[28] See Bate, *The Genius of Shakespeare*, 191–200.

[29] See Richard Ellmann, *James Joyce* (New York: Oxford UP, 1959), 406.

[30] See *The Letters of D. H. Lawrence*, ed. J. T. Boulton et. al. (Cambridge: UP, 1979–93), 407 (vol. 3), 342 (vol. 4).

[31] The enthusiasm of George Gissing was typical. See letter of 24 April 1881, in *Letters of George Gissing*, ed. A. and E. Gissing (London: Constable, 1927), 96.

[32] Against this, of course, is the fact that Joyce's *Portrait of the Artist as a Young Man* does record precisely an acute crisis of faith. The difference may be that for Joyce's Stephen the crisis occurs within the context of an adolescent sexual development and is primarily moral and aesthetic. The contrast, say, with the religious crisis described by Edmund Gosse in *Father and Son* is instructive.

[33] Cf. Peter Ackroyd, *T. S. Eliot* (London: Hamilton, 1984), 316.

[34] "Goethe as the Sage," *On Poetry and Poets*, 209.

[35] Ted Hughes, "The Poetic Self: A Centenary Tribute to T. S. Eliot," in *Winter Pollen* (London: Faber, 1995), 268–92 (particularly 269–73).

[36] See "The Poetic Self," in *Winter Pollen*, 269–76.

[37] See, for example, Ted Hughes, *Shakespeare and the Goddess of Complete Being* (London: Faber, 1992), 31.

Goethe's Orientalism

David Bell

THE ENGLISH-SPEAKING WORLD was an alien world for Goethe — more so, perhaps, than is at first sight apparent. Much of his literary life was spent appropriating alien worlds, however, and if Shakespeare was one of the first great "others" in his life, he was certainly not the last. Goethe's most explicit discussion of literary and cultural difference is to be found in the *Noten und Abhandlungen zu besserem Verständnis des West-östlichen Divans*. The *Noten und Abhandlungen*, and the *Divan* itself, owe a great deal to the pioneering work of the British Orientalist Sir William Jones. In recent years, though, Anglo-American literary criticism has become sceptical of the purportedly academic and cultural movement of "Orientalism" and has sought to uncover its hidden political agenda. My contention, in this paper, is that Goethe's Orientalism is untouched by this Anglo-Saxon critique; indeed, as far as Goethe is concerned, the critique itself is evidence of the continuing difficulty the English-speaking world experiences in understanding Goethe's "otherness."

The epigraph to Goethe's *Noten und Abhandlungen* is sufficiently well-known for it to be cited out of context, as if it were a statement claiming general validity:

> Wer das Dichten will verstehen,
> Muß ins Land der Dichtung gehen;
> Wer den Dichter will verstehen,
> Muß in Dichters Lande gehen. (*HA* 2, 126)

Interpreted broadly, the suggestion is clear: to achieve understanding of the poet behind the poetry, we need to enter the country of that poet. Goethe, of course, had no firsthand experience of the East, of the land of Hafiz, Ferdusi or Nisami, whose work inspired him and whom he claims to empathise with. The journey to the East is, as has long been recognised, an imaginary one, where the poet wishes to be regarded "als ein Reisender [. . .], dem es zum Lobe gereicht, wenn er sich der frem-

den Landesart mit Neigung bequemt, deren Sprachgebrauch sich anzu-
eignen trachtet, Gesinnungen zu teilen, Sitten aufzunehmen versteht"
(2, 127).[1] Equally, if we interpret the verse more specifically in context,
applying the term "Dichter" to Goethe himself, then it becomes a kind
of justification for the inclusion of the *Noten und Abhandlungen*: the
reader is referred first to the poetic world created in the poetry, but to
understand the poet, he must enter "his" country, which he seeks to
present in the essay and which indeed he adopts ambiguously as his own
in the poetry by taking on the guise of Hatem, combining this with the
role of traveller. In both cases, therefore, we are dealing with an imagined country, not a real country that has been experienced at first hand.
A question then poses itself at this juncture: Are we dealing here with
that kind of "Orientalism" that consists of an invented Orient, one that
imposes a vision that tells us more about Western culture than Eastern?
Neither the *Divan* nor the *Noten und Abhandlungen* mean to present
an objective representation of the Orient as it "really" is or was; the title, after all, indicates that it is "west-östlich." Still, the work as a whole
is certainly a "representation" in that it presents a constellation of images and ideas said to be oriental, with which the poet engages and in
conjunction with which his own poetry arises.

The idea that in the work of European Orientalists since the eighteenth century, the Orient is "represented," indeed fabricated, is central
to the landmark study Orientalism by Edward Said, first published in
1978, where he cites Marx's *Eighteenth Brumaire of Louis Bonaparte*,
"sie können sich nicht vertreten, sie müssen vertreten werden."[2] Not
surprisingly, Goethe and his contemporaries can refer to the "Orient"
in an apparently unproblematic way, and colleagues with whom Goethe
discussed his plans relating to the *Divan* can comment with apparent
neutrality about his "Orientalism": Sulpiz Boisserée, for example, notes
that Goethe's *Divan* represents "Aneignung des Orientalismus" and
continues with reference to the *Noten und Abhandlungen*, "Er las mir
eine sinnreiche Introduction, eine Exposition des ganzen Orientalismus
und seines eigenen Verhaltens dazu vor."[3] Here, nothing more is intended than to indicate Goethe's attempt to familiarise himself with the
Orient and to present it to the readers of his poems, so that the poetry
of both East and West, and in particular this special "west-östlich" poetry, will be better understood.

In this post-colonial age, however, it is not surprising that the nature of this approach to the Orient should be subject to stringent criticism in the light of cultural theory. One of the most fundamental
characteristics of Orientalism in its more general sense is identified by

Said as an acknowledgement of the fundamental *difference* between East and West:

> Orientalism is a style of thought based upon an ontological and epistemological distinction made between "the Orient" and (most of the time) "the Occident." (2)

At the root of this style of thought is a relationship of power. Orientalism is a means of coming to terms with the Orient, perceived as "the Other"; more than that, it is the imposition of a political vision predicated not only on the "otherness" and difference of the Orient, but also on the assumption of its cultural inferiority, thereby providing the justification for colonial and imperialist domination, for Western hegemony. It has been the function of Orientalism to tame and control the Orient through investigating it, categorising it, *knowing* it with such comprehensiveness that it becomes subject to Western control. As Said puts it, "Orientalism, which is the system of European or Western knowledge about the Orient, thus becomes synonymous with European domination of the Orient" (197). The Orient is, therefore, an entirely artificial construct, created in a process Said calls "Orientalizing the Orient,"[4] which is an instrument of political and cultural dominance, "a Western style for dominating, restructuring, and having authority over the Orient"(3). Its origins can be identified in the post-Enlightenment age and in its origins and its development is primarily a British and French "cultural enterprise," at least until the dominance of the USA since the Second World War. The men who laid the foundations for this discourse were men like Sir William Jones (1746–94) and Silvestre de Sacy (1758–1838), both of whom played a significant role in informing Goethe's understanding of the Orient and the preparation of the *Divan* and the *Noten und Abhandlungen*. In political terms the defining moment is Napoleon's occupation of Egypt in 1798–99, which despite its military failure can be seen as a paradigm of the process of political and cultural appropriation, encapsulated in the massive *Description de l'Égypte*, published in twenty-three volumes (1809–28), which was both *symbolic* of Western dominance in the way it reduced, classified and controlled the available knowledge about the contemporary Orient, and *instrumental* in providing a basis for the colonial dominance that was founded in this period, just as Jones's work provided a similar basis for the development of British rule in India.

This is clearly a simplification of Said's argument, but it raises interesting questions about the nature of Goethe's approach. This paper aims to consider Goethe's Orientalism in the light of these perspectives.

It will be helpful to turn to Said once again, where he recapitulates some of the key "dogmas" of Orientalism as he defines it:

> One [dogma] is the absolute and systematic difference between the West, which is rational, developed, humane, superior, and the Orient, which is aberrant, undeveloped, inferior. Another dogma is that abstractions about the Orient, particularly those based on texts representing a "classical" Oriental civilization, are always preferable to direct evidence drawn from modern Oriental realities. A third dogma is that the Orient is eternal, uniform, and incapable of defining itself; therefore it is assumed that a highly generalized and systematic vocabulary describing the Orient from a Western standpoint is inevitable and even scientifically "objective." A fourth dogma is that the Orient is at bottom something either to be feared (the Yellow Peril, the Mongol hordes, the brown dominions) or to be controlled (by pacification, research and development, outright occupation whenever possible). (300–301)

Based on these "dogmas," an essentialist view of the Orient is created, indeed the Orient itself is "Orientalised," that is, created in the image of these dogmas, conforming to the stereotypes and prejudices and providing the foundations for a self-justifying colonial will to power. Although Said concedes that the inauguration of a systematised discourse of Orientalism underpinning Western dominance of the Orient was really the work of a generation later than that of Jones and Goethe, it is nevertheless made plain in the case of Jones that his contribution was seminal:

> To rule and to learn, then to compare Orient and Occident: these were Jones's goals, which, with an irresistible impulse always to codify, to subdue the infinite variety of the Orient to "a complete digest" of laws, figures, customs, and works, he is believed to have achieved." (78)

Equally, though, Said concedes that he neglects the German dimension (18–19). Goethe is seen firmly as part of the phenomenon whereby the Orient is restructured, reflecting broad trends and prejudices as well as personal idiosyncrasies. He makes much of the fact, rightly, that Goethe's Orient in the *Divan* has no basis in direct experience of the "real" Orient, and this is seen as confirmation of the role played by "the literary crowd" (168) in exploiting the copious material made available by pioneers like Jones and Sacy. That Goethe participates in a discourse about the Orient in the sense taken over by Said from Foucault may well be the case, but the aim here is to examine more closely and critically the nature of that attitude and vision, expressed in the *Divan* and the *Noten*, and to question whether Said's approach can help us to understand the poet and his chosen world, despite all the illuminating and cogent insights that his essay throws on European culture.

It is not difficult to find evidence in the *Divan* and Goethe's explanatory apparatus to support the view that he is presenting a restructured version of the Orient determined not only by a Western perspective, but also by a projection from a remote and supposedly "classical" past. The opening poem of the *Divan*, "Hegire," is cited by Said (167–68) as evidence of this kind: "Flüchte du, im reinen Osten / Patriarchenluft zu kosten," and again, "Dort, im Reinen und im Rechten, / Will ich menschlichen Geschlechten / In des Ursprungs Tiefe dringen" (*HA* 2, 7). The Orient is, evidently, seen as a place of purity and refuge from the turmoil of the day. It invites us to return to our origins, where our thought and our language reflect a greater closeness to our divine source. Further, the poet envisages sweeping us off on a journey that seems to contain all the "Oriental" clichés one could wish for: shepherds and oases, caravans in the desert, shawls, coffee and musk, bandits cowering in the dark, bathhouses and taverns, love-songs, veiled lovers and houris. We are presented with something strange and exotic, unfamiliar and crucially, in Said's terms, fundamentally different or "other." This would seem to be borne out further in the following poem "Segenspfänder," which introduces the reader to what the poet takes to be strange and unfamiliar religious customs and artefacts: "Talisman," "Amulette," "Inschrift," "Abraxas," and "Siegelring." Indeed, the whole rationale of providing the *Noten und Abhandlungen* is to facilitate "besseres Verständnis" of something that is strange and different. We seem, then, to be witnessing here evidence of one of the axiomatic principles that underpin Orientalism: the assumption of a fundamental difference or otherness that must be explained and understood, and therefore tamed and brought under control, assimilated to a view of the Orient that is created by the Western perspective.

The motifs, images, landscapes, and cultural and religious references that inform the poems of the *Divan*, and which Goethe culled from his prodigious reading of Orientalists and their translations of Oriental poetry and other sources, are consistent with the tendency to view the Orient as exotic, mysterious, and pure: there is arguably a display in Goethe of what Said calls "Orientalizing the Orient." We are likely to find evidence for many of the key facets of Orientalism thus defined, not only in the poems, which do indeed "represent" an imagined, rather than a real world, but more importantly, perhaps, in the *Noten und Abhandlungen* — more importantly because they suggest how Goethe actually viewed the Orient, and how it relates to his poetry.

A casual reading of the *Noten* reveals that Goethe frequently speaks of the "Orient" and "Orientals" in a manner suggesting generalisation and stereotyping. We must remember, however, that Goethe's vision is derived from a reality transmitted through and refracted by translations of literary and religious sources going back many centuries: the most recent of the seven major poets commented on in the *Noten*, Dschami, died in 1494. Despite this massive range in time, however, the Orient is perceived as eternal and unchanging; Goethe refers to it as "unwandelbar" (*HA 2*, 168). This is reflected in poems such as "Unbegrenzt" and "Im Gegenwärtigen Vergangenes," and appears to be an example of what Said calls "synchronic essentialism" (240). While Goethe shows sensitivity to historical change, including the evolution of poetic forms and traditions, he attempts to make the Oriental world that informs the *Divan* accessible and intelligible by appealing to an essentialist vision of this kind: an Orient that encapsulates "Reinheit," the paradisiacal world familiar from the Old Testament,[5] a world that is both old and new, where heaven and earth seem closer together. These are familiar motifs in many of the poems.

We find other explanatory perspectives in the *Noten*, designed to facilitate the reader's understanding of the *Divan* itself. These perspectives rely on identifying and isolating the difficult, different or strange, viewing them as essentially *characteristic* and *typical*, but requiring explanation before they can be assimilated by the Western mind. Said, of course, sees a will to control as implicit in this discourse, which is then, in a period later than Goethe's, more explicitly translated into an instrument of colonial power. Such aspirations are not attributed to Goethe as such, but suggest that he perpetuates the image and is influential in transmitting it. Said, in fact, identifies Goethe as the source of Marx's "conceptions about the Orient," conceptions which see the role of England in India as bringing about a revolution through the destruction of the old "Oriental" order, part of a necessary process that inevitably involves human suffering. To suggest that from suffering may come regeneration, Marx quotes "An Suleika" from the "Buch des Timur" (Said 153–54). While we cannot blame Goethe for Marx's conceptions or misconceptions, it is true that the latter finds support when Goethe writes about "Oriental despotism," for instance. Goethe acknowledges that there will be difficulties for the Western reader of Oriental poetry when confronted with the unfamiliar, but the main problems do not come from their religion, fables, parables, or spirituality:

> Was aber dem Sinne der Westländer niemals eingehen kann, ist die geistige und körperliche Unterwürfigkeit unter seinen Herren und Oberen, die sich von uralten Zeiten herschreibt, indem Könige zuerst an die Stelle Gottes traten. (*HA 2*, 169)

Goethe, then, gives sustenance to the idea, exposed by Said as a part of the discourse of superiority, that the Orient lacks a true (i.e. Western) concept of freedom.

Goethe also apparently believes that the Oriental is essentially given to "Sinnlichkeit," when, for example, he suggests that poetry, "Diese Spiele einer leichtfertigen Einbildungskraft [. . .] waren der orientalischen Sinnlichkeit, einer weichen Ruhe und bequemem Müßiggang höchst angemessen" (*HA* 2, 145). This "Sinnlichkeit," however, is combined with a spirituality: "Der höchste Charakter orientalischer Dichtkunst ist, was wir Deutsche *Geist* nennen, das Vorwaltende des oberen Leitenden" (*HA* 2, 165), and this proximity of the earthly and the divine, "das Sinnliche" and "das Übersinnliche," are seen as constituting the characteristic mysticism of the East. Again we are confronted with examples of a superficial image projected on to the Orient, examples of that process of creating or "Orientalising" the Orient for the purpose of assimilating it to Western ways of thinking.

To argue this view, however, is to adopt a particular historical and cultural perspective that is not necessarily, or at least not exclusively, valid in the attempt to "understand the poet," and is certainly not adequate to describe the nature of Goethe's attitude, nor the role the Orient plays in his poetry. Far from finding a process that consists of "Orientalising the Orient," we discover that Goethe actually urges something very different on us when we are faced with the difficulty of responding to products of a different culture:

> Wollen wir an diesen Produktionen der herrlichsten Geister teilnehmen, so müssen wir uns orientalisieren, der Orient wird nicht zu uns herüberkommen. Und obgleich Übersetzungen höchst löblich sind, um uns anzulocken, einzuleiten, so ist doch aus allem Vorigen ersichtlich, daß in dieser Literatur die Sprache als Sprache die erste Rolle spielt. Wer möchte sich nicht mit diesen Schätzen an der Quelle bekannt machen! (*HA* 2, 181)

It was the same spirit that motivated Sir William Jones in his linguistic endeavours, although the aspirations to such linguistic knowledge voiced here by Goethe were destined to remain limited. The notion of "Orientalising ourselves" implies the possibility of a *real* understanding, based on a willingness to move one's position, which can have positive results without assuming a position of superiority, control, and domination. Goethe, like Jones, realised that what he was presenting was unfamiliar to his readers, hence the need to make it more intelligible by expanding our horizons in a new direction, and changing our (Western) assumptions by "Orientalising ourselves." Nevertheless, acknowledgement of cultural difference does not require the acceptance of *fundamental* or *ontological* difference, which Said maintains is at the root of Orientalism, and explains the need to *create* an Orient in order to subdue it. Goethe does not accept this ontological difference; on the contrary, the assumption of something common underlies the enterprise that he takes on in the *Divan*, otherwise the task of "Orientalising ourselves" would be futile. For Goethe there is no absolute difference or divide. We think, stereotypically, of East and West as distant poles; but Goethe suggests the truth is an underlying oneness:

> Bist du von deiner Geliebten getrennt
> Wie Orient vom Okzident,
> Das Herz durch alle Wüste rennt;
> Es gibt sich überall selbst das Geleit,
> Für Liebende ist Bagdad nicht weit. (*HA* 2, 75)

It is no surprise that the motif of lovers' separation and oneness, which is so predominant in the "Buch Suleika," should be used to make this suggestion about the relationship of East and West. Goethe's encounter with the East — through the poetry of Hafiz, and the myriad sources he devoured from the work of men like Jones, Diez, and Hammer — was primarily a personal encounter that has consequences for his poetry above all. It was never his goal, even in the *Noten und Abhandlungen*, to present the "real" Orient as if it were some objectively existing entity. The Orient of the *Divan* is principally derived from and mediated by literary sources; these are not objectively valid representations of some "Oriental" essence, but manifestations of cultural and literary diversity and achievement, which represent truths about human reality and spirituality, as do their Western counterparts. Intellectual and imaginative effort on Goethe's and the Westerner's part, and a willingness to put aside Western preconceptions, are required in order to appreciate it. This is what Goethe means by "Orientalising ourselves." It harks back to the relativism and "Einfühlung" advocated years before by Herder. The actual product of this "Einfühlung" in this instance is the poetry of the *Divan* itself, that hybrid "west-östlich" variety that is only possible because there is a perceived commonality and a shared vision that blurs the distinctions of East and West.

Goethe placed great value on the lines he adapted, indirectly, from the Koran in "Talismane":

> Gottes ist der Orient!
> Gottes ist der Okzident!
> Nord- und südliches Gelände
> Ruht im Frieden seiner Hände. (*HA* 2, 10)

He found Hammer's rendition of the Koranic verses (Sura 2, 115)[6] as a motto to the *Fundgruben des Orients* (1809–18) and twice incorporated his version on an ornamented design in his own hand that might well have served as a motto for the *Divan*.[7] Said interprets these verses (one of few specifically referred to) as evidence of Goethe finding in the Orient "completion and confirmation of everything one had imagined" (167). However, they seem to suggest the covalency and equal validity of all cultures, viewed as coexisting in the hands of God. The fact that these lines derive indirectly from the Koran, but are used by Goethe to speak to Western and Christian ears, is further evidence that he sees value in an approach that is predicated neither on an assumption of absolute difference, nor on a presumed relationship of superiority.

A brief example will illustrate this concept in Goethe's approach to the Orient. The example centres on the supposed "mysticism" of the East. The "mystical" and "spiritual" Orient is a familiar stereotype, frequently opposed to the "rational" West with its strong sense of the real. In the hands of Orientalists, the convenient dichotomy is used to create, to "Orientalise," the Orient so that it can be known and subdued. Orientalists have also debated whether certain kinds of Oriental poetry should be interpreted as mystical or as sensual-erotic. Goethe's response to this question appears to transcend the assumptions implicit in Said's theory, and set up new productive links between the poetry of East and West. Essentially, Goethe sees in the poetry of Hafiz and the Orient a close proximity between the earthly and the divine, that which is "sinnlich" and that which is "übersinnlich"; this lies behind the apparently mystical view that sees the presence of the divine in the earthly. Goethe's attention may have been drawn to this by Orientalists of the day, like Joseph von Hammer and J. G. L. Kosegarten.[8] In Kosegarten's review of the *Divan*, for example, which recognises Goethe's use and adaptation of these ways of seeing the world, he describes it as something fundamentally mystical:

> Bei den Moslemischen Völkern ist er [der Mystizismus] sehr stark hervorgetreten, sie nennen das dem sinnlichen Auge verborgene Grundseyn, *das wirkliche*, das von den Sinnen wahrgenommene aber *das bildliche*, anstatt daß wir es wohl umgekehrt zu machen pflegen, und z.B. die Sehnsucht nach dem Ewigen nur bildlicherweise Liebe nennen. Sie hingegen nennen das Gefühl für die göttliche Vollkommenheit [. . .] *amor verus*, die sinnliche Liebe aber [. . .] *amor metaphoricus*, letztere ist ihnen nur eine in der Sinnenwelt vorkommende Abspiegelung der ersteren.[9]

This may seem to support Said's argument, for the imposition of a Western "explanation" on something unfamiliar. However, in Goethe's hands it is entirely different. Goethe achieves his insight through empathy with Hafis and others, empathy related to an outlook that Goethe also shares. It is not about attaching labels, such as "mysticism," which Kosegarten cannot get away from. More recently, Annemarie Schimmel cut through this problem in appreciating Islamic mysticism, by showing that the arguments for both the "sensual-erotic" and the "mystical" are wide of the mark. Poets such as Hafiz create "new relations between worldly and otherworldly images, between religious and profane ideas; [. . .] and the tension between the worldly and the religious interpretation of life is resolved, in the poems of the outstanding masters of this art, in a perfect harmony of the spiritual, psychic, and sensual components."[10] This is the way in which Goethe reads Oriental poetry, and, perhaps more importantly, the way in which he emulates in the *Divan*. On Goethe's part, then, there is a great sense of kinship, a shared religious and poetic outlook, which causes him to regard himself as Hafiz's "twin" (*HA* 2, 23). There is no sense of division; no sense of superiority, cultural or otherwise; no agenda of control; and certainly none of the disdain, hostility, and fear that Said locates at the heart of Orientalism.

Thus, in Goethe's view, we see an underlying oneness without fundamental or ontological difference, and without the Orient existing in the mind of the West as some alien "other." However, this view seems to be at odds with the reality of an obvious difference in customs, religion, statecraft, and literary convention. It is no easy process to penetrate through the preconceptions and prejudices, for which there was plenty of fuel in the writings of early Orientalists and explorers, not to mention hostile Christians. The object of such a process is not to represent the "real" Orient; this is not possible anyway, since there is, in Goethe's view, no such essence to be represented. We need help, however, in confronting the superficial differences, if we are to reach awareness of the underlying unity. In the *Noten und Abhandlungen*, Goethe is at pains to give us this help. Our cultural taste will find certain ideas unpalatable, but this does not mean that the culture from which they spring is degenerate, fundamentally alien, or inferior. Such elements are the "Abraxas": talismans portraying (to Westerners) grotesque images:

> Doch *Abraxas* bring ich selten!
> Hier soll meist das Fratzenhafte,
> Das ein düstrer Wahnsinn schaffte,
> Für das Allerhöchste gelten.
> Sag' ich euch absurde Dinge,
> Denkt, daß ich Abraxas bringe. (*HA* 2, 9)

The last lines indicate a wider application than the context of the individual poem "Segenspfänder." Such elements may seem grotesque, but must not blind us or confuse us. Accepting them as part of the whole is a prerequisite for a meaningful interaction with this non-Western culture; they should not mislead us into thinking that the Orient is something fundamentally alien.

Said's arguments have provided us with one perspective from the English-speaking world (though his origins give him a unique position from which to comment). Now let's take a little further some of the comparisons previously made between Goethe and Sir William Jones, an authority from the English-speaking world whom he refers to in the *Noten* as one of his "teachers" (*HA* 2, 245–46). Jones was a colonial administrator and, while passionately interested in the languages and poetry of the East, especially India, he may legitimately be viewed as an instrument of that colonial power. This is the role assigned to him in Said's analysis. Indeed, on his journey out to India, in a list comprising twenty-six items containing, legal, political, historical, scientific, commercial, literary, and aesthetic subjects, Jones noted as one of the many "objects of enquiry" that he intended to pursue in India the "Best Mode of governing Bengal" and aspired to attain "*a complete knowledge of India.*"[11] Nevertheless, it is interesting to note that reassessments of his work at the recent bicentennial (1994) include the defence of Jones in the face of this critique of Orientalism.[12] He is said, for example, to have set out "to combat the insularity of European thought,"[13] to have argued "that Persian poetry could provide the needed counter to European staleness."[14] It is neither possible nor appropriate in this context to determine the validity of Said's criteria in relation to Jones, but a comparison with some aspects of Goethe's approach may be illuminating in relation to my argument about the nature of Goethe's "Orientalism."

Goethe shared Jones's enthusiasm and genuine love of Oriental poetry, and like Jones, believed it could have a rejuvenating effect on European poetry. Indeed, it may have contributed, along with a constellation of other factors, to rejuvenation in a personal sense with respect to Goethe and his creativity. Early on, in his "Essay on the Poetry of Eastern Nations" (1771), for example, Jones argues that "our European poetry has subsisted for too long on the perpetual repetition of the same images, and incessant allusions to the same fables," and that familiarity with other literary cultures would create "a more extensive insight into the history of the human mind."[15] This stands in contrast to Said's argument, which suggests that the Orientalist agenda, from Jones onwards, is based on the "idea of regenerating a fundamentally lifeless Asia" (154), that is, giving it life, creating it in order to control it. Goethe shares Jones's openness to new stimuli, but he differs in two important respects. First, he was not a colonial administrator or representative of a political authority, ruling over a foreign culture; and second, he responded to this new cultural material primarily as a poet. Both of these factors feed into the criticisms Goethe makes of Jones amid the praise and recognition in the *Noten und Abhandlungen*. In the chapter entitled, ominously, "Warnung," he reproves Jones for the extent to which he compares Oriental poets with the classics of Greece and Rome. He recognises the factors that led Jones down this route in the face of powerful classical prejudices in England, but goes on to point out the dangers and harmful aspects of such an approach:

> Er kannte, schätzte, liebte seinen Orient und wünschte dessen Produktionen in Altengland einzuführen, einzuschwärzen, welches nicht anders als unter dem Stempel des Altertums zu bewirken war. Dieses alles ist gegenwärtig ganz unnötig, ja schädlich. Wir wissen die Dichtart der Orientalen zu schätzen, wir gestehen ihnen die größten Vorzüge zu, aber man vergleiche sie mit sich selbst, man ehre sie in ihrem eignen Kreise, und vergesse doch dabei, daß es Griechen und Römer gegeben.[16]

We may well be reminded of Horace when reading Hafiz, of Homer when reading Ferdusi, but the unavoidable danger in such an approach, for all Jones's sincerity, is that by making the very comparison we are inadvertently adopting the European standard as the norm, resulting in worthless value judgements that will inevitably point to the *inferiority* of, say, Ferdusi, because Homer is set up as the ultimate standard against which all others are measured. In rejecting this approach, Goethe is actually moving closer to the goal that Jones, in a sense, also shared, but which, perhaps, he could not see so clearly – namely, an understanding of different cultures that is achieved without the presumption of a relationship of power or domination. It is a genuine cosmopolitanism and deserves, if anything does, the epithet "multicultural." The basis of Goethe's approach behind the fusion that is properly described as "west-östlich" is one that presupposes a fundamental bond between equals. Comparisons may be necessary to promote understanding, but those comparisons must never be reduced to relative value judgements and verdicts of inferiority and superiority. Such a view is, of course, central to Goethe's concept of "Weltliteratur," itself one of the clearest manifestations of Goethe's openness to multicultural perspectives. If we add to this the personal dimension, whereby the cultural openness leads to an enrichment of the creative process and an incremental step in individual growth ("Werden"), we must conclude that the notion of "Orientalism" as a mode of cultural and political discourse does not adequately enable us to understand the nature of

Goethe's Orientalism. We find there no trace of the condescension and disdain, even hatred and hostility, that Said identifies as an inherent feature of Orientalism as it developed from the late eighteenth century.

This does not invalidate Said's thesis regarding the use of knowledge about the Orient or the agenda in whose service it has been applied. Marx's recourse to Goethe as a source for his views on the Orient is not evidence that those views are supported in Goethe. It has been stressed throughout this essay that Goethe's *Divan* does not purport to represent the real Orient, and Said is wrong to state that the *Divan* is "set" in the Orient (157). It is ironic therefore, that in the end, the objectives of both Goethe and Said may be convergent.

Said writes passionately of his goal to combat "the Orient-versus-Occident opposition" and the need to straddle the "permanent divide that my book quite specifically abjures."[17] This paper has attempted to demonstrate that Goethe, too, seeks to overcome this divide. That is not to say he is entirely free of prejudices. How could he be at a time when knowledge of other cultures was so deficient? — arguably, it still is. Through the medium of the *West-östlicher Divan* and its apparatus, he does further the cause of "multiculturalism, rather than xenophobia and aggressive, race-oriented nationalism" (336), which Said aspires to. It has not been argued here that Goethe writes wholly counter to the emerging cultural discourse, so to speak; from our historical perspective, it can be seen as intimately related to a broader pattern. The case argued here, however, is that a proper reading of Goethe and the *Divan*, together with an accurate conception of his Orientalism, can contribute to overcoming an artificially constructed and fundamental divide, one which Goethe does not recognise any more than does Edward Said.

Notes

[1] See also Esin Ileri, *Goethes "West-östlicher Divan" als imaginäre Orient Reise* (Frankfurt: Lang, 1982).

[2] Edward W. Said, *Orientalism* (Reprint of 1978 edition with new Afterword, Harmondsworth: Penguin, 1995), 21.

[3] *GG* 2:312 (3 August 1815). Compare Goethe's comment in a letter to J. F. Cotta, 16 January 1816, referring to the proposed announcement of the *Divan*, "worin ich von meinem Orientalismus vorläufige Rechenschaft gebe," *WA* 4, 26, 216.

[4] Said, 5, 67, 87, 167.

[5] See "Alt-Testamentliches," *HA* 2, 206–7.

[6] "To Allah belongs the east and the west. Whichever way you turn there is the face of Allah." Quoted from *The Koran*, translated with notes by N. J. Dawood, 4th revised edition, (Harmondsworth: Penguin, 1974), 344.

[7] See Hans Albert Maier, ed., *Goethe. West-östlicher Divan. Kritische Ausgabe der Gedichte mit textgeschichtlichem Kommentar*, 2 vols. (Tübingen: Niemeyer, 1965), 2, 86–87.

[8] Johann Gottfried Ludwig Kosegarten (1792–1860) studied under Silvestre de Sacy and was appointed Professor of Oriental Studies in Jena in 1817. Goethe sought his advice and assistance regularly during his work on the Divan.

[9] J. G. L. Kosegarten, "Rezension von: West-östlicher Diwan. Von Goethe," *Allgemeine Literatur-Zeitung vom Jahre 1819*, in E. Lohner, ed., *Studien zum West-östlichen Divan Goethes*, Wege der Forschung, 287 (Darmstadt: Wissenschaftliche Buchgesellschaft, 1971), 173–89 (180).

[10] Annemarie Schimmel, *Mystical Dimensions of Islam* (Chapel Hill: U of North Carolina P, 1975), 288.

[11] See A. J. Arberry, *Oriental Essays: Portraits of Seven Scholars* (London: Allen & Unwin, 1960), 62, 70.

[12] *Objects of Enquiry: The Life, Contributions, and Influences of Sir William Jones (1746–1794)*, edited by Garland Cannon and Kevin R. Brine (New York & London: New York UP, 1995). See K. R. Brine, "Introduction," 1–19 (4); Garland Cannon, "Oriental Jones: Scholarship, Literature, Multiculturalism, and Humankind," 25–50 (48); David Kopf, "The Historiography of British Orientalism, 1772–1992," 141–60 (155).

[13] Brine (3), referring to the contribution by O. P. Kejariwal, "William Jones: The Copernicus of History," 102–15.

[14] Cannon, 30.

[15] Quoted in Kejariwal, 106.

[16] *HA* 2, 182–83. A similar criticism is raised in the section specifically on Jones in the chapter "Lehrer," *HA* 2, 245–46.

[17] Said, 336. See also 28, where he writes of his aspiration to "eliminate" the "Orient" and the "Occident" altogether.

What Gets Lost? A Look at Some Recent English Translations of Goethe

John R. Williams

I AM NOT going to talk here about translation theory or translation methodology, but I will begin by quoting a translation theorist I much admire — not least because he allows himself a degree of scepticism towards his own discipline. In 1982 Leif Ludwig Albertsen wrote:

> Im Laufe der letzten zwanzig Jahre [and we can add on nearly another twenty years by now] hat sich global eine strukturierte Übersetzungswissenschaft entwickelt, für die jede Übersetzung ein großes Problem bedeutet, an das nur mit einer elaborierten Strategie heranzutreten ist. In diesem Zusammenhang scheint das Übersetzen von Dichtung so überaus problematisch, daß die ohnedies schlecht bezahlten Übersetzer fast als leichtsinnige Toren dastehen, die unüberlegt eine Arbeit auf sich nehmen, ohne zu bedenken, daß diese Arbeit allenfalls auf ungenügende und vielleicht irreführende Weise auszuführen ist. . . . Manche Theoretiker möchten denn auch behaupten, daß die Übersetzung von Dichtung eigentlich nicht möglich sei.[1]

Albertsen goes on to remark that the study of literary translation has been taken over by linguists. Institutes for *Übersetzungswissenschaft* have grown up, periodicals have been founded — all of which ought by now to have brought the art, or craft, or skill of literary translation to a peak of perfection — "vorausgesetzt," as Albertsen wisely adds, "diese Linguisten verstehen etwas von der Kunst und haben recht" (9).

We are constantly reminded that the translation of poetry is impossible in principle; yet the sheer number of relatively successful translations of Goethe into English over the last thirty years or so defies that principle. To give a brief and certainly incomplete survey,[2] we have had the Boston/Suhrkamp and Princeton edition of the *Collected Works* in twelve volumes by various authors; Walter Arndt's translation of both parts of *Faust*; Barker Fairley's prose version of *Faust*, which has recently been revived in Nicholas Boyle's Everyman edition; John Prudhoe's *Faust Part One* (and his *Iphigenie* and *Tasso*); Stuart Atkins's

Faust; David Luke's *Faust*; Martin Greenberg's *Faust*; and Philip Wayne's Penguin translation of *Faust*, which is (astonishingly) still in print. We have had Robert David MacDonald's heavily adapted *Faust* for the Glasgow Citizens' Theatre and the Lyric Hammersmith, and Howard Brenton's truly awful translation for the Swan Theatre, Stratford-upon-Avon. (The stage performance, in spite of the translation, was exhilarating). Dan Farrelly's *Urfaust* was published in 1998, and my own translation of Part One, the *Urfaust* and the Walpurgisnacht scenarios appeared in 1999. We have had *Die Wahlverwandtschaften* by H. M. Waidson, by Mayer and Bogan, by R. J. Hollingdale, by Judith Ryan, and most recently by David Constantine; *Werther* by Mayer and Bogan and by Michael Hulse; Waidson's translation of the *Wilhelm Meister* novels, John Russell's translation of the *Theatralische Sendung*, and a re-issue of Carlyle's *Wanderjahre*; Francis Lamport's *Egmont*, John Arden's quirky *Götz von Berlichingen* ("Ironhand"), David Luke's *Iphigenie*, and Alan Brownjohn's *Tasso*. In the poetry, we have had David Luke's translation of the *Roman Elegies*, "The Diary," and a further selection of Goethe's *Erotic Poems*; Michael Hamburger's *Roman Elegies* and other poems; John Whaley's *Selected Poems* was published in 1998, as was the revised edition of his 1974 *West-östlicher Divan*; and David Luke's *Selected Poetry*, which appeared in 1999. We have had Elisabeth Stopp's *Maxims and Reflections*; D. J. Enright's *Sayings of Goethe*; W. H. Auden and Elizabeth Mayer's *Italian Journey*; T. J. Reed's translation of the Italian Diary for Frau von Stein; and all kinds of selections from the conversations and the writings on science, art, and literature. Jim Reed has also edited a selection of poems in translation for the Gregynog Press, which appeared in 2000. Just how many translations of *Faust* there have been into English, I do not know. I would hazard a guess that we are not far off the hundred mark; we shall have a clearer picture when Derek Glass publishes his comprehensive bibliography of twentieth-century English translations of Goethe for the English Goethe Society.

Hence, there is no lack of brave or foolhardy attempts to perform the theoretically impossible and translate Goethe's poetry (or his prose) into English. As any translator would readily agree, there is no such thing as a perfectly adequate or "Platonic" translation of poetic language from one language or culture into another, and any number of metaphors and analogies have been thought up to describe this flawed process: squaring the circle; dancing in chains; poetry is what gets lost in translation; *traduttore — traditore*.

The Anglophone translator of Goethe's verse is perhaps in a particularly fortunate position because of the close affinity between English and German in stress patterns, and hence in metrical constructions. Take this simple (but carefully chosen) example: when Marcellus in *Hamlet* (act 1, scene 4) says "Something is rotten in the state of Denmark," Schlegel's translation loses very little in terms of metre: "Etwas ist faul im Staate Dänemarks." Even the trochaic inversion in the first four syllables is reproduced in the German; the only difference I can detect is that Schlegel's line is decasyllabic (or catalectic), where Shakespeare's is hendecasyllabic. To be sure, something is lost — in this case, semantically; the pun on "state" as *Staat* or *Zustand* is not immediately obvious in German (though most educated Germans will recognize it anyway because they know the original). This is not to say, of course, that Schlegel's Romantic rhetoric is not fundamentally different from Shakespeare's Baroque rhetoric.

The affinity of stress between English and German, however, means that the Anglophone translator finds him or herself virtually obliged to translate German verse into its approximate metrical equivalent — simply because it is possible to do so. The translator is deprived of the freedom, even the fun, that translators into Romance, Slavonic, or Asiatic languages might have in choosing their own *sprachspezifisch* equivalents to Goethe's poetic wizardry. To take the example of *Faust*, that "metrical pandemonium," as Christian Wagenknecht nicely describes it,[3] every metrical and strophic form has a fairly satisfactory English equivalent: *ottava rima, Knittelvers, Madrigalvers*, adonics, amphibrachs, dactylic verse (even Andreas Heusler's so-called "false dactyls"),[4] folksong strophes, blank verse, "Spanish" trochees, *terza rima*, the neo-classical forms of iambic trimeter, trochaic tetrameter, choric odes. Whatever metrical challenges Goethe presents in both parts of *Faust* can be rendered more or less satisfactorily into English; even the alexandrine, used parodically and satirically in the fourth act of Part Two, can be made to sound as pompous and stilted in English as Goethe makes it sound in German.

Every translator of Goethe's verse into English is confronted with the terrible problem of rhyme. To rhyme or not to rhyme is an agonizing choice either way: you're damned if you do, you're damned if you don't. The fact that most English translations of *Faust* do rhyme, and scan as well, shows clearly enough that it can be done — not perfectly, perhaps, but well enough. One of the great boons to the translator of *Faust* is the wonderful flexibility of the *Madrigalvers* in which the greater part of the work is written; and Goethe exploits to the full the prosodic freedom of that idiom, which extends to metre as well as rhyme. Goethe varies the number of stresses per line from one to six, and uses all manner of rhyming patterns — *aabb, abab, abba*, single unrhymed *Waisen*, and whole chains of monorhyme. One of the most striking examples of monorhyme is Mephisto's speech *ad spectatores* at the end of the second *Studierzimmer* scene (lines 1856–67), where there are six rhymes in the space of twelve lines: *gegeben / Streben / Leben / kleben / schweben / übergeben*. One might think the translator can only try to reproduce that kind of virtuosity at the risk of his or her sanity, and a check through a dozen or so English translations reveals only two who have attempted it. Bayard Taylor does it with the help of some very quaint vocabulary (*gave him / drave him / enslave him / deprave him / lave him / save him*) (Taylor, 53). David Luke succeeds triumphantly, and even throws in a seventh rhyme for good measure: *blind / mind / behind / kind / bind / find / signed* (Luke, *Faust I*, 56).

Rhyme is clearly the most refractory, most frustrating, and most arbitrary challenge facing the translator, more especially where the translator cannot exploit the freedom of Goethe's *Madrigalvers* and is compelled to mould the verse to the intractable schemes of *ottava rima, terza rima*, sonnet, or quatrain. Albertsen even suggests that the translator must here be twice as good (in a technical sense) as the original poet — "denn ihm hilft seine Sprache nicht, sie ist vielmehr sein Gegner, dessen Besonderheiten er zu überwinden hat" (10). The original poet can take rhyme as his starting point, or he can scrap a rhyme and start again; the translator is severely hampered by the limited and arbitrary selection of rhymes available to him to render the sense of a passage. Again, the Anglophone translator might seem to have an advantage here, for between two cognate languages, exact rhyming equivalents are occasionally to be found; but these cases are so sporadic and unpredictable that they help very little in practice (*Stein / Bein / allein*: stone / bone / alone; *Brot / tot / rot*: bread / dead / red; *frei / drei / sei*: free / three / be; etc.).

It is scarcely surprising, then, that some translators give up the unequal struggle, forgoing rhyme in order to do justice to other aspects of poetic expression. Barker Fairley used prose as a matter of principle for his *Faust* translation — though even he uses some rhyme for the prosodic wooing of Faust and Helen, and appears also to scan Brander's Song of the Rat in a rough-and-ready way (Fairley, 1999, 985–86 and 797–98). Stuart Atkins follows Goethe's metres scrupulously, but uses rhyme only very occasionally: for some of the songs and jingles (lines 2126–49, 2211–40, 2540–51) and for the wooing of Faust and Helen (lines 9346–55, 9377–84, 9411–18). Even here, though, Atkins reproduces Goethe's internal rhyme only once in the eight lines of their final *rapprochement* (*away / say* in lines 9411–12). Walter Arndt and David Luke both tackle the internal rhyme here; Bayard Taylor rhymes internally only once, and Philip Wayne and Louis MacNeice not at all.

The critic (even the critic/translator) can scarcely censure a considered judgement on the part of a translator to dispense with rhyme; and even the translator who wrestles with the intractable problems of rhyming is often forced to concede defeat, to sacrifice a felicitous rhyme for a less successful version in order to do justice to the sense, which must be paramount. As David Luke points out (*Faust I*, 1i), there is a point for every translator at which rhyme becomes an impossibly expensive luxury. On the other hand, it seems to me that little is gained, indeed almost everything is lost, by Martin Greenberg's decision to escape the "bondage of Riming" by recourse to half-rhyme (e.g. *spring / green, earth / wealth, effectual / criminal*: Greenberg, *Faust Part Two*, 1). Indeed, Greenberg does not always contrive even half-rhyme; and his rendering of the iambic trimeter (which he misguidedly calls "classical hexameter"), the trochaic tetrameter and even the choric odes of *Vor dem Palaste des Menelas zu Sparta* into "regular pentameter verse" sells all the passes at once — especially when we ponder a line of "regular pentameter": such as "How the world unfolds for you yourself's able to see" (137 = *Faust*, line 8911). Walter Arndt puts the case for rhyme vehemently in a sharp polemic against Barker Fairley:

> What could be a more saddening act, on the part of a revered Goethe scholar, than this methodical wrecking operation, performed by the ponderous steel ball of a paradoxical "prose accuracy," upon the whole splendidly intricate body of Goethe's metric architecture? What could be plainer than the fact that in the transference, the bringing home of a work of poetry from another language, fidelity and prose are mutually exclusive goals? (360)

David Luke agrees with Arndt (with his theory, if not with his practice) that rhyme and meaning are, as it were, symbiotic (Luke, *Faust Part One*, 1). This is a difficult proposition to prove, even by means of individual example; and we are forced back on not entirely convincing assertions that since Goethe saw fit to write *Faust* in rhymed verse, it can only be adequately translated into rhymed (and metrical) verse, or that unrhymed versions of *Faust* "sound rather flat." Does this mean that *Faust* can never be adequately translated into languages that have no end rhyme — of which there are many? Would the absence of rhyme disturb a reader in another language who did not know the rhymed German *Faust*, or was unaware that the original was in rhyme?

Nevertheless, it seems to me that the charge of "flatness" against unrhymed versions of *Faust* (let alone against prose versions) is not without substance. Even in Stuart Atkins's impeccable metrical translation, there is an important dimension missing to the verse. My own principal reservation about Barker Fairley's version (apart from the fact that it is in prose) is that his constant use of the full stop reduces Goethe's diction not simply to prose, but to a clipped, abrupt, and quasi-telegraphic style that deprives even his prose of any rhythmic effect. Take, for example, lines 1740–51: "Don't be afraid of me breaking the contract. My full effort and energy is what I promise. I aimed too high. I'm only fit to be in your class. The great Earth-Spirit has rejected me. Nature is closed to me. I can't think. I'm sick of learning, have been for ages. Let us spend our passions, hot in sensual deeps" (Fairley 788).

It is true that in English, Goethe's *Knittelvers* can sound alien, mechanical, and uncomfortably bumpy — more so, perhaps, than in German. Rhymed alexandrines can sound even more stilted and relentless in English than in German, but this is the effect that Goethe also exploits in the fourth act of *Faust Part Two*. It might even be argued that it is inappropriate to translate *Faust* into rhymed English, since no playwright writes in rhyme nowadays. This is true enough; but no one has, to my knowledge, proposed that Shakespeare's verse (say in *A Midsummer Night's Dream*) should be de-rhymed for theatrical production, and it is worth noting that the *Faust* versions of Robert David MacDonald and Howard Brenton (both emphatically and expressly done for modern stage performance) carefully retained Goethe's rhymes.

This does not make it any easier to define just what does get lost in unrhymed translation. Goethe's lines are often strongly profiled by his use of end rhyme; to see what we would be missing, we only have to imagine: "Da steh' ich nun, ich armer Tor, / Und bin so klug als wie vordem;" or: "Heiße Magister, heiße Doktor auch, / Und ziehe schon an die zehen Jahr' / Herauf, herab und kreuz und quer / Meine Schüler an der Nase herum." It is one of my few reservations about David Luke's impressive *Faust* translation that he is frequently forced into quasi-prosaic enjambement, where Goethe stops the sentence or phrase with a pithy or emphatic end rhyme — for example, in lines 1338–44 or 1349–56. However, Luke has done more than justice to Goethe's rhyme for the most part — especially to the monorhyme chain in Mephisto's soliloquy mentioned above, where the accumulation of rhyme reinforces the Devil's crescendo of triumphant malice as he anticipates Faust's perdition.

There are several occasions in *Faust* where rhyme, or the absence of rhyme, or the switch from rhymed to unrhymed verse, or indeed the switch from verse to prose, works to striking effect. Faust's *Wald und Höhle* monologue was written in blank verse, surely at least in part to recall the interior monologues of Shakespeare's figures; and the contrast between this medium and Mephisto's sarcastic *Madrigalvers* from line 3251 is all the more striking. The stark transition at the end of the

Walpurgisnachtstraum from the whispered *pianissimo* of the insect orchestra to the brutal realism of *Trüber Tag. Feld* is reinforced by the change from rhymed verse to prose. The drastic cultural, geographical, and historical shift from Faust's farewell to Helen at the beginning of act 4 (lines 10039–66) to Mephisto's bizarre entry in seven-league boots is vividly expressed in the shift from unrhymed iambic trimeter (Faust is, as it were, still speaking in Greek) to the rhymed *Madrigalvers*, denoting a new sphere of Faustian activity on German soil. Most dramatic of all is the *coup de théâtre* at the beginning of act 3, where the chaotic polyphony of exuberant rhymed verse in the *Meerfest* scene gives way to the solo voice of Helen speaking in unrhymed trimeter: "Bewundert viel und viel gescholten, Helena. . . ." All this — and, I believe, much more — is lost in unrhymed versions of *Faust*.

The most notable recent translations of Goethe's poems are John Whaley's *Selected Poems* and his revised *West-östlicher Divan*, and David Luke's three volumes: the *Roman Elegies and "The Diary,"* the *Erotic Poems*, and the *Selected Poetry*. I also discovered an impressive translation of "Das Tagebuch" by D. M. Black in the Scottish poetry magazine *Gairfish* (1993). Whaley in particular, with his versions of the sonnets, the *ottava rima* poems, and the *terza rima* of "Im ernsten Beinhaus," demonstrates convincingly that translators into English can cope with hendecasyllabic rhymed verse, although Anglophones constantly complain that English is severely disadvantaged in this respect compared with German or Italian. In his version of "Urworte. Orphisch," Whaley exactly reproduces Goethe's metrical pattern, down to the alternation of eleven and ten-syllable lines in the stanza *Eros*; Luke uses decasyllabics throughout, except for the final couplet of the stanza *Daimon*. Indeed, in these two lines, Whaley and Luke come strikingly close to each other:

> Nor any time nor any power can shatter
> Imprinted form informing living matter.
>
> (Whaley, *Selected Poems*, 123)

> For neither time nor any power can shatter
> The evolving life-form of imprinted matter.
>
> (Luke, *Selected Poetry*, 191)

Whaley also sustains feminine endings throughout his translation of "Das Tagebuch" (which Luke and Black do not), except for the very last couplet: "By two strong powers within us and above: / By *Duty* much, endlessly more by *Love!*" This seems reasonable enough; in order to conclude the poem, as Goethe does, on the word *love*, a decasyllabic line is unavoidable — the only way to contrive a feminine ending would be to invert the words *love* and *duty*, or to recast the line

altogether. Both Luke and Black do this — but they both also end up
with decasyllabics, respectively: "To Duty much, to Love far more we
owe," and: "Duty does much; Love, infinitely more!" These three
translations of "Das Tagebuch" are more adequate in all respects than
John Frederick Nims's notorious "Playboy" version, which unfortunately found its way into the first volume of the Suhrkamp/Princeton
Collected Works (180–89). That volume is altogether a most peculiar
rag-bag of translations by various hands; some are excellent, some
(Christopher Middleton's "Kennst du das Land" or "Dämmrung
senkte sich von oben") I find quite bizarre.

John Whaley's impressive command of rhyme makes his *West-
östlicher Divan* a pleasure to read. To cite only one example, his "Phä-
nomen" does full justice to metre, rhyme and sense:

Wenn zu der Regenwand	Phoebus on high receives
Phöbus sich gattet,	Rain cloud's embraces,
Gleich steht ein Bogenrand	Rainbow enshadowed weaves
Farbig beschattet.	Colourful traces.

(Whaley, Divan, 27)

Whaley is less successful with Goethe's distichs; some of his pen-
tameters, and even some of his hexameters, are metrically awkward. In
particular, he falls into the tempting trap of inserting an extra *Senkung*
between the hemistichs of the pentameter:

And had Luna delayed to kiss the beautiful sleeper
    Jealous Aurora for sure would quickly have kissed him awake.
Hero caught sight of Leander at the revels, and the lover
    Hurled himself hot from the feast into the nocturnal tide.
Rhea Silvia, princess and virgin, wanders down to the Tiber
    Meaning to draw some water, and there she's seized by the god.

(Whaley, Selected Poems, 57)

The second, third, fifth, and sixth lines of this passage do violence
even to Goethe's relaxed handling of the distich. At the risk of sounding
like one of the "Herrn der strikten Observanz," I would suggest some
simple changes to restore the rhythm:

And had Luna delayed to kiss the beautiful sleeper
    Jealous Aurora for sure soon would have kissed him awake.
After Leander and Hero had met at the revels, the lover
    Hurled himself hot from the feast into the nocturnal tide.
Rhea Silvia, princess and virgin, goes to draw water
    Down at the Tiber's edge, where she is seized by the god.

Whaley's translation of "Der Gott und die Bajadere" is exemplary in terms of rhyme, metre, and sense (as is Luke's); but Whaley does allow his bayadère to lapse disconcertingly into pidgin English when she says: "Give him back, I tomb defy!" (*Selected Poems*, 75).

David Luke handles the distichs of the *Roman Elegies* and the *Venetian Epigrams* with more prosodic confidence than Whaley. His translation of *Faust* is also admirably scrupulous in the reproduction of both rhyme and metre, of both modern and classicizing verse; readers without German can readily appreciate the extraordinary variety of Goethe's poetic expression from Luke's version. All the more startling, then, is his uncharacteristic lapse in the translation of "Der König in Thule," where he gives Goethe's carefully contrived masterpiece of laconic verbal and metrical simplicity a rollicking rhythm that recalls nothing so much as the nursery rhyme "Old King Cole was a Merry Old Soul." What is more, he also supplies internal rhymes of which there is no trace in the original:

> They feasted long with wine and song,
> And there with his knights sat he,
> In the ancestral hall, in his castle tall
> On the cliffs high over the sea.
>
> (Luke, *Faust I*, 86–7)

Luke has also reproduced this version in his *Selected Poetry* (19).

I would like to focus now rather myopically on a particular and very intriguing problem in the translation of *Faust*, namely on the words of the *Erdgeist* in lines 501–9, and quite especially on the last two lines of this passage, on the image of the "sausende Webstuhl der Zeit." This is a metaphor that causes much trouble to critics, and perhaps even more to translators. Technically, the greatest challenge to the translator is to find satisfactory rhymes, and also to reproduce the vividly mimetic dactyls Goethe uses (as Heine was also to do in "Die schlesischen Weber") to suggest the rhythmic process of handloom weaving. But there are semantic problems here, too. The translator must try to convey the sense of toil and effort implied in *so schaff' ich*; the creative, as it were, manufacturing process of *und wirke*; and the sense of *sausend* — that is, whether this is to be understood aurally, kinetically, or both.

In other words, *sausend* is an odd term to associate with a handloom, whether we understand it aurally as "humming," "thrumming" or "whirring," or kinetically as "hurtling" or "flying." A handloom, in my experience, doesn't hum or whirr; it clatters and thumps and shakes and rattles as the weaver stamps on the treadles that operate the moving parts. We might prefer to translate this as "the clattering loom of time" — but that is not what Goethe wrote. Nor does it make more sense if we understand *sausend* as "hurtling" or "flying" (as in "er saust durch die Gegend"): *ein Webstuhl saust ja nicht durch die Gegend*, it stays put, for all that it shakes and rattles and shudders. What does move, of course, what does *sausen* in both senses of the word, is the shuttle as it is catapulted at dizzying speed through the sheds, the strung warps, to create the *Zettel und Einschlag* of the woven fabric. If we take "der sausende Webstuhl der Zeit" as *pars pro toto*, then, it might be appropriate to settle for the "humming loom," "the whirring loom" — or even, more dubiously, "the hurtling loom" or "the speeding loom of Time."

The intriguing point about this metaphor, and more particularly about Goethe's use of the term *sausend*, is that we might reasonably conclude that it is an image inspired by the eighteenth-century proto-industrial revolution — that is, by the invention of the flying shuttle by John Kay in 1733. Kay's invention revolutionized the working of the handloom by means of a catapult mechanism that hurled the shuttle from one side of the loom to the other; and we can safely assume that Goethe would have known of this relatively recent invention, whether from his reading of the *Encyclopédie*,[5] or from his firsthand experience of the cottage industries of Saxe-Weimar. However, it appears that the weaver's shuttle had been used as a metaphor of speed or transience for centuries, if not for millennia, before the invention of the flying shuttle. In the Authorized Version of the Book of Job (7, 6) there is the well-known lament: "My days are swifter than a weaver's shuttle, and are spent without hope" — or, in the Lutheran version: "Meine Tage sind leichter dahingeflogen denn eine Weberspule, und sind vergangen, daß kein Aufhalten dagewesen ist." The image of the weaver's shuttle as a metaphor of transience is clearly an ancient one, but the biblical metaphor is scarcely relevant to the words of the Erdgeist. Goethe's image is not a metaphor of the brevity or transience of human life, but rather one of a constant and busily creative activity on the part of the "geschäftige Geist" — that is, one based on the manufacturing or fabrication processes of the handloom. Here is the passage, followed by nine English translations:

> In Lebensfluten, im Tatensturm
> Wall' ich auf und ab,
> Webe hin und her! (*Variant*: Wehe hin und her!)
> Geburt und Grab,
> Ein ewiges Meer,
> Ein wechselnd Weben,
> Ein glühend Leben,
> So schaff' ich am sausenden Webstuhl der Zeit,
> Und wirke der Gottheit lebendiges Kleid.
>
> (*Faust*, lines 501–9)

In flood of life, in action's storm
I ply on my wave
With weaving motion
Birth and the grave,
A boundless ocean,
Ceaselessly giving
Weft of living,
Forms unending,
Glowing and blending.
So work I on the whirring loom of time,
The life that clothes the deity sublime.
　　　　(Philip Wayne, 1949)

In the floods of life, in the storm of
　　　　work,
In ebb and flow,
In warp and weft,
Cradle and grave,
An eternal sea,
A changing patchwork,
A glowing life,
At the whirring loom of Time I
　　　　weave
The living clothes of the Deity.
　　　　(Louis MacNeice/E. L. Stahl,
　　　　1949)

I seethe within the floods of life,
In stormy action's wave
I weave and wander free:
Both birth and grave,
Eternal·sea,
Chequered patterns changed by strife,
Radiance of glowing life.
I weave at the humming loom of time
The living veil of the Divine.
　　　　(John Prudhoe, 1974)

In tides of living, in doing's storm,
Up, down, I wave,
Waft to and fro,
Birth and grave,
An endless flow,
A changeful plaiting,
Fiery begetting,
Thus at Time's scurrying loom I
weave and warp
And broider at the Godhead's living
　　　　garb.
　　　　(Walter Arndt, 1976)

In the tides of life, in action's storm,
I surge and ebb,
move to and fro!
As cradle and grave,
as unending sea,
as constant change,
as life's incandescence,
I work at the whirring loom of time
and fashion the living garment of God.
　　　　(Stuart Atkins, 1984)

In life like a flood, in deeds like a
　　　　storm
I surge to and fro,
Up and down I flow!
Birth and the grave
An eternal wave,
Turning, returning,
A life ever burning:
And thus I work at Time's whirring
　　　　wheel,
God's living garment I weave and
　　　　reveal.
　　　　(David Luke, 1987)

Wherever life ebbs and flows
Wherever its battles rage
I weave my presence.
The womb, the grave,
The eternal sea,
The constant change,
Busy at time's spinning wheel,
I shape the godhead's outer self.
(Dan Farrelly, *Urfaust*, 1998)

In all life's storms and surging tides
I ebb and flow
From birth to grave,
Weave to and fro,
An endless wave
Through all life's glowing
Fabric flowing.
On time's humming loom, as I toil
      at the treads,
For God's living garment I fashion
      the threads.
(John R. Williams, 1999)

In floods of life, in storms of action, I range up and down. I flow this way and that. I am birth and the grave, an eternal ocean, a changeful weaving, a glowing life. And thus I work at the humming loom of time, and fashion the earth, God's living garment.
(Barker Fairley, 1970)

Philip Wayne's version seems to me to be flawed in several respects. It takes up two lines more than the original; it indulges in the quaint inversion "So work I on the whirring loom of time"; the last two lines have five stresses to Goethe's four; and no attempt is made to reproduce the dactylic (or, more technically, amphibrachic) rhythms of the original. MacNeice chooses not to rhyme here (in his and Stahl's translation generally, rhymes come and go unpredictably); and despite the fact that he has no *Reimzwang*, there is no attempt at rhythmic mimesis in the last two lines. One might also question "the storm of work" for *im Tatensturm*. In Prudhoe's version, "seethe" and "strife" have no equivalent in the original; "strife" appears to be a blatant result of *Reimzwang*, and I would have preferred "Within the seething tides [or floods] of life" to "I seethe within the floods of life." Prudhoe has only one dactyl in the last two lines. Arndt's version is interesting, but in the end not very convincing. He evidently intends to render "Wall' ich auf und ab" by "Up, down, I wave" — but it sounds as if he is translating *winken*, not *wallen*. His "waft" is presumably a translation not of *webe*, but of the variant *wehe* in the *Ausgabe letzter Hand* and the *Weimarer Ausgabe*. Arndt's rhymes are frankly duff ones: *plaiting / begetting* and *warp / garb*. He appears to understand *sausend* as a kinetic image — but the notion of a "scurrying loom" is odd. His last two lines are rhythmically jumbled, especially the last line: "And broider at the Godhead's living garb."

Atkins, who is free from *Reimzwang*, is able to give a close account of the sense, though he takes some liberty with the repeated *as*. His "move" in the third line is evidently based on the variant *wehe*: his translation is expressly based on the *Ausgabe letzter Hand*. He also re-produces the essential elements of the last two lines, rendering *schaffen* as "work" and *wirken* as "fashion"; and he reproduces some of Goethe's dactylic rhythms — but only fifty percent. However, we miss the profiling of Goethe's lines by means of rhyme, and the last couplet in particular sounds flat against the original.

Luke does rhyme, and rhymes well; he also realizes two-thirds of the dactylic potential of the last two lines. But he switches the metaphor drastically from that of the weaver's loom to that of the spinning-wheel, which loses the whole reference and resonance of the image. However, in his revision of these lines for inclusion in his translations of the poems, Luke restores the weaving image: "At Time's whirring loom I work and I play, / God's living garment I weave and display" (*Selected Poetry*, 17). Dan Farrelly's *Urfaust* version also uses the image of the spinning-wheel, which is all the more unaccountable since he has no constraint of either rhyme or metre; and "I *shape* the godhead's outer self" is scarcely appropriate in terms of either spinning or weav-ing. In my own version I have tried to respect both meaning and meta-phor of the original, perhaps at the expense of literal sense equivalence; I have aimed at reproducing in full the rhythmic effect of the last two lines, and to convey the essential meaning of *schaffen* and *wirken* re-spectively by means of "toil" and "fashion." Barker Fairley's version, for all that it is in prose, is not an exact sense equivalent of the original. "I flow" is neither *webe* nor *wehe*; he inserts "*I am* birth and the grave"; and he introduces a surely unnecessary gloss to the final image by ex-plaining what is meant by "God's living garment" (the earth).

Such myopic pedantries should not obscure the fact that we are fortunate to have modern Goethe translations of generally high quality available; this is an encouraging sign at a time when public Anglophone interest in Goethe is at a relatively low ebb, especially in Britain. Trans-lations can be illuminating, not only to readers without German, but also to the student of German literature, provided that they are used intelligently in conjunction with the original, not as mere cribs. Goethe should be retranslated by every generation, just as he should be reread and reinterpreted; examples of computer-generated literary translation are reassuring in their hilarious absurdities, indicating that this is a task for which human intelligence will be required for some time to come.

Notes

[1] Leif Ludwig Albertsen, "Zur Problematik der Übersetzung von Dichtung," in: *Schriften der Theodor-Storm-Gesellschaft* 32 (1983): 9.

[2] Full details of the translations quoted are given in the list of "Works Cited." In the following, translations will be referred to by translator and page number.

[3] Christian Wagenknecht, *Deutsche Metrik. Eine historische Einführung* (Munich: Beck, 1981), 46.

[4] See Andreas Heusler, *Deutsche Versgeschichte*, vol. 3 (Berlin & Leipzig: De Gruyter, 1929), 397–400.

[5] Vol. 9, 190–1, s.v. LAINE: *de la navette angloise.*

Goethe and Irish German Studies 1871–1971

Eda Sagarra

GOETHE IN IRISH GERMAN studies of bygone days hardly seems a topic to engender excitement among scholars, though it did provoke passion among Irish Germanists of the day. If the main source of their academic excitement paralleled what was happening in Britain — namely our predecessors' attempt to assert their claims against those of the classicists, and allowing our students of German to read and take examinations based as much on Goethe and Schiller as their Anglo-Saxon primer — the Irish battles were fought out on a very small stage. Nor are there compensatory claims to be made for Irish Goethe pedagogy or scholarship, at least not before the last third of the twentieth century, even if it was an Irish university student who produced the first verse translation of Goethe's *Faust Part I* in 1815. Even here, however, disappointment awaits: the author, an undergraduate, was not even a student of German, but of law (and later Regius Professor of Civil Law at Trinity College Dublin), John Martin Anster (1793–1867)[1] from Charleville, Co. Cork. Anster published his rendering of *The Bride of Corinth* with William Blackwood in 1819; the following year his unfinished *Faust* translation appeared in *Blackwood's Magazine.*[2] The value of the present exercise, then, lies in the general area of *Wissenschaftsgeschichte*, the history of our discipline, and in what it tells us about the ideological premises (which their authors would have likely denied) on which the syllabuses were based

In order to provide context for the debate, a brief description of the Irish university education system may be helpful. Like our civil service, our currency, and our banking system (though not our monetary policy), the Irish university system was modelled on, and remains in many respects similar to, its British counterpart — as a system, that is. Its operation is rather different. There are now seven universities in the Republic of Ireland, five of them with departments teaching and doing research in *Germanistik*. The University of Dublin, founded by Elizabeth I in 1591, is the oldest; however, it never grew beyond one college, Trinity. (The relations between university and college are too complex to detain us here.[3]) The German department goes back to 1776,[4] its honours undergraduate course to 1871.[5] Maynooth, a secular university since 1997, began life as a pontifical university in 1795, while Sir Robert Peel was responsible for the creation of the Cork and Galway university colleges in 1846. These were known, along with Queen's Belfast, as the Queen's Colleges, but were immediately dubbed by their opponents, including the Irish Catholic bishops, as the "godless colleges" because of their nondenominational character.[6] Although the reference is useful for purveyors of *Paddywitze*, it holds some importance in explaining the manner in which Goethe's place, and that of the classical era generally, was later established — and defended — in the curriculum of those colleges. This is also true of University College Dublin, formerly John Henry Newman's Catholic University, founded in 1854.[7] The Queen's University, which had been the examining body for the Cork and Galway colleges, as well as for Belfast, was superseded for the first two in 1879 by the Royal University, a purely examining body. In 1909 Queen's Belfast became an independent university, as the other colleges had been reconstituted with Dublin to form the National University of Ireland, with Maynooth being given status as a so-called "recognised college." However, the decision to found the National University was a controversial one. The fact that it was "nobody's darling"[8] proved paradoxically useful in helping it to survive and, in due course, prosper. It was only at the end of the century (in 1997), following protracted debate and in the context of the massive expansion of Ireland's third-level education system, that the four colleges of Cork, Dublin, Galway, and Maynooth finally became independent universities.

Trinity had several merits, and its Fellows enjoyed numerous perquisites in the nineteenth and most of the twentieth centuries. However, the college did not feel an urgent need to extend these perquisites to its graduate students in modern languages. While the university provided an education at undergraduate level, it did not appear to take seriously the postgraduate training of students of modern languages, not even in the first decades of the twentieth century. Indeed, there do not appear to be any records of successful graduate students in German at Trinity before the mid-1940s, when Hans Reiss received his doctorate.[9] By contrast, the National University of Ireland inherited from the old Royal University a well-endowed travelling studentship scheme, which financed postgraduate study abroad for its modern language graduates. Where money is available, there are usually students to take it, and the

National University scheme proved to be an abiding attraction. However, since few male students read modern languages, during the period under discussion, apart from those at Trinity, virtually all takers were women. This explains why German studies in Ireland, again apart from Trinity, were dominated by Irish women from the beginning of the twentieth century to the late 1960s, all of whom had studied in Germany, Austria, and/or Switzerland.[10] The appointment of Tim Casey, then a lecturer at Queen's, to the chair of German in Galway on 1 January 1967, marks both the end of the domination of the petticoat regiment in German studies in the National University of Ireland, and in a very real sense the beginning of the era in which Irish *Germanistik* developed its own profile.[11]

The first concern, in attempting to assess the position of Goethe in the Irish university curriculum, must be one of method. As Gilbert Carr wrote in his seminal article on syllabus and ideology in the university curriculum in 1976, "There are no historical eye-witness accounts of lectures or classes." But both methodology and ideology of university curricula, he goes on to say, can be explored in "University Calendars, parliamentary papers, unpublished Board and Council Minutes, examinations papers and prescribed texts."[12] I would add to this list the area of published work, occasional writings and radio broadcasts of academics. The media, then as now, played a prominent rôle in influencing public attitudes in Ireland on university matters.

The University of Dublin was allegedly long known in Cambridge and Oxford circles as "the silent sister."[13] Whether nineteenth- and early twentieth-century modern linguists at Trinity were too busy talking to write is not clear, but few of them gave the academic community the benefit of their researches. In this, they were similar to their colleagues in the younger Irish universities. Germanists in the National University were even less forthcoming. There was little institutional encouragement to do so. Well into the twentieth century, French and German remained, in the eyes of the university establishment, a tool rather than a discipline.[14] The idea that modern languages could have equal status with classics or English was strenuously resisted in the older British universities. One of the chief advocates of change in Ireland, (Albert) Maximilian Selss, was the German liberal appointed in 1866 to the Trinity chair, and a graduate of Tübingen. He prefaced his *Brief History of the German Language* as follows:

> To assist in vindicating for modern languages such a place of honour besides the long-established Classics of Greece and Rome is one of the objects which the writer has proposed to himself in the compilation of this sketch. (Selss 1885, iv)

He inaugurated the honours course in 1871, in which Goethe texts had pride of place. Over his forty or so years in office, Goethe — or rather a particular version of Goethe — played a significant role in the Trinity curriculum. Still, Selss was not afraid to introduce contemporary authors, including towards the end of his tenure, the Naturalists. In 1909, however, his successor promptly turned back the clock with regard to literature. Robert Alan Williams, later Schröder Professor at Cambridge, excised Heine, Hauptmann, and Sudermann from the syllabus and reduced the time devoted to literature, putting the focus on the *Nibelungenlied* (and Hebbel's *Nibelungen*) rather than Goethe and Schiller. He established, in the process, a course of the kind encountered by the young Walter Bruford as a first-year student at Cambridge in 1911, namely one "of a severely philological nature."[15] The course was no doubt designed to win the respect of the classicists, but it proved to be a cul-de-sac. Yet the underlying principles of the curriculum were not seriously challenged before the 1970s. Williams was more interested in his other appointment, the lectureship in Anglo-Saxon, a link that was not broken until Lionel Thomas came to Trinity in 1958. Over the three-quarters of a century between the Crimean War and the 1918 Leathes Commission, set up to enquire into the teaching of modern languages in British universities,[16] successive Royal Commissions reported on and castigated the Dublin university authorities for failure to move with the times. However, they cut little ice with the Fellows, who remained impervious to arguments about the need to rethink the role of modern languages in the curriculum. Equally, the 1902 Royal Commission described the arts course of the Royal University as extremely academic and impractical,[17] but to little effect. Perhaps, since a significant proportion of those taking the examinations of the Royal University were women, the role of literature in the examination syllabus was regarded by its authors as enhancing young ladies' accomplishments and therefore appropriate.

The records regarding curriculum and examinations are more complete and more accessible for Trinity College than for any other university. Consequently, Trinity College will provide the main focus of the following discussion. The German syllabus at Trinity, over the century succeding the inauguration of the honour course in 1871, reveals that Goethe had an established place throughout. But what kind of a place? And which Goethe?

Trinity's approach was no different from other British German departments of the day in its advocacy of set texts, nor in the fact that the choice was often dictated by what the professor and his colleagues had edited. These were not critical editions, such as are used today in the sophister years, but German texts with English introduction, notes, and comments, and perhaps translation of difficult passages or phrases. (Many older colleagues will have inaugurated their publishing careers with such editions. The problem with our predecessors in German literary, as opposed to linguistic, studies, was that they often ended them there.) Selss, like his predecessor and fellow liberal Ignatius Abeltshauser in the 1840s, 1850s, and early 1860s, and, from an opposing perspective, his successor Williams, had decided views on the matter of what should and should not be included in the teaching and examination syllabuses. Selss was the author of the history of German literature recommended for the freshman German course, *A Critical Outline of the Literature of Germany*, the first edition of which had appeared in 1865. (This was followed, between 1880 and 1896, by four subsequent, enlarged editions.) These were duly advertised at the beginning of the university calendar as a textbook for students to purchase. The bulk of this survey of German literature, from the earliest times to the era of the edition, was devoted to the chapters on German classical authors, with the longest devoted to Goethe.[18] For years these works constituted a significant element of the examination syllabus in German. Language students were prompted to think of their German authors as engaged in competition, each against the rest; so, too, in Selss' literary history, and in his edition of what he rather infelicitously termed Goethe's minor poems (he meant "shorter"), notional "marks" are awarded to Goethe's individual works. Those which "perform well" are included, and successive University of Dublin Calendars set them out, along with the relevant portions of the Outline, as the texts on which students would be examined. Selss proceeds on the premise that "the great national authors of Germany coincide only with the end of the last [=eighteenth E. S.] century," adding in parenthesis: "unless, indeed, we should claim for the medieval bards the title of national poets, which their now discarded dialect and their solely antiquarian importance forbids us to attribute to them" (Selss 1880, 15). While the Romantics figured in the freshmen years, only the sophomores studied Goethe, Schiller, and Lessing. Selss, along with numerous contemporaries and immediate successors, had scant respect for the Romantics, which is evident from this reference, in a generally dismissive account of his own century, couched in terms of competitive sport: "The Romantic School sets the fashion at first, but soon Heine and the Young Germans drive them off the field" (Selss 1880, 16).

Götz, Egmont, and *Faust* he declares baldly to be the best works of Goethe, and the syllabus generally reflected the professor's views. (This is not surprising, because there were no other lecturers.) On the matter

of canonical literature in German and its capacity to "compete" with
and even "vanquish" the received canon of the classical poets, Selss felt
himself on sure ground. In the preface to his edition of Goethe's *Faust*,
he acts as advocate in his own cause:

> Meanwhile, the modern languages and their literatures have partly suc-
> ceeded in dethroning the ancient Classics from the supreme position
> they once held in our educational system. A book, therefore, so teem-
> ing with thought as the *Faust* of Goethe, which has a scholar for its
> hero, and might have been written specially for the benefit of Univer-
> sity students, ought not any longer be left unedited. (Selss 1880a, v)

While the Goethe-Schiller *Briefwechsel* for the years 1794–97 figured briefly on the sophister syllabus for 1900, neither Goethe's scientific works, nor the great works of Goethe's late middle and old age
were deemed by Selss to be worthy of the student's attention:

> Whatever was written by him [Goethe] subsequently to this [i.e. after
> *Hermann und Dorothea*] shows a decided decline in clearness and vig-
> our and a leaning towards oriental mysticism. Neither his contribution
> to optics and botany, nor his singular novel on wedded life, called *Elec-
> tive Affinities* (1809), nor his *Autobiography* (1811–31), are at all com-
> parable, in their literary value, to his earlier writings. (Selss 1896, 148)

However, like many Germans of his generation, the "patriotism" of
Hermann und Dorothea appealed to Selss, and despite his strictures,
selected books from *Dichtung und Wahrheit* appeared in the mid 1870s
as part of the honour course (though they failed to retain their place),
in common with the once popular *Wilhelm Meisters Lehrjahre*. Similarly, the balance in favour of Goethe's early poems is evident in Selss's
1880 edition, a favourite set text. Only brief extracts from the *Römische
Elegien* and two six-line verses from the *Divan* are included here, while
successive editions of his literary history contain severe strictures on the
latter, only surpassed by his stern dismissal of *Faust II*:

> The second part is but a feeble composition; and it contains Faust's
> adventures in the domain of science, art, court life, and politics. The
> story is obscured by the introduction of allegorical and symbolical fig-
> ures . . . but seldom a passable scene, or even a dramatic dialogue, is
> offered to the reader who has patience enough to look for them. (Selss
> 1880a, 157)

To encourage interest in German authors at school, Selss edited an
English edition of Christoph Schmid's perennially popular and much-
translated children's story *Die Ostereier*. His college teaching texts, his
history of literature, and editions of Goethe were designed to help the
process of "dethroning the ancient classics from the supreme position

they once held in our educational system" (Selss 1880a, 157). Despite his conviction of the importance of the German classics, however, the teaching of literature in his department appears to have been broadly dictated by the requirements of acquiring a proper level of competence in reading the written language. He speaks of his decision to edit Goethe's *Faust* in order to combat the many bad translations extant, and his critical comments are designed to help the students to get grips with what is linguistically obscure. He favoured a strictly biographical approach to the "interpretation" of Goethe texts, but this need not surprise us. He took an independent line within that approach, when he declared that it wouldn't matter in what order one read the two hundred plays of Kotzebue, but in the case of Goethe, as for Shakespeare, the key to the works of great men is "the life" and the chronological linking of life and work. This, he says, is the key to a proper appreciation of the whole man (Selss 1880a, vi.).

In establishing Goethe as *the* classical German author in the teaching and examining programme of students of German at Dublin, Selss seems to have been in tune with the trends of his contemporaries in imperial Germany. Under his predecessor, Abeltshauser, in the 1840s and 1850s, Schiller appears to have featured more prominently in the professorial lectures. Certainly Trinity students, including the famous Irish patriot Thomas Davis, writing in several successive numbers of the *Dublin University Magazine* in the 1830s and 1840s, had translated Schiller's poems along with those of the Young Germans, but not those of Goethe. In Selss's manual, the *Deutsche Styl- und Redübungen* of 1886, published in Dublin to provide material for German composition, he offers quaint evidence of his regard for Goethe's stature in an imagined literary hierarchy. Among the model sentences he includes as No. 86 is the following:

> It is usual at present to regard Schiller only as second author of Germany, and to put him after the author of *Faust*. The decision is founded on the fact that Goethe's was on the whole a more original mind than that of his friend and rival. Schiller has not created any new style of art, but only repeated the historical drama and the ballad-style which before were known, and employed by others. Goethe, on the other hand, has created a philosophical drama in his Faust, and a species of lyrics in his Gedichte, which were new in their kind, and which contain a large number of original ideas. (Selss 1886, 32)

More so than in the older British universities, Irish students even in the nineteenth century were preoccupied with the usefulness of languages for employment. In the mid 1850s, the University of Dublin had negotiated the right to administer qualifying examinations for the

Indian civil service for its students. A chair of Arabic had been established in 1855, and Hindustani added to its title in 1866, Persian in 1873. A lectureship, and from 1862 a professorship, in Sanskrit and comparative philology had also been created. The recognition of the importance of German for applicants for the Indian civil service undoubtedly helped the subject, and in the literary history of 1873 by Gostwick and Harrison, prescribed for these candidates and for the sophister honours course from the 1870s, Max Müller's dictum receives particular emphasis:

> Accordingly, where a knowledge of German is rated so high, says Max Müller, it is but fair that the examiners should insist on something more than a conversational knowledge of the language. . . . Candidates may fairly be required to know something of the History of German Literature. [19]

Knowledge about, rather than of, seems to have been the keyphrase, and Gostwick and Harrison briskly pigeonhole German literature from 380 to 1870, or 1880 in their second edition, into "departments": scientific, philosophic, poetic, and theological. How well the 108 successful Trinity candidates for the Indian service between 1855 and 1877 were actually familiar with Goethe's *Faust* is impossible to reconstruct. One suspects that at best they had the capacity to construe.

One significant development in the area of modern languages was the admission in 1904 of women to take degrees at the University of Dublin: many took modern languages — and gained significant success at moderatorship. (Cambridge women, who had successfully read for a degree, but were not allowed to graduate, were offered recognition of their degree by Dublin University. By 1907, some 720 women had travelled to Dublin to take their degrees, and their fee payments helped to build Trinity Hall, a hostel for women students.) [20]

While Selss selected and tailored Goethe's works in his idealistic view to develop the German moderator's aesthetic sense, and while the syllabus of the civil service examinations was designed to promote the imperial cause, the concerns of syllabus designers and teachers in the new National University of Ireland in 1909 (and for almost the half-century that followed) were somewhat different. University Colleges Cork, Dublin, and Galway were not godless colleges — quite the reverse. They specifically aimed to provide Catholic university education for Catholic students. The Trinity Vice-Provost had in 1906 dismissed the suggestion that the University of Dublin broaden its intake by providing degree courses for "the commercial classes." He declared himself determined that the University of Dublin should not become a "charity school" for "poor and ignorant" Catholic peasants who were much more useful as "agriculturalists."[21] The National University was designed, *inter alia*, to do precisely this for the children of those "ignorant Irish peasants." National University teachers had to be mindful of the force of the Irish bishops' ire over the mid-nineteenth century Queen's colleges. Even more topical, in the first decade of the century (the time of the National University's foundation), was the Modernist controversy in the ranks of the Catholic church, which even in Ireland claimed its intellectual martyrs. For German academic teachers in Ireland, there was the additional prejudice, which I personally can recall encountering as a student in Dublin in the 1950s, that, while French, Italian, and Spanish were "Catholic languages," German was a "Protestant language," the language of the Reformation. Ironically, given the venom that German liberal Protestants reserved for the Jesuits in and after the *Kulturkampf*, if German was taught at all in Catholic schools in mid-twentieth-century Ireland, it tended to be in Jesuit schools, which carried social cachet, and in the better-off convents. Be that as it may, one or two German teachers in a department of the National University between 1910 and the later 1960s occupied those positions through the inertia of the authorities rather than their own learning; some lecturers, according to anecdote, experienced little intellectual difficulty in suggesting to their pupils, most of them convent girls, that Goethe was really a Catholic at heart. Others, such as the first woman appointee to a chair in modern languages in these islands (in 1910), Mary Ryan of Cork, preferred to focus on Catholic authors, such as Caritas Pirckheimer, or later, Hans Carossa or Gertrud von le Fort. She published on them in such journals as the *Irish Rosary* or the *Irish Ecclesiastical Record*, but also in Carl Muth's liberal Catholic journal *Hochland*.[22] Ryan, who was effectively in charge of modern Continental languages at Cork for two decades, published one article on Goethe in the *New Ireland Review* 26 (1903) under the title of "The Faust Legend and Goethe's Faust."

Mary Macken of University College Dublin, who had spent a year in an Ursuline convent in Berlin as a schoolgirl and later studied under Karl Breul at Cambridge, became the doyenne of German and Goethe studies in Ireland from the 1920s to the 1950s. She went out of her way publicly, through occasional publications and radio broadcasts, to establish Goethe's personal credentials as capable of harmonisation with Christian and Catholic teaching. To protect herself, she sought the authority of the Jesuit order to prove her point and chose to place most of her numerous articles on German literature and *Landeskunde* in the influential Jesuit periodical, *Studies: An Irish Quarterly Review of Letters, Philosophy and Science*. One of her most pointed articles on Goethe appeared here in 1932 in the form of a review of a recent work by a German Jesuit, with the unlikely name of Friedrich Muckermann, whom she described as "the first Catholic writer to attempt, in a work of any length, a synthesis between Christianity and Goethean idealism."[23] Mary Macken, who had studied at Berlin, knew Germany and Austria well; she spent most summers there and travelled on a number of occasions to Weimar. She actually visited Weimar in 1932, the bicentenary of the poet's birth, as the representative of the National University and part of a delegation sent by the young Irish Free State to Weimar. This occurred shortly after the Nazis assumed power in the so-called Free State of Thuringia. She described her experiences vividly a number of years later in a radio talk broadcast by Radio Éireann on 1 September 1949, which was subsequently published in *Studies* (Macken 1949). In the same article, she demonstrated, in her colourful and allusive prose, that she was thoroughly abreast of the current debates on Goethe in Germany in 1949, something that could not be said of her Irish colleagues in the 1940s and 1950s. She was a friend and correspondent of Hermann Bahr, about whom she wrote a lengthy article (Macken 1926). She also referred to "well-known contemporary Catholic writers such as Hermann Bahr and Hans Carossa, in whom the beautiful Goethean form and tradition lives and flourishes without detriment to their belief and its practice" (Macken 1932, 662). Though it is hard for the modern reader to appreciate, she was attempting here to legitimise the role of Goethe and German literature from the eighteenth and nineteenth centuries as part of the undergraduate curriculum of her Dublin German department. The years affected were between 1910 and 1950, when clerical control of the university was still very real. Mary Macken prospered in her stratagem, as her most eminent pupil, Tim Casey, recalls.

Goethe studies in the other colleges of the National University remained at a low ebb, dominated for forty years as they were, until the late 1960s, by university teachers who taught assiduously but published virtually nothing. The Galway professor, Margaret Shea, allegedly turned down a German embassy scholarship for her students in the inter-war period, for fear of endangering her pupils' "moral character" (Fischer, 2, 113–14.). Only in Maynooth did the German refugee scholar, John Hennig, publish on Goethe and provide informed instruction on German humanist culture, but this to students of theology rather than German, and without any status that a permanent position would have given him.[24]

An initial survey of the university examination papers set reveals that the two systems were not so far apart in the ideological premises underlying their curricular objectives, at least with regard to the literature and essay elements. Two samples, both from the period 1900 and 1914, must suffice:

The Royal University degree examination in German of 1900 required candidates answering German literature to "Give the chief features of the leading characters in *Hermann und Dorothea*, and (to) show that it is a thoroughly German poem, full of healthy patriotism" (Fischer 2, 119). By 1914 the Trinity moderators were asked: "What would Goethe think of modern German Kultur?" Alternatively, by analogy with the notion of the "two Germanies," the candidates could "Show that the Prussian contribution to German literature during your period is negligible" or "Draw a parallel between the Swiss spirit of freedom as depicted by Schiller and that of modern Belgium."[25] (Examinations, we recall, were taken in the autumn, that is, in this case some weeks after the outbreak of the 1914 War.) One year later, the philologist Williams, now professor at Queen's, had been succeeded by Gilbert Waterhouse, who, following some years as a Lektor in Leipzig, acted briefly as war correspondent from Germany. Two years later, Waterhouse would state in a public lecture, immediately printed in pamphlet form, that the only purpose of learning German was to beat the Germans at every level — on the battlefield, the laboratory, the market, and the factory floor, and that the only justification for learning German would be in self-defence.[26]

Ireland, after the founding of the Free State in 1922, became in many senses an intellectual backwater. German declined radically in the schools and few lamented its passing. An exception might seem to have been William Stockley, professor of English at University College Cork, when he declared that German should indeed be taught, because Germany was the land of congresses and Irish students should be encouraged to attend them. But what he meant — and said — were congresses such as the German *Katholikentage*.[27] Trinity language departments were less authoritarian, and no doubt, given the range of Waterhouse's intellectual interests and publication record, more intellectually exciting. By the beginning of the 1930s, however, Waterhouse left for Queen's, and Samuel Beckett had long since departed to France to exchange an uncertain life in Paris for that of teaching French at Trinity. When modern languages underwent a process of *aggiornamento* after the Second World War, French and Spanish were the initial beneficiaries, attracting a series of learned and gregarious men to their chairs. The German chair was initially down-graded to a senior lectureship when the new incumbent, Lionel Thomas, came to Dublin in 1958, though the chair was reinstated during his term of office. Little curricular or institutional innovation occurred during his tenure, but almost immediately following the appointment of Hugh Sacker in 1971, a radical revolution took place.

I have implied that the late 1960s and early 1970s marked a kind of watershed in German studies in Ireland. Though changes occurred in all sorts of ways, it was primarily a matter of personalities and new appointments. The positivists retired, moved on, or died. All four Irish chairs of German were filled between 1967 and 1974. By now, German professors had two, three, or even four colleagues to share the work of their departments. This was truly a case of Hegel's dictum that a quantitative change can bring about a qualitative change. Although I was not in Ireland then, the Trinity experience provides the most immediate example of the consequences of that generational shift.

Following Hugh Sacker's appointment to the Trinity chair in 1971, the German syllabus was redesigned from the bottom — defined, probably for the first time in its two-hundred-year history, in terms of perceived needs and objectives.[28] The bulk of students of German at that time came from Northern Ireland, with its excellent tradition of teaching modern languages in grammar schools. This, coupled with the four-year degree course, allowed for a degree of specialist literature teaching that was hitherto unknown. Goethe was a principal beneficiary. The teaching of the classical period was systematised, and late Goethe was finally given a recognised position in the curriculum. His poetry was introduced to junior freshmen as part of the small-group teaching of textual analysis. The early dramas of Goethe (and Schiller) featured now in the freshman seminars, which laid emphasis on close reading skills. Moreover, Goethe became an important vehicle for integrating the teaching of literary theory into the undergraduate curriculum. At sophomore level, seminars on the *Bildungsroman* now included both *Wilhelm Meisters Lehrjahre* and the *Wanderjahre*, as well as *Der grüne Heinrich* and *Der Zauberberg*. Käthe Friedemann and Franz Stanzel were read in conjunction with *Die Wahlverwandtschaften*.

Offered several times as a seminar, the *Divan* proved to be a clever and popular choice. This was true in part because it was novel. Students had not encountered anything like it before, and they responded with alacrity to the beauty of the text and to the concept of the poetic cycle. Early Goethe poems had been on the A-level syllabus for Northern Ireland students, and, as Northern students respect authority, they had absorbed the notion of a "right" and a "wrong" interpretation. In their view, James Boyd, as an Oxford professor, clearly had authority on his side. The new syllabus, including the *Divan*, provided a salutary shock to the certainty that there was "*an*" interpretation of the poetic text to be discovered by hard work and the reading of secondary literature.

The *Divan* also introduced them, though the term was not current then, to the concept of intertextuality.

However, by the mid 1970s, as the euphemistically labelled Northern "troubles" began to influence student choice, the Northern students preferred to study in Scotland or Northern England rather than at Trinity. Their places were taken by students from schools in the Republic. This created all sorts of difficulties for the teaching of German literature. Protestant and Jewish students from the Republic at Trinity usually did British school exams (A-levels) and the Trinity Matriculation exam, both of which had literature papers. German was one of three A-level subjects. These students had read German set texts and could read German with reasonable fluency. Most, being from middle class backgrounds, had had their school-arranged exchange. Catholic students did the Leaving Certificate, with students doing some eight subjects in the final year. There was no oral component, and German, taught as a dead language, was generally their fourth language, after Irish, Latin, and French. Apart from students from well-to-do boarding schools, few of them would have heard German spoken, let alone be able to speak it themselves.[29] The "literature component" of the Leaving Certificate examination in the 1960s and 1970s was little short of a farce. As sole examiner for seven years, and as author of seven annual reports making that point, I can speak from experience. I doubt that anyone ever read them. Certainly the reports were never acted upon. In the 1980s, literature was simply dropped from the Leaving Certificate modern languages curriculum, though the issue has since been re-opened by the National Council for Curriculum and Assessment as part of its fundamental redesign of the school examinations. Up to the 1970s, the literature component of the Leaving Certificate consisted in "writing an appreciation" of a poem, often something patriotic by Freiligrath, such as *Die irische Witwe*, prepared by the pupils' school teacher and learnt by rote for regurgitation in the written examination. Inviting these students to read the German classics before the end of their second year proved a recipe for disaster. However, things changed with time, following the slow but systematic improvement in the standard of teaching German at school, and the dramatic increase in the number of students taking German at school and university. By the 1980s, both at Trinity and in Irish university German departments generally, it became clear that teaching Goethe, or indeed German literature in general, to students who were either bilingual, or who had a profound post-colonial awareness of language, was an exciting enterprise.

This, I think, is what my younger Irish colleagues find today; but that is only part of the story. The other part belongs to the history of modern Irish *Germanistik*, which needs to be told, at another time and in another place, by those Goethe scholars who were Irish Germanists, in the sense that they taught and published from their Irish base, but were, with few exceptions, British or German by origin. This paper is a modest tribute to them.

Notes

[1] Paul Foley Casey, "John Martin Anster: His Contributions to Anglo-German Studies," *Modern Language Notes*, 96 (1981): 654–66 (here 656). The translation was not completed until 1835.

[2] Edinburgh, June 1820, 635–658. Casey reminds us that it thus pre-dated Carlyle's influential essays (Casey, 657).

[3] Aidan Clarke, Erasmus Smith's Professor of Modern History and a former Vice-Provost of the College, offers a succinct analysis in: "Responsibility: the administrative framework," in Charles H. Holland, ed.: *Trinity College Dublin and the Idea of a University* (Dublin: Trinity College Press, 1991), 89–103.

[4] For an appropriately sceptical account of the origin and development of the modern languages chairs at Trinity see Richard Cox, "A Curious History: Two Hundred Years of Modern languages," in: Holland, 255–69.

[5] See Maurice Raraty, "The Chair of German at Trinity College, Dublin 1775–1866," in: *Hermathena. A Dublin University Review*, 53–62.

[6] The best account of this complex saga is Donal Kerr, *Peel, Priests and Politics. Sir Robert Peel's Administration and the Roman Catholic Church in Ireland, 1841–46*, Oxford Historical Monographs (Oxford: Clarendon Press, 1982), chapter 7: The "Godless Colleges," 290–353.

[7] On the context of Newman's foundation see Louis McRedmond: *Thrown among Strangers. John Henry Newman in Ireland* (Dublin: Veritas, 1990).

[8] Donal McCartney, *The National University of Ireland and Eamon de Valera* (Dublin: The University Press of Ireland, 1983), 8.

[9] Hans Reiss, "Sieben Jahre in Irland 1939–46. Mein Weg in die Germanistik," in: *Jahrbuch der deutschen Schillergesellschaft* 40 (1996): 409–432.

[10] Incidentally, both Helen Watanabe-O'Kelly of Oxford and I are "products" of that scheme, as is Tim Casey of Galway, each of us having had our doctoral studies funded by a NUI Travelling Studentship.

[11] I review the development of German studies in the last third of the twentieth century in: Sagarra (1999): 117–30.

[12] Gilbert J. Carr, "Literary historical Trends and the History of the German Syllabus at Trinity College, Dublin, 1873–1972," *Hermathena. A Dublin*

University Review 121 (1976). Modern Language Teaching. Trinity College 1776–1976: 36–55 (here 37).

[13] See James Lydon, "The Silent Sister: Trinity College and Catholic Ireland," in: Holland, 29–53.

[14] Richard Cox, a Cambridge graduate in French and German but speaking from his perspective as a lecturer in the department of French, of "the theoretical muddle in the formal curriculum," would suggest that this situation obtained well into the second half of the twentieth century (Cox, 262).

[15] Walter H. Bruford, *First Steps in German Fifty Years Ago. The Presidential Address to the Modern Languages Research Association 1965* (Leeds: Modern Languages Research Association, 1965), 8.

[16] Sir Stanley Leathes, Secretary to the Civil Service, chaired the "Government Commission on the position of modern languages in the educational system of Great Britain" from 1916 until his submission of the 200-page report in April 1918.

[17] Carr, 40.

[18] In the 1880 second edition, chapters 16–20, and part of 27 ("Goethe's latest works").

[19] In the first edition only: Preface, v–vi.

[20] Eda Sagarra, "From the Pistol to the Petticoat? The Changing Student Body 1592–1992," in: Holland, 105–127 (here 122–4).

[21] Royal Commission on Trinity College. First Report, 1906, quoted in Carr, 40.

[22] The standard study of German in the Irish education system (as well as the media, etc.) is Joachim Fischer, *Das Deutschlandbild der Iren 1890–1939*, University of Dublin Ph.D., 1996, 2. Vols., vol. 1, 112. Published as Joachim Fischer, *Das Deutschlandbild der Iren 1890–1939. Geschichte, Form, Funktion* (Heidelberg: C. Winter, 2000).

[23] Mary Macken, "Friederich Muckermann S. J.," in: *Studies* 21 (1932): 657–62 (here 659).

[24] Hennig's output was substantial, given his circumstances as a refugee (his wife was Jewish and he had spent some time in a concentration camp). Much of it appeared under the aegis of the Royal Irish Academy's Proceedings.

[25] Carr, 48.

[26] Gilbert Waterhouse, "The War and the Study of German. A Public Lecture Delivered in Trinity College Dublin on 29 May 1917" (Dublin: Dublin University Press, 1917), 3.

[27] Fischer, 96–97. The link is in fact much older, as Geraldine Grogan has shown in her study of what political Catholicism in mid-nineteenth-century Germany owed to Ireland, or rather, to Daniel O'Connell's political vision

and strategic skills: *The Noblest Agitator. Daniel O'Connell and the German Catholic Movement 1830–1850* (Dublin: Veritas, 1991).

[28] See also David Little, "A New German Syllabus," in: *Hermathena* 121 (1976). Modern Language Teaching. Trinity College 1776–1976, 69–79.

[29] I recall administering a matriculation examination oral to a candidate from James Joyce's old school, Belvedere College, in the late 1970s. He was fairly accurate but not at all fluent. It was, he said, the first time he had tried speaking German, his sixth language (with Greek, Latin, Irish, French, and Spanish).

Notes on Contributors

DAVID BELL has studied and worked in Cambridge and Basel and is currently Senior Lecturer and Chair of the Department of German Studies in the Victoria University of Manchester. He published *Spinoza in Germany from 1670 to the Age of Goethe* in 1984 and has written on Goethe's religious thought.

MATTHEW BELL is Lecturer in German at King's College London. He studied Ancient Greek, Latin, and German at Oxford (Balliol College), and wrote his Ph.D. thesis on anthropological conceptions in Goethe's writing (*Goethe's Naturalistic Anthropology: Man and Other Plants*, 1994). He has published articles on Lessing, Goethe, and Schiller, and he is currently working on a study of psychological theory in Germany from 1700 to 1830. His other main interest is the reception of classical literature in the eighteenth century.

NICHOLAS BOYLE is Professor of German Literary and Intellectual History and Head of the Department of German at Cambridge University. He has been a Fellow of Magdalene College since 1968. His publications include *Goethe. Faust Part One* (1987), *Goethe. The Poet and the Age* (Volume 1, 1991; Volume 2, 2000), and *Who Are We Now? Christian Humanism and the Global Market from Hegel to Heaney* (1998).

JANE K. BROWN, Professor of Germanics and Comparative Literature at the University of Washington, is former president of the Goethe Society of North America. She has written several books on Goethe, particularly on *Faust*, and published essays on Goethe, Droste-Hülshoff, Shakespeare, Mozart, Schubert, and the *Lied*. Her most recent book is *Ironie und Objektivität: Aufsätze zu Goethe* (1999).

HOWARD GASKILL is Reader in German at the University of Edinburgh. Originally a Hölderlin specialist, he has become increasingly interested in Scottish-German literary relations, in particular the phenomenon of Ossianism. He is the editor of *Ossian Revisited* (1991), *The Poems of Ossian and Related Works* (1996), and (with Fiona Stafford) *From Gaelic to Romantic: Ossianic Translations* (1998). He is currently editing a volume of essays on Ossianic reception for Athlone's "Reception of British Authors in Europe" project.

KARL S. GUTHKE, Kuno Francke Professor of German Art and Culture, Harvard University, was trained at the Universities of Heidelberg and

Texas. He has taught at the Universities of California (Berkeley) and Toronto, and has been Visiting Professor at the Universities of Colorado and Massachusetts. He has published books, in English and German, on Matthew Gregory Lewis, Lessing, Haller, Hauptmann, and literary life in the eighteenth century, as well as several collections of his essays. Among recent publications are *The Last Frontier: Imagining Other Worlds, from the Scientific Revolution to Modern Science Fiction* (1990), *B. Traven: The Life Behind the Legends* (1991), *Last Words: Variations on a Theme in Cultural History* (1993), *Die Entdeckung des Ich* (1993), *Trails in No-Man's Land* (1993), *Schiller's Dramen: Idealismus und Skepsis* (1994), *The Gender of Death* (1999), and *Der Blick in die Fremde: Das Ich und das andere in der Literatur* (2000). Professor Guthke is a member of Sidney Sussex College, Cambridge, England, and a former Fellow of the Institute of Advanced Studies in the Humanities in Edinburgh, the Humanities Research Centre in Canberra, and the Wolfenbüttel Research Centre. He is a Corresponding Fellow of the Institute of Germanic Studies, London.

JOHN GUTHRIE studied at the University of Western Australia, Tübingen and Cambridge (Corpus Christi College) and has taught at the Universities of Leicester, Leeds, and since 1984 at Cambridge, where he is Fellow in German and Director of Studies in Modern Languages at New Hall, and Newton Trust Lecturer in the Department of German. He has written books on Lenz and Büchner and Droste-Hülshoff, and edited Büchner's *Woyzeck*. He is currently working on a project on the language of German drama in the period 1750–1815.

PETER MICHELSEN is Professor Emeritus at the University of Heidelberg. He has published extensively on the literature of the German Classical period and on Anglo-German literary relations. His books include *Laurence Sterne und der deutsche Roman des 18. Jahrhunderts* (2nd edition, 1972), *Der Bruch mit der Vater-Welt. Studien zu Schillers "Räubern"* (1979), *Der unruhige Bürger. Studien zu Lessing und zur Literatur des 18 Jahrhunderts* (1990), and *Im Banne Fausts. Zwölf Faust-Studien* (2000).

H. B. NISBET is Professor of Modern Languages (German) at the University of Cambridge and Fellow of Sidney Sussex College. His main research areas are the German Enlightenment as a movement, the work of Lessing and Herder, the German Classical tradition, and science and philosophy in the eighteenth and nineteenth centuries.

CATHERINE W. PROESCHOLDT obtained her Diploma as a Librarian in 1967 and started work at the Central Theological Library. From 1979 to 1982 she read Modern and Medieval Languages at Cambridge University (King's College), and in 1990 completed her Ph.D. on the reception of Goethe in British periodicals with the CNAA. Since then she has been working as a freelance writer and translator, as well as teaching at Cambridge University.

JAMES SIMPSON is Senior Lecturer in German and Director of Combined Honours at the University of Liverpool. His most recent monograph is *Goethe and Patriarchy: Faust and the Fates of Desire* (1998), and he is currently working on a study of Brecht.

NICHOLAS SAUL studied at Cambridge and lectured at Cambridge and Trinity College Dublin before taking the Chair at the University of Liverpool in 1998. He specialises in German literature and intellectual history from the eighteenth century to the present day. He has written monographs on *Poetry and History in Novalis and in the Tradition of the German Enlightenment* (1984) and *"Prediger aus der neuen romantischen Clique." Zur Interaktion von Romantik und Homiletik um 1800* (1999). He has recently edited books on *Schwellen* (1999) and *The Body in German Literature around 1800* (1999), and published the first edition of Clemens Brentano's drama *Zigeunerin* (1998).

EDA SAGARRA studied in Dublin, Freiburg iBr, Zurich, and Vienna (where she obtained her doctorate). She has lectured at Manchester University (1958–75) in German and in German history for students of literature and language, as well as for the WEA. She was Chair of German at Trinity College Dublin from 1975–98, and is currently involved in education policy in Ireland and Europe. She is a former Secretary of the Royal Irish Academy, current Chairman of the Irish Research Council for the Humanities and Social Sciences, and Irish member on the European Science Foundation Humanities Committee and Pro-chancellor, Dublin University.

ELINOR SHAFFER, FBA, is Senior Research Fellow, School of Advanced Study, University of London, and Research Director and Series Editor of the project on *European Critical Traditions: The Reception of British Authors in Europe*, a multi-volume series published by Athlone Press. She has published widely on Romanticism, in particular Coleridge studies, and, more generally, on the relation between English and German thought. *"Kubla Khan" and The Fall of Jerusalem: The Mythological School in Biblical Criticism and Secular Literature, 1770–1880* was published in 1975, followed by a series of articles on related themes, including "The Hermeneutic Community: Coleridge and Schleiermacher," in *The Coleridge Connection* (1990), and "Goethe and George Eliot: 'hearing the grass grow,'" PEGS (1997). Her latest publication is "Religion and Literature" in the Romanticism volume of the *Cambridge History of Literary Criticism*. Her essay on English and German biography in the nineteenth century will appear in the British Academy millennial volume on Biography (2001). She is currently preparing *Coleridge On Criticism: Shakespeare* in the series *Coleridge's Writings* (Palgrave). A volume on *The Reception of Coleridge in Europe* will appear in the European Critical Traditions series.

PETER SKRINE read Modern and Medieval Languages at Cambridge (Corpus Christi College) and in 1963 was awarded the Doctorat d'Université of the University of Strasbourg. In 1962 he was appointed Assistant Lecturer, then Lecturer, and in 1977 Senior Lecturer in German at the University of Manchester. His first book, *Naturalism* (with Lilian Furst), appeared in 1971; *The Baroque: Literature and Culture in Seventeenth-Century Europe* in 1978; and *Hauptmann, Wedekind and Schnitzler* followed in 1989. In that year he was appointed to the Chair of German at the University of Bristol, becoming Chairman of the School of Modern Languages at Bristol University in 1991–94. In 1997 his *Companion to German Literature* (co-authored with Eda Sagarra of Trinity College, Dublin) was published. In 1998 he became the Chairman of the newly founded South-West Group of the Elizabeth Gaskell Society, and in 1999 he was invited by the Bath Royal Literary and Scientific Institution to give a lecture on "Goethe and His English Readers" to commemorate Goethe's 250th anniversary. In 2000 he was awarded the titles of Professor Emeritus and Senior Research Fellow by the University of Bristol. He is the author of some fifty articles and over 140 reviews.

ROGER STEPHENSON holds the William Jacks Chair of German Language and Literature at the University of Glasgow. His publications include *Goethe's Wisdom Literature* (1983), *Goethe's Conception of Knowledge and Science* (1995), and articles on various aspects of modern German thought and literature, in particular Weimar Classicism.

JOHN R. WILLIAMS studied at Oxford (St. John's College), Heidelberg, and Manchester, and has taught at UMIST and St Andrews. His main interests are Goethe and the *Goethezeit* and literary translation. Publications include articles and reviews in most British and German periodicals; contributions to *Goethe-Handbuch, Vol. 1* (1996); *Goethe's Faust* (1987); *The Life of Goethe. A Critical Biography* (1998); and *Goethe: Faust. The First Part of the Tragedy with the unpublished scenarios for the Walpurgis Night and the Urfaust* (1999).

Works Cited

Ackroyd, Peter. *T. S. Eliot*. London: Hamilton, 1984.

Adler, Jeremy. "The Aesthetics of Magnetism: Science, Philosophy and Poetry in the Dialogue between Goethe and Schelling." In *The Third Culture: Literature and Science*. Translated by Carol Scully, edited by E. S. Shaffer. Berlin and New York: De Gruyter, 1998. 66–102. (For the original German language version of this paper, see *Goethe-Jahrbuch* 112 (1995): 149–65.)

———. *"Eine fast magische Anziehungskraft." Goethes "Wahlverwandtschaften" und die Chemie seiner Zeit*. Munich: C. H. Beck, 1987.

Albertsen, Leif Ludwig. "Zur Problematik der Übersetzung von Dichtung." In: *Schriften der Theodor-Storm-Gesellschaft* 32 (1983): 9–13.

Alford, R. G. "Englishmen at Weimar." *PEGS* 5 (1889): 191–92.

Arberry, A. J. *Oriental Essays: Portraits of Seven Scholars*. London: Allen & Unwin, 1960.

Arens, Hans. *Kommentar zu Goethes "Faust I."* Heidelberg: Winter, 1982.

Arndt, Walter, trans., and Cyrus Hamlin, ed. *Faust. A Tragedy*. New York: Norton, 1976.

Arnold, Matthew. *Complete Prose Works of Matthew Arnold*. Ed. Robert Henry Super. Michigan: Ann Arbor, 1960–77.

———. *The Letters of Matthew Arnold*. Ed. Cecil Y. Lang. Charlottesville and London: UP of Virginia, 1996–.

———. *Letters of Matthew Arnold 1848–88*. Ed. George William Erskine Russell. London: Macmillan, 1895.

———. *Poetical Works of Matthew Arnold*. London: Macmillan, 1897.

Ashton, Rosemary. *George Eliot: A Life*. London: Hamish Hamilton, 1996.

———. *The German Idea. Four English Writers and the Reception of German Thought 1800–60*. Cambridge: Cambridge UP, 1980.

———. *The Life of Samuel Taylor Coleridge: A Critical Biography*. Oxford: Blackwell, 1996.

———, editor. *Versatile Victorian: Selected Writings of George Henry Lewes*. London: Bristol Classical P, 1992.

Atkins, Stuart. *Goethe's "Faust." A Literary Analysis.* Cambridge, MA: Harvard UP, 1958.

———, trans. *Faust I and II.* In *Goethe. Collected Works in 12 Volumes,* vol. 3. Cambridge, MA: Suhrkamp, 1984. New ed., Princeton: Princeton UP, 1994.

Auden, Wystan Hugh. *Collected Poems.* ed. E. Mendelson, London: Faber, 1976.

Aufenanger, Jörg. *Hier war Goethe nicht: Biographische Einzelheiten zu Goethes Abwesenheit.* Berlin: Kowalke, 1999.

Bahr, Erhard. *The Novel as Archive: The Genesis, Reception, and Criticism of Goethe's "Wilhelm Meisters Wanderjahre."* Columbia, SC: Camden House, 1998.

Barbauld, Anna Letitia. "Seláma: An Imitation of Ossian" (1774). http://miavx1.muohio.edu/~leaporm/barbauld/selama.htm.

Bate, Jonathan. *The Genius of Shakespeare.* London: Picador, 1997.

Bäumler, Alfred. *Das Irrationalitätsproblem in der Ästhetik des 18. Jahrhunderts bis zur Kritik der Urteilskraft.* Darmstadt: Wissenschaftliche Buchgesellschaft, 1967 [1923].

Beam, Jacob N. "A Visit to Goethe." *Princeton University Library Chronicle* 8 (1947): 115–22.

Beattie, James. *Essay on the Immutability of Truth.* Edinburgh, 1771.

Bechler, Zev. "'A Less Agreeable Matter': The Disagreeable Case of Newton and Achromatic Reflection." *British Journal for the History of Science* 8 (1975): 101–26.

Bell, Matthew. "Sorge, Epicurean Psychology, and the Classical *Faust.*" *Oxford German Studies* 28 (2000): 83–131.

Benjamin, Walter. "Goethes Wahlverwandtschaften." In *Walter Benjamin. Gesammelte Schriften,* vol. I, 1. Edited by Rolf Tiedemann and Hermann Schweppenhäuser. Frankfurt a.M.: Suhrkamp, 1980. 123–201.

Betteridge, H. T. "Macpherson's Ossian in Germany, 1760–1775." Diss., London, 1938.

Beutler, Ernst. *Essays um Goethe.* 4th ed., vol. 1. Wiesbaden: Dieterich, 1948.

———. "Von der Ilm zum Susquehanna. Goethe und Amerika in ihren Wechselbeziehungen." In: *Essays um Goethe.* 5th ed. Bremen: Schünemann, 1957: 580–629.

Bhabha, Homi. *The Location of Culture.* London and New York: Routledge, 1994.

Birus, Henrik. "Am Schnittpunkt von Komparatistik und Germanistik. Die Idee der Weltliteratur heute." In *Germanistik und Komparatistik. DFG-Symposion 1993*. Edited by Henrik Birus. Stuttgart, Weimar: Metzler, 1995. 439–57.

Black, D. M., trans. *Johann Wolfgang von Goethe: The Diary*. In *Gairfish. Bridge of Weir*: Gairfish, 1993: 130–35.

Blackbourn, David. *The Long Nineteenth Century*. London: Fontana, 1997.

Blair, Hugh. "A Critical Dissertation on the Poems of Ossian." In *The Poems of Ossian and Related Works*. Edited by Howard Gaskill. Edinburgh: Edinburgh UP, 1996.

Böhme, Gernot. "Ist Goethes Farbenlehre Wissenschaft?" In Böhme. *Alternativen der Wissenschaft*. Frankfurt a. M.: Suhrkamp, 1980, 123–53.

Boyd, James. *Goethe's Knowledge of English Literature*. Oxford, 1932.

Boyle, Nicholas. *Goethe, "Faust. Part One."* Cambridge: Cambridge UP, 1987.

———. *Goethe: The Poet and the Age. II. Revolution and Renunciation (1770–1803)*. Oxford: Clarendon P, 2000.

———. *Who Are We Now? Christian Humanism and the Global Market from Hegel to Heaney*. Notre Dame: Notre Dame UP; and Edinburgh: T. & T. Clark, 1998.

Bräuning-Oktavio, Hermann. *Herausgeber und Mitarbeiter der Frankfurter Gelehrte Anzeigen 1772*. Tübingen: Niemeyer, 1966.

Brill, Barbara. *William Gaskell 1805–84: A Portrait*. Manchester: Manchester Literary and Philosophical Publications, 1984.

Broadie, Alexander, ed. *The Scottish Enlightenment: An Anthology*. Edinburgh: Canongate, 1997.

———. *The Tradition of Scottish Philosophy: a New Perspective on the Enlightenment*. Edinburgh: Polygon, 1990.

Brooke, Rupert. *The Collected Poems of Rupert Brooke*. London: Sidgwick & Jackson, 1918.

Brown, Jane K. "*Die Wahlverwandtschaften* and the English Novel of Manners." *Comparative Literature* 28 (1976): 97–108.

———. "The Tyranny of the Ideal: The Dialectics of Art in Goethe's *Novelle*." *Studies in Romanticism* 19 (1980): 217–31.

Bruford, Walther Horace. *Culture and Society in Classical Weimar*. Cambridge UP, 1962.

———. *First Steps in German Fifty Years Ago. The Presidential Address to the Modern Languages Research Association 1965*. Leeds: Modern Languages Research Association, 1965.

———. "Some Early Cambridge Links with German Scholarship and Literature II." *German Life and Letters* 28 (1974–5): 233–45.

Burke, Edmund. *The Correspondence of Edmund Burke*. Edited by George H. Guttridge. Cambridge UP, 1961.

Burton, Robert. *The Anatomy of Melancholy*. 3 vols. Oxford: Oxford UP, 1994.

Butler, Elsie Mary. *Byron and Goethe: Analysis of a Passion*. London: Bowes and Bowes, 1956.

Cannon, Garland, and Kevin R. Brine, eds. *Objects of Enquiry: The Life, Contributions, and Influences of Sir William Jones (1746–1794)*. New York and London: New York UP, 1995.

Capper, Charles. *Margaret Fuller: An American Romantic Life*. The Private Years. New York and Oxford: Oxford UP, 1992.

Carlyle, Thomas. *Critical and Miscellaneous Essays*. 2nd ed. London: Chapman and Hall, 1842.

———. "Life of Schiller." In *The Works of Thomas Carlyle*, XXV. Centenary edition, 30 vols. Edited by. H. D. Traill. London, 1896–1899.

———. *Sartor Resartus and On Heroes, Hero-Worship and the Heroic in History*. London: Dent, 1964.

Carr, Gilbert J. "Literary Historical Trends and the History of the German Syllabus at Trinity College, Dublin, 1873–1972." *Hermathena. A Dublin University Review* 121 (1976). Special number: *Modern Language Teaching. Trinity College 1776–1976*: 36–55.

Casey, Paul Foley. "John Martin Anster: His Contributions to Anglo-German Studies." *Modern Language Notes*, 96 (1981): 654–65.

Cassirer, Ernst. *Die Philosophie der Aufklärung*. Tübingen: Mohr, 1932.

Ceasar, James W. *Reconstructing America: The Symbol of America in Modern Thought*. New Haven, London: Yale UP, 1998.

Chaos. Reprint, Bern: Lang, 1968.

Clark, Robert J. *Herder: His Life and Thought*. Berkeley and Los Angeles: U of California P, 1955.

Clarke, Aidan. "Responsibility: the Administrative Framework." In Holland, ed., 89–103.

Cogswell, Joseph C. "On the Means of Education, and the State of Learning, in the United States of America." *Blackwood's Edinburgh Magazine* 23 (February 1819): 546–53.

———. "On the State of Learning in the United States of America," *Blackwood's Edinburgh Magazine* 24 (March 1819): 641–49.

Coleridge, Samuel Taylor. *Collected Letters of Samuel Taylor Coleridge*. Edited by E. L. Griggs. 6 vols. Oxford and New York, 1956–1971.

———. *The Collected Works of Samuel Taylor Coleridge*. Edited by Kathleen Coburn. Princeton, NJ: Princeton UP; London: Routledge, 1969– .

———. *The Complete Poetical Works of Samuel Taylor Coleridge*. Edited by Ernest Hartley Coleridge. 2 vols. Oxford: Oxford UP, 1912.

———. *The Confessions of an Inquiring Spirit*. Edited by Henry Nelson Coleridge. London, 1840.

———. *The Confessions of an Inquiring Spirit*. 2nd ed. Edited by Sara Coleridge. With an Introduction by J. H. Green and a Note by Sara Coleridge. London, 1849.

———. *The Confessions of an Inquiring Spirit*. With an Introduction by J. H. Green and a Note by Sara Coleridge. Edited by H. St. J. Hart. Stanford: Stanford UP, 1957.

Cooper, James Fenimore. *The Last of the Mohicans* (1826).

———. *The Pilot* (1824)

———. *The Pioneers, or the Sources of the Susquehanna* (1823)

———. *The Prairie* (1827).

———. *The Red Rover* (1827).

———. *The Spy* (1821)

Cox, Richard, "A Curious History: Two Hundred Years of Modern Languages." In Holland, ed., 255–69.

Crabb Robinson, Henry. *On Books and Their Writers*. Edited by Edith J. Morley. London, 1922.

Dawood, N. J., trans. *The Koran*. 4th revised ed. Harmondsworth: Penguin, 1974.

De Quincey, Thomas. *Collected Works*. Edited by David Masson. London: A & C Black. 18.

DeLaura, David Joseph. *Hebrew and Hellene in Victorian England: Newman, Arnold and Pater*. Austin and London: U of Texas P, 1969.

Diderot, D., and J. d'Alembert, eds. *Encyclopédie, ou Dictionnaire raisonné des sciences, des arts et des métiers*. "Neufchastel: Faulche" (in fact Paris), 1751–1765.

Downes, George. *Letters from Continental Countries*. Dublin: Currie, 1832.

Dublin University Calendars for the years 1872–1950. Dublin: Dublin UP.

Duck, Michael J. "Newton and Goethe on Colour: Physical and Physiological Considerations." *Annals of Science* 45 (1988): 507–19 (esp. 518).

Duncan, Bruce. "'Emilia Galotti lag auf dem Pult aufgeschlagen.' Werther as (Mis)reader." *Goethe Yearbook* 1 (1982): 42–50.

Eibl, Karl, Fotis Jannidis and Marianne Willems, eds. *Der junge Goethe in seiner Zeit. Texte und Kontexte. Sämtliche Werke, Briefe, Tagebücher und Schriften bis 1775. In zwei Bänden und einer CD-ROM.* Frankfurt a. M.: Insel Verlag, 1998.

Eliot, George. *Essays of George Eliot.* Edited by Thomas Pinney. London: Routledge and Kegan Paul, 1963.

———. "The Morality of Wilhelm Meister." In *Essays of George Eliot.* Edited by Thomas Pinney. New York: Columbia UP; London: Routledge and Kegan Paul, 143–47.

Eliot, Thomas Stearnes. *On Poetry and Poets.* London: Faber, 1957.

———. *Selected Essays.* 3rd ed. London: Faber, 1951.

———. *The Use of Poetry and the Use of Criticism: Studies in the Relation of Criticism to Poetry in England.* 2nd ed. London: Faber, 1964.

Ellmann, Richard. *James Joyce.* New York: Oxford UP, 1959.

Engel, Eduard. *Goethe.* Berlin: Concordia, 1910.

Englische Miscellen. Tübingen 1800–1807.

Fairley, Barker, trans. *Faust.* Toronto: University of Toronto Press, 1970. Reprinted in: Boyle, Nicholas (ed.). *J. W. von Goethe: Selected Works.* London: David Campbell (Everyman's Library), 1999: 747–1049.

Falk, Johannes. *Goethe aus näherem persönlichem Umgange.* Berlin: Morawe u. Scheffelt, 1911.

Farrelly, Dan (Translator). *Urfaust by Johann Wolfgang von Goethe in Brechtian Mode.* Dublin: Carysfort P, 1998.

Faust, Albert Bernhardt. *The German Element in the United States,* vol. 2. Boston: Houghton Mifflen, 1909.

Fearon, Henry Bradshaw. *Scizzen von America, entworfen auf einer Reise durch die Vereinigten Staaten in den Jahren 1817 und 1818.* Jena, 1819.

Fick, Monika. *Das Scheitern des Genius. Mignon und die Symbolik der Liebesgeschichten in "Wilhelm Meisters Lehrjahren."* Würzburg: Königshausen & Neumann, 1987.

Fink, Karl J. *Goethe's History of Science.* Cambridge: Cambridge UP, 1991.

Fischer, Joachim. *Das Deutschlandbild der Iren 1890–1939.* U of Dublin Ph.D. 1996, 2 vols. Forthcoming in Anglistische Studien. C. Winter, Heidelberg.

Fitzpatrick, W. J. *The Life of Charles Lever.* London: Chapman and Hall, 1879.

Ford, Ford Maddox. *The Good Soldier.* New York: Vintage, 1983 [1927].

Ford, Franklin L. *Europe 1780–1830.* London: Longman 1983.

Forster, Norman. "Henry Crabb Robinson and Goethe: Part II." *PEGS,* New Series, 8 (1931): 1–129.

Franke, Willibald. *Die Wahlfahrt nach Weimar*. Leipzig: Dieterich, 1925.

Friedrich, Theodor and Lothar J. Scheithauer. *Kommentar zu Goethes "Faust I."* Stuttgart: Reclam, 1959.

Gadamer, H. G. *Wahrheit und Methode*. Tübingen: Mohr/Siebeck, 1975.

Gall, Ludwig. *Meine Auswanderung nach den Vereinigten-Staaten in Nord-Amerika im Fruehjahr 1819 und meine Rueckkehr nach der Heimath im Winter 1820*. Trier: Gall, 1822.

Ganz, P[eter] F. *Der Einfluß des Englischen auf den deutschen Wortschatz*. Berlin: E. Schmidt, 1957.

Gaskell, Elizabeth: *The Letters*. Edited by J. A. V. Chapple and Arthur Pollard. Manchester: Manchester UP, 1966.

Gaskill, Howard. "'Blast, rief Cuchullin . . .!': J. M. R. Lenz and Ossian." In *From Gaelic to Romantic*. Edited by Fiona Stafford and Howard Gaskill. Amsterdam: Rodopi, 107–18.

———. "Hölderlin und Ossian." *Hölderlin-Jahrbuch* 27 (1990/91): 100–30.

———. "The 'Joy of Grief': Moritz and Ossian." *Colloquia Germanica* 28 (1995): 101–25.

———. "Tieck's Juvenilia: Ossianic Attributions." *Modern Language Review* (forthcoming).

Gillies, Alexander. *A Hebridean in Goethe's Weimar*. Oxford: Blackwell, 1969.

———. *Herder und Ossian*. Berlin: Junker und Dünnhaupt, 1933.

Gissing, George. *Letters of George Gissing*. Eds. Algernon and Ellen Gissing. London: Constable, 1927.

Goethe, Johann Wolfgang von. *Wilhelm Meisters Lehrjahre* [1795]. *Gesamtausgabe*. 22 vols. Stuttgart: Cotta, 1940–1963. VII: 9–708. Translated by Thomas Carlyle as *Wilhelm Meister's Years of Apprenticeship*. 3 vols. 1824.

———. *Conversations of Goethe with Johann Peter Eckermann*. Translated by John Oxenford. Edited by J. K. Moorhead. New York: Da Capo Press, 1994.

———. *Selected Writings*. London: Everyman, 1999.

Gostwick, Joseph, and Robert Harrison. *A Critical Outline of German Literature*. 1873. 2nd ed. London and Edinburgh: Williams and Norgate, 1883.

Granville, A. B. *St. Petersburgh: A Journal*. London: Colburn, 1828.

Grave, S. A. *The Scottish Philosophy of Common Sense*. Oxford: Clarendon P, 1960.

Greenberg, Martin (Translator). *Faust Part Two*. New Haven & London: Yale UP, 1998.

Grogan, Geraldine. *The Noblest Agitator: Daniel O'Connell and the German Catholic Movement 1830–1850*. Dublin: Veritas, 1991.

Gudde, Erwin G. "Aaron Burr in Weimar." *South Atlantic Quarterly* 40 (1941): 360–88.

Guthke, Karl S. *Der Blick in die Fremde: Das Ich und das andere in der Literatur*. Tübingen: Francke, 2000.

———. *Die Entdeckung des Ich*. Tübingen: Francke, 1993.

Hapgood, Norman. *The Stage in America: 1897–1900*. New York and London: Macmillan, 1901.

Hauhart, William Frederic. *The Reception of Goethe's Faust in the First Half of the Nineteenth Century*. New York: Columbia UP, 1909.

Hazlitt, William. *Collected Works*. Edited by Alfred Rayney Waller and Arnold Glover. London: J. M. Dent, 1902–1906.

Hennig, John. *Goethe and the English-Speaking World*. Bern: Lang, 1988.

———. *Goethes Europakunde*. Amsterdam: Rodopi, 1987.

———. "Goethe's Interest in British Meteorology." *Modern Language Quarterly* 10 (1949): 321–37.

———. "Goethe's Relations with Hüttner." In: *Modern Language Review* 46 (1951): 404–18.

———. "Irish descriptions of Goethe." *PEGS* 25 (1956): 114–24.

Hentschel, E. C. *The Byronic Teuton: Aspects of German Pessimism 1800–1933*. London: Methuen, 1940.

Hentschel, Uwe. "Goethe und die Reiseliteratur am Ende des achtzehnten Jahrhunderts." In: *Jahrbuch des Freien Deutschen Hochstifts*, 1993: 93–127.

Herder, Johann Gottfried. *Schriften zur Ästhetik und Literatur 1767–1781*. Edited by Gunter E. Grimm. Frankfurt a. M.: Deutscher Klassiker Verlag, 1993.

———. *Volkslieder, Übertragungen, Dichtungen*. Edited by Ulrich Gaier. Frankfurt a. M.: Deutscher Klassiker Verlag, 1990.

Heselhaus, Clemens. "Die Wilhelm-Meister-Kritik der Romantiker und die romantische Romantheorie." *Nachahmung und Illusion*. Edited by Hans-Robert Jauß. Munich, 1964.

Heuer, Otto. "Eine unbekannte Ossianübersetzung Goethes." *Jahrbuch des freien deutschen Hochstifts* (1908): 261–73.

Heusler, Andreas. *Deutsche Versgeschichte*. 3 vols. Berlin & Leipzig: de Gruyter, 1925–1929.

Heyd, Michael. *"Be sober and reasonable." The Critique of Enthusiasm in the Seventeenth and Early Eighteenth Centuries*. Leiden: E. J. Brill, 1995.

Höcker, Wilma. *Der Gesandte Bunsen als Vermittler zwischen Deutschland und England*. Göttingen: Musterschmidt, 1951.

Hölderlin, Friedrich. *Sämtliche Werke.* Edited by Friedrich Beissner. Stuttgart, 1951.

Holland, Charles H., ed. *Trinity College Dublin and the Idea of a University.* Dublin: Trinity College P, 1991.

Holmes, Richard. *Coleridge: Darker Reflections.* London: Harper Collins, 1998.

——. *Coleridge. Early Visions.* Harmondsworth: Penguin, 1989.

Home, Henry [Lord Kames]. *Loose Hints Upon Education.* Edinburgh, 1781.

Horowitz, Joseph. *Wagner Nights: An American History.* Berkeley: U of California P, 1994.

Hueffer, F. M. *When Blood is Their Argument: An Analysis of Prussian culture.* London: Hodder & Stoughton, 1915.

Hughes, Ted. *Shakespeare and the Goddess of Complete Being.* London: Faber, 1992.

——. *Winter Pollen.* London: Faber, 1995.

Hume, David. *Principal Writings on Religion including "Dialogues Concerning Natural Religion" and "Natural History of Religion."* Edited by J. C. A. Gaskin. Oxford: Oxford UP, 1993.

——. *A Treatise of Human Nature.* Edited by A. D. Lindsay. London: Dent, 1911 [1738].

——. *A Treatise of Human Nature.* Edited by L. A. Selby-Bigge, revised by P. H. Nidditch. Oxford: Oxford UP, 1978.

Ileri, Esin. *Goethes "West-östlicher Divan" als imaginäre Orient-Reise.* Frankfurt a. M.: Lang, 1982.

Jameson, Anna. *Winter Studies and Summer Rambles in Canada.* London: Saunders and Ottley, 1838.

Jones, Trevor D. "English Contributors to Ottilie von Goethe's *Chaos.*" *PEGS,* New Series, 9 (1931–33): 68–91.

Keating, William H. *Narrative of an Expedition to the Source of St. Peter's River, Lake Winnipeek [. . .]* 2 vols. Philadelphia, 1824.

Kerr, Donal. *Peel, Priests and Politics: Sir Robert Peel's Administration and the Roman Catholic Church in Ireland, 1841–46.* Oxford Historical Monographs. Oxford: Clarendon P, 1982.

Keudell, Elise. *Goethe als Benutzer der Weimarer Bibliothek.* Weimar, 1931; reprinted Leipzig: Zentralantiquariat der DDR, 1982.

Killy, Walther. *Von Berlin bis Wandsbeck.* Munich: Beck, 1996.

Koenig, Gustav Adolf. "Ossian und Goethe, unter besonderer Berücksichtigung von Goethes Übersetzungstechnik aus dem Englischen." Diss., Marburg, 1959.

Kosegarten, Johann Gottfried Ludwig. "Rezension von: West-östlicher Diwan. Von Goethe," *Allgemeine Literatur-Zeitung vom Jahre 1819.* In *Studien zum West-östlichen Divan Goethes,* Wege der Forschung, 287. Edited by Edgar Lohner. Darmstadt: Wissenschaftliche Buchgesellschaft, 1971. 173–89.

Kriegleder, Wynfried. "Wilhelm Meisters Amerika. Das Bild der Vereinigten Staaten in den *Wanderjahren.*" *GoetheJbWien* 95 (1991): 15–32.

Kuehn, Manfred. "The Early Reception of Reid, Oswald, and Beattie in Germany." In *Journal of the History of Philosophy* 21 (1983): 479–95.

———. *Scottish Common Sense in Germany, 1768–1800: A Contribution to the History of Critical Philosophy.* Kingston & Montreal: McGill-Queen's UP, 1987.

Lactantius. *Works.* Translated by W. Fletcher. Edinburgh: T. & T. Clark, 1871.

Lämmert, Eberhard. "Der Dichterfürst." In *Dichtung, Sprache, Gesellschaft: Akten des IV. Internationalen Germanisten-Kongresses in Princeton.* Ed. Victor Lange and Hans-Gert Roloff. Frankfurt: Athenäum, 1971. 439–55.

Lamport, F[rancis] J. "Goethe, Ossian and *Werther.*" In *From Gaelic to Romantic: Ossianic Translations.* Eds. Fiona Stafford and Howard Gaskill. Amsterdam: Rodopi, 97–106.

Landgraf, Hugo. *Goethe und seine ausländischen Besucher.* Munich: Deutsche Akademie, 1932.

Lawrence, David Herbert. *The Letters of D. H. Lawrence.* Eds. James Thompson Boulton, et al. Cambridge: Cambridge UP, 1979–1993.

Lawson, Richard H. *Edith Wharton and German Literature.* Studien zur Germanistik, Anglistik und Komparatistik Bd. 29. Bonn: Bouvier, 1974.

Lewes, George Henry. *The Life and Works of Goethe.* 2 vols. London, 1855; 2nd rev. ed., 1864.

———. *The Life and Works of Goethe.* 1855. London: J. M. Dent & Sons, 1908.

Lewis, M[atthew] G[regory]. *The Life and Correspondence of Matthew Gregory Lewis.* 2 vols. London: Colburn, 1839.

Lewis, R. W. B. *Edith Wharton: A Biography.* NY, Evanston, San Francisco, London: Harper & Row, 1975.

Lichtenberg, Georg Christoph. *Schriften und Briefe.* Edited by Wolfgang Promies. 4 vols. Munich: Hanser, 1967–92.

Little, David. "A New German Syllabus." *Hermathena* 121 (1976). Modern Language Teaching. Trinity College 1776–1976. 69–79.

Livingston, Donald W. *Philosophical Melancholy and Delirium: Hume's Pathology of Philosophy.* Chicago: U of Chicago P, 1998.

Long, Orie W. *Literary Pioneers.* Cambridge, MA.: Harvard UP, 1935.

Luden, H., ed. *Reise des Herzogs Bernhard zu Sachsen-Weimar durch Nord-Amerika.* 2 vols. Weimar, 1828.

Luke, David, trans. *Faust. Part One.* Oxford: Oxford UP, 1987.

———. *Johann Wolfgang von Goethe: Selected Poetry.* London: Libris, 1999.

Lydon, James. "The Silent Sister: Trinity College and Catholic Ireland." In Holland, ed. 29–53.

Mackall, Leonard L. "Mittheilungen aus dem Goethe-Schiller-Archiv." In *Goethe Jahrbuch* 25 (1904): 1–37.

Macken, Mary. "Friederich Muckermann S. J." *Studies* 21 (1932): 657–62.

———. "The Goethe Bi-Centenary." *Studies* 38 (1949): 403–12.

MacNeice, Louis and E. L. Stahl, trans. *Faust Parts I and II.* London: Faber & Faber, 1951.

Macpherson, James. "A Specimen of the Original of Temora." In *The Works of Ossian, the Son of Fingal, in two Volumes, translated from the Gaelic Language by James Macpherson.* Vol. 2. London: Beckett and Dehondt, 1765. 289–309.

———. *The Poems of Ossian and Related Works.* Edited by. Howard Gaskill. Edinburgh: Edinburgh UP, 1996.

Maier, Hans Albert, ed. *Goethe. West-östlicher Divan. Kritische Ausgabe der Gedichte mit textgeschichtlichem Kommentar.* 2 vols. Tübingen: Niemeyer, 1965.

Maierhofer, Waltraud. "Perspektivenwechsel: Zu *Wilhelm Meisters Wanderjahre* und dem amerikanischen Reisetagebuch Bernhards von Sachsen-Weimar-Eisenach." *Zeitschrift für Germanistik*, N.S. 3 (1995): 508–22.

Mandelkow, Karl Robert. *Goethe in Deutschland: Rezeptionsgeschichte eines Klassikers.* 2 vols. Munich: C. H. Beck, 1980–1989.

Manuel, Frank E. *The Changing of the Gods.* Hanover, NH: U of New England P, 1983.

Marquardt, Hertha. *Henry Crabb Robinson und seine deutschen Freunde.* Vol. 1. Göttingen: Vandenhoeck u. Ruprecht, 1964.

Matussek, Peter, ed. *Goethe und die Verzeitlichung der Natur.* Munich: C. H. Beck, 1998.

McCartney, Donal. *The National University of Ireland and Eamon de Valera.* Dublin: The UP of Ireland, 1983.

McRedmond, Louis. *Thrown among Strangers: John Henry Newman in Ireland.* Dublin: Veritas, 1990.

Medwin, Thomas. *Conversations of Lord Byron.* London: printed for Henry Colburn, 1824.

———. *Journal of the Conversations of Lord Byron.* London: printed for H. Colburn, 1824.

Michelsen, Peter. Review of Lawrence Marsden Price, *Die Aufnahme englischer Literatur in Deutschland 1500–1960*. Ins Deutsche uebertragen von Maxwell F. Knight. (Bern and Munich: Francke Verlag, 1961). *Göttingische Gelehrten Anzeigen* 220 (1968): 239–282.

Middleton, Christopher, ed. *Goethe. Selected Poems*. In *Goethe. Collected Works in 12 Volumes*. Vol. 1. Cambridge, MA: Suhrkamp, 1983. New ed., Princeton: Princeton UP, 1994.

Miller, Johann Martin. *Siegwart. Eine Klostergeschichte* (1776). Stuttgart: Metzler, 1971.

Minden, Michael. *The German "Bildungsroman": Incest and Inheritance*. Cambridge: Cambridge UP, 1997.

Moritz, Karl Philipp. *Andreas Hartknopf* (1786). Ed. Hans Joachim Schrimpf. Stuttgart: Metzler, 1968.

Moses, Montrose J. *The Life of Heinrich Conried*. New York: Thomas Y. Crowell, 1916.

Müller, Pia. *Johann Christian Hüttner's "Englische Miscellen."* Würzburg: Triltsch, 1939.

Neubauer, John. "'Die Abstraktion, vor der wir uns fürchten.' Goethes Auffassung der Mathematik und das Goethebild in der Geschichte der Wissenschaft." In Volker Dürr and Géza von Molnár, eds., *Versuche zu Goethe. Festschrift für Erich Heller*. Heidelberg: Lothar Stiehm, 1976. 305–20.

Nisbet, Hugh Barr. "Goethes und Herders Geschichtsdenken." In *Goethe-Jahrbuch* 110 (1993): 115–33.

Novalis. *Schriften*. Edited by Richard Samuel. H. J. Mähl, G. Schulz. Darmstadt: 1968.

Oellers, Norbert, and Robert Steegers. *Treffpunkt Weimar: Literatur und Leben zur Zeit Goethes*. Stuttgart: Reclam, 1999.

Oxenford, John. *The Auto-Biography of Goethe. Truth and Poetry: From My Own Life*. London: Henry G. Bohn, 1848.

Pascal, Blaise. *Pensées*. Edited by L. Brunschvicg. Paris: Hachette, 1966.

Pascal, Roy. "Herder and the Scottish Historical School." *Publications of the English Goethe Society* 14 (1939): 23–42.

Pfund, Harry W. "George Henry Calvert, Admirer of Goethe." In *Studies in Honor of John Abrecht Walz*. Lancaster, PA: Lancaster P, 1941. 117–61.

Pochmann, Henry A. *German Culture in America: Philosophical and Literary Influences 1600–1900*. Madison: U of Wisconsin P, 1957.

Prawer, S[iegbert] S. *Breeches and Metaphysics: Thackeray's German Discourse*. Oxford: Legenda, 1997.

———. "Thackeray's Goethe: A 'Secret History.'" *PEGS*, New Series, 62 (1993): 1–34.

Priestley, Joseph. *An Examination of Dr. Reid's Enquiry into the Human Mind on the Principles of Common Sense, Dr. Beattie's Essay on the Nature and Immutability of Truth, and Dr. Oswald's Appeal to Common Sense in Behalf of Religion.* London, 1774.

Propper, M. von. "Zur Anatomie einer Meisterfälschung: *Goethes Gespräch mit dem russischen Grafen S.*" *GoetheJbWien* 78 (1974): 5–26.

Prudhoe, John, trans. *Faust Part One.* Manchester: Manchester UP, 1974.

Pütz, Peter. "Werthers Leiden an der Literatur." In *Goethe's Narrative Fiction: The Irvine Goethe Symposium.* Edited by Wiliam J. Lillyman. Berlin and New York: de Gruyter, 1983. 55–68.

Ramsay, David. *Geschichte der Amerikanischen Revolution aus den Acten des Congresses.* Berlin, 1795.

Raraty, Maurice. "The Chair of German at Trinity College, Dublin 1775–1866." *Hermathena. A Dublin University Review,* 53–62.

Raverat, Gwenyth. *Period Piece: A Cambridge Childhood.* London: Faber, 1960 [1952].

Ray, Gordon N. *Thackeray.* Vol. 2. New York: McGraw-Hill, 1958.

Reid, Thomas. *Analysis of Aristotle's Logic.* Edinburgh, 1806.

———. *Enquiry into the Human Mind on the Principles of Common Sense.* Edinburgh, 1764.

Reiss, Hans. "Sieben Jahre in Irland 1939–46. Mein Weg in die Germanistik." *Jahrbuch der deutschen Schillergesellschaft* XL (1996): 409–32.

Robertson, John George. "Goethe and Byron." *Publications of the English Goethe Society* 2 (1925): 1–132.

Robinson, Henry Crabb. *Diaries, Reminiscences, and Correspondence of Henry Crabb Robinson.* Ed. Thomas Sadler. London: Macmillan, 1869.

———. *Henry Crabb Robinson on Books and Their Writers.* Edited by Edith Julia Morley. London: Dent, 1938.

Röder-Bolton, Gerlinde. *George Eliot and Goethe: An Elective Affinity.* Amsterdam and Atlanta: Rodopi, 1998.

Rothmann, Kurth. *Erläuterungen und Dokumente. Johann Wolfgang Goethe. Die Leiden des jungen Werther.* Stuttgart: Reclam, 1997.

Ryder, Frank. "George Ticknor and Goethe: Boston and Göttingen." *PMLA* 67 (1952): 960–72.

———. "George Ticknor and Goethe: Europe and Harvard." *MLQ* 14 (1953): 413–24.

Sagarra, Eda. "From the Pistol to the Petticoat? The Changing Student Body 1592–1992." In Holland, ed., 105–27.

———. "German Studies in Ireland. History and Reminiscence." In *Vermitt-lungen. German Studies at the Turn of the Century. Festschrift für Nigel B. R. Reeves*. Edited by Rüdiger Görner und Helen Kelly-Holmes. Munich: iudicium, 1999. 117–30.

Said, Edward W. *Orientalism*. Reprint of 1978 ed. with new Afterword. Harmondsworth: Penguin, 1995.

Sammons, Jeffrey. *Ideology, Mimesis, Fantasy: Charles Sealsfield, Friedrich Gerstäcker, Karl May, and Other German Novelists of America*. Chapel Hill and London: U of NC, 1998.

Santayana, George. *Reason in Common Sense*. New York: Dover, 1980 [1905].

———. *Three Philosophical Poets: Lucretius, Dante, and Goethe*. Cambridge: Harvard UP, 1945 [1910].

Schimmel, Annemarie. *Mystical Dimensions of Islam*. Chapel Hill: U of NC P, 1975.

Schings, Hans-Jürgen. "Fausts Verzweiflung." *Goethe-Jahrbuch* 115 (1998): 97–123.

Schlegel, Friedrich. *Kritische Friedrich-Schlegel-Ausgabe*. Edited by Ernst Behler, J.-J. Anstett, and Hans Eichner. Munich, Paderborn, Wien: F. Schöningh, 1958–.

Schöffler, Herbert. "Ossian. Hergang und Sinn eines großen Betrugs." In *Deutscher Geist im 18. Jahrhundert: Essays zur Geistes- und Religions-geschichte*. 2nd ed. Göttingen 1967. 135–81.

Schöne, Albrecht. *Goethes Farbentheologie*. Munich: C. H. Beck, 1987.

Schultz, Arthur R. "Goethe and the Literature of Travel." *JEGP* 48 (1949): 445–68.

Schulz, Gerhard. *Exotik der Gefühle: Goethe und seine Deutschen*. Munich: Beck, 1998.

Schütze, Jochen. *Goethe-Reisen*. Wien: Passagen, 1998.

Scott, D. F. S. "English Visitors to Weimar." *GLL*, New Series, 2 (1949): 330–41.

———. *Some English Correspondents of Goethe*. London: Methuen, 1949.

Selss, Albert M. *A Brief History of the German Language, with Five Books of the Nibelungenlied*. Edited and annotated by Albert M. Selsss. London: Longmans, Green, & Co., 1885.

———. *A Critical History of German Literature*. London: Longmans, Green, & Co: 1865; 2nd: 1880 (=1880b); 3rd: 1884; 4th: 1890; 5th: London, New York and Bombay: Longmans, Green & Co., 1896.

———. *Deutsche Styl- und Redeübungen or Lessons in German Composition*. Dublin: William McGee, 1886.

———. *The Easter Eggs by Dean von Schmid*. 3rd ed. Edited with notes and a commentary. Dublin: Edward Ponsonby, 1905.

———. *Goethe's Faust. Part I*. The German Text, with English notes. For the use of students of modern literature. London: Longmans, Green, & Co., 1880 (=1880a).

———. *Goethe's Minor Poems*. Selected, annotated and rearranged by Albert M. Selss. London: L. Trübner & Co.; and Dublin: Hodges, Foster & Co., 1875.

Sepper, Dennis. *Goethe Contra Newton: Polemics and the Project for a New Science of Color*. Cambridge: Cambridge UP, 1988.

Seth, Andrew. *Scottish Philosophy: A Comparison of the Scottish and German Answers to Hume*. Edinburgh & London: Blackwood, 1885.

Shaffer, E[linor] S. "Goethe and George Eliot: 'hearing the grass grow.'" *PEGS* (NS), LXVI (1997): 3–22.

———. "The Hermeneutic Community: Coleridge and Schleiermacher." In *The Coleridge Connection*. Edited by Richard Gravil and Molly Lefebure. Festschrift for Thomas McFarland. London: Macmillan, 1990. 200–29.

———. *"Kubla Khan" and The Fall of Jerusalem: The Mythological School in Biblical Criticism and Secular Literature, 1770–1880*. Cambridge: Cambridge UP, 1975.

———. "Metaphysics of Culture: Coleridge and Kant's 'Aids to Reflection.'" *Journal of the History of Ideas* (April-June, 1968), 199–218.

———. Review of *Shorter Works and Fragments (Collected Coleridge XI)*. *Review of English Studies* NS 49 (1998): 96–97.

Sharps, J. G. *Mrs. Gaskell's Observation and Invention*. Fontwell: Linden P, 1970.

Shelley, Percy Bysshe. *The Letters of Percy Bysshe Shelley*. Edited by Frederick L. Jones. 2 vols. Oxford: Clarendon P, 1964.

Sidgwick, Henry. *Outlines of the History of Ethics*. London: Macmillan, 1888.

Simpson, James. *Matthew Arnold and Goethe*. Cambridge: Modern Humanities Research Association, 1979.

Siskin, Clifford. *The Historicity of Romantic Discourse*. New York and London: Oxford UP, 1988.

Skrine, Peter. "Mrs. Gaskell and Germany." *The Gaskell Society Journal* 7 (1995): 37–49.

———. *Susanna and Catherine Winkworth: Clifton, Manchester and the German Connection*. Croydon: The Hymn Society, 1992.

Soret, Frédéric. *Zehn Jahre bei Goethe*. Leipzig: Brockhaus, 1929.

Spender, Stephen. *The Making of a Poem*. London: Hamish Hamilton, 1955.

Spinner, Kaspar Heinrich. *Der Mond in der deutschen Dichtung von der Aufklärung bis zur Spätromantik*. Bonn: Bouvier, 1969.

Stafford, Fiona J. *The Last of the Race: The Growth of a Myth from Milton to Darwin.* Oxford: Oxford UP, 1994. 232–60.

Stephenson, R. H. *Goethe's Conception of Knowledge and Science.* Edinburgh: Edinburgh UP, 1995.

———. *Goethe's Wisdom Literature: A Study in Aesthetic Transmutation.* Bern: Lang, 1983.

———. "'Man nimmt in der Welt jeden, wofür er sich gibt': the Presentation of Self in Goethe's *Die Wahlverwandtschaften*." *GLL* NS XLVII (1994): 400–6.

Stern, Ludwig Christian. "Die ossianischen Heldenlieder." *Zeitschrift für vergleichende Litteraturgeschichte* 8 (1895): 50–86, 143–74.

Strich Fritz. *Goethe und die Weltliteratur.* Bern: Francke, 1946.

Taylor, Bayard, trans. *Faust: A Tragedy.* 3rd ed. London & New York: Ward, Lock, 1890.

Theodores, Tobias. "On the Study of the German Language." In *Introductory Lectures on the Opening of Owens College, Manchester.* London, Cambridge, Manchester, 1852.

Tieghem, Paul van. "Ossian et l'ossianisme au XVIIIᵉ siècle." In *Le Préromantisme.* Vol. 1. Paris: Rieder, 1924, 195–287.

Voßkamp, Wilhelm. "Utopie und Utopiekritik in Goethes Romanen in *Wilhelm Meisters Lehrjahre* und *Wilhelm Meisters Wanderjahre*." *Utopieforschung. Interdisziplinäre Studien zur neuzeitlichen Utopie.* Edited by Wilhelm Voßkamp. 3 vols. Stuttgart: Metzler, 1982. 3, 228–49.

Wadepuhl, Walter. *Goethe's Interest in the New World.* 1934. Reprint, New York: Haskell House, 1973.

———. "Hüttner, a New Source for Anglo-German Relations." In *The Germanic Review* 14 (1939): 23–27.

Wagenknecht, Christian. *Deutsche Metrik: Eine historische Einführung.* Munich: Beck, 1981.

Wahl, Hans. Ed. *Briefwechsel des Herzogs-Grossherzogs Carl August mit Goethe.* 3 vols. Bern: Lang 1971.

Wanniek, Erdmann. "*Werther* lesen und Werther als Leser." *Goethe Yearbook* 1 (1982): 51–92.

Warden, D. B. *Statistical, Political and Historical Account of the United States of North America.* Edinburgh, 1819.

Waterhouse, Gilbert. "The War and the Study of German: A Public Lecture Delivered in Trinity College Dublin on 29 May 1917." Dublin: Dublin UP, 1917.

Wayne, Philip, trans. *Faust Part One.* Harmondsworth: Penguin, 1949.

Webb, Timothy. *The Violet in the Crucible: Shelley and Translation.* Oxford: Clarendon P, 1976.

Wehler, Hans Ulrich. *Die Herausforderung der Kulturgeschichte.* Munich: Beck, 1998.

Wenzel, Manfred. "'Die Abstraktion, vor der wir uns fürchten.' Goethe und die Physik." *Freiburger Universitätsblätter* 35, Heft 133 (1996): 55–79.

Whaley, John, trans. *Goethe: Selected Poems.* Introduction by Matthew Bell. London: J. M. Dent, 1998.

———. *Johann Wolfgang von Goethe: Poems of the East and West (West-östlicher Divan).* Introduction by Katharina Mommsen. Bern: Lang, 1998.

Wharton, Edith. *The Age of Innocence.* New York: Modern Library, 1999 [1920].

———. *A Backward Glance.* New York, London: D. Appleton-Century, 1936 [1933].

———. *The Custom of the Country.* New York: Bantam, 1991 [1913].

———. *The Reef.* New York: Collier, 1986 [1912].

———. *The Writing of Fiction.* New York: Simon and Schuster, 1997. [NY: Scribners, 1924].

Wiethölter, Waltraud, ed. *Goethe. Die Leiden des jungen Werthers.* Frankfurt a. M.: Deutscher Klassiker Verlag, 1994.

Wild, Reiner. *Goethes klassische Lyrik.* Stuttgart: J. B. Metzler, 1999.

Wilde, Oscar. *The Letters of Oscar Wilde.* Edited by Rupert Hart-Davis. London: Hart-Davis, 1962.

Wilkinson, Elizabeth M., and L. A. Willoughby. *Friedrich Schiller: On the Aesthetic Education of Man. In a series of letters. Edited and translated, with an Introduction, Commentary and Glossary of Terms.* Oxford: Clarendon P, 1982 [1967].

Williams, John R., trans. *Faust: The First Part of the Tragedy with the Unpublished Scenarios for the Walpurgis Night and the Urfaust.* Ware, Herts: Wordsworth, 1999.

Willoughby, L[eonard]. "Goethe Looks at the English." *MLR* 50 (1955): 464–84.

———. *Samuel Naylor and "Renard the Fox."* London and New York: Milford, 1914.

Winkworth, Catherine. *The Christian Singers of Germany.* London: Macmillan, 1869.

Winkworth, Susanna. *Letters and Memorials of Catherine Winkworth.* Clifton: R. Austin and Son, 1886.

Witte, Bernd, et al., eds. *Goethe Handbuch*. 4 vols. Stuttgart: Metzler, 1996–1999.

Wordsworth, William. *Wordsworth's Literary Criticism*. Edited by Nowell Charles Smith. London: Henry Frowde, 1905.

Wuthenow, R. R. "Reisende Engländer, Deutsche und Franzosen." *Rom-Paris-London*. Edited by Conrad Wiedemann. Stuttgart: Metzler, 1988. 90–10.

Zantop, Susanne. *Colonial Fantasies. Conquest, Family and Nation in Precolonial Germany, 1770–1870*. Durham, London: Duke UP, 1997.

Zarncke, F. "Ueber den fünffüßigen Jambus bei Lessing, Schiller und Goethe" *Kleine Schriften 1: Goetheschriften*. Leipzig: Eduard Avenarius, 1897. 309–428.

Zart, G. *Einfluß der englischen Philosophie seit Bacon auf die deutsche Philosophie des 18. Jahrhunderts*. Berlin: Dümmler, 1881.

Zeller, Bernhard, ed. *Weltliteratur: die Lust am Übersetzen im Jahrhundert Goethes. Eine Ausstellung des deutschen Literaturarchivs im Schiller-National-museum Marbach am Neckar*. Marbacher Kataloge 37. Marbach, 1989.

Zeydel, Edwin Hermann. "The German Theater in New York City, with Special Consideration of the Years 1878–1914." *Deutsch-Amerikanische Geschichtsblätter: Jahrbuch der Deutsch-Amerikanischen Historischen Gesellschaft von Illinois* 15 (1915): 255–309.

Index